WITHDRAWN

Learning To Be Moral

Studies in Applied Philosophy
Series Editors: Brenda Almond and Anthony O'Hear

Published

Geoffrey Brown
The Information Game:
Ethical Issues in a Microchip World

Paul Crittenden
Learning To Be Moral
Philosophical Thoughts about Moral Development

Igor Primoratz
Justifying Legal Punishment

Learning To Be Moral
Philosophical Thoughts about Moral Development

Paul Crittenden

HUMANITIES PRESS INTERNATIONAL, INC.
New Jersey ◇ London

First published 1990 by Humanities Press International, Inc.,
Atlantic Highlands, NJ 07716 and 3 Henrietta Street, London WC2E 8LU

© Paul Crittenden, 1990

Library of Congress Cataloging-in-Publication Data

Crittenden, Paul.
    Learning to be moral: philosophical thoughts about moral
development / Paul Crittenden.
        p. cm. — (Studies in applied philosophy)
    Includes bibliographical references.
    ISBN 0–391–03668–8
    1. Moral development.   2. Ethics.   I. Title.   II. Series: Studies
in applied philosophy (Atlantic Highlands, N.J.)
BF723.M54C75   1990
155.2'5—dc20   89–29748
                                                            CIP

British Library Cataloguing in Publication Data

Crittenden, Paul.
    Learning to be moral: philosophical thoughts about moral
development. – (Studies in applied philosophy).
    1. Moral development
    I. Title II. Series
    155.2'5
    ISBN 0–391–03668–8

Printed in the United States of America

For Jascha

Contents

Preface

The first part of this book is concerned with the main contemporary accounts of how human individuals come to be moral beings. The topic of moral development is of obvious importance for anyone with an interest in social and cultural forms; parents and educators, in particular, are likely to have a practical interest in the matter as well. But in the division of labor which has characterized the growth of academic disciplines, contemporary study of the nature and patterns of moral development is undertaken mainly in psychology, as part of child and developmental psychology, with ramifications in social psychology and social theory generally. Philosophers, with the notable exception of philosophers of education, have not been greatly interested in the topic, and the study of ethics in philosophy departments has proceeded, for some time, largely without reference to developmental questions. This was not the case in the past. Philosophers, beginning with Plato and Aristotle, characteristically gave close attention, in their discussion of moral questions, to the ways in which moral beliefs and practices are acquired. Theories of morality and moral development thus went hand in hand. The neglect of this aspect of moral inquiry in contemporary philosophical practice has had unhappy consequences for moral philosophy itself and for the disciplines which have taken up the concern.

Among contemporary accounts of moral development, versions of social learning theory are probably the most widespread and deeply entrenched. Social learning theory, with roots in empiricist science and behaviorism, has typically eschewed concern with historical and conceptual issues in morality in order to get on with empirical research and the establishment of scientific conclusions. In fact, such empirical research has been driven to a considerable extent by moral theory (whether its presence is acknowledged or not) which is partial or otherwise unsatisfactory. Social learning theory, however, takes many forms, and my discussion of it in chapter two will include attention to a version which moves toward a more developed account of moral and other relevant philosophical issues.

The other main accounts of moral development which I discuss in this study can be associated readily with particular theorists: Freud, Piaget, and Kohlberg. Freudian psychoanalytic theory, which has had close connections with social learning theory in the empirical study of moral development, was also put forward as purely scientific in outlook, where this is taken to exclude, among other things, a philosophical point of view. In fact, Freudian theory incorporates moral and other philosophical elements from the past, some of which are deeply problematic. More generally, a considerable part of the force of Freud's ideas arises from his capacity for philosophical inquiry, even though he was unwilling to acknowledge the philosophical presuppositions and implications of his thought.

Jean Piaget was as much a philosopher as a psychologist. His views on the development of moral judgment in the child reflect an informed grasp of moral theory, especially in the traditions associated with Rousseau and Kant and in nineteenth- and early twentieth-century sociological inquiry. In his case, therefore, the account of moral development (or a significant aspect of it in moral judgment) is accompanied by an explicit, albeit brief, treatment of moral theory. This could not be said to apply, however, to much of the subsequent empirical research generated by Piaget's ideas. In any case, the sources of Piaget's moral theory are quite narrow, and the theory, on the basis of which his empirical inquiries proceeded, can be shown to be unsatisfactory.

Lawrence Kohlberg, whose life-work was devoted primarily to the study of moral development in the context of moral education, also drew consciously on moral philosophy, both ancient and modern, in the elaboration of his views. But once again, the choice of moral theory on which Kohlberg drew was both narrow and problematic. Once again, a great deal of empirical inquiry on the basis of Kohlberg's moral stages has been undertaken on questionable premises or with assumptions which were largely unexamined. In fact, the problems in Kohlberg's account of moral development emerge most clearly when attention is given to its philosophical underpinnings, especially in connection with his views about the more mature stages of moral growth. This criticism was brought forward significantly from within the Kohlbergian research program in the work of Carol Gilligan in the early 1980s. Gilligan has argued that Kohlberg's moral stages fail to capture satisfactorily the moral experience of women in particular. I think that her criticism is well-founded in a quite general sense, but a considerable part of the strength of her case is that it reflects, though in unstated ways, themes which reach back to Greek ethical thought, and which embody a richer approach to moral issues than the various ideas which have been prominent in modern theories of ethics and related accounts of moral development.

Against this background, the second part of the book consists of a series of historical studies of major accounts of morality and their developmental ramifications in the writings of the philosophers. The rationale for these studies is set out in the introduction to Part Two; these pages could be read immediately, if the reader wishes, after this Preface. Part Three provides a brief conclusion in which many questions are left open, but in which some main threads of argument are drawn together.

The empirical study of moral development in children over the past fifty years is quantitatively far in excess of all previous studies in past history.

(This is connected with the immense growth of educational institutions this century and has no direct bearing on the quality of the inquiry, past or present; other factors are involved in the growth, especially in regard to the forms it has taken.) The extensive study of the topic has gone on over a period which has also witnessed widespread controversy and uncertainty about the nature of morality and moral authority, a consideration which in itself raises problems for attempts to treat moral development in a purely scientific way. The problematic status of morality in our culture is connected in part with the changing authority of religion in this domain. Among other pertinent factors, it reflects the impact of ideas drawn from the thought of a number of major modern critics of morality such as Marx, Freud, and Nietzsche. Some of these issues are taken up in chapter one, prior to the discussion of accounts of moral development and the historical studies.

I began writing this book during some months of study leave which I spent at the Australian National University in Canberra in 1986. But the germ lies in a paper on morality and moral development which I contributed to a collection called *The Developing Child*, which was produced in connection with the International Year of the Child 1979, and which appeared, a little after the event, in 1981. I discussed the plan of the book with Genevieve Lloyd in 1986, and have greatly appreciated her advice and encouragement over many years.

I am grateful to the University of Sydney for the opportunities I have had for teaching and research as a member of the Department of General Philosophy. Versions of one or another chapter of the book were read to seminars at Sydney and Canberra in particular; I have profited greatly from the critical response and interest of many of the participants. I have also learned a great deal from students who have taken part in my graduate seminars on morality and moral development and related topics. I have been helped in various ways in this project by many different people over the years; they include Brian Crittenden, Benjamin Gibbs, William Ginnane, Kim Lycos, Anselm Müller, David Novitz, and Lloyd Reinhardt. Brenda Almond's response to the plan of the book and its first chapters gave me considerable encouragement. One's debt of gratitude, especially in connection with a topic such as this, runs back over many years to include many teachers and friends. In particular, I acknowledge my gratitude to my parents who were for me the givers of life and nourishment and the best of teachers from birth (to adapt a remark of Aristotle's about parents and children). I am grateful to colleagues in the Department of General Philosophy, John Burnheim and György Markus in particular, and also to Veronica Leahy and Patricia Bower for their secretarial help and warm interest in my work. Finally, I wish to thank my wife, Nadia, for her encouragement and involvement and support.

Sydney N. S. W., Australia

PART ONE
Morality and Moral Development

1. Morality in Question

1. Moral and Developmental Questions

Very young children are not moral agents. They do various things (in a limited way at first) and have various things done to them, but they are not properly held responsible for their behavior. This is entirely reasonable since very young children have no ideas or beliefs about good and evil and no sense of the possibility of choosing courses of action. The process of becoming a moral agent is gradual and complex, involving both maturational development and a great deal of learning — that is to say, the process depends in part on the growth of natural or inborn capacities which are characteristic of human beings and, in part, on experience in response to a very wide and variable range of environmental factors.

Various questions immediately suggest themselves in regard to this process. Consider the following group. How does the process of becoming a moral agent occur? Does the process follow any set patterns or stages of development? If so, do these patterns vary significantly in form or content across different cultures and types of societies and across time? What is the relative importance of maturational and environmental factors in the process, and how are they related? Or, how much is due to natural growth and how much to learning from "external" sources, such as social influences, in the development of our moral views? What role does teaching play in moral development?

Setting aside the further issue whether these questions are all well-formed, now consider a related but different set of questions. What are the conditions and characteristics of moral maturity? That is, how should the preferred outcome of the process of moral development be characterized? What is involved in being a *moral* agent, in being able to assess matters — our own behavior or the behavior of others for example — from a moral point of view? How do we know what is morally good and morally bad? Is it possible to have knowledge at all in this field as distinct from prejudice or irrational conviction or merely local belief (derived, for example, from one's social class or religious upbringing)? Are there any general moral truths or basic principles which moral agents could be expected to acknowledge? What are the grounds of morality? What authority does it have? On the assumption that moral beliefs and practices can be taught to children in some sense, what should be taught to them and by whom (and by what authority)?

2

Questions of the first sort are likely to be raised in the writings of psychologists or sociologists dealing with moral development as part of the study of child development. The issues might be taken to have something of a scientific character, amenable to empirical investigation, testing and measuring, and the like. Questions of the second sort will be found more readily in discussions about morality, whether at an ordinary and practical level — as when parents wonder about the moral upbringing of their children — or in the more formal setting of books or courses on ethics by philosophers. There is a common view among the more scientific-minded that this second group is composed of intractable questions which can be answered only in dependence on an assumed moral position in the first place and which, being concerned with values, are endlessly and tiresomely debatable.

Whether the two sets of questions can be properly divided off from one another is itself a question of importance in moral and social inquiry. It is clear that they are at least interdependent in various ways. People engaged in scientific study might say that, from a scientific point of view, they are concerned only with what counts as moral beliefs and practices for the subjects of their inquiry; their own views regarding morality, they would say, are irrelevant. But moral considerations enter into their own procedures: truthfulness in recording data for example. Furthermore, psychologists could not present an account of moral development without drawing on their own views about the nature of morality: they could not otherwise identify the development as moral. How would an anthropologist or sociologist identify any of the beliefs and practices of a people as *moral* beliefs and practices in the absence of all beliefs on their part about the character of moral goodness and badness? In general, empirical investigation of moral development presupposes ethical views and theory of one sort or another (though social scientists are often unwilling to acknowledge the point).

On the other hand, ethical studies which have no concern with the ways in which people acquire moral beliefs and practices assume a false abstraction from the conditions of human life in which morality has its place. In any case, parents and others with the responsibility of caring for children, if they have time to think about the matter in a theoretical way at all, would be concerned with questions of both types. They would want to know, for example, whether there are regular stages of moral development through which children pass and how their progress might be helped or hindered. Equally, they would have views about the desirable outcome of moral development, some notion of the specific qualities of character and behavioral habits which go with moral maturity. Theory should follow the example of practice here. In short, theoretical inquiries in psychology or sociology which deal with moral development need to go hand in hand with a substantive interest in the major questions of ethics, and ethical inquiry needs to be related to the realization of the relevant ideas and principles in individual and social life.

The need to relate accounts of moral development to ethics proper is underlined by the climate of controversy and dispute which now surrounds morality. The period of unprecedented research in psychology in regard to moral development over the past half century has also been a period of vast, if not unprecedented, dispute and uncertainty regarding moral values and the nature of morality. Ironically, research has expanded along with a growing problem in specifying the object under research: what it is that research in moral development is a study *of*. This is not sheer coincidence, though of course the growth in research and the proliferation of moral dispute are each additionally associated with other complex sets of factors. Thus Freudian psychoanalytic theory, for example, has given rise to considerable experimental research in the developmental field. At the same time, it has been a major factor in bringing aspects of the traditional conception of morality into question. Again, a certain amount of research in the field of moral development is prompted specifically by the desire to assess the impact at this level of the more general change and uncertainty in moral understanding. Contemporary controversy about the nature of morality provides a common — though not exhaustive — matrix both for an understanding of morality and for the consideration of accounts of moral development. It is possible, and fruitful, to approach them together by this path.

Controversy about morality reflects the widespread upheaval of our time, associated with the rapidly changing social conditions of the modern era and the sense of a future which appears especially uncertain and threatening. Moral thinking is the attempt to provide a theoretical and practical answer to such questions as: How should we live? What constitutes human fulfilment and happiness? What principles and general rules of conduct (if any) are needed to safeguard and promote the well-being of individuals and societies and the world of which human beings are a part? What qualities of character (virtues) typify a good human being? Morality bears particularly on matters relating to birth and death, sexual relations, social relations within and beyond communities. Given the scope of these matters, it is hardly surprising that morality should come under scrutiny at a time of rapid change. Indeed, social change and upheaval have often been linked with dissatisfaction with hitherto accepted moral views and practices. Those who oppose change in these conditions standardly invoke the threat to established moral beliefs and practices as the major reason for their conservative stand. Their opponents frequently call for change in the name of promoting a more enlightened and more just — and hence morally better — social order.

The evidence of current moral controversy is most obvious perhaps in connection with specific issues. These include aspects of modern warfare, for authenticity in the exercise of one's god-like freedom is the requirement that one's fundamental choice of being be purged of bad faith; this demand then shapes the range of possible genuine values and corresponding character traits — truthfulness, integrity, courage, and so on — along recognizably traditional lines. At the same time, existentialism with its mixture of defiance and despair reflects a widespread uncertainty about the nature and foundations of morality, and a sense that, whereas human life once had meaning effortlessly conferred on it by God, its meaning now is put in question or has been lost.

Some current ideas, many with a long and interconnected history, can be linked with this experience of loss of meaning which is commonly associated with the separation of morality from religion. There is the idea that morality is subjective in the sense of being nothing more than a matter of personal conviction or feeling, that one is free to choose one's own moral values of whatever sort one likes, that morality is private and individual and should not make demands of a public sort, that moral views are relative to particular groups or individuals and hence valid and binding only in their given framework, that there is no fixed or general content to morality, and that in moral matters one opinion is as good any any other since morality is a field in which there are no authorities and no experts, that moral beliefs are neither true nor false since there is no such thing as moral facts of which there could be knowledge.

The current prevalence of these ideas may be linked historically and psychologically with the decline of religious belief and its separation from morality. But the claims might all be disputed without resort to religion. One way to show that there is something wrong with the main force of these claims would be to consider the situation of parents or others responsible for bringing up children. Responsibility for bringing up children involves the obligation of introducing them to some range of moral beliefs and practices. This is in any case inescapable since no form of life can exclude moral values: the process is built into the way in which children are treated and got to act or allowed to act. It follows that those who have this role are authorities in morals in their sphere; the children learn about morality and moral behavior through them. The authority, it is true, may be exercised badly, whether through ignorance or ill-will, or excess or defect, in one form or another. This consideration, however, only underlines the idea of authority in morals, viz., that the role is subject to standards of assessment and can be exercised well or badly. The role of authority itself also builds in a range of requirements and obligations.

Those who exercise parental authority are obliged to care for the children in their charge. They are not at liberty to interpret this in any way they choose any more than Humpty Dumpty in Lewis Carroll's *Through the Looking Glass* could make words mean whatever he wanted them to mean. No one could just decide, for example, that physical or mental cruelty exercised on children will count as taking care of them and constitute virtuous behavior in their "chosen" repertoire of moral values. Nor could anyone reasonably claim that such cruelty is a purely private matter beyond the bounds of public interest or concern. Parental authority in morals is ordinarily subject to public judgment and checks to some extent, even in fragmented societies in which major emphasis is placed on the values of private enterprise at all levels; hence parental authority is exercised in the context of a wider social authority in regard to morality. In summary, the claims that there are no authorities in morals, that morality belongs only to the sphere of the private, and that it is entirely a matter of personal choice with no fixed content, are false. This is compatible with recognizing, what is in any case obvious, that in the domain of morality a great many matters are uncertain and controversial, that authority is often abused, and that innumerable claims are false or unwarrantable.

Religious authorities sometimes continue to argue as if the current climate of uncertainty and dogmatic subjectivism in morality was the consequence of its separation from religion. They are thus given to proclaiming that moral confusion and disagreement will be overcome only by a return to religious belief and practice. It may be that the history of moral experience in our culture supports this contention — the biblical story of Moses descending from the mountain with the tables of the law handed down to him by God is deeply engrained in consciousness. It may then be a psychological fact for many people, an acquired feature of their thought and feeling, that morality and religion stand or fall together. But this contention, as I noted above, overlooks the existence of non-religious-based moral theories and systems and the historical relationship which they have with religion-based morality in Western culture. Again, it overlooks the major religious ethical tradition which recognizes that moral beliefs and practices cannot be justified merely by the voice of authority, not even by the authority of God.

The major philosophical objection to the attempt to ground morality on religious authority was set out clearly and succinctly by Plato in his dialogue, the *Euthyphro*.[2] In discussion with Socrates, the young Euthyphro, a somewhat naive and overconfident expert on religious matters, seeks to locate the basis of piety and impiety (and, by implication, virtue and vice generally) in divine approval and disapproval respectively. Socrates leads him to agree that divine approval or disapproval of forms of behavior, supposing that we have access to it, could not simply be an arbitrary exercise of authority, but would itself have to rest on grounds which relate directly to the goodness or badness of the behavior in question. In other words, reference to divine authority does not tell us what makes behavior good or bad and hence does not supply an ultimate basis or court of appeal. Euthyphro, defeated by Socrates in argument, nevertheless goes away apparently unchanged in his convictions at the end of the dialogue. In this he serves as a type of the fundamentalist religious believer. But it is also fair to remind ourselves that the force of Plato's argument has long been acknowledged by major authorities in the history of Christianity.

It is clear that religious believers, even when they accept the general separability of morality from religion, could still defend the viability of the basic content of their moral tradition. It is clear, too, that for themselves they would continue to think of morality in a religious setting; and in that setting, the moral development of children would go along with — and be treated as part of — their religious outlook. In this framework, moral goodness is understood typically as an expression of the love of God, and moral badness is interpreted as sin, which is conceived essentially as an infringement of the relationship of love of God. Furthermore, religious belief gives rise to some specific moral practices and attitudes, for example, obligations relating to prayer and worship and a specific sense of gratitude to God. Again, a religious way of life, lived seriously, constitutes a form of life, a way of living in the world, and hence a distinctive morality in one sense of the term. It is clear that morality in the senses just indicated cannot be separated from its realization within religion. It would be an illusion, however, on the part of religious believers to think that they have some independent source of moral insight or knowledge unavailable to others. Short of moral dogmatism — of which everyone is capable — they have to rely on resources which are generally available.

Religious belief, it is true, may provide a distinctive and specific motivation for moral behavior, notably by way of the promise of reward or the threat of punishment, especially in a postulated future life. But this specific motivation is not essential to morality; and whether it is effective in promoting morally good behavior, as some religious leaders suppose, is open to question. One obvious consideration here is that, in focusing attention on individual salvation in the world to come, religion could lead to the neglect of certain moral concerns in the present world. The major test case in this regard concerns matters of justice in the socio-political order. The New Testament proclaimed a conception of human equality in the message that "there is neither Jew nor Greek, slave or freeman, male or female"; but in accepting established civil authority, Christianity went along with the oppressive institution of slavery. Later, with the acquisition of political power, the Christian Church exercised its own forms of political oppression especially in relation to "outsiders" and dissenters. More recently, many Christians have been a powerful voice for social justice in different parts of the world. But the current dispute in the Roman Catholic Church concerning liberation theology in Latin America is testimony to the tensions in Christianity between involvement with the world and withdrawal from it. In short, motivation for moral behavior arising from a religious base appears to be something of a two-edged sword.

A further consideration here is that a strong religious emphasis on motivation in terms of (eternal) rewards and punishments appears to clash with the moral ideal of doing right for the right motive, that is, for the sake of what is good itself. Motivation in terms of reward and punishment belongs to the early stages of moral development and does not fit well with any reasonable ideal of moral maturity (including the ideal of unselfish love which is upheld in Christianity). A commitment to morality which operates primarily on the basis of a system of rewards and punishments is necessarily immature.

Taking account of these factors, one could agree that the historical loss of religious certainty is certainly connected with the growth of moral uncertainty and the sense that there is nothing to set limits and provide a bulwark for moral behavior. But there is no reason to think that this situation could be resolved, except in a dogmatic way, merely by a revival of religious belief. The value of the moral teaching of religious leaders — Popes and bishops, Ayatollahs, Church Moderators, and so on — needs to be looked for in the teaching itself, not in their position of authority. While religion, as history and current example attest, can constitute a powerful force in morality (for good or ill, as history and current example also attest), it does not in itself provide an answer to the question of the sources or grounds or content of morality.

3. Critics of Morality (1): Marx and Freud

MARXISM AND MORALITY

There is a dispute about morality, also of a general sort, arising from the Marxist critique of morality. Marxist thought standardly holds that morality is an ideological device for the support of an oppressive class society. The moral development of the child, in this view, would be the process by which a person comes to accept as natural the values and structures of capitalist society. Moral development so-called would be seen more generally as a central component in the process by which capitalist society ensures its reproduction. Parents, especially working-class parents, are seen as the unwitting means, together with the education system in general, by which the process is accomplished. In general, moral beliefs are taken to be determined by social class.

However serious and plausible this critique might be, it has certain curious features. The most obvious anomaly is that, beginning with Marx himself, the critique is usually conducted in an atmosphere of high moral sentiment approaching in fervor the religious denunciation of sin. In a word, Marx regarded capitalism as an evil social order, for all his acknowledgment of its inevitability as a stage of development and its realization of features of permanent value. Thus, the rejection of morality is made in part from a moral standpoint. The anomaly can be cleared up if it is allowed that Marx was thinking of morality in a very specific way in the

context of condemning it, viz., as a system of ideas and practices support-
ing class oppression, and more specifically, the system of beliefs and
practices which draws people into accepting the values of capitalist society
and which presumes to justify that society and its values.[3]

It might be obvious that morality so defined is the consecration of
something which incorporates immoral components and which is subject
to criticism from a more enlightened moral standpoint. The criticism
cannot be intelligibly taken, however, as a blanket objection to morality. It
cannot even be taken as an argument against morality as understood and
practiced in the capitalist era, for it would be absurd to suggest that all the
morality of this time has had a predominantly oppressive role: moral
concern has sometimes inspired opposition to oppression and served as
the basis for the critical rejection of capitalist values and the reform of social
practices. The focus of Marx's criticism needs to be taken, therefore, in a
fairly precise and limited sense.

Marx in fact did not say very much about morality in a future socialist
society, but he suggested in *The German Ideology* that communism "shatters
the basis of all morality." But once again, "morality" needs to be understood in this context as something like "oppressive class morality."
Alternatively, the idea of there being no morality in the socialist society of
the future could be compared to the Christian idea that morality —
conceived as a set of rules which prescribes some forms of behavior and
proscribes others — has no place in heaven. In the meantime, socialism in
the normative sense in which some Marxists use the term has nowhere
been realized; and one might say that human societies remain in need of
morality, not least to combat oppression and other forms of injustice in
socialist as well as capitalist societies.

While Marx was fundamentally concerned with issues other than morality, he nevertheless subscribed to a moral outlook in a broad but important
sense.[4] He was profoundly influenced by Greek thought throughout his
life, and upheld in his writings an Aristotelian-type ideal of the good life
for human beings: self-actualization for the individual, the development of
one's potential in a range of worthwhile human endeavors, within a
unified and integrated community. In relation to capitalist social relations,
this ideal entails the overcoming of alienation in human life, especially in
relation to the conditions of human work. More generally, it encompasses
the satisfaction of physical and social needs of individuals within the
community, with particular emphasis on scope for the exercise of cre-
ativity, and with autonomy for all. It could be objected, with good reason,
that Marx failed to work out the details of his ideal of self-actualization and
that its presentation, in relation to socialism, was marked by utopian
elements. He did not acknowledge the role it played in his criticism of
capitalist morality; furthermore, he did not properly acknowledge the
strong presence of a similar ideal of self-actualization in Western ethical

thought, in the ethics developed by medieval thinkers on the basis of Aristotle's writings, for example, or in Hegel's ethical thought.

In summary, Marx's broad conception of morality is more traditional than his better known remarks about morality might allow; and his critique of morality is correspondingly less sweeping than it might at first appear. From a more adequate ethical vantage point, it is directed at morally objectionable features of the capitalist era (though not restricted to it): exploitation of human and natural resources, acquisitive materialism, greed, mindless consumerism, the fragmentation of social relations, ruthless competitiveness and individualism. Given the influence of these features in conventional moral belief and practice, the critique is directed at forms of immorality which masquerade as morality. Its particular strength lies in the unmasking of ideological elements in conventional morality, especially in its public and institutional forms.

The deceptively sweeping appearance of this critique exacts a price. There is the temptation for Marxist critics to simplify grossly or to misrepresent in other ways the general moral theories and beliefs of Western ethical thought, and to underestimate the capacity for self-criticism in the tradition. The appearance of excess in the critique also weakens its impact at the levels at which it is most pertinent, as bearing on forms of deception and injustice in the modern era. Again, the illusion that Marxism has achieved a general and compelling critique of morality promotes a belief among its adherents that ethics or moral philosophy is no concern of theirs. Thus, while Marxism has helped to provoke awareness of a significant range of matters which are pertinent to morality, Marxist thinkers have contributed very little to the development of moral inquiry.[5]

In conclusion, there is no good reason to accept the view that morality is inevitably manifested as oppressive class-morality, or as nothing but this, or that the moral development of children is necessarily a smokescreen term to cover the process of their induction into their place in the galaxy of the "values" of exploitation, greed, competitive individualism, and so on. This is not to suggest that class factors do not exercise considerable influence on moral beliefs and practices; nor is it to deny that they have affected the practice of moral philosophy from its primary constitution by Plato and Aristotle in ancient Athens. The weaknesses in the general Marxist critique do not destroy the force of specific criticisms. On the other hand, the criticisms have force insofar as they point to a more adequate moral standpoint.

MORALITY AND FREUDIAN THEORY

Freudian psychoanalytic theory has had major reverberations in contemporary thinking about morality; it has also been a major influence on theory and research in the field of moral development. Consideration of the latter topic will be taken up in the next chapter. For the present, I want to take note of Freud's conception of morality and of the main implications of Freudian thought for moral questions.

In commenting on Freud's denial that psychoanalysis has "moral" implications beyond those of the scientific attitude in general, Ronald de Sousa writes aptly:

> Yet any comprehensive vision of human nature such as [Freud] provides must have implications for the nature of happiness, and for the relation of man's natural capacities to his normal or ideal state.[6]

It is also obvious that Freud's conception of the unconscious and his emphasis on the role of instincts in human behavior has considerable bearing on the idea of personal responsibility and agency and on our understanding of motivation. There is also his account of conscience in terms of the notion of the super-ego.

Freud, it is well known, was profoundly critical of religion as a deep and harmful illusion which pretends at once to serve three roles in human life: it seeks to provide an explanation of the origin of the universe; it supplies a major source of consolation in life's difficulties and holds out the promise of ultimate happiness; and it claims to provide the ground and authority for ethical precepts in the conduct of life. Religion, in Freud's diagnosis, "is an attempt to master the sensory world in which we are situated by means of a wishful world which we have developed within us as a result of biological and psychological necessities." Again, it is the wishful extension of the relations of the child to its parents to a universal expression. Ethical precepts in particular are presented to children by their parents and are inculcated by a system of loving rewards and punishments. In the religious transposition of this experience, as Freud explains it, "their parents' prohibitions and demands persist within them as a moral conscience. With the help of this same system of rewards and punishments, God rules the world of men."

In rejecting religion in the name of a scientific "world-view," Freud did not also reject morality. On the contrary, he acknowledged its necessity and pointed to the need to find some basis for ethical demands other than religion:

> the ethical demands on which religion seeks to lay stress need, rather, to be given another basis; for they are indispensable to human society and it is dangerous to link obedience to them with religious faith.[7]

This point could hardly be stated more clearly. Freud nonetheless contemplated the idea that cultural forms generally — moral and political beliefs, art, and even science — are all illusions, that is to say, products of wishful thinking. He raises this question in fact in *The Future of an Illusion*:

> Having recognised religious doctrines as illusions, we are at once faced by a further question: may not other cultural assets of which we hold a high opinion and by which we let our lives be ruled be of a similar nature?[8]

Having raised the question, Freud sets it aside at this point. But in the lecture of 1933 to which reference was made above, he defended scientific inquiry against the suggestion that it is illusory. At the same time, he readily acknowledged that art is an illusion: it is a defensible illusion, however, on the grounds that it is "almost always harmless and beneficent; it does not seek to be anything but illusion."[9] (Freud also observes that philosophy is illusory, but he sets it aside as of no great concern since philosophy, he considered, was of interest to so few people.)

The development of the argument in The Future of an Illusion leads eventually to a consideration of the status of moral belief. Given the premise that the prohibition on killing and the other precepts of civilization do not rest on divine sanction, it becomes necessary to look for their basis in a purely human origin. Freud's answer is that the source of moral precepts is found in reason. His argument starts from a position which is evocative of the Hobbesian version of a pre-social state — the so-called state of nature — which consists of a war of all against all. Faced with insecurity of life in these conditions, men (and women) unite into a society which prohibits killing on the part of individuals and which takes on authority to punish offenders with death. Thus, reason in the form of social necessity determines what has to be done to secure human life. The same form of argument is then extended to moral and social precepts generally — though, as Freud points out, many actual moral precepts fail to meet the test of rationality because they are, in his words, "an expression of selfishly narrow interests or a conclusion based on insufficient premisses."[10]

Freud's appeal to reason, it should be noted, is put forward as a rational reconstruction of moral belief, not as original history (of which he sought to give an account in Totem and Taboo). In The Future of an Illusion, as elsewhere in his writings, Freud emphasizes the power of the passions and instinctual demand: there is a prevailing idea that arguments are of no avail against the passions. Even so, it is clear that Freud seeks to find in reason and intellect a growing normative influence in human life.

This consideration does not enter satisfactorily, however, into his account of morality. For Freud, reason is located, as we have just seen, in the domain of social relations or in the conditions in which social relations come into being. Reason is portrayed, therefore, as lying outside human nature proper, which for him is realized in the individual and which consists, in the individual, of a web of instincts:

Psychological — or, more strictly speaking, psycho-analytic — investigation shows . . . that the deepest essence of human nature consists of instinctual impulses which are of an elementary nature, which are similar in all men and which aim at the satisfaction of certain primal needs.[11]

Chief among the instincts with bearing on morality (in which the needs and demands of the human community are introduced) is a cruel aggressiveness. This is manifested according to Freud as a "primary mutual hostility of human beings," and it "reveals man as a savage beast to whom consideration towards his own kind is something alien."[12]

Morality in this preconceived setting is understood as a set of rules and sanctions imposed on the individual from outside and from above (so to speak) in the interests of the community. Morality, imposed by society or civilization or reason, is thus necessarily in conflict with human nature and natural desire in the individual. In some sources, furthermore, Freud treats moral rightness as merely the expression of a form of violence which is stronger than individual violence. There is an example of this in his letter to Einstein, "Why War?" (1932), where he locates the origins of moral right in the union of violent individuals against individual violence and argues in conclusion:

> Thus we see that right is the might of a community. It is still violence, ready to be directed against any individual who resists it; it works by the same methods and follows the same purposes. The only real difference lies in the fact that what prevails is no longer the violence of an individual but that of a community.[13]

Freud's developmental account of morality, as we shall see, holds that the process works only by reliance on psychical reaction-formations in which — beginning with the fear of punishment and loss of love — individual aggressiveness is turned back on its possessor in the form of conscience. The moral rules of the community are thus internalized as inhibitions on original instincts, but they remain weak, always under threat from the basic natural forces.

Freud does not supply much argument for his thesis of original aggressiveness and the "primary mutual hostility of human beings." The evidence is hardly more than anecdotal and relates in any case to violence manifested *within* a social setting (atrocities in war and so on).[14] This latter consideration points to a central weakness in the whole account, its abstract individualism. Freud attempts to work with a conception of individuals as somehow complete human beings without reference to social relations (which are treated as outside the essence of human nature). He does not succeed in the attempt any more than did Hobbes in his portrayal of "presocial" human beings in the opening chapters of *Leviathan*. The account appears to work only because it smuggles in reference to social dimensions of existence, but it thereby undercuts itself.

In the terms of the model, nature and culture (society, civilization) are distinct and opposed; instincts, the properties of individuals, fall on the side of nature; reason and morality, since they involve social relations, fall on the side of culture. But for the reason indicated, the model itself is radically flawed. It can be argued that we become social and moral beings only through a process of learning. But this does not mean that we are not social beings by nature any more than the fact that we have to learn to speak a language would imply that human beings are not naturally language-users. Characteristic human desires and forms of behavior are inconceivable apart from a social setting. Culture in one form or another therefore enters into any satisfactory account of human nature; so too do reason and morality. Once this is recognized, the view that culture is *essentially* restrictive vis-à-vis the individual and in opposition to natural desire collapses. While various cultural forms, including moral rules, may inhibit desire and growth because they are unsatisfactory, culture is nevertheless the medium in which human desire and growth are possible in the first place.

It is also important to note that Freud's "might is right" account of morality (as in *Civilization and Its Discontents*) is at odds with his attempt to find the ground of morality in a normative account of reason and his defense of civilization (in *The Future of an Illusion*, for example). Curiously, the espousal of the "might is right" account undermines the desired distinction between nature and culture since it reduces everything to the same level of force or violence. Freud thereby denies himself access to the ground on which a critical assessment of morality and of specific rules would be possible. He certainly envisaged such an undertaking in various writings; furthermore, the whole psychoanalytic program builds in the idea of normal human development within a social setting. But this is bedevilled in Freudian theory as a whole by the conception of moral rules as lying outside human nature and in conflict with natural desire.

4. Critics of Morality (2): Nietzsche

The interpretation of Nietzsche's views is notoriously a matter of dispute. Part of the difficulty is that he had so much to say on the topics he discussed, so many different points and insights, and so many different ways of making the same point, none of them complete. There is also the consideration that he put on a number of masks, adopted different voices, and perhaps laid false trails. Nevertheless, Nietzsche claimed a general unity for his thought. Within the limitations of a short inquiry, I will present an interpretation which does justice to this claim in regard to his views about morality.

To a considerable extent Nietzsche's writings on this topic take the form of a critique of moralities and moral philosophies hitherto. I will argue that his critique is illuminating in important respects, in part because it is less subversive than it is regularly taken to be. Nietzsche did not undertake to provide a detailed blueprint for a revised account of morality. Nevertheless, it is possible to find in his project for a revaluation of all values a definite approach to this goal. I will argue that his account, once again, is illuminating and defensible in important respects, in part because it is more traditional than Nietzsche would allow. His views are marred, however, by a degree of extremism and ambivalence; and there is a great weakness in his account inasmuch as his central moral ideal is unworkable. I will argue that this weakness is connected with Nietzsche's failure to take account of developmental considerations in his thinking about morality.

MASTER MORALITY AND SLAVE MORALITY

Nietzsche is sometimes described as a moral nihilist, and on occasions he would refer to himself as an immoralist. This could suggest that there is no place for morality in his thought, specifically that his philosophy of the future, in the words of one of his best known books, lies beyond "good and evil."[15] But this popular conception of Nietzsche is ill-founded. He was a profound critic of nihilism which he saw as symptomatic of the modern age, especially as a consequence of the crisis of religious belief and the associated general crisis of confidence in the values of Western civilization. And what he saw as lying beyond good and evil was not immorality or amorality, but a more satisfactory way of grounding values in the natural world.

The basis of the popular misconception of Nietzsche lies in part in his characteristic use of hyperbole: in his writings, exaggeration is developed to the level of an art-form.[16] The other main factor lies in the scope of his critical attack on traditional moral systems and on arguments for morality based on religious belief or philosophy. The sweep of his criticism is more or less universal. His critique of moralities hitherto and of all moral philosophies is thus seen — not least by Nietzsche himself in many places — as the critical repudiation of morality itself.

In writing on morality, Nietzsche put particular stress on the diversity of moral systems. This is linked in *Thus Spoke Zarathustra* with the idea that "no people can live without evaluating; but if it wishes to maintain itself it must not evaluate as its neighbour evaluates."[17] So he speaks of ancient Greek and Persian, ancient Jewish and modern German tables of value, of a thousand peoples and a thousand different goals or ways of marking out good and evil, and, as yet, no goal for humanity as a whole. More prosaically in *Beyond Good and Evil* (hereafter *BGE*), he observes:

> The diversity of men is revealed not only in the diversity of their tables of what they find good, that is to say in the fact that they regard diverse goods as worth striving for and also differ as to what is more or less valuable, as to the order of rank of the goods they all recognise — it is revealed even more in what they regard as actually *having* and *possessing* what they find good. (*BGE* 194)

In keeping with the emphasis on diversity, Nietzsche refers to the need for a typology of morals: one might then approach and discover the problems of morality by comparing *many* moralities. Such an undertaking is begun in Part 5 of *Beyond Good and Evil* and taken up more fully in *On the Genealogy of Morals*.[18] But for all the emphasis on diversity, illuminated by his capacity for observing subtleties in human attitudes and his imaginative — though not very plausible — reconstructions of history, the typology of morality offered in these sources is essentially simple:

> In a tour of many finer and coarser moralities which have ruled or still rule on earth I found certain traits regularly recurring together and bound up with one another: until at length two basic types were revealed and a basic distinction emerged. There is *master morality* and *slave morality* — I add at once that in all higher and mixed cultures attempts at mediation between the two are apparent and more frequently confusion and mutual misunderstanding between them, indeed sometimes their harsh juxtaposition — even within the same man, within *one* soul. (*BGE* 260)

With this distinction, the general scope of Nietzsche's moral inquiry is revealed: while master morality points toward his ideas regarding the revaluation of all values, slave morality constitutes the primary object of his critique. The distinction can be explained fairly — though certainly not completely — in the following way (with particular reference to the first essay of *On the Genealogy of Morals*).

Master morality consists essentially of an untrammelled, proud expression of human powers on the part of members of a group who, as individuals, act without reference to others. Such individuals constitute an elite almost by definition. In a highly implausible historical hypothesis, Nietzsche associates this form of life (and morality) with ruling groups in early societies, typically conceived as a powerful and aggressive warrior caste. "Good" in the eyes of this morality consists in being a person who lives in the way indicated, achieving great deeds of one sort or another. (Nietzsche is insouciant about this, but in context one is to think of courageous, fearless, warlike deeds.) To be "bad" from this point of view is simply to be one of the general run of people who do not assert themselves in the specified way and whose lives are subject to conformity and constraint in the pursuit of petty goals. Nietzsche describes this latter form of life in general as "herd morality."

Slave morality, in Nietzsche's hypothesis, is a form of herd morality which arose in reaction against master morality. Its origin lies in a sense of envy and desire for revenge on the past of the weak against the strong. The great driving force of this morality is *ressentiment* — resentment — the desire for revenge for one's inferiority, hatred of the strong and healthy (which becomes, through punishment and guilt, a form of self-hatred as well).[19] In establishing itself, slave morality effected a revaluation of the values of master morality: thus, pride in power and achievement was replaced by passivity, and the virtue of humility was esteemed as a cloak for weakness; again, self-reliance gave way to relations of dependence and pity was invoked as a mask for resentment.

The major reversal, as Nietzsche conceives it, lies in the conception of good in slave morality and the invention of the *antithesis* of good and evil. In master morality, the good is a joyful expression of one's being which occurs without comparison of oneself with others: the noble person "conceives the basic concept 'good' in advance and spontaneously out of himself and only then creates for himself the idea of 'bad'" — the bad being, in effect, those who are deficient in regard to the characteristic qualities of the good. In this case, "good" and "bad" are not opposites, but points on a continuum which relates to degrees of power. This order is reversed in slave morality: evil is now the dominant idea; and good and evil, differently understood, are set up as *opposites*. (In reference to slave morality, Nietzsche uses the term "evil" in place of "bad" to mark the contrast.)[20] The slave, acting out of reaction, begins with reference to the other, the "good man" of master morality, and it is precisely this man and the values exhibited in his life which are now nominated as *evil*. The *good* in slave morality is then specified negatively and by way of comparison as the opposite of what is evil. Slave morality, it can be seen, does not *create* values or affirm life; its values are constructed negatively out of the rejection of the values of the other. In making these remarks in *On the Genealogy of Morals* (hereafter GM), Nietzsche concludes with a reference to "that dangerous slogan . . . inscribed at the head of my last book *Beyond Good and Evil*. At least this does *not* mean 'Beyond Good and Bad'" (*GM* I, 17). The general form of a Nietzschean prescription for morality is thus made clear.

The contrast of master and slave moralities provides the key to large areas of Nietzsche's thought. It relates immediately to his notoriously polemical attack on Christianity, for he considered that the Christian "table of value" is the primary historical expression of slave morality. This relates in turn to his critical account of nihilism in the later nineteenth century, for nihilism is diagnosed as the outcome of slave morality. The overcoming of nihilism, which is linked with Nietzsche's idea of the "Overman" (*Übermensch*), would then consist of a revaluation of slave values which would take its general form from the idea of master morality. The contrast of master and slave moralities relates to Nietzsche's basic cosmological principle according to which the universe is composed of two sorts of forces, active and reactive, each of which is associated with a characteristic "will to power" (which is force considered from an internal point of view) — will to power expressed as affirmation (the action of active forces) and negation (the action of reactive forces).

History, according to Nietzsche's hypothesis, has seen the triumph of reactive forces, leading to the decline of humanity manifested in nihilism.

This is witnessed, he argues, in the mediocre, sickly, herd-minded individual in the social, political, and cultural life of modern Europe. While the primary focus of his attack in this context is Christianity, its scope extends to socialism, anarchism, liberal democracy, and just about everything modern, as merely secularized versions of Christian values. Indeed, in Nietzsche's more hyperbolic turn, it might seem that nothing human escapes the net:

> [The] instinct of revenge has so mastered mankind in the course of millennia that the whole of metaphysics, psychology, conception of history, but above all morality, is impregnated with it. As far as man has thought, he has introduced the bacillus of revenge into things.[21]

In spite of massive simplification and dubious historical hypotheses (such as concern Christianity and the relation of the modern world to ancient societies), Nietzsche's typology of morality has significant force. It offers a penetrating account of the syndrome of resentment and its role in constituting a pervasive origin of moral judgments. This goes along with sharp critical insight into human foibles and the all-too-human capacity for self-deception, pretension, and creating a gap between lofty rhetoric and sordid reality especially in the domain of morality.

In Nietzsche's account, resentment and the desire for revenge are connected with the repression of basic emotions and affects. What his diagnosis points to is the extent to which realized moral systems, expressed in a will to condemn and punish and in opposition to spontaneous enjoyment, get their character from the attempt to curb inclination and desire and the passions in the name of duty (for example). Such moralities, in Nietzsche's phrase, are recipes to counter the passions; or again, as he observes, "the moralist's mania . . . demands not the control but the extirpation of the passions. Their conclusion is ever: only the emasculated man is the good man" (*BGE* 198).

As we saw in connection with Freud, this way of thinking about morality is not uncommon. With Nietzsche's analysis at hand, it is possible to see that morality, past and present, frequently operates along these lines: in significant practical respects, it arises out of fear, as Nietzsche says, fear of the passions, fear of freedom, fear of the other person (see *Beyond Good and Evil*, 201). In such a situation there is the likelihood of an unrecognized conflict between the practice of a morality and some of its demands. Most moralities, and notably Christian morality, would characterize revenge, ill-will, lack of respect for others, hatred, and the like, as immoral. Yet these are precisely the attitudes to which Nietzsche points in his account of slave morality. Apart from the spirit of revenge, the resentment-filled person (or morality) is marked by ill-will manifested as an inability to admire or respect or love others, by a willingness to impute blame, and by an attitude in which pain is linked essentially to guilt and punishment.

Nietzsche's account of this type of personality offers a powerful instrument of criticism of a great deal of moral thinking and practice. But, as we saw in the case of Marx, the criticism is itself offered from a moral standpoint. Nietzsche's insight into the prevalence of elements of resentment in moral judgment and behavior is importantly a *moral* insight. But critique is then carried to the point of caricature. Nietzsche is drawn to treat elements of resentment as both inescapable and all-conquering in relation to morality; and in his attack on Christianity and modern social movements, he writes as if the pure type of slave morality had been fully and universally realized. In truth, Nietzsche's critique of the resentment-filled person finds common ground with the traditions of which he is critical.

There is one major respect, however, in which Nietzsche's discussion of Christian morality in particular appears to go beyond the possibility of common ground, viz., his repudiation of the value of pity or compassion in human relations. Here, it seems clear, Nietzsche places himself entirely outside the bounds of common morality. When attention is given to context, however, the matter is not so straightforward.

It is noteworthy that some proponents of Stoic morality in the late classical world also rejected pity as a moral virtue, mainly on the grounds that it is incompatible with an adequate conception of the central moral requirement for self-sufficiency and detachment in the wise man.[22] The Nietzschean context for this consideration, constituted immediately by the complex of master and slave morality, is in fact broadly similar. The primary target of the attack is pity as manifested in slave morality — in other words, pity which is associated with an underlying hatred for and denial of life, "a depressive and contagious instinct [which] thwarts those instincts bent on preserving and enhancing the value of life";[23] or again, what he attacks is a pity which wallows in a cult of suffering, which always interprets pain in terms of guilt and punishment, and in which the sufferer is always a victim:

> There exists almost everywhere in Europe today a morbid sensitivity and susceptibility to pain, likewise a repellent intemperance in lamentation, a tenderization which, with the aid of religion and odds and ends of philosophy, would like to deck itself out as something higher — there exists a downright cult of suffering. (*BGE* 293)

Earlier in the same paragraph Nietzsche speaks of pity of a different sort, the pity "of man who is by nature a *master* — when such a man has pity, well! *that* pity has value!" The stoic dimension of Nietzsche's approval of pity of the right sort is clear from a related passage:

> The noble human being too aids the unfortunate, but not, or almost not, from pity, but more from an urge begotten by superfluity of power. (*BGE* 260)

Thus, the pity of which Nietzsche is critical is not properly a moral virtue at all even if it is decked out in this way; and his characterization of pity of this sort as a form of moral pathology is a further exercise of *moral* insight. This standpoint is muddied, however, in Nietzsche's writings. He tends to treat all manifestations of pity, in Christianity and the modern world generally, as instances of debased, "slave" pity; and there is affirmation in his writings of forms of appropriation, injury, violence, the aggressive manifestation of strength over weakness, and so on, in connection with master morality. He would defend this as an affirmation of life against the life-denying character of slave morality. But here the question arises as to what sort of strength and what of life are being affirmed. It is possible to extract a defensible interpretation from what he says on this matter (one in which his position is not, for example, an affirmation of the successful and callous bully), but he leaves himself open to misinterpretation. Apart from this, Nietzsche's whole characterization of current forms of morality — Utilitarianism, Kantian ethics, Christian morality, and so on — depends on ridicule as much as argument. In being justifiably critical of elements in the constitution of these moral positions, he goes on to treat them as if they were pure realizations of slave morality. Nietzsche's rhetoric runs on well beyond the force of his argument. This same consideration applies to his otherwise illuminating discussion of the related topic of nihilism.

Nietzsche observes at the beginning of *The Will to Power* (hereafter *WP*):

> What does nihilism mean? *That the highest values devaluate themselves*. The aim is lacking; "Why?" finds no answer. (*WP* 2)

The French philosopher Gilles Deleuze suggests that this remark relates to a secondary and derived sense of nihilism, the colloquial sense in which nihilism consists in the denial of values and the sense that the world is empty of meaning and purpose.[24] But from where does secondary nihilism come? The proposal is that it arises out of the historical collapse of the expression of nihilism as the *will to nothingness* which is realized most typically for Nietzsche in Christian belief. Nihilism in this primary sense means an attitude which accords the *value of nil* — no value — to life; hence, nihilism means the depreciation of life. This comes about, as Nietzsche portrays it, on the basis of a fiction, the invention of *another* world in which higher values — God, ultimate truth, goodness — are located. In the process, the real world, this world, is depreciated, becoming a world of appearances only, a world without value. It is in this sense that Nietzsche holds that Christian belief constitutes in itself the primary form of nihilism. Reactive or secondary nihilism ensues when these *highest values devaluate themselves* — that is to say, when belief in the values of the other world loses its hold (the death of God). The loss of belief in transcendental values is then hypothesized as leading to the denial of all values.

Nietzsche's account of these matters is illuminating to a degree; the problem once again is that he takes one specific feature of a situation and projects it as the whole. There is the tendency in human experience, manifested most characteristically in religion, to seek value in some other world. Sometimes this projection is connected with a depreciation of this world: strands of this sort are readily identifiable in Christianity and other religions; but just as characteristically (and perhaps more so) it goes with an affirmation of value in this world. Similarly, the loss of faith in a transcendental world may be followed by a general denial of value and a sense of forlorn and fearful emptiness (such as Matthew Arnold captured in his poem "Dover Beach"). This is a significant theme in nineteenth- and twentieth-century experience. But again, the transition to reactive nihilism is not inevitable, nor is it even characteristic of modern experience. Nietzsche in fact recognized this and bemoaned the apparent ease with which a religious view of the world was giving way to secularized forms of religious values. His conviction was that the full experience of nihilism *should* follow the collapse of the age of faith, for only in this way could a thorough and worthwhile revaluation of values be effected in European culture. His position, then, was to will the advent of nihilism, without directly being a party to it, as the necessary step toward overcoming the phenomenon of decadence or the total loss of value associated with the triumph of reactive forces.

THE REVALUATION OF VALUES

The general character of a Nietzschean revaluation of values has already been indicated in the discussion of master and slave moralities. In this context, master morality points the way to the idea of the *Übermensch*, that is, the one who has overcome the general human entanglement in herd or slave morality.[25] What is involved in this overcoming is, in Nietzschean terms, the return of *active* forces (as against the reactive forces of slave morality). It is a vision of the creation of new values. But it is necessary to give this vision more content and to consider what could be its ground.

In his general critique of moralities hitherto, Nietzsche rejected philosophical attempts of the previous century to ground morality on conscience or inner moral sentiments, on the one hand, or on a rational grasp of moral law, as in Kant's notion of the categorical imperative, on the other. In pressing this argument in *The Gay Science* (335) he went on to propose:

> Let us therefore *limit* ourselves to the purification of our opinions and valuations and the *creation* of our own new tables of what is good. . . .
> We . . . *want to become those we are* — human beings who are new, unique, incomparable, who give themselves laws, who create themselves.

In a comment on this passage, Alasdair MacIntyre sees Nietzsche as seeking to replace reason with "some gigantic and heroic act of the will" in which each individual takes on the task of inventing a new table of what is good; and he concludes that this venture — the invention of self-willed values by each individual — "would constitute the core of a Nietzschean moral philosophy."[26] What Nietzsche offers in the MacIntyre interpretation is a prophetic irrationalism: the presentation of a problem which defies rational solution and which, as such, captures the condition of bureaucratically managed modern societies.

This interpretation certainly captures a theme in Nietzsche's writings. Moreover, MacIntyre shows how it was picked up by Max Weber in his account of bureaucratic rationality — that is, the rationality which consists in matching means to ends purely on grounds of economic efficiency. In this framework, Weber drew on Nietzsche in particular as one who holds that values are created by human decisions and are purely subjective.[27] For all that, the projection of this theme as the core of a Nietzschean moral philosophy is mistaken: it entirely overlooks major elements in his project for a revaluation of values.

Rather than endorsing an arbitrary choice of self-willed values, Nietzsche seeks to ground values in the natural world. Here, as elsewhere in his thought, the primary inspiration is drawn from Greek sources. A morality as Nietzsche portrays it is a way of interpreting the world (expressive in particular of how we respond emotionally to the world). The principle for assessing such interpretations as better or worse — and, in effect, as having a claim to greater or lesser truth — is drawn from an understanding of nature, more precisely a normative understanding of nature as manifesting a proper balance and state of health. In Nietzsche's terms, the morality of a people is the voice of its will to power, the way in which it seeks to express itself in terms of an understanding of the world. Allowing for the simplification in his moral typology, the will to power of a morality is either an expression of predominantly active, affirmative, healthy forces, or predominantly reactive, negative, and sick forces. But the determination whether a force or combination of forces is one or the other is *not* itself a matter of will. Forms of slave morality are anti-natural because they are directed against human passions and instincts:

> Formerly one made war on passion itself on account of the folly inherent in it: one conspired for its extermination — all the old moral monsters are unanimous that *"il faut tuer les passions"*.

Against this Nietzsche espouses a principle of ethical naturalism:

> I formulate a principle. All naturalism in morality, that is all *healthy* morality, is dominated by an instinct of life — some commandment of life is fulfilled through a certain canon of "shall" and "shall not", some hindrance and hostile element on life's road is thereby removed. *Anti-natural* morality, that is virtually every morality that has hitherto been taught, reverenced and preached, turns on the contrary precisely *against* the instincts of life — it is now a secret, now loud and impudent *condemnation* of these instincts.[28]

Nietzsche's project for a revaluation of values is presented most charac-teristically as a *reversal*. It consists in the idea of overturning the central reactive values of slave morality in favor of a return to nature. But here the "return to nature" is understood not as the attempt to go back to some postulated former condition, but as a going forward, or beyond, or up — "up into a high, free, even frightful nature and naturalness, such as plays with great tasks, is *permitted* to play with them."[29] This is the move toward the Übermensch, the beyond-human being. Nietzsche is anxious to distin-guish his conception of relevant nature from Aristotelian naturalism or the understanding of nature in Stoicism or in Rousseau's moral thought. But the *form* of argument is not different.

The Nietzschean project of reversal is accompanied by a certain ethical ideal of the life-affirming human being as creative artist, as magnanimous and noble, as a self-sufficient and sovereign individual — in contrast to the life-denying person characterized by mediocrity and pettiness, self-serving pity, and an underlying hatred of self and others. Affirmative values are values of life as light and active and joyful, the values of dance, laughter, and play. The primary demand, then, in the creation of new values would be to seek to go beyond moral and political orders based on resentment and repression. The resentment-filled person, as we saw, is characterized by passivity, a spirit of revenge, ill-will toward others, a festering memory of wrong done and the inability to forget, a willingness to impute blame, an attitude in which pain is associated with guilt and the need for punishment.

The core of a Nietzschean morality would be the creative reversal of these reactive values, to be filled out by the ideal of self-sufficiency together with the range of qualities which might be associated with the creative artist and sovereign individual. This includes an emphasis on self-mastery and on discipline in one's life as the condition of achievement in any worthwhile domain, be it virtue, art, music, dance, reason, spiritu-ality (see *BGE* 188). There is also the ideal of developing creative powers as richly as one can and holding them together in unity. (It should now be clear that the sorts of power and strength properly associated with Nietz-sche's revaluation of values are quite different from those which mark the heroes of "original" master morality, even if he would insist that there are important underlying continuities.) The development of one's powers would be linked, finally, with the ideal of "becoming what one is."

Nietzsche introduced this phrase in *The Gay Science* and then used it as the subtitle of his account of his work, *Ecce Homo: How One Becomes What One Is*.[30] The phrase, which is less than perspicuous, is associated with being a creator of values, and conveys the sense of a principle of authen-ticity. In this connection, it is perhaps suggestive of the idea of self-realization: realizing one's self as a whole in one's activities (an idea already noted in the brief discussion of Marx, and one which will recur in connection with Aristotle and Hegel).

The above program is a far cry from the bald affirmation of the will which MacIntyre and others attribute to Nietzsche. Considered as a whole, his position is much less subversive than it has regularly been taken to be. Indeed, it has much in common with a conception of morality which might be drawn from Greek ethical naturalism. There are elements of Aristotle and the Stoics in particular. What makes it appear subversive is that the spirit and tone of Nietzsche's enterprise are drawn from the defiant but ill-considered assertion of nature over convention made by Callicles in Plato's *Gorgias*.

Nietzsche's attempt at a revaluation of all values, which began, as he came to recognize, in his first work, *The Birth of Tragedy*, was left uncompleted at the time of his mental collapse in 1889. A satisfactory study of his project would need to take full account of the collection of notes published posthumously as *The Will to Power*, along with writings which he published in the 1880s, especially *The Gay Science*, *Thus Spoke Zarathustra*, *Beyond Good and Evil*, and *On the Genealogy of Morals*. The interpretation I have put forward relates to all these sources, but much has been omitted — much of the force and subtlety and detail of Nietzsche's thought, and also much of the extremism, exaggeration, disdain for everything of which he was critical, and the apocalyptic and cataclysmic tone of his writing (elements of which are all significant in setting the character of his writing, making it fascinating to many readers and repellent to others, but in any case immensely powerful). There is, however, one theme to which attention needs to be given.

Nietzsche was opposed to the idea that there could be just one satisfactory morality embracing all human beings. This is connected with his perspectivism, his insistence in Alexander Nehamas' words that "every view is only one among many possible interpretations, his own views, particularly this very one, included."[31] Specifically in the domain of morality, it is connected with the idea that there are many different types of peoples, many different types of human beings, hence many different forms of life, ideals and goals. (Morality for Nietzsche relates especially to the whole style or character of the life of a person — or a people.) This embraces his plea for diversity against the drive for universality, and his opposition to the strong emphasis on conformity and constraint in traditional morality. More deeply, it concerns his longing for a flowering of genius which might somehow carry European culture beyond its critical breakdown to a new sense of unity and purpose. What he opposes in this context is a petty-minded mediocrity:

Lofty spiritual independence, the will to stand alone, great intelligence even, are felt to be dangerous; everything that raises the individual above the herd and makes his neighbour quail is henceforth called *evil*; the fair, modest, obedient, self-effacing disposition, the *mean and average* in desires, acquires moral names and honours. (*BGE* 201)

The Nietzschean idea of the creation of values also belongs to this context. In its primary application, it is the task of outstanding thinkers, writers, artists, or "men of action" who forge a new way of thinking about or experiencing life, and who enrich people's experience generally and make it possible for others to see things differently — Shakespeare, Mozart, Goethe, to take outstanding examples to whom Nietzsche alludes. But the creation of values in this way is obviously rare. Taken in a broad or general sense, it is the task of assuming responsibility for values in one's own life as against acting out of mere conformity to rules laid down by others. In this sense, the creation of values by the individual is a necessary condition of moral maturity. Once again, this has nothing to do with the subjective invention of values.

In Nietzsche's elitist point of view, "few are made for independence — it is a privilege of the strong" (*BGE* 29). For most people, guidance is found in the "human herd," in family groups, communities, tribes, nations, states, churches, as he observes in *Beyond Good and Evil* (199). The Nietzschean emphasis on diversity over conformity is made against this background. But what Nietzsche fails to acknowledge is the degree of generality (and traditionalism) in his own account of values after the revaluation. Nietzschean virtues include, on reflection, such traditional values as honesty, truthfulness, justice, courage, self-control, love of others, unwillingness to bear grudges or impute blame, and the acceptance of life — and of death. There is, however, a significant lacuna. The virtues just listed have social and political implications. But in his concern for lofty spiritual independence and a high, free nature such as plays at great tasks, Nietzsche does not take up in any detailed way the moral questions of human association. Aspects of common life fall under his critical eye on innumerable occasions, but in his espousal of a "pathos of distance" there is no attempt to take up the issues positively. This is a major weakness.

In a basic sense, the problem arises from within the terms of his typology of moralities and relates to the topic of moral development. Social relations in the framework of master and slave moralities are treated primarily as the expression of reactive forces (hence as "herd" or "slave" morality). The master is by contrast a sovereign individual and his own legislator. As self-sufficient, his virtues are thought of as realized in his own person without reference to others (except perhaps to those others who are his equals in lofty independence). The theme of self-sufficiency is persistent in Western moral thinking — it can be associated readily with Aristotle in one way, in another with the Stoics, and in different ways again with Rousseau and Kant. The problem is to find an appropriate balance between self-sufficiency as a value and the need for and value of relationships with others.

In his moral thinking, Nietzsche sets this problem aside, and so far as masters are concerned, independence and self-sufficiency stand alone.

Nietzschean masters — and the Nietzschean Übermensch as an ethical ideal — are presented as if they erupted into the world with all their creative forces and life-affirming will to power fully developed from within. But this is a romantic illusion. Human beings, even very superior human beings, come into possession of their powers only through a long process of maturation in relationships of essential dependence on others. Human self-sufficiency can be achieved only in relation to others.

Nietzsche's exposure of critical problems in the domain of moral belief and practice cuts deep, and his attempt at a revaluation of values, while open to serious question, marks a major contribution to a necessary project. But for all his concern with the natural history and genealogy of morals, Nietzsche overlooked the basic considerations which bear on the history of the growth of moral awareness in the individual. Much can be extracted from his account of master and slave moralities, as I hope to have indicated; and his general approach is defensible as a version of ethical naturalism. But the Nietzschean moral ideal as a whole collapses in the light of his neglect of developmental considerations.

2. Moral Development: Social Learning and Psychoanalytic Theories

Reference was made early in chapter one to two general factors in the process of becoming a moral agent, the maturation of inborn capacities and experience. Theories of moral development are often classified on the basis of which of these two factors they emphasize the more. Accounts which put particular stress on the role of experience and learning in moral development belong, in general, to the empiricist tradition of Western intellectual history. This approach is committed in broad terms to the view that all knowledge and ideas are derived from experience (and that knowledge and ideas are to be understood essentially as possessions of individuals); consideration of what is inborn is then restricted, more or less, to the acknowledgment that the organism is capable of learning. This emphasis has been particularly strong in English thought since the late seventeenth century and is dominant in the self-image of much science and social science. Accounts which, by contrast, analyze moral development more as the natural growth of inborn capacities belong to the rationalist tradition of thought in which the human mind or reason is held to make a significant contribution to our knowledge and understanding distinct from experience alone (as the precondition of making sense of experience, for example). This emphasis has been particularly common in French and German thought since Descartes restructured the whole conception of knowledge in the seventeenth century. It was associated for a time with the thesis that the human mind is endowed with innate ideas as the condition of meaningful experience, ideas of a general and non-experiential sort such as principles of logic, but some recent versions have appealed more directly to empirical data, as in Noam Chomsky's account of language-learning or in an evolutionary theory of knowledge as espoused, for example, by Sir Karl Popper.

Rationalist and empiricist approaches are also reflected in different historical traditions in moral theory (as I will show more fully in later chapters). Empiricist accounts are related most directly to versions of Utilitarian ethical views which developed in the eighteenth and nineteenth centuries. Cognitivist or rationalist accounts are linked more typically with the late eighteenth-century rationalist ethics of Immanuel Kant, with its conception of individual autonomy and the rationality (and universality) of rules of morality. There are also links with Rousseau for whom moral maturity is a matter of development according to nature. The character of each tradition, and the contrast between them in relation to moral development, is expressed succinctly by John Rawls. In seeking to fit his own account of justice as the ground of social order into a developmental structure, Rawls observes that in the empiricist/utilitarian tradition,

> right conduct is conduct generally beneficial to others and to society (as defined by the principle of utility) for the doing of which we commonly lack an effective motive, whereas wrong conduct is behaviour generally injurious to others and to society and for the doing of which we often have a sufficient motive. Society must somehow make good these defects. This is achieved by the approbation and disapprobation of parents and others in authority, who when necessary use rewards and punishments ranging from bestowal and withdrawal of affection to the administration of pleasures and pains. Eventually by various psychological processes we acquire a desire to do what is right and an aversion to doing what is wrong.

In the rationalist tradition of moral learning, he continues,

> moral learning is not so much a matter of supplying missing motives as one of the free development of our innate intellectual and emotional capacities according to their natural bent. Once the powers of understanding mature and persons come to recognise their place in society and are able to take the standpoint of others, they appreciate the mutual benefits of establishing fair terms of social cooperation. We have a natural sympathy with other persons and an innate susceptibility to the pleasure of fellow-feeling and self-mastery, and these provide the affective basis for our moral sentiments once we have a clear grasp of our relations to our associates from an appropriately general perspective.[1]

The empiricist emphasis in moral development is now found primarily in social learning theory. This approach, which has its basis in behaviorism, is deeply entrenched in contemporary psychology, especially in the United States. Social learning theory covers a number of fairly different accounts of moral development, but the basic common element — which is inevitably very general — is the view that moral development can be fully accounted for by learning brought about by environmental stimuli. Perhaps the best known version of learning theory is to be found in the writings of B. F. Skinner; H. J. Eysenck also incorporates elements of a radical version of learning theory in his treatment of moral development. Some other prominent social learning theorists provide modified versions which seek to take greater account of cognitive considerations.

The dominant contemporary form of the rationalist tradition is called cognitive developmental theory; its leading exponent has been Lawrence Kohlberg. Kohlberg's work on moral development, based in important ways on the views of the Swiss psychologist and philosopher Jean Piaget, has been the basis of a major research program over the past thirty years.

To social learning and cognitive developmental theories there must be added Freudian psychoanalytic theory. Psychoanalytic theory cannot be comfortably accommodated in either of the two dominant traditions. Nevertheless it shares important characteristics with the empiricist approach and has exercised considerable influence on the direction of experimental research undertaken by social learning theorists. In the present chapter, therefore, I will discuss psychoanalytic theory together with social learning theory, and the discussion of cognitive developmental theory will be taken up in the next chapter. This division of the topic is somewhat artificial since the theories overlap in various ways. Nevertheless they reflect different historical approaches and theoretical emphases and need separate treatment. Each is open to a variety of criticisms, but any attempt to move toward a satisfactory understanding of moral development would need to take account of them and to incorporate elements from each.

1. Social Learning Theory

Social learning theory holds that moral formation consists in the acquisition of rules or norms of behavior which are taken in from one's external environment.[2] Through a process of learning, which is sustained initially by external forces, the individual is got to observe certain rules, essentially on the basis of rewards and punishments. But the acquisition is complete only when individuals, in some sense, have taken the rules on as "their own," in a process of internalization.[3] The primary evidence of this is that the individual regularly observes the rules without (immediate) dependence on the external forces which initiated them.

The relevant rules are identified as rules set by society, mediated to the individual by parents or teachers or other social agents in the environment. The rules, it is assumed, are to be described as "prosocial": that is, they are directed to forms of individual behavior which are (or are thought to be) of benefit to others (as against antisocial behavior which is typically seen as being of benefit to the agent in the form of immediate satisfaction). Benefit here, it could be noted, has the sense of satisfaction, typically the experience of pleasure, on the part of individuals. The question of how (and in what sense) human beings learn to be altruistic provides a central focus of concern for the approach.

The human organism in this setting is seen, in a manner of speaking, as unformed clay, able to be molded in a great variety of ways. (The favorite traditional metaphor is that the mind, considered apart from experience, is a *tabula rasa*, a slate or page on which nothing has been written.) How individuals turn out depends on what happens to them in experience, in effect, on their education; what social/moral rules a person learns (and eventually internalizes) depends on his or her social learning history.

The metaphor of the *tabula rasa* conveys on first impression a neutral picture of the presocial behavior of the individual; one would expect that such behavior would be neither "prosocial" or "antisocial" in the terms of the theory. But in fact the metaphor of emptiness cannot be pushed too far even in social learning theory. What the theory emphasizes is a view of human beings in which instincts and feelings — passions, emotions — are original and dominant. It holds as a rule that the basic motivation of behavior is the satisfaction of biological needs (associated with instincts and feelings), and that the organism is marked by the desire or drive to maximize gratification in their regard. This marks out a sense of what is *natural* in regard to human beings. The organism is "programmed" to seek its own satisfaction without reference to others. The learning theorist is not committed thereby to the view that infant behavior is typically selfish and antisocial (though some writers proceed to use these terms, as if babies were just small versions of older children or adults).[4] Nevertheless, the original picture of the human organism as dominated by asocial instincts and feelings sets the terms in which moral learning is envisaged.

In a situation in which the individual is set over against its social environment, the learning consists essentially of motivational development by which the original feelings and their gratification become attached to socially imposed objects and forms of behavior. The learning in question relates primarily therefore to artificially induced changes in the person's feelings, especially in connection with objects of attachment. Cognitive considerations, understanding and evaluation, enter the picture only in a secondary way (though they are accorded a greater role by some social learning theorists). The point of the process is to supply the individual with affective motivation, otherwise thought to be absent, for conforming to moral standards (understood as social norms). Thus moral development proceeds as a form of training — reinforcement schedules — based originally on rewards and punishments to produce the appropriate desires and aversions.

The general thesis that moral development depends essentially on learning is hardly open to question. The significant issues concern rather the conditions and character of the learning in question and how the account is related to a more general understanding of the individual and social character of human life. Social learning theorists, who are self-avowedly scientific in outlook, might be inclined to treat the latter concern as typically philosophical and therefore not *their* concern. But, in fact, they have already entered the field with the original picture of the human organism.

The major contention of social learning theory, against this philosophical background, is that learning proceeds according to laws, most pertinently the Law of Effect. This proposes, in ordinary parlance, that people (or other capable organisms such as rats) will respond to stimuli in ways which secure them rewards rather than punishments. In a critical discussion of social learning theory, Thomas E. Wren summarizes the law in the context of morality as stating that "a moral agent comes to adopt the morality that he does because its adoption has resulted in more reinforcing events."[5] Reinforcement here, as Wren points out, can be related to an expectancy account of motivation according to which desire is directed primarily to anticipated pleasure. Or it can be linked with a "tension- or drive-reduction" account according to which pleasure is treated primarily as the resolution of desire (the decrease in a "needstate"). The relevant learning procedures can be summarized conveniently as classical conditioning, related forms of reinforcement through reward and punishment (as in Skinnerian operant conditioning), learning through observation (the "power of example"), and forms of explanation and reasoning.

CONSCIENCE AS A CONDITIONED REFLEX

A resolutely non-cognitivist account, it is clear, will put major emphasis on forms of conditioning. This can be illustrated by reference to what H. J. Eysenck says about the developed nature of conscience:

> Our contention will be that conscience is simply conditioned reflex and that it originates in the same way as phobic and neurotic responses . . . in other words when the child is going to carry out one of the many activities which have been prohibited and punished in the past (—the slap, the moral shaming, or whatever the punishment may be), then the conditioned automatic response would immediately occur and produce a strong deterrent, being as it were, unpleasant in itself.[6]

Eysenck's account is part of an attempt to explain how external rules and precepts are "internalized" by a subject so as to give rise to moral (socially approved) behavior in appropriate circumstances. What is offered is the idea of conscience as conditioned anxiety, effected primarily through punishment. In the model (classical conditioning), behavior which is regarded by others as bad, naughty, or wicked constitutes a conditioned stimulus which is naturally reinforcing inasmuch as it gives rise to immediate satisfaction for the individual. This is changed, however, by the introduction of punishment for the behavior, viz., an unconditioned stimulus which evokes the unconditioned response of pain which is experienced as unpleasant and fearful. Given sufficient experience of the association, we would expect, in Eysenck's words, that "anxiety (conditioned fear) would gradually become the conditioned response to carrying out or even contemplating the naughty action, and that this immediate negatively reinforcing consequence would discourage both contemplation and execution of the action in general. This conditioned anxiety is experienced by the child as 'conscience'."

Eysenck commends his account on the grounds that "it makes use of well-established principles based on detailed laboratory experiments" and leads to testable results. This espousal of an avowedly scientific standpoint is combined with a robust rejection of any view in which moral conduct (identified as "moral" conduct) is thought to involve responsible decision-making behavior in accordance with rational (philosophical) principles.[7]

This claim to scientific purity is bedevilled by the non-scientific assumptions it embodies, such as the picture of human beings as dominated by motivation associated with the satisfaction of biological drives. It would be naive to maintain that this model is the fruit of pure observation and scientific testing. Patently, it expresses an understanding of human nature which involves aspects of a philosophical sort and which in turn bears on subsequent observation and experiment. Given the way in which motivation is specified in the account, it is not surprising that natural and moral behavior are seen to be in conflict or that moral development is explained in terms of the acquisition of motives through a process of conditioning which both exploits and overcomes "natural" motivation.

It is also clear, at a more general level, that Eysenck's whole conception of science and scientific procedure—leaving aside the question of its adequacy—presupposes a philosophical standpoint. Furthermore, it builds in evaluative components which presumably involve responsible decision-making behavior, for example, judgments about the use of punishment in testing conditioning processes, truthfulness in collating data, and so on. This consideration points to the very limited conception of morality and moral learning in the account as a whole. It can be allowed that forms of conditioning and reinforcement play a considerable role especially in the early stages of development. Again, there is reason to hold that a good part of the motivation for moral behavior is supplied early in life before the individual has any grasp of the cognitive content and point of moral obligation. But conscience is presented here as a conditioned, automatic response: it appears in the manner of an alarm bell in a clock or security system (allowing that a person's consciousness has to enter the picture and that feelings would have to be measured in some non-circular way). There is a startling lack of attention to the variety of forms of learning and the growth of cognitive elements in experience; nor is there any consideration of the extent to which children from an early stage manifest affective behavior which is not self-directed (e.g., sympathy, concern, love, trust). Finally, an adequate account of the development of conscience—or of anything else for that matter—should consider what it is like in its developed and mature state. What is offered in this radical account is, at best, an idea of conscience which is fixed at an early or profoundly arrested stage of development. It is an account of moral conduct in the absence of moral agents.

In Eysenck's emphasis on classical conditioning (and biological factors), the moral agent effectively disappears; the agent is conceived, rather, as a field on which forces contend. What the person "does" is what is determined by the strongest force, or a resolution of forces, at a given time, in keeping with the relevant laws and the person's history. B. F. Skinner espouses a similar view in his behavioristic stance: "A person is not an originating agent; he is a locus, a point at which many genetic and environmental conditions come together in a joint effect."[8] Notwithstanding his emphasis on operant conditioning, Skinner is drawn to make the extraordinary claim that in human action, the environment acts on the perceiving person, the person does not act on the environment.[9]

This standpoint reflects a conviction that agency and talk of the "self" involve postulating what Eysenck calls "a meaningless and improbable mentalism" which is inconsistent with scientific inquiry. Such reductionism, however, appears to take too short a way with the evidence of familiar experience concerning agency and related ideas such as responsibility, human powers of evaluation and reflection, including self-reflection, and the human capacity to grasp meanings and to act meaningfully. The recognition of these powers does not yield a conception of the human agent as an absolute point of origin who creates a world out of nothing, or of an inaccessible, pure self. One reason for this is that the person who grasps meanings and acts meaningfully is necessarily a being with social relationships, an individual who has a social history as part of his or her personal and physical reality. The self, the person, the agent, can be thought of as identical with the human being, that is, a living body of a certain sort with a range of broadly identifiable powers and relationships.

CONSCIENCE AS COGNITIVE AND EVALUATIVE

Many social learning theorists have expressed dissatisfaction with a narrow, behaviorist-type account of moral learning. Their approach has shown up particularly in two ways: greater attention to cognitive and evaluative considerations in relation to moral judgment and conduct, and an attempt to give force to the idea of self-regulation in connection with the internalization of moral values. Thus, Walter Mischel and Harriet N. Mischel, for example, speak of "a cognitive social-learning approach to morality and self-regulation"; they espouse a conception of the self as the person, as living and acting organism.[10] Approaches of this sort have also been built on greater attention to human social behavior, child-rearing practices, and the variety of forms of learning (beyond a focus on the immediate effects of reward and punishment), and have given more attention to philosophical considerations regarding moral judgment and agency. But while writing from within this general approach, Justin Aronfreed complained (in 1977) that although these theories assume that their mechanisms of learning will account for the transmission of values from socialized agents to children, they do not deal developmentally with either the cognitive or affective dimensions of values:

Social-learning theories, even in their most sophisticated extensions, restrict values to the role of an inferred cognitive mediator of overt behavior. They do not really address the question of how values gain control over the child's actions. And since these theories also do not examine the nature of representational thought, they can hardly be expected to illuminate the contribution that moral judgment makes to the development of conscience.[11]

In a number of writings, most notably in his study, *Conduct and Conscience* (hereafter *CC*), Aronfreed has sought to develop a more satisfactory version of social learning theory in application to moral learning.[12]

In keeping with a major theme in social learning theory, Aronfreed's work is focused on internalization or the acquisition of internalized control of behavior. This concerns in context the development of the person as a moral agent with a capacity for self-regulation and for action in accordance with recognized evaluative standards of good and bad in human conduct. As an initial account of internalization, Aronfreed offers the view that "we might consider an act to be internalized to the extent that its maintenance has become independent of external outcomes—that is, to the extent that its reinforcing consequences are internally mediated, without the support of external events such as reward or punishment" (*CC* 18). This assumes that the primary learning experience of the behavior-types follows a pattern of conditioning and reinforcement by external controls. The primary working criterion of internalization, then, is that the behavior continues to occur in appropriate circumstances independently of previously established external consequences (the original reinforcing elements). The basic test for this is that it occurs in the absence of surveillance. In learning theory terms, the conduct would not continue unless it had reinforcing consequences; when conduct occurs, therefore, in the absence of external support, the conclusion to be drawn is that "its reinforcing consequences must somehow be carried in its intrinsic correlates" (*CC* 34). In short, it is necessary to take account of the cognitive determinants of conduct, specifically the development of the power to represent and evaluate one's own behavior.

The emphasis on the "intrinsic correlates" of conduct is related to Aronfreed's idea of conscience. This has its starting point in a broadly traditional conception:

> *Conscience* is the term that has been used traditionally to refer to the cognitive and affective processes which constitute an internalized moral governor over an individual's conduct. (*CC* 2)

For purposes of the study, Aronfreed treats morality as being concerned essentially with the welfare of others. This has some bearing on his view that the current notion of conscience includes considerably more than matters of moral judgment: "It is used, for example, to refer to value orientations which support self-denial of pleasure, effort in the face of adversity, and other self-directive patterns of behavior" (CC 5). One could say, however, that this comment points to a narrow conception of morality which is characteristically modern—a narrowness which, in the history of ethics, has been associated with the assumption of a problematic opposition between self and other. Aronfreed does not follow this path, however; while he works with a somewhat narrow (and unexamined) conception of morality, he embraces a more than ample conception of conscience. The province of conscience, he proposes, consists of "those areas of conduct where social experience has attached substantial affective value to the child's cognitive representation and evaluation of its own behavior" (CC 6). There is very little reference to moral content in the study, but concern with a recognizably wide range of moral values—care for others, justice, integrity, truthfulness, and so on—clearly falls within this province.

Aronfreed is concerned in dealing with conscience to give full play to the cognitive processes of representation and evaluation. But cognitive elements (the "intrinsic correlates" of conduct) have no practical force in the view which he puts forward. If they are to lead to action, they have to be linked up with "the affective, inarticulate, and impelling forces of conscience" (CC 2).

I will have occasion in later chapters to show how this proposal reflects a misleadingly sharp separation between reason and the emotions which developed in modern thought, especially from the seventeenth century. This separation is connected in Aronfreed's study with a misconception of classical Greek moral thought in the writings of Plato and Aristotle. The Greeks, according to Aronfreed, thought of moral judgment as an essentially rational phenomenon, and "did not perceive in it the powerful affective components which we are now inclined to regard as indispensable to internalized control over social conduct" (CC 2). This comment completely overlooks the very explicit emphasis which Plato and Aristotle placed on habit formation and the education of the emotions in the young in their accounts of moral development. It is true that in their different ways Plato and Aristotle saw moral judgment as essentially rational. But as Aristotle in particular argued, there is such a thing as *practical reason*, that is, reason which embodies motivational force and leads to action; again in this understanding, emotions may embody cognitive components. It appears that, in thinking that the Greeks concentrated on rationality to the exclusion of affectivity in moral judgment, Aronfreed is wrongly imputing to them his own modern conception of reason.[13]

While Aronfreed departs from the Greeks in separating cognitive and affective processes, he is one with them in thinking that the two elements need to be brought together to account for moral conduct. One of the ways in which he describes their relationship in this venture is to say that the cognitive elements mediate affectivity. "The internalized status of an act is a function of the mediation of affectivity by its intrinsic correlates" (CC 66). Alternatively, he speaks of the connection as one in which the affective elements become directly attached to the intrinsic correlates (having been attached originally to the external outcomes of the behavior) (CC 44, 54). The second model expresses Aronfreed's more consistently held view, in which behavior is determined fundamentally by affective forces, but the emphasis on cognitive factors gives rise to a certain ambivalence in his position. Thus cognitive elements are accorded a more controlling role in the first model.

The conception of affectivity involved in this account is essentially simple. In Aronfreed's words, "affective states may be divided into two basic classes: *positive* (pleasurable) and *aversive* (unpleasant or painful) states" (CC 45). Corresponding to this dichotomy, stimuli in the child's environment may be credited with positive or aversive properties to the extent that they bring about related affective states in the child (whether the experience of their affective value has an innate basis or is something that is acquired, as is the case with major classes of social stimuli). An organism, it is assumed, will act so as to maximize pleasurable outcomes and avoid what is unpleasant. On the same basis, affective control (hence behavioral control) is either positive or aversive in character.

So far as it concerns moral behavior, control in the primary stages of learning is provided by external monitors in the form of parents and other social agents who use rewards and punishments of various sorts. With internalization, control passes increasingly to the internal factors of representation and evaluation exercised by the individual. In dealing with the relevant mechanisms of learning, Aronfreed holds that the shift or transfer takes place essentially through a process of conditioning (CC 44). The initial focus in the account thus concerns externally imposed reinforcing or suppressive techniques, with particular attention being given to the effectiveness of punishment. But this emphasis is set against the acknowledgment that, in large measure, autonomous conduct does not rest on the child's training as a conditionable animal; it is related rather to "the kind of learning that is made possible by the child's remarkable cognitive capacities" (CC 67). He thus directs attention to the representational and evaluative powers of language and thought, concentrating in particular on the importance of observational learning and imitation and on empathic and vicarious experience.

The particular concentration on representation among cognitive skills appears curiously narrow and passive. A representation is understood as a *cognitive template* of behavior, "in the sense that the structure and topography of the behavior are stored for reproduction" (CC 79). What is imagined is that the "template" may be a simple (mental) copy of behavior or something more abstract and structural with internal rules and operations which allow for behavioral variations. In a sense, representation is intended to stand here for a wide variety of cognitive skills: powers of observation and discrimination, the coding and storing of information, memory retrieval, imagining and rehearsing, forming generalizations and abstractions, making judgments, forming plans. Cognitive skills have the role of identifying situations and facilitating behavior, but the issue of *which* behavior ensues is made a function of affective forces. What is missing in the account of cognitive capacities under the title of representation is attention to the notion of *understanding* (understanding language, behavior, social practices, and so on, as involving practical engagement with others) together with acting for a reason, as contrasted with having some sort of internal picture of behavior routines and reproducing them (perhaps with variations) on occasions in response to a dominant dispositional force.

The character of Aronfreed's version of social learning theory is opened out significantly, however, by his emphasis on evaluation as a cognitive dimension of conscience. This leads him to distinguish between a number of different kinds of evaluative control over conduct, ranked along a "continuum of *internal versus external orientation*" (CC 34). Thus, moving from a more external to a more internal orientation, there is: evaluation of behavior in which standards are taken from others and in which one is concerned fundamentally with the immediate consequences of the conduct for oneself; evaluation on the basis of standards or practices of people whom the agent esteems or sees as authorities, but without particular reference to immediate consequences for the self; evaluation on the basis of standards involved in maintaining satisfactory affiliative or contractual relationships in a society; or, again, evaluation involving "broader principles which are oriented to the intrinsic goodness or rightness of the effects on [one's] actions upon the welfare of others" (CC 35).

This sequence could suggest a feasible schema of moral development. Indeed, it is broadly comparable to Kohlberg's stages of moral judgment (which I discuss in the next chapter). It bears comparison, perhaps more loosely, with a developmental schema which can be found in Aristotle's ethical writings (discussed in chapter four). The comparability does not suggest that Aronfreed is committed to a Kohlberg-type thesis of sequential stages of moral orientation (nor is a thesis of this sort to be found in Aristotle for that matter). In being critical of Kohlberg's thesis, however, Aronfreed moves to the other extreme of being ambivalent about accepting the idea of *moral* development at all beyond the course of socialization. He is drawn to the possibility that

> the fundamental cognitive and affective substance of values remains relatively unchanged after it has been established in the course of socialization, but . . . the values become subordinated to representation in various forms or structures which differ in their abstractness, complexity, and sensitivity to later social influence. (CC 263–64)

Aronfreed does not offer any view about the upper boundary of the course of socialization; at the same time, all of the evaluative schemata listed earlier are put forward as "capable of controlling conduct without any concrete reference to external consequences of reward or punishment" (*CC* 35), and hence as manifesting internalized control. That is, he appears unwilling to make any evaluative distinction between motivation which arises fundamentally from the desire to please someone or in obedience to an authority and motivation based on reflection regarding human welfare. He appears committed, it could be said, to a doctrine of the homogeneity of motivation.

Aronfreed's standpoint in the passage quoted above could be connected with an unwillingness to evaluate different schemata of moral judgment, arising in part from a sensitivity to differences among people from different backgrounds and across different societies. In any case, it reflects the characteristic view of social learning theory that moral reasoning and thinking about human relations and criteria of right and wrong in general have no real bearing on moral motivation and conduct, on the grounds that everything is laid down (cognitively and affectively) at a relatively early stage and remains relatively unchanged. Yet it seems clear that forms of motivation connected with obligations in a society as a whole or in response to more general principles become possible only when a person has acquired a corresponding level of knowledge and experience and capacity for general thought; in other words, the differences in the evaluative schemata do not appear to be restricted purely to features of the representational level.

It is necessary to look more closely at what Aronfreed says about evaluation. In his analysis of evaluative thought, Aronfreed draws attention to both cognitive and affective elements. The cognitive dimension in evaluation, he suggests, could be treated as a set of classificatory operations which make use of a representational base linked with awareness of one's social environment. He continues:

> However, an evaluative structure is not merely a cognitive schema for the economical coding of information. It is the quality and magnitude of the affectivity that becomes associated with particular classifications which permit the structure to enter into the operations of value and to exercise some control over behavior. (*CC* 278).

One could argue that, in this account, the affectivity associated with a person's (moral) values is treated as the outcome of reinforcing schedules. It falls on the same level as other affective or motivational forces and competes with them, and if it is strong enough, it results in moral conduct of the appropriate sort. What is missing from this "one-level, non-hierarchical picture of human motivation," as the philosopher T. E. Wren describes it, is "any suggestion of a higher order of motivation whose object is the ordinary first-order motivations or sets of motivations that are keyed to the environment."[14]

The reference to a higher order of motivation draws on a notion of *self-intervention* developed by William P. Alston. Self-intervention according to Alston is the idea that "one may do something to change one's motivational processes from what they would otherwise have been." The suggestion is that it occurs typically when a person exercises virtue or responsibility in difficult circumstances: one draws back from doing something to which one is attracted or gets oneself to do something one was initially reluctant to do. The intervention (such as getting oneself to help a difficult acquaintance, or exercising patience, courage, or kindness, rather than taking an easy way out) obviously arises from motivation itself, but the motivation presents itself at a different level from the primary motivational forces: it manifests second-order or higher-level reflection on the relevant motivational field. More generally, it brings into play the idea of the human agent as capable of stepping back from a situation and reflecting on it and taking control of the course of events. The objection against a single-level analysis of motivation is that, in obliterating the distinction of levels, it does away with a central element of psychological and moral experience and is consequently unable to provide a satisfactory account of self-regulation and moral agency.

Alston argues specifically that Aronfreed's notion of evaluative structure fails to escape this objection. Even though the idea of conscience as internalized control emphasizes the subject's evaluative cognition of his behavior, motivation is located in the positive or negative affective associations set down in one's socialization. Everything is made to rest on affective anticipations. In this case, no explanation of the possibility of self-intervention is forthcoming, and, in Alston's words, "internalized control by conscience differs from the more rudimentary sort only by inserting into the picture the cognitive content of self-judgment."[15]

The relevance of this criticism reflects the extent to which the thesis of the Law of Effect continues to constitute the general framework of Aronfreed's account of conscience. On the other hand, there are recurrent indications in his writings of an alternative and enlarged view of motivation and agency. The primary treatment of different kinds of evaluative control along a continuum of internal versus external orientation provides an example. This sequence could be taken to point to an account in which affectivity comes to be linked progressively with a person's grasp of moral principles and their place in the social order (and in which the outcome of behavior in terms of positive or aversive states is no longer the controlling factor). There is also an element of ambivalence, as I noted earlier, in the way in which Aronfreed presents the relationship of cognitive and affective elements in relation to moral conduct. More significantly, T. E. Wren has argued that a hierarchical account of motivation can be found in

Aronfreed's treatment of guilt and shame as moral feelings in Chapter
Nine of *Conduct and Conscience*:

> Aronfreed there envisions an agent for whom at least two action-guiding
> principles are not only hierarchical in the sense of directing other motiva-
> tions but also truly loaded with affect: those of not harming others and of
> keeping in good social standing.[16]

The two principles are derived from the analysis of guilt and shame
respectively. In this account, guilt and shame and fear constitute distinct
forms of the general aversive state of anxiety which arises in the context of
the child's response to (moral) transgression. Each feeling is accorded its
own cognitive structure in this setting (though it is allowed that the
relevant structures are not mutually exclusive). Fear in response to transgression involves centrally the idea of aversive consequences—
punishment—emanating from an external source (parents, social agen-
cies). It fits clearly enough into the standard pattern of motivation offered
by social learning theory. Guilt arises by contrast on the ground of the
moral evaluation of one's behavior; it is a form of anxiety which is properly
based on "one's cognition of the harmful consequences of one's actions for
others" (CC 247). Finally, the cognitive housing of shame is related to the
visibility before others of the transgression: "The essence of shame is a
cognitive focus on the appearance or display of that which ought not to
show" (CC 249).

It is clear that guilt and shame presuppose considerable learning experience. But the critical question is how they operate as motivational influences on behavior. According to Wren:

> Aronfreed clearly believes that in cases of guilt and shame the general
> distress of anxiety is administered internally, through a set of cognitions
> which are self-referring and hierarchical in a way that the expectations
> characterizing fear are not.[17]

This observation may not appear so compelling in the case of shame. But it
is interesting to note that shame has long been associated with the acquisition of an internal principle of behavior, notably in Aristotle's ethics.
Furthermore, Aristotle draws an explicit contrast, as we shall see, between
shame and fear of punishment as motives for behavior. Nevertheless,
shame presents itself as a form of fear, specifically the fear of disrepute,
allied with the desire to be well thought of by parents and other significant
figures in one's social world. But shame can also be linked with the
acquisition of a more detached sense of what is noble or honorable, and an
awareness of the value of common traditions and standards of behavior
and the importance of social affiliations in a worthwhile life. In this light,
one could say that shame supplies a motivational basis which is both
different from and more developmentally advanced than the fear of punishment; at the same time, it points to an immature or incomplete stage of

moral development. (In Aronfreed's schema of evaluative control, shame could be linked perhaps with the form in which people evaluate their actions, "with respect to the standards or practices of those whom they hold in esteem or authority, without necessarily being oriented towards the consequences which their actions will have for themselves" [CC 35]).

The idea of a distinct motivational base is even more apparent in the case of guilt, for the idea of guilt which Aronfreed brings forward is clearly normative—that is, it builds in a standard by which guilt can be judged appropriate or not, viz., "one's cognition of the harmful consequences of one's actions for others" (CC 47). Guilt in this case draws its force centrally from an understanding of morality and its place in human life as a source of action-guiding principles. It is in marked contrast to guilt in the form of feelings laden with fear and elements of self-hatred which could be seen as the product of reinforcement which lacks the relevant rational basis. Aronfreed's treatment of guilt points, in short, to the idea of a distinct (and illuminating) motivational base for moral behavior. But he does not offer any account of its provenance or its special role.[18]

This absence might be linked with Aronfreed's broad commitment to the scientific (causal) model of explanation generally espoused in social learning theory. To that extent, his emphasis on cognitive and evaluative elements in conscience and behavior exists without proper attention to the non-causal explanatory notions of meaning, understanding, and interpretation to which they might be connected more readily. For all its wealth of detail and scope, the study proceeds without sustained attention to such notions as agency and action, the development of self-consciousness, responsibility, virtue, and character. Nor is much attention given to later stages in the development of the child's conscience or to the idea of mature moral attainment. This is effectively closed off, as we have seen, by the idea that the fundamental cognitive and affective substance of values remains relatively unchanged once it is established. The significance of this closure can be indicated by reference again to the idea of self-intervention.

The capacity for reflecting on one's motivational processes and taking steps to change them clearly belongs to a later stage of development, though of course it builds on earlier forms of self-evaluation and control. Not to take account of its developed form is to leave out an arguably central element in our understanding of what it is to be a human agent. Self-intervention, as we have seen, is located typically in situations of potential conflict (between what one should do and what one is inclined to do, for example). The more general phenomenon of which it is part is the human capacity for forming second-order desires, viz., desires that one have certain (first-order) desires. This is expressed in what Charles Taylor suggests is the distinctively human power "to *evaluate* our desires, to regard some as desirable and others as undesirable," a power to evaluate desires not simply on the basis of outcomes but with reference to their qualitative worth as meeting standards (noble or base, life-affirming or life-denying, serious or frivolous, good or bad, virtuous or vicious) and as belonging to forms of life which are similarly subject to appraisal.[19]

The types of issues concerning agency which have just been noted cannot be fully articulated in Aronfreed's treatment of conscience. Many of the relevant ideas are made explicit, up to a level, in what he says, or they lie not far below the surface. Indeed, there is a loose but genuine sense, as I have suggested, in which an Aristotelian-type conception of moral formation, beginning with the early establishment of habits, can be found in his writings. But the scope for the development of the ideas is closed off by the basic framework and presuppositions of social learning theory.

A COMMENT ON EMPIRICAL STUDIES

In keeping with normal practice in psychology, social learning theory has been accompanied by extensive empirical research on aspects of moral development. The characteristic theses are commonly presented as conclusions drawn from empirical studies or as hypotheses confirmed by the studies. It is clear, however, that empirical work does not take place in the absence of theory, reflecting views about the nature of scientific inquiry in general and the specific field of application, in this case morality and moral development. There is no "pure" vantage point from which these matters can be marked out, observed, described, and explained.

The most general theoretical conflict in this field concerns the whole status of psychology (and related social sciences) as *science*: whether psychology, in all its branches, can or should proceed in the manner of a natural science (of which physics is the paradigm); or whether it is, in important respects, a "hermeneutical" science concerned with understanding and interpreting phenomena which, of their nature, cannot be captured by the explanatory patterns applicable in mechanics or physics (in part because human beings, the subjects of the inquiry, are themselves self-interpreting animals). I have touched on this issue already in suggesting that in Aronfreed's study of conscience, elements of a hermeneutical sort sit uneasily with a more general causal framework. More hardline theorists such as Eysenck do not have this problem since they unequivocally assume a thesis of causal determinism and an essentially mechanistic model of the subject as demanded by a "scientific" outlook. This is frequently accompanied by an atomistic conception of the individual as a complete whole without attention to the way in which social relationships (beginning with the society of the infant and its mother or nurturer) constitute the condition of *human* existence.

The issues in this dispute regarding the appropriate patterns of explanation in psychology are too large and complex to be unravelled here. My own general theoretical commitment is already obvious, and my line of argument is one of seeking to reflect critically on theoretical aspects of rival accounts in the field and of trying to show that theoretical considerations drawn mainly from philosophical reflection are properly part of the relevant data.

Empirical studies relating to morality face formidable difficulties, both conceptual and methodological. The difficulties begin with the question of *what* is being studied (which brings in the widespread conflict and uncertainty regarding morality), of how moral beliefs and attitudes and pieces of behavior and practices relevant to their acquisition are to be identified, of how testing should proceed regarding these items and their relationships, and of what conclusions can be drawn from studies of particular groups against a particular theoretical background (in which the moral, social, and scientific outlook of the experimenters may play some part). While there is evidence of widespread sensitivity to these difficulties, research programs characteristically have their own dynamic and set the framework and terms within which inquiry proceeds. It is not entirely surprising that many social learning theorists find support in empirical studies for the view that moral judgment is not very closely related to moral conduct, and that many cognitive-developmental proponents, by contrast, find support for the opposite conclusion. The difficulties in this matter are well illustrated by Augusto Blasi's careful discussion in 1980 of moral cognition and moral action and his review of empirical literature. Writing from within a cautious adherence to Kohlberg's cognitive-developmental approach, Blasi concludes:

> The body of research reviewed here seems to offer considerable support for the hypothesis that moral reasoning and moral action are statistically related. This statement, however, should be qualified as soon as one looks at the findings in more detail. Empirical support, in fact varies from area to area . . . .[20]

It is possible that sensitivity to difficulties (as well as the difficulties themselves) is connected with the fact that extensive research in some important areas has been disappointingly inconclusive or banal. The range of opinion and disagreement across research sources appears to reflect fairly closely the related range of views in the community.

Social learning theorists, and psychologists influenced by psychoanalytic theory, have devoted considerable research to the role of parental discipline in the early moral formation of the child and to the topic of the internalization of moral standards. Particular attention has been given to such forms of discipline as physical punishment and the expression of anger, and more "psychological" forms such as parental explanation and reasoning allied with a focus on the withdrawal of affection. (Aronfreed describes the latter disciplinary habits as *induction*, "because they inscribe a pattern of learning that induces internalized monitors of the child's anxiety in response to an anticipated or committed transgression."[21] One writer concludes a review of the research on this topic as follows:

There is . . . disappointingly little general agreement. The best-supported findings seem to be that some degree of familial affection and support favours moral development, and that the children of parents who *reason* with their children or use *induction* techniques are likely to function at a higher moral level.[22]

Assuming this assessment is correct, it is surprising that there is not more general agreement on the matter; the question why it is lacking would be an interesting research topic in itself. The lack of agreement is also disappointing. On the basis of ordinary experience and on ethical grounds, one could argue that parental affection is normally both a natural inclination and also a moral virtue; and it is difficult to see how a child could survive, much less flourish as a human being, without a fair degree of genuine care and affection.[23] One could also argue that the ability to exercise insight and reasoning in the sphere of morality is a necessary (though not sufficient) condition for moral maturity. It would then be a matter for astonishment if behavior of these kinds did not contribute significantly to the moral development of children.

2. Freudian Psychoanalytic Theory

Some elements of the Freudian view of moral development emerged in chapter one, notably Freud's genetic account of morality as social violence, his idea of a rational basis for morality, and aspects of his conception of human nature. In going further into the topic, I shall not discuss its various aspects in detail, much less deal with the development and modification of Freudian views in the writings of such authorities as Wilhelm Reich, Melanie Klein, or numerous other Freudian theorists. A broad characterization of the topic and a modest assessment of its contribution to an understanding of the topic must suffice.

Psychoanalytic theory—like social learning theory—takes a basically hedonistic view of human nature. More specifically, the human organism is thought of as seeking maximal satisfaction, the source of satisfaction being identified as libido or sexual "instinct." Notoriously, Freud held that sexuality is characteristic of human life from its beginning. Again, as in social learning theory, the process of moral development is equated by and large with socialization, and it is seen as taking place in the context of conflict between natural drives characteristic of the individual and the demands of society or civilization.

THE DEVELOPMENT OF THE SUPER-EGO

In Freudian theory the critical stage of moral development is centered on the Oedipal conflict. The resolution of the conflict involves a process of coercion and instinctual renunciation resulting in the development of the super-ego, broadly a notion of conscience, in the form of guilt-motivated internalization of parental authority. At the same time, the resolution is the

condition of growth toward emotional maturity and the key to the individual's basic character (which according to the account is largely set by age 5
or 6).

The general pattern of moral development begins with the young child
experiencing frustration and hostility in response to parental intervention
that cuts across natural desire, but anxiety over punishment, especially the
dread of the withdrawal of affection and loss of love, leads to the repression of hostility to the parent. In this situation the child is led to accept the
rules, specified mainly as prohibitions, laid down by his parents as agents
of society, and in the process, he is made to think of the rules as embodying goodness in some objective sense. In asking how a person arrives at a
judgment of what is good and bad, Freud argues that it must arise from an
extraneous source since the capacity to distinguish good and bad is not
original or, so to speak, natural:

> Here, therefore, there is an extraneous influence at work, and it is this
> that decides what is to be called good or bad. Since a person's own
> feelings would not have led him along this path, he must have had a
> motive for submitting to this extraneous influence. Such a motive is
> easily discovered in his helplessness and his dependence on other
> people, and it can best be designated as fear of loss of love. If he loses the
> love of another person on whom he is dependent, he also ceases to be
> protected from a variety of dangers. Above all, he is exposed to the
> danger that this stronger person will show his superiority in the form of
> punishment. At the beginning, therefore, what is bad is whatever causes
> one to be threatened with loss of love. For fear of that loss, one must
> avoid it.[24]

The idea of identification plays a key role in Freud's account of the process.
The child's acceptance of the external rules is sustained by a growing desire
for identification with parents and especially with the parent of the same
sex. Identification consists of an emotional tie in which the child, anxious
to retain parental affection, seeks to imitate the parent as much as possible,
an endeavor which includes importantly the "introjection" of parental
moral values and norms. Once again, the Oedipal situation is seen as the
crucible in which the process of identification, relative to each parent, is
worked out in its basic and major form. Freud's own discussion of these
matters is predominantly (and notoriously) male-oriented and culture-
bound, though it is presented as universal. In a footnote added in 1920 to
the *Three Essays on Sexuality* (1905), he asserted:

> Every new arrival on this planet is faced by the task of mastering the
> Oedipus complex; anyone who fails to do so falls a victim to neurosis.[25]

The Oedipus complex is seen as arising in the male child in connection
with the desire to be identified with the father and to possess the mother
sexually; the child has a love-hate relationship to his father. But primarily

because of a perceived threat of castration, he is led to give up the desire to possess the mother. The Oedipus complex is thereby repressed—or rather, in the case of (ideal) normal development, it is destroyed or abolished by the castration complex. In this process the super-ego is brought into being "as the heir of that emotional attachment which is of such importance for childhood" (the Oedipus complex). Its nucleus lies in the introjection of parental authority: with the abandonment of the Oedipus complex the child enters a more complete identification with his father and a subordinate identification with the mother; in identifying with parents and adopting their moral standards (the severe moral standards of its parents' *super-ego*), the child takes on the role of exercising self-directed judgment and punishment for moral misdemeanors. In this connection the super-ego also plays the role of maintaining an ego ideal: it is "the representative for us of every moral restriction, the advocate of a striving towards perfection."[26]

This formation of the super-ego is gradual and may never get worked out properly. In Freud's terms, it is not merely a question of its existence, but of its relative strength and sphere of influence. Later on the child takes on the influence of those who stand in the place of parents such as teachers and ideal models; in this way it moves toward a more impersonal character which helps to provide a basis for the subordination of the super-ego to considerations of reason more than authority at a later stage. But in the meantime, the major motivation for observing the dictates of morality has been secured: self-punishment takes the form of guilt-feelings which, against the background of early experience, are deeply feared. In order to avoid them, the child seeks to observe the moral norms it has imbibed.

A corresponding version of the Oedipus complex, though rather in the manner of an afterthought, is postulated for the female child.[27] In the pre-Oedipal phase, girls (like boys) are primarily attached to their mothers. But in the hypothesized normal Oedipal phase, they come to harbor feelings of hostility to the mother and now transfer their primary attachment to the father, the parent of the opposite sex. This is effected mainly, so Freud supposes, by a female version of the castration complex, associated with penis envy, in which the child comes to believe that, because of her mother, she has in fact been castrated. In this case, the castration complex, rather than resolving the Oedipus complex as it does for boys, is precisely the means by which it develops. Here, according to Freud, is a fundamental difference between the sexes, and one which has moral ramifications.

How is the Oedipus complex dealt with in girls? Freud's view is that while girls also develop a super-ego, they are likely to remain in the Oedipal phase for an indeterminate length of time: the complex may be slowly abandoned, or it may persist long into adult life. Woman's super-ego, it is claimed, is less developed. There is a predominance of envy in woman's mental life and hence a weak sense of justice:

The fact that women must be regarded as having little sense of justice is no doubt related to the predominance of envy in their mental life; for the demand for justice is a modification of envy and lays down the condition subject to which one can put envy aside.[28]

And again:

I cannot evade the notion (though I hesitate to give it expression) that for women the level of what is ethically normal is different from what it is in men. Their super-ego is never so inexorable, so impersonal, so independent of its emotional origins as we require it to be in men. Character traits which critics of every epoch have brought up against women—that they show less sense of justice than men, that they are less ready to submit to the great exigencies of life, that they are more often influenced in their judgements by feelings of affection or hostility—all these would be amply accounted for by the modification in the formation of their super-ego which we have inferred above.[29]

In putting forward his comparative account of the Oedipus complex, Freud noted that it rested on a handful of cases and waited on further confirmation. But claims which "critics of every epoch have brought up against women" are taken simply as data to be explained, not as matters to be questioned. (I will take up this topic again in connection with a number of different moral theorists and critics of women; Freud's proposal is criticized by Carol Gilligan, as we shall see in chapter three.)

The internalization of norms constitutes a major phase of development in the growing child. Freud speaks of this process as a great change in the subject, while allowing that many adults remain at an infantile stage of observing precepts only when they fear that their non-compliance might be discovered:

A great change takes place only when the authority is internalized through the establishment of a super-ego. The phenomena of conscience then reach a higher stage. Actually, it is not until now that we should speak of conscience or a sense of guilt. At this point, too, the fear of being found out comes to an end; the distinction, moreover, between doing something bad and wishing to do it disappears entirely, since nothing can be hidden from the super-ego, not even thoughts.

But the moral norms are still represented as lying outside the individual's natural self, for the whole process is sustained by a channelling of the subject's original aggressiveness back against itself:

This we can study in the history of the development of the individual. What happens in him to render his desire for aggression innocuous? Something very remarkable. . . . His aggressiveness is introjected, internalized; it is, in point of fact, sent back to where it came from — that is, it is directed towards his own ego. This is taken over by a portion of the ego which sets itself over against the rest of the ego as super-ego, and which now, in the form of "conscience", is ready to put into action against the ego the same harsh aggressiveness that the ego would have liked to satisfy upon other, extraneous individuals. The tension between the harsh super-ego and the ego that is subjected to it, is called by us the sense of guilt; it expresses itself as a need for punishment.[30]

If one were to observe that the specified process does not constitute *moral* development in any proper sense, Freud might agree if only because he implies in places that moral development is illusory (or delusory). In the essay "The Disillusionment of the War" (1915), he proposes that the primitive instinctual impulses which constitute the deepest essence of human nature are subject in their long development to reaction-formations which give only a false appearance of higher morality:

> These primitive impulses undergo a lengthy process of development before they are allowed to become active in the adult. They are inhibited, directed towards other aims and fields, become commingled, alter their objects, and are to some extent turned back upon their possessor. Reaction-formations against certain instincts take the deceptive form of a change in their content, as though egoism had changed into altruism, or cruelty into pity.[31]

But Freud is also drawn to say that egoistic instincts may be transformed into social and altruistic attitudes under the influence of erotism — "that is, by the human need for love, taken in its widest sense." The illusion in this case is concerned not with the possibility of moral development (which is conceded), but with the common tendency to exaggerate the number of people who, as a matter of fact, get very far in this direction. Freud's inclination, made explicit in part by the experience of the war, was to think that genuine moral change is rare and that, for a very large number of people, morality does not go deep. Both themes — that moral development is illusory or that it occurs but is uncommon — can be found in Freud's writings. It is not easy to say which position is more characteristic of his thought.

Freud placed great, even excessive, weight on the original and early stages of human development in the individual. With that emphasis, and taking a line from the postulate of original instinctual impulses to the emergence of the super-ego, one might treat the process of moral formation — and of socialization generally — as the dynamic resolution of a conflict of instinctual drives. In the process, the id-instincts, or libinal impulses, become subject to the self-preservative or ego-instincts which are shaped by the implanted moral beliefs and unconscious fears of punishment (which compose the super-ego). This account of development is espoused by the Freudian psychologist J. R. Maze in his book, *The Meaning of Behaviour*.[32] It is put forward as the view to be found by and large in Freud's writings, up to about 1923, on the developed structure of the human mental apparatus. In Maze's words:

What gives moral beliefs their binding force, what motivates people actually to behave in accordance with them, is the underlying fear that they will be punished if they do not. These fears become unconscious, largely because the guilt-making circumstances in which they were acquired become subject to repression, whereas the moral beliefs are consciously held as objectively true, rather than as restrictions imposed on one by the threat of sanctions. The economic value of this is that it enables the person to believe that he is adopting certain inhibitions of his instinctual impulses as a matter of virtue, of principled renunciation, whereas if he retained in consciousness the realisation that he had given in to the arbitrary demands of others, that would be humiliating and painful. (171)

In proposing the Freudian thesis that, "the socialisation of children can readily be interpreted as the setting of instinctual drives against one another," Maze explicitly goes beyond Freud in minimizing the role of rational considerations:

The ego functions in accordance with the reality principle, and opposes the tendencies of the id, only insofar as that is effective *in securing its own gratification*. Its policies are not dictated by Reason but by its own consummatory programs. The moral convictions that a person embraces are embraced by, or forced upon, the ego, as beliefs about what it must do in order to protect itself from frustration. These beliefs, together with the unconscious fears of punishment, constitute Freud's "superego". Moral behaviour, then, is to be seen as a special sort of functioning of those drives which compose the ego. . . . Morality functions to persuade individuals to forego real-world gratifications in favour of the assurance of "virtue". (172)

This account is question-begging in important respects. It assumes that the individual can be treated as a complete system without reference to moral notions and independently of social relations. It further assumes that moral demands — treated necessarily as arising from the demands of others — are arbitrary of their nature. It also assumes that the individual is oriented to some exhaustive set of fixed "real-world gratifications" which are necessarily in conflict with "virtue."

But even if the original picture were to be accepted, there is a further question whether the account could be the whole story inasmuch as the delusion regarding morality, which is supposed to be built into its formation, cannot properly survive its exposure. Even if the claim were originally true, awareness of how one acquired moral beliefs and the related motivation would produce a change in the conditions in which the process is bound. Awareness constitutes a new stage of development. Unless it is treated as purely epiphenomenal, it would create the conditions for a new or different moral response. But what might be brought about by awareness of this view of early development would be affected by maturing cognitive and emotional growth in any case. Even when the original assumptions are conceded, therefore, the characterizations of moral behavior which Maze presents relate at best to an arrested stage of development, as if the story of the super-ego and moral understanding were complete at the age of six.

Freud, as Maze acknowledges, did not restrict his own account to the primary stage of development; it can now be seen that he had good reason to concede some place to later developments. The super-ego, having absorbed the norms of authority figures and society generally, undergoes a new round of conflict in adolescence before — ideally — taking on a more settled and less dominant role. With the weakening of the super-ego, rational considerations are able to play a more effective role in moral thought and practice; its weakening could be treated therefore as a major condition of growing moral maturity. The consideration of Freud's thought is thus brought back to the idea of a normative element in his understanding of morality and moral development.

HUMAN MATURITY

One major vein in the normative element in Freud's thought lies in his commitment to an idea of human maturity. He was sharply insistent on the difficult and conflictual character of development, on the idea that it can never be complete, and on the prevalence of suppression, self-deception, and rationalization in the moral domain. Nevertheless, he held out a conception of human growth which embraces such conditions as autonomy and independence, self-mastery, a capacity for self-criticism, a stable grasp of reality, and the capacity to act rationally in the real world. In the Freudian account these conditions have to be related in some way to the development of original instincts; at the same time, they carry implications in relation to emotional and cognitive growth which go beyond the postulated original base. Furthermore, the ideas carry moral import, albeit of a general sort, for they are concerned with the conditions of human self-realization and happiness. Indeed, as Ilham Dilman suggests, maturity is itself a moral category: "We have to use moral categories in elucidating what maturity means — such categories as responsibility, steadfastness, dependability, loyalty, seriousness, courage, integrity and others."[33] It is additionally clear that Freud put a particular emphasis on a sense of justice (as against envy) as a mark of maturity (hence his hypothesis regarding different levels of what is ethically normal for men and women).

The specified conditions of maturity can all be considered as self-regarding in important respects and as dimensions of individual growth. This is enough to suggest that a conception of morality as entirely determined by (arbitrary) social demands from outside the individual and as necessarily involving conflict with individual desire is mistaken. The way is open for thinking of moral development in some important respects as part of the internal growth of the organism. On the other hand, the conditions are all other-regarding and involve social relations as well: none of them could be attained by an individual except in a network of social interaction in which, broadly speaking, respect for them as values is upheld in a form of mutual concern. Development necessarily incorporates inner- and outer-related elements which are themselves inter-dependent. It is specifically linked in maturity with the capacity to love another person.

Freud's account of these matters focuses especially on the working out of libinal drives toward genital organization in the subject. Normal development, then, has to be contrasted with the manifestation of neuroses and perversions, which Freud speaks of in the summary at the end of the *Three Essays on Sexuality* (1905) as "on the one hand inhibitions, and on the other hand dissociations, of normal development." In related fashion, there is the contrast to be made with forms of fixation (in which features of earlier stages of development are carried over into adulthood) and regression. The topic also brings in his views about character and character-types. Or rather, the whole account Freud gives of development could be seen in terms of his treatment of character.[34]

Character, as Freud presents it, is linked especially with emotional growth. Its formation revolves around the way in which the child learns to deal with libinal pleasure in the original context of parental control — whether it reacts away from pleasure in the process of developing an excessively harsh super-ego or whether it clings to it in some fixated way and becomes the slave of libinal drives, or whether, ideally, it finds some way of incorporating the demands of both super-ego and id in a dynamic resolution. The presence of normative and moral elements could then be filled out in the contrast between forms of infantile or immature character and mature character.

Freud's view that character is already formed in some definitive sense at the age of five or six years is consistent with his general outlook. At the same time, it is problematic in the light of the general notion of character as embracing established capacities for action and emotional response and settled patterns of relationships. It also makes it difficult for him to draw out the necessary contrast between immature forms of character in the child and the manifestation of immature character carried over into adulthood. As for the fully mature character-type, Freud's view is that it would consist in a balance of all three elements, ego, super-ego, and id; but this type, as he says — the *erotic-obsessional-narcissistic* type — "would no longer be a type at all: it would be the absolute norm, the ideal harmony."[35] The ideal is presented as an ideal of emotional maturity. But this has general moral import in connection with its relation to happiness, and the idea of the mature character could be filled out only with reference to a range of moral categories, especially the notion of responsibility and of virtues such as courage, truthfulness, fairness in dealing with others, and so on.

The discussion has shown that the Freudian account of development, as it bears on moral development, is not purely a moral psychology. It incorporates a conception of morality, albeit in broad terms, in its very understanding of development and maturity. This dimension cannot be eliminated in favor of a reductivist, scientific, "value-free" interpretation without leading to a collapse of the whole theoretical framework. Furthermore, the relevant conception of morality goes beyond the explicitly acknowledged understanding which is given in terms of social demands imposed on the individual from outside. It goes beyond this to encompass aspects of the internal growth of the human subject, which significantly presupposes a social context.

CRITICAL REFLECTIONS

Questions about the nature of development postulated in Freudian theory, and its moral implications, abound. While Freud's general theory is of obvious power, the major constitutive elements such as the theory of libido, identification and the Oedipal complex, and the notion of the super-ego, are all problematic to a greater or lesser degree. It is a major problem, commonly observed, to know how the theory in its various aspects is to be tested, to know what evidence could be invoked for or against it. What would show, for example, that there is such a thing as the Oedipus complex or that it belongs to the causal network of libido, identification, and super-ego (and neuroses) in the way in which Freud depicts it? Freud's own inquiries were based on limited clinical data such as provided by the "Little Hans" case;[36] yet he confidently asserted its universality across gender (allowing for differences as noted above) and culture and time; and he went on to assign it a central place in the birth of civilization itself (in *Totem and Taboo* [1912–13]).

The emphasis on the Oedipus complex as the uniquely critical phase of development has been challenged by various Freudians in various ways, by Melanie Klein and Jacques Lacan, for example, to name two very different theorists. Malinowski and others have raised serious questions, on the basis of anthropological data, about its universality, though Malinowski held that it is universal within the family structure of patriarchal societies. Others again have seen it as a phenomenon which arises only in families in which certain specific conditions obtain in the relations between parents and children.

In a sympathetic discussion of the topic, Dilman concludes with Malinowski that the appeal to the Oedipus complex (in *Totem and Taboo*) to account for the origins of culture is unsatisfactory on grounds of circularity: the postulated occurrence of the complex presupposes the existence of culture already.[37] This is as conclusive an objection as any could be. With regard to its relevance to individual development, Dilman seeks to provide a general and conciliatory view. Freud's contribution in developing the idea of the Oedipus complex is placed in his drawing attention to "the problematic character of individual development irrespective of its social context":

[Freud] recognised that there are emotional problems bound up with the development of the child, problems concerning his relationships with his parents. . . . At the core of these problems is the conflict between his dependent attachment to his mother, the ideal of greater independence embodied in his father, and the threat of turning this in phantasy into a tyrannical assertion of paternal rights over the mother, reacting to it on that basis.

It would be difficult to disagree with Dilman's general interpretative comment regarding the problematic character of individual development. On the other hand, his Oedipal-type specification of the core problem does presuppose, in fact, definite forms of family and social structure. As for the proper resolution (or dissolution) of the complex, which is the condition for avoiding neuroses, Dilman proposes:

Freud believes that a stable relationship with the parents presupposes love and affection, and that the capacity for such love can only be achieved when conflicting emotions do not hinder autonomy and do not, in turn, reinforce dependency. They will do so until they are faced and lived through.[38]

Once again, it would be difficult to disagree with this proposal either in general or as expressive of the broad spirit of Freud's thought. At the same time, it appears to fall well short of the strong and specific claims which Freud made regarding the Oedipus complex and its role in the development of the human subject.

Psychoanalytic theory, as I have indicated, shares some basic ideas with social learning theory in its approach to moral development. These include a hedonistic view of human nature and of motivation for behavior. More specifically, each approach characterizes moral development essentially as the acquisition of motives for behavior contrary to natural inclination, with the outcome being effected by a system of rewards and punishments (which sets up a second-order level for the achievement of satisfaction). Moreover, each holds that the significant occurrences connected with moral development are already effected before the child is capable of exercising reason in their regard. Subsequent conformity with moral rules is then explained by the workings of a pre-rational mechanism or a continuing fear of punishment. In broad terms, therefore, psychoanalytic theory, no less than social learning theory, incorporates specific philosophical views about human nature and the nature of morality which give prior shape to the whole inquiry. Its specific findings and clinical practices are not vitiated by this consideration, for every possible view reflects a philosophical standpoint of some sort, but the assessment of the findings and practices needs to be referred back to the original philosophical conceptions, and the conceptions need to be considered in their own right.

I have already criticized some of the relevant presuppositions in connection with social learning theory and in the earlier discussion of Freud's moral views, viz., the thesis of original aggressiveness, instinctual drives as constituting the human essence, the idea of reason as lying outside human nature proper, and the exaggerated individualism which involves a conception of the human subject as abstracted from all social relations (and which is connected in turn with a questionable idea of radical conflict between individual and society, nature and culture, passions and reason, natural inclination and morality).

The restricted role accorded to cognitive factors is particularly significant in the developmental context of morality. The view that motivation for moral behavior is substantially laid down before the child is properly aware of what is going on is not in question. As I have already pointed out, this general idea was already espoused in the writings of both Plato and Aristotle on ethics and education. It is part of the common wisdom. Freud, it is true, has given it particular force by couching it in a complex and powerful account of early child-parent relationships, but key elements in his account are problematic. This applies to the idea of the super-ego, given its supposed causal basis in the complex. The super-ego is additionally put in question by the broad exclusion of cognitive elements from its formation and operation.

The view that conscience is an inverted form of original aggressiveness, which is Freud's more general characterization, rests heavily on ill-supported and largely unexamined ideas regarding human nature. (Perhaps it draws some appearance of support from instances of adult self- and other-hatred manifested as moral fervor.) Freud's more detailed account, however, starts from a considerably more plausible beginning in holding that the original motivation of moral behavior is the child's desire to enjoy the affection of its parents, mixed with fear of losing their love. This idea, which might be seen as enjoying the advantages and disadvantages of obviousness, can also be found in the writings of Plato and Aristotle (and many others). The question then turns on how the context of this motivational account is filled out and what is said in regard to subsequent development.

In the matter of context, all the problematic aspects of the Freudian philosophical standpoint come into play: the thesis of original aggressiveness, the exaggerated individualism, and so on. Furthermore, the contextual picture Freud supplies is thin, consisting of the promulgation of rules curbing natural desire, the use of reward and punishment, and the processes in which love and fear in relation to parents come to be attached to moral rules and behavior. In omitting a great deal, this picture misconstrues moral development.

The child's whole emotional and cognitive development, granted a desirable situation of loving care and attention, with reasonable sympathy, encouragement, mutual enjoyment, and so on, is already moral in character. Moral learning and growth in the form of affective response to parental treatment precedes and extends well beyond a focus on rules. Again, this picture would need to be filled out by attention to the way in which the child, in learning language, comes to acquire a moral vocabulary, and the way in which this vocabulary is related in its life, not simply to rules, but as much to attitudes and feelings and incipient forms of virtue — concern for others, friendship, gratitude, trust, generosity, care for one's environment (for example, in relation to plants, household pets, toys), courage, patience, truthfulness, and the like.

Such considerations suggest that the basic affective response which serves as the motivating factor in regard to morality in the young child is filled out by increasing awareness and practical knowledge and growth toward responsibility, all of which has bearing on the child's moral growth. The process never takes place in ideal conditions, and it is reasonable to suppose that it is always accompanied by occasions of considerable conflict, difficulty, and clash of wills between parent and child. One could also expect that a good deal of moral formation takes the form of repressive measures (or excessively indulgent treatment) which inhibit the child's development toward maturity. Nevertheless, when attention is given to a wider context, it seems clear that the normal moral development of children is considerably richer in the first motivational phase than the Freudian framework is able to recognize.

The same consideration applies to the account of subsequent development: the period of Oedipal conflict, repression of desire, identification with the (male) parent, the establishment of a transformed motive for moral obedience, and the buried fear of punishment through guilt in the reign of the super-ego. Once again, and with increasing unreality, the wider context of the child's moral experience is filtered out of the picture. It is questionable whether a good deal of moral life — attitudes, feelings, beliefs, dispositions, behavior — falls remotely into the postulated pattern of submission to conscience under threat of guilt. In many moral contexts, reference to conscience at all is strained or inappropriate, and where it is appropriate, it is questionable whether it has to be understood as universally tyrannical. This model seems to arise from a concentration on situations of conflict and certain types of personalities, allied with a prior conception of morality as the internalization of repressive and arbitrary external rules. Given this understanding of conscience, it is difficult to see how mature moral agency is possible even as an ideal. The adoption of an internalized set of standards in the form supposed by the theory would weaken a person's capacity to assess social norms and conventions critically and to exercise responsible independence in moral judgment and action.

Freud, as we have seen, espouses a conception of maturity which has definite moral ramifications. At this stage of development, cognitive considerations are accorded a significant role: in Freud's terms, they have particular bearing on the way in which the ego, the reality principle, holds a balance of control in relation to both super-ego and id. But how is this to be understood? It is not clear, for example, in the light of the allocation of roles in the psyche, how moral insight or moral understanding or moral perception would be explained. Freud says little about the later stages of growth toward maturity. His emphasis falls on the formation of the super-ego, and the recognition of later development is qualified by the idea of the controlling power of early development. Furthermore, the Freudian apparatus for portraying normal adult moral life is very limited. In Freud's defense it could be said that he took the importance of rationality for granted, including its importance in affective growth and emotional well-being, in order to stress the insufficiently recognized influence of instinctual elements and the decisive influence of early childhood experience. This is a fair point up to a point. On the other hand, there are serious problems in the views which are explicitly espoused, and a huge gap is opened up between the account of the formation and operation of the super-ego and the conception of the morally mature adult, so briefly sketched, at the other end of the process.

I will conclude with a brief comment on empirical research in this context. Empirical inquiry inspired by psychoanalytic theory in the field of moral development has focused on two areas. The first is the question of the internalization of moral standards in response to forms of parental discipline; the second concerns the process of identification and imitative modelling in the child-parent relationship. There has been extensive inquiry in both areas, much of it conducted by social learning theorists. But the work in connection with internalization has been largely inconclusive (as noted earlier). With reference to the topic of identification, M. L. Hoffman concluded a discussion of empirical findings with the remark:

> We conclude only that a great deal more research is needed before a definitive statement about the role of identificatory and modelling processes in moral development may be made.[39]

An important part of the difficulty is connected with the task of fixing the meaning of the key notions for purposes of testing and measurement (a pervasive problem in psychoanalytic theory). There is every reason to think that Hoffman's cautious conclusion remains valid. Nevertheless, the broad significance of the power of example is hardly a matter for doubt, and the human tendency to identify with and imitate others, especially when there are strong bonds of affection, is a commonplace which is of obvious importance for the moral development of children.

3. Moral Development: Cognitive Developmental Theory

The classification and assessment of types of moral character has long been a matter of interest in moral inquiry. Modern moral philosophy has tended to concern itself with more formal matters, however, and questions about types of moral character, and the related topic of virtues, have been widely neglected. The interest has been taken up more vigorously, often in a self-consciously empirical way, by psychologists. Numerous examples of moral typology have been proposed in this century. In classifications which range across some four to eight different types, most lists include the conformist-submissive and the independent-autonomous types.[1] In the context of psychology there has been a concern with trying to identify the background conditions which might be associated with the development of the various types. Freud's reflections on character-types are of this kind, given added urgency by his view that character is determined in early childhood in the immediate aftermath of the Oedipal conflict.

The classic example of work in relation to virtues or character traits is the study made by Hartshorne and May in the late 1920s in which a very large number of school-aged children were tested, for honesty and self-control in particular, over a range of situations offering opportunities for lying, cheating, and stealing.[2] On the basis of finding low positive correlations across different situations, Hartshorne and May concluded that behavior is highly specific and that there is insufficient evidence of unified character traits. In this view, there are honest and dishonest acts, but not honest or dishonest people. These findings would no doubt fit with a social learning account. But equally, Lawrence Kohlberg appealed to them as part of his case for replacing an emphasis on character traits in moral education with a cognitive developmental approach in which emphasis is placed on forms of moral reasoning. On the other hand, Hartshorne and May's methodology and findings have been challenged by a number of investigators.[3]

The emergence of cognitive developmental theory can be related to the classificatory ambitions of both character-type and virtue schemata. This approach, developed first by Jean Piaget in the early 1930s and extended by Lawrence Kohlberg since the late 1950s, attempts to classify types of moral outlook on the basis of stages of cognitive development from early childhood to maturity. Piaget's research led him to conclude that children's thinking about moral issues moves from a heteronomous to an autonomous stage (dividing around the age of ten or eleven). Kohlberg, on the basis of work mainly with adolescents and Piaget's more general theory of cognitive stages, was led to postulate that there are no less than six stages of successively more adequate forms of moral reasoning. In putting forward this account, he repudiated the idea of character traits. Citing the Hartshorne and May study — and his own studies on this basis — Kohlberg argued that the "bag of virtues" approach (as he called it) was arbitrary, vague, relativist, and, indeed, empty. Thus he took the view that there are no traits of character corresponding to the virtues and vices of conventional language. Terms like honesty, responsibility, friendliness, courage, and so on, are to be thought of as merely evaluative labels. In place of a "bag of virtues," Kohlberg's plan has been to rely on one virtue alone, justice, conceived as a universal principle, "a rule of choosing that we want all people to adopt always in all situations."[4] Whether reliance on justice alone is satisfactory, or whether Kohlberg's account is ultimately so very different, will be matter for later discussion.

Piaget's and Kohlberg's attempts to classify moral stages mainly on cognitive considerations are in marked contrast to psychoanalytic and social learning theories. With the emphasis on the acquisition of mental capacities and levels of understanding, there is a broad assumption that emotional development will move at a comparable pace. In contrast to the empiricist and Freudian approach, no particular emphasis is placed on the acquisition of guiding motives in relation to morality. The general outlook is that the child who is able to think about moral questions in a certain way will have corresponding feelings in their regard, sufficient to guide behavior. In that case, the question of special motivation does not arise.

This conviction reflects in part the primary focus of research in cognitive developmental theory. Piaget and Kohlberg are concerned with classifying children's "moral level" on the basis of their responses to stories or hypothetical dilemmas which concern the behavior of others; the question of how children are motivated in regard to their own behavior does not properly arise (even if inferences are drawn). There is also a difference in the theoretical starting point. In contrast to the other theories, the cognitivist emphasis takes a generally optimistic view of human nature and of the child's capacity for moral growth, and the sharp oppositions between nature and morality, individual and society, are muted. Piaget in particular was familiar with Freud's thought and was influenced by it in some respects in elaborating his own views. But neither Piaget nor Kohlberg accepted psychological or ethical hedonism, and their outlook on the relations of individual and society was very different.

The provision of a motive for moral behavior is all-important in Freudian and social learning accounts for, by nature, the motivational make-up of the individual is treated as essentially "anti-moral." A sufficient motive for moral behavior then *has* to be implanted from outside, a violent process with an inevitable legacy of conflict. Piaget or Kohlberg can allow for conflict of various sorts between individual inclination and moral norm, but in their terms, the social and moral growth of the individual can be treated as broadly natural.

With respect to the different historical strands in moral theory, rationalist and empiricist, Kohlberg in particular has sought to find a place for both. Within a cognitive framework, the principle of utility is associated with the fifth stage of moral development, subsumed under a universal formal principle of justice at the sixth and final stage. In this way, Kohlberg's higher stages encapsulate the prevailing wisdom of ethical and political theory in the modern era, an ordered conjunction of Utilitarianism and Kantian ethics. This wisdom, however, is not necessarily the last word: Utilitarian theory and Kantian ethics have each been subjected to considerable criticism, and Kohlberg's version of them has been challenged significantly from within his own research program, notably by Carol Gilligan in her book *In a Different Voice*.[5] Gilligan argues that the Piaget-Kohlberg accounts, while put forward in general terms, are systematically biased to a male point of view and male standards of judgment; women's ways of conceptualizing morality are either ignored or relegated to immature stages of moral growth. A study of Piaget and Kohlberg as the major exponents of the cognitive developmental theory needs to be accompanied, therefore, by a consideration of Gilligan's different voice. This voice, I argue, does not speak the last word either, but in important ways it picks up themes and concerns which reach back beyond Kant and the Utilitarians to an earlier and more satisfactory conception of moral wisdom.

1. Piaget: The Development of Moral Judgment

Piaget's developmental psychology consists importantly of a complex and, in part, speculative account of stages of cognitive development from birth to maturity.[6] The account includes a detailed structural theory of the human organism in genesis and of the conditions of structural stability and change in development. Piaget's work on moral development is part of this general theory, but in a rather loose and peripheral way. What he says about stages and their sequence in connection with moral thinking needs to be related to the more general theory at various points, and is certainly consistent with it. Nevertheless, the treatment of children's moral thinking does not depend on his general account of structure and stages of cognitive development in a detailed way. This is connected with the fact that Piaget's study of moral thinking was undertaken at a relatively early stage in his work and was restricted in scope. His views on morality and moral development are contained almost entirely in a single source, *The Moral Judgement of the Child* (hereafter *MJC*), published in French in 1932 and in an English translation the same year.[7]

FROM CONSTRAINT TO COOPERATION

Piaget holds that children's moral thinking, once they advance beyond the pre-moral stage of the infant years, moves through a sequence of two stages. In the years from about the age of four or five to nine, their views about morality are dominated by the authority of parents or other adult figures. This marks the primary stage of moral growth, heteronomous morality or the morality of constraint. Then, from around the age of ten, the influence of the peer group becomes much more significant, and in this setting of broad social equality, children move toward moral autonomy, the morality of cooperation which, fully developed, is the mature stage of moral growth.

Put in the broad terms of an advance from heteronomous to autonomous morality, the Piagetian proposal has an air of normative inevitability. What gives it interest and force is the detail in which the two stages are assembled and explicated in conjunction with the chosen method of inquiry. Piaget's method consisted in telling children stories, typically pairs of stories inviting comparison, relating to simple moral situations — stories about children telling lies, taking things, breaking things, situations involving reward and punishment and matters of justice. The children were asked a series of questions designed to elicit their judgment on a range of aspects raised by the stories: whether one piece of behavior was better or worse than another, the relevance of intention and motive and context in judging behavior, whether and in what ways punishment might be expected for wrongdoing, and so on. The assessment of the replies then yielded a characteristic profile for each of the two age-groups over a range of criteria.

In the foreword of his book, Piaget expressed the hope that his approach to the topic would be taken up and tested by other psychologists in differing social environments. His preliminary piece of work, as he called it, has in fact given rise to a vast number of studies, and it was a major influence in the development of Kohlberg's more complex and bolder theory of moral stages. But before considering Piaget's moral stages in more detail, we need to take some account of his moral theory, that is, of what he takes morality to be. While the specific elements of the two stages have been studied and tested extensively by psychologists, Piaget's moral theory has gone largely unexamined. This philosophical neglect is connected in part with the preoccupations of modern moral philosophy, in part with the fact that Piaget did not write extensively on the topic. A consideration of his views is important nonetheless, for they shape his inquiry. In a structural context, as Piaget has pointed out, the pyramid of knowledge does not so much rest on foundations as hang by its vertex, the ideal point toward which it moves.[8]

In an anecdotal but telling passage about early moral training, Piaget laments the fact that the majority of parents believe too much in morality:

"How much more precious," he observes, "is a little humanity than all the rules in the world" (*MJC* 191). This homely suggestion could be met with the comment that humanity might be thought of as part of morality as much as rules. But this consideration does not enter into Piaget's formal, and normative, specification of morality. In his view, the essence of morality is constituted by rules and respect for rules:

> All morality consists in a system of rules, and the essence of all morality is to be sought for in the respect which the individual acquires for these rules. (*MJC* 13)

Piaget does not discuss what is distinctive about moral rules, nor how they might be related to other relevant considerations such as notions of virtue and vice, or of good and bad. Moral rules are rules which children (and everyone) can be expected to recognize as moral and as defining what is good and bad; they are introduced, therefore, simply by way of example in the test stories. With this large assumption, the progress of the inquiry is set out in one move.

Piaget begins with an investigation of rules in a non-moral sphere. What he and his colleagues examined primarily in this regard was the way in which boys at different ages observed the rules of the game of marbles and expressed their ideas about them as rules. Girls' games, Piaget reports, were found not to exhibit the same emphasis on complex codified rules, but, on the basis of an inquiry relating to a simple version of hide-and-seek played by girls, the investigators claimed to find substantially the same pattern of respect for rules among girls and boys in the respective age-groups.[9]

There is a primary stage — which covers a more complex series of stages regarding the practice and then the consciousness of rules — in which the rules of marbles (and hide-and-seek, one may surmise) are thought of as sacred, immutable, imposed by a higher authority, demanding unilateral respect.[10] This stage is dominant from about the age of six. But then consciousness, following on increasing practical cooperation with peers, gradually yields an entirely different conception of rules from around the age of ten or eleven:

> Autonomy follows upon heteronomy: the rule of a game appears to the child no longer as an external law, sacred in so far as it has been laid down by adults; but as the outcome of a free decision and worthy of respect in the measure that it has enlisted mutual consent. (*MJC* 65)

From the rules of the games children play, attention turns to their ideas about specifically moral rules laid down by adults. Parallel attitudes are then uncovered across the relevant age-groups: the five-to-nine-year-old children think of moral rules as sacred, immutable, imposed by a higher authority, demanding unilateral respect. This is the stage of heteronomous morality or the morality of constraint or the age of moral realism as Piaget also calls it. Following a process in which rules are interiorized and generalized, a new consciousness develops on the basis of cooperation with peers (and later with adults). With cooperation there comes a sense of reciprocity and mutual respect and the idea that moral rules, especially the rules of justice as equity, are the outcome of mutual consent or social agreement. The child thus grows into the adult world of the morality of cooperation (except, of course, that many adults exhibit immature moral understanding).

Piaget's idea of morality — the essence of morality as respect for rules and the ideal of moral maturity in particular — shapes the whole of his inquiry. Some caution is called for here given that Piaget's primary concern is with testing cognitive capacities exhibited in moral judgment. But this does not make a substantial difference. What is being tested, how testing proceeds, and how results are classified and assessed are all matters which are shaped significantly, though not exclusively, by the given understanding of morality. In the light of this understanding, the presentation of the method and the research findings constitutes the major part of Piaget's study (the first three chapters). Moral theory is then taken up in a more direct way in the fourth and concluding chapter, in which Piaget is drawn to compare his findings with views about morality then current in sociology and social psychology (the views of Emile Durkheim in particular).

At this point of the study, the two stages are identified with corresponding types of morality, each associated with a characteristic type of social relation. In summary form, morality is heteronomous (immature) when a person — child or adult — stands in an unequal relation to moral authority (society, "elders," tradition, parents). Morality is autonomous (mature) when a person, in relations of equality and solidarity with others, assumes individual and subjective responsibility in moral matters. This constitutes, in Piaget's words, true or rational morality. His research findings, which are essentially descriptive in intent, are thus inextricably tied to a definite (albeit very general) normative conception of morality and of the way in which moral development should proceed.

The two types of questions which were set out early in chapter one above are obviously relevant to Piaget's study. Questions of the more philosophical sort would be addressed primarily to Piaget's "true morality" (MJC 402), especially the reasonableness and plausibility of the content and form of his ideal of moral maturity. There is also a more general question concerning the adequacy of thinking of morality as consisting essentially of a certain set of rules, whatever sort of respect they command. Questions which have in fact been put to Piaget's findings have come more frequently, however, from psychological standpoints in which the moral theory is taken at face value. Such questions ask whether, or to what extent, children in the respective age groups, in one or other sample from this or that social environment, exhibit the range of features which characterize the moralities of constraint and cooperation which Piaget found in his group of children in Switzerland; whether, or to what extent, children progress from one stage to the other, and whether there is a consistent or unified pattern of progress across the range of features; whether, or to what extent, the operative explanatory factors cited by Piaget in relation to stages can be verified or supported for different groups.

The main features of moral realism as Piaget depicts it consist in a unilateral respect for rules as sacred, absolute, immutable; an emphasis in moral assessment on overt behavior and its perceivable consequences with little or no recognition of the relevance of intention; the belief that punishment inescapably follows wrongdoing as the work of God or nature if not of parents or teachers; and the belief that the rules laid down determine rightness and wrongness authoritatively. The morality of cooperation, by contrast, reflects a respect for rules as social agreements based on mutual respect among the parties concerned. In this case, there is room for recognizing different points of view. Rules may be changed in appropriate circumstances; punishment for wrongdoing is not treated as automatic or inevitable; the agent's intention is seen as significant in assessing behavior; and rightness and wrongness arise out of the requirements set by cooperation. The unilateral respect of moral realism shows up characteristically in an acceptance of authority as commanding obedience and of its right to administer reward and punishment in unequal and even arbitrary ways. With mutual respect, by contrast, the emphasis falls on a measured response of the parties concerned when punishment is in question, together with a strong insistence on principles of equality in the distribution of goods.[11]

The most pervasive feature of moral realism as Piaget portrays it is the egocentrism of the young child. Egocentrism in this context is not a moral quality, but a general feature of cognitive immaturity: broadly, it consists in the young child's limited capacity for distinguishing between self and the external world. Typically, the young child externalizes subjective features of its experience and is unable to grasp that there are points of view other than its own. Moral rules are *reified* in this mentality — hence the name "moral realism" — and are thought of as absolute and immutable. The child's emotional dependence on its parents and the power of parental constraint also feeds into this way of thinking: a unilateral respect for moral rules flows from the child's feelings of awe and respect for parents who are the source of the rules (*MJC* 184–94). The transition beyond this stage is treated as essentially a matter of general cognitive growth, specifically in a series of "decentrations" in which the child comes to appreciate different points of view and acquires a more objective and more flexible understanding of the relevant issues. But as part of this development, Piaget puts particular stress on the growing child's experience of reciprocity with peers precisely as associations of cooperation. The world of parental and adult authority which so dominated the child in its first years gives place to the experience of engaging in moral judgment and decision in a society of equals.

PROBLEMS OF AUTHORITY
Piaget was explicitly aware of problems in his method of inquiry and was cautious in drawing conclusions. In contrast with his work in some other cognitive domains, he held that there was no case for talking of clearcut stages in moral psychology (*MJC* 267). Subsequent research appears to have provided some support for Piaget's developmental thesis in broad terms, but results in regard to more specific claims have been mixed.[12] The presence of problems could be inferred too from more general studies of Piaget's developmental psychology.

To take one pertinent example, egocentrism may be generally less significant than Piaget took it to be. In Margaret Boden's words, "Piaget's claims about egocentrism have not gone unchallenged, and it seems that, although he has identified an important aspect of thinking that is especially prominent in young children (because they are so reliant on perception, which necessarily involves a point of view), he underestimates the extent to which even infants can put themselves in another's place."[13] There is evidence that children who fall into the age group for moral realism (from around age five) do not treat rules as immutable; what they are likely to think is that rules can be changed, but only by adults. Their perception that they do not have the power to do this is perhaps an expression of realism in a more ordinary sense! More generally, indeed, the sense of reification associated with Piaget's "moral realism" is obscure enough to make assessment difficult. It might be that children who are interpreted as "reifying" rules do not have anything like an adequate grasp of the notion of rules. Egocentrism may reasonably be linked with a rigid and otherwise immature sense of moral rules in young children, but the hypothesis that it constitutes the ground of a stage of morality with the specified features in any tightly knit way is less compelling.

The idea of a stage has to be loosened in other ways. There is evidence that children respond in different ways to different issues. Personal, social, and cultural factors are almost certainly relevant in this regard, but there is the more general consideration, which must affect all testing in this domain, that the moral sphere is not a seamless web. Children's progress along the Piagetian dimensions (recognition of the relevance of intention, for example) within each stage and from one stage to the other is apparently uneven, nor are the stages self-contained.[14]

Research concerned with Piaget's second stage has concentrated largely on its two major conditions, peer relations and the experience of cooperation, on the one hand, and relative independence from adult constraint, on the other. Once again, the evidence of studies appears mixed.[15] But rather than looking into this evidence more directly, I propose to consider some related questions of a more philosophical sort.

Piaget's account of morality embodies a loosely specified idea of moral maturity. It is the idea of a person who cooperates with others as equals, who accepts individual responsibility, who is flexible and open to different points of view, and who enters into moral commitments by choice and in agreement with others rather than under constraint. The central virtue in a life of this sort is a sense of justice as fairness animated by a spirit of cooperation (*MJC* 347–49). This is obviously normative and ideal in character, as an account of moral maturity is bound to be, though the several elements have at least prima facie plausibility. It becomes clear on closer inspection, however, that Piaget's thinking in this area contains a measure of more questionable idealization.

The site of the problematic ideal can be found in Piaget's frequent references to democracy in connection with morality (*MJC* 65–76, 325, 346, 362–63). The guiding theme is that, in a democracy, law is the product of the collective will of the sovereign people. The form of the morality of cooperation is thus expressed in what Piaget sees as the essence or principle of democracy. Furthermore, he portrays democracy as the peak of historical evolutionary development, an advance beyond previous ages of theocracy and gerontocracy. The signal mark of the development is the extent to which social arrangements, being founded on the cooperation and mutual consent of equals, escape the constraints of past generations. The child in moving from heteronony to autonomy, from the morality of constraint to the morality of cooperation, thus re-creates the Piagetian conception of the movement of history.

Piaget's loose historical thesis associating rational morality with democratic ideas could imply that, outside democracy, the achievement of moral maturity is impossible. On the available evidence from other cultures (and from the past) this is a highly implausible thesis. It is true that Piaget's remarks on this theme are made in passing. There is no doubt, however, that he subscribed to a broad thesis of the kind in question. Thus he points to the affinity of his results in child psychology with the results of the historical or logico-sociological analyses of the French philosophers Léon Brunschvicg and Henri Lalande, and he suggests that Brunschvicg's work on the progress of consciousness in Western philosophy "is the widest and most subtle demonstration of the fact that there exists in European thought a law in the evolution of moral judgements which is analogous to the law of which psychology watches the effects throughout the development of the individual" (*MJC* 396).[16] Such ideas set the climate of thought within which Piaget's empirical inquiries proceeded. It is not entirely surprising, then, that the evidence of growing moral maturity among children is found primarily in their relations with one another in a postulated democratic society of equals. In taking this line, Piaget was consciously, albeit respectfully, setting himself against the views of Emile Durkheim.[17]

For Durkheim, morality consists of a body of rules sanctioned by society and imposed authoritatively by the social group on the individual. Through discipline in their upbringing, individuals interiorize the moral law of society, and through the development of bonds of social attachment, they are led to value it. On these lines, Durkheim seeks to account for morality in terms of two essential properties, duty and good:

> Duty is morality insofar as it commands. It is morality conceived of as an authority that we must obey because, and only because it is authority. The good is morality conceived as a desirable thing that attracts our wills to it spontaneously, quickening our desire for it. Now it is readily seen that duty is in fact society insofar as it imposes rules on us, specifies limits to our natural inclinations; while the good is society insofar as it constitutes a richer reality than our own individual selves and in which we cannot be involved without enriching ourselves.

Duty and good are complemented in this account of morality by a third element, autonomy or self-determination. This, in the interpretation Durkheim offers, consists fundamentally in the awareness and acceptance of the necessity set by the moral law of society (it does not rest in a pure property of the will, as Kant had proposed):

> We liberate ourselves through understanding; there is no other means of liberation. Science is the wellspring of our autonomy. In the moral order there is room for the same autonomy; and there is place for no other. Since morality expresses the nature of society and since this nature is no more directly apprehended by us than the nature of the physical world, individual reason can no more be the lawmaker for the moral world than for the physical world.[18]

Piaget was thus faced with a powerful account of morality in which the idea of duty remains paramount and in which constraint and cooperation are brought into harmony. His most telling argument against the Durkheimian account is that, contrary to Durkheim's own convictions, it leaves no room for critical intervention in the moral sphere. This is so because the normative force of morality is located entirely in the power of social sanction. There is no room for a distinction between what is the case in regard to moral rules and what ought to be, between what is and what would be better. Moral beliefs and practices are laid down by social authority with the weight of unshakeable tradition; the task of the individual, under threat of moral sanction but with the promise of enrichment, is to maintain the given beliefs and practices (*MJC* 344–47). Piaget's case against Durkheim is well taken. (He might have invoked Plato's argument in the *Euthyphro* against attempts to base morality on the word of an authority.) But there is a case for thinking that, in seeking to resolve the problem in the terms set by Durkheim, Piaget moved to the other extreme. Piaget's response to Durkheim is to espouse a sharp division between constraint and cooperation — and between duty and good — with each being assigned to distinct types of morality and to distinct stages in the development of moral judgment. In Piaget's own account of these matters, almost nothing is said about the need to learn how to accept and to exercise authority. There is a first stage, when authority is imposed from above in an unequal relationship of constraint in which cooperation is excluded. There is then a second stage, which consists of freely consenting equals who cooperatively agree on rules in a situation in which constraint has no place.

The focus on authority in each of these stages is overly narrow, albeit in different ways. At the first stage, heteronomous constraint is built into the situation by definition: the rules are set by others, and the child is required to obey. What is missing in this negative emphasis on authority is attention to the content of the rules and the more general context in which they operate. It may be that parental authority is commonly exercised in forms of arbitrary constraint, but in that case it is exercised badly. The element of constraint is properly located within a set of conditions which are necessary for the child's well-being and growth. The primary part of parental authority is to provide these conditions and to care for the child to the point where it is no longer needed or justified. But the whole process is one in which a good deal of cooperation between parents and children is needed from an early stage.

Piaget's idea of authority at the level of consenting equals is also narrowly based, but in a different way. The reference points for this stage relate initially to the attitude of adolescents to the rules of marbles, according to which "a rule is conceived as the free pronouncement of the actual individual minds themselves," something dependent on their collective will (*MJC* 70–71). The same attitude is then found to hold in the moral sphere, especially in relation to justice, which is seen to rest on equality and reciprocity in such a way that "justice can only come into being by free consent" (*MJC* 319).

The range of reference points to which Piaget alludes is remarkably limited. Even in the sphere of games, children learn to play games such as chess and football as well as marbles; and part of the enjoyment of playing these games is connected with developing skills in accordance with the built-in conditions of the game and the rules and traditions derived from "elders" and past generations. Something similar goes on in learning to play a musical instrument or in learning mathematics, a foreign language, or any number of skills. Respect for the rules of chess is not unilateral or heteronomous in the Piagetian sense, but neither does it arise in a context of equality in which the rules are conceived as the free pronouncement of the individual mind or the product of the collective will of the players. In these contexts, there is both constraint and cooperation, freedom and necessity, dependence on others and scope for autonomy.

The contexts of authority relevant to adolescent experience are much more extensive, of course, than the activities just mentioned. Questions of authority, for example, are involved in children's relations to parents, teachers, officeholders in various institutions (the bus driver, the librarian, the shopkeeper), and so on. Moreover, children quickly become aware of these dimensions of authority and have views about what is fair and unfair in their regard. But even if one's attention is restricted to games, the transition from the experience of games of a particular sort to related conclusions regarding moral attitudes is remarkable. It is reasonable to suppose that the discovery of the connection was shaped, if not predetermined, by Piaget's views regarding the democratic ideal as the expression of rational morality and by his concern, in opposition to Durkheim, to draw a sharp distinction between cooperation and constraint.

Piaget was critical of the way in which Durkheim concentrated on social relations between children and adults and failed to consider the distinctive social relations in the groups which children form among themselves (*MJC* 361). His own account is affected by the opposite bias. More precisely, it suffers from a limited focus on types of authority. For Piaget, authority is either external and imposed in a situation of inequality, or it is internal and free in a context of mutual respect and agreement among equals. Piaget's anxiety to avoid any element of constraint is well illustrated by his individualistic account of the notion of *common morality*. In place of the Durkheimian idea of a body of beliefs and practices imposed on the individual by society, Piaget seeks to define common morality as no more than a sum of relations between individuals, the sum of their different but related individual moral perspectives (*MJC* 350–51).[19]

Piaget's account of authority (beyond the stage of constraint) bears some similarity to Rousseau's idea of legitimate civil authority. This consists of a full participatory democracy in which freedom and authority are reconciled inasmuch as the person who obeys the law has also willed it. The Rousseauian proposal has been subjected to a good deal of criticism, not least in regard to the possibility of implementation (and the injunction that the citizen who is unwilling to obey must be forced to be free). In any case, it has never been realized in any large-scale instance, and one may be a little skeptical of Piaget's idea that democracy of this sort is realized among young adolescents in relation to moral rules. What Piaget offers as a factual account of experience relevant to morality appears fanciful, whether among adolescents or adults.

Even if the Piagetian picture were true in fact, it could still not account for the authority of rules as moral rules. Consider the claim in regard to justice, that "resting as it does on equality and reciprocity, justice can only come into being by free consent" (*MJC* 319). A group of peers, we suppose, agree on a set of rules governing their behavior. Allowing that the rules have an appropriate form and content — which is not a matter of mere decision, whether individual or collective — the question arises as to what would constitute the rules as rules of justice. If one says that it is the authority of the group acting in free consent, the rules are rendered arbitrary and immune to criticism. In that case, Piaget's democratic account would be no better off than Durkheim's direct resort to the authority of society. As we saw in connection with Plato's *Euthyphro*, the agreement — which serves as an authority — would need to be referred back to some other ground, presumably considerations about the nature of justice and its place in human relations and questions about human harm and welfare. Piaget acknowledges this element of control, in effect, in his emphasis on mutual respect and the idea that cooperation sets necessary preconditions on the choice of rules. But the recognition of this dimension is obscured by idealized elements in his conception of democratic procedures and authority in this context. These factors shape his conception of moral maturity and cast their influence back on his empirical inquiries in the domain of moral judgment.

Piaget comments in the foreword to his study:

> In a sense, child morality throws light on adult morality. If we want to form men and women nothing will fit us so well for the task as to study the laws that govern their formation. (*MJC* 9).

His concern is with moral judgment in the developing child, not with moral philosophy or questions about the nature of morality or moral education in an immediate sense. But a conception of morality, shaped by an ideal of individual autonomy free of relationships of authority, sets the character of the primary inquiry. It is not so much that child morality is used to throw light on adult morality, as that a normative conception of morality on the basis of adult social and political relations shapes the search for laws in the domain of moral formation. For all the wealth of ideas, philosophical and psychological, in Piaget's work on moral judgment, what seems to be needed in the end is a more rigorous study of stages of development in the light of a more fully worked out and more adequate conception of morality and its forms. Lawrence Kohlberg's work on moral development might be thought to have satisfied these related needs most fully.

2. Kohlberg: The Saga of Moral Stages

Where Piaget spoke of two stages of moral development, Lawrence Kohlberg puts forward six; where Piaget spoke of moral stages in a loose sense, Kohlberg proposes that the stages in his account are to be understood in the strong sense of Piagetian stages of logical and cognitive development (with which, with some qualifications, the moral stages are aligned).[20] Kohlberg follows Piaget in focusing on moral reasoning as the central issue in moral development; he also takes his cue from Piaget in concentrating on moral judgment in the domain of justice. In many writings Kohlberg appears to treat justice as covering everything of importance in morality, but this was disavowed in the latest writings in response to criticism. Kohlberg eventually came to present his theory as being — and as always having properly been — a rational reconstruction of the ontogenesis of justice reasoning (justice being seen as the core of morality).[21]

THE SYSTEM OF STAGES

Kohlberg's six moral stages — stages of moral judgment — are distributed in pairs across three levels of development: pre-conventional, conventional, and post-conventional.

Pre-Conventional Level

STAGE 1:

> *Heteronomous morality or stage of obedience and punishment*. What is right is set by rules which the child obeys to avoid punishment and out of deference to superior power of authorities. Egocentric point of view.

STAGE 2:

> *Stage of Individual instrumental purpose and exchange*. What is right is related to rules insofar as they serve immediate interests, one's own or the acknowledged interests of others, with a view to meeting one's own needs and interests in a world in which one must recognize that others have interests too. Concrete individualistic point of view.

Conventional Level

STAGE 3:

> *Stage of mutual interpersonal expectations, relationships, and conformity*. What is right and good is related to the expectations of the people with whom one lives, and to some more general expectations connected with roles. Emphasis on concern for others, being well thought of, relations of trust, loyalty, respect, gratitude, and related rules and authority which support stereotypical good behavior. The point of view of the individual as having shared feelings and agreements with other individuals.

STAGE 4:

> *Social system and conscience stage*. What is right is set by one's duties in society, the need to uphold social order and to maintain the welfare of society, group or institution, with a view to keeping the system going, and out of sense of conscience. Emphasis on rules and authority in this context. Acknowledgment by the individual of a general societal point of view different from interpersonal agreements or motives.

Post-Conventional or Principled Level

STAGE 5:

> *Stage of social contract or utility and individual rights.* Awareness of variety of values and of values as relative to one's group; what is right is nonetheless the upholding of the relative rules (as a rule) to ensure impartiality and because "they are the social contract"; moreover, some values, life and liberty in particular, are non-relative and ground rights which must be upheld in any society. Commitment to laws on the basis of one's social contract with a view to the welfare and protection of the rights of all; emphasis on the principle of utility, "the greatest happiness for the greatest number." The prior-to-society point of view — that of a "rational individual aware of values and rights prior to social attachments and contracts."

STAGE 6:

> *Stage of universal ethical principles.* What is right is specified by reference to self-chosen ethical principles; particular laws and agreements are upheld as usually valid insofar as they rest on principles which are universal principles of justice with overriding force: "the equality of human rights and respect for the dignity of human beings as individual persons." Commitment as a rational person to the validity of the universal principles. *"Perspective of a moral point of view* from which social arrangements derive" — the perspective of the rational individual recognizing the nature of morality.

This account of moral stages was fully elaborated by the early 1970s.[22] Revisions and modifications were to follow, as we shall see, but these do not affect the substance of the general claims which Kohlberg makes in regard to the stages. These can be summarized as follows: (a) the moral stages constitute distinct or qualitatively different ways of thinking about or solving the same problems (relating to justice); (b) stages are "structured wholes" with an underlying thought organization, and individuals are consistent in their level of moral judgment; (c) stages constitute hierarchical integrations, forming an order of increasingly differentiated and integrated structures to fulfil a common function; (d) the stages form an invariant sequence in individual development, moving progressively from less to more integrated structures; stages are not skipped, regression does not occur (though advance is not guaranteed), and the invariant sequence, which holds universally, is not substantially affected by social epoch or cultural class or gender differences; (e) the six stages form a complete set; (f) movement through the stages is conceived on the model of an interaction between organismic structuring tendencies and the structure of the outside world, the social environment in particular (capacity for judgment is closely dependent on opportunity for role-taking).[23]

These claims were the conclusion of research which had begun in the 1950s as a cross-sectional study of the ways in which children and adolescents (all male subjects) responded to a range of hypothetical dilemmas.[24] This was followed by a major longitudinal study of some 58 subjects from the original group and a variety of smaller longitudinal and cross-sectional studies in different cultures (yielding some cross-cultural comparisons). While acknowledging the need for modifications, Kohlberg continued to report in the mid-1980s that studies confirmed his thesis of a culturally universal invariant sequence of stages, specifically Stages 1 to 5.[25] In relation to the stages in general, children up to around age ten are placed in Stage 1 or 2; after that age, the majority of people are assessed as being in Stage 3 or 4; Stages 5 and 6 define an adult level of attainment.

The purpose of organizing the moral-judgment interviews around hypothetical dilemmas, backed up by the elaborate scoring system, is to determine a person's level of moral reasoning. It is not concerned, therefore, with the views a person holds, but rather with the sorts of thinking or reasoning they employ in expressing the views. It is not so easy, however, to effect the desired separation of form and content this concern envisages. By the 1970s some anomalous results had emerged — notably, an apparent regression in early adulthood of some subjects from Stage 4 or higher to Stage 2 or 3, and an apparent leap by some from Stage 3 to Stage 5. These problems arose, as Kohlberg came to argue, from the admission of too much content into assessment and from inadequacies in the definition of Stage 4. His eventual solution was to postulate a transitional or intermediate stage, Stage 4½, between the conventional and the post-conventional levels. What had appeared as regression could then be reinterpreted as partial progress on the grounds that while the *content* of judgment was typical of an earlier stage (e.g., in its relativism), the level or character of argument was higher. In a later modification, Stages 3 and 4 were subdivided into (A) and (B) substages: (A) as the original stage, (B) as a version marked by the beginnings of principled-stage thinking, with an orientation to autonomy, mutual respect, and reversibility rather than the heteronomy which is characteristic of the (A) substage, and with an "intuition of a hierarchy of values, e.g. of life over property in the Heinz dilemma."[26] When a revised scoring system was eventually put in place in the late 1970s, many adolescents who had previously been ranked at a higher level were reclassified into one or other substage of Stages 3 and 4. At this point, Stage 5 came to be treated as uncommon, and the attainment of Stage 6, which was dropped from the scoring manual entirely, was seen as altogether rare.

Taken as a whole, Kohlberg's theory offers a scientific account of the development of moral reasoning; as such, it claims to be true for all times and places. Moral reasoning according to the theory is manifested as the grasp of a set of rules which reflect a stage or structure of adaptation of the individual to his or her environment in relation to conflicts concerning rights and duties. The claim is that the rules exhibit increasing generality and adequacy, with the more particular, more limited, lower stages being subsumed into the higher stages. The process arrives in the end (Stage 6) at a set of formal moral principles, specifically of justice conceived as a universal, impartial, rational principle of equality, reciprocity, and cooperation, which in application yields an ultimate, rational resolution of conflict in its domain.

What is exhibited at Kohlberg's Stage 6 is a deontological view of ethics, associated especially in the history of ethical thought with Kant (see chapter seven below). In this view, duties arise prescriptively from the rational agent's awareness of universal ethical principles, the moral law; the rational moral agent is autonomous in respect of these duties; moral principles are marked out by a criterion of universality; and the fundamental principle is that persons are to be treated as ends in themselves, never as means. Stage 5 reflects a different conception of justice associated rather with Utilitarian theory, guided by the non-deontological principle of utility, "the greatest happiness of the greatest number" (see chapter eight below). In this understanding, duty does not arise in its own right (as in a deontological view), but in virtue of serving to promote pleasure or happiness (that is to say, human good). Kohlberg's depiction of this stage includes the "perspective of the social contract," specifically the idea that moral and political obligation — and the social order as a whole — can be thought of as the product of an implicit agreement among individuals to respect mutual rights, beginning with the right to life. What is offered, then, in the case of each stage at the post-conventional level is the idea of formal principles of justice arising out of equality and the conditions of cooperation. Particular moral content is thus ostensibly excluded. At the same time, the principles in question are characteristic of the two main schools of ethical liberalism, Utilitarian and Kantian ethics respectively.[27]

In putting forward a view according to which formal principles of justice grow with normal cognitive development, Kohlberg could take a strong position with respect to moral education. He could argue against value-neutrality in the name of justice, without having to appeal to particular value-content or specific values other than justice; and armed with the case for universal principles, he could argue against ethical relativism. It is important to keep in mind that Kohlberg characteristically put his views forward in the educational context; that is, he was concerned to argue that education in keeping with the stages provides the proper and only satisfactory basis for moral education.[28] According to the theory, the stage sequence is invariant. But progress through the stages is seen to depend on environmental conditions, on the quality of teaching and especially on the opportunity for role-taking to which children have access. A common hypothesis in this context has been the idea that advance is facilitated by exposure to examples of reasoning at one stage above a subject's current stage.

What were the sources of Kohlberg's account of levels and stages in moral development? Bill Puka, a philosopher who is critical of philosophical criticism of Kohlberg as too abstract and general, says that the Kohlbergian stage descriptions are interpretations derived from (empirical) data.[29] This is implausible for Stages 5 and 6: each is patently a version of a philosophical ethical theory. Each of these theories, Utilitarianism and Kantianism, has connections with Greek and medieval thought, but each, in different ways, is characteristically a modern doctrine with deep roots in social, political, and economic experience in Europe since the seventeenth century. Furthermore, each view (and the idea of a social contract as well) has been given strong contemporary expression, notably in the writings of R. M. Hare and John Rawls (philosophers who have clearly influenced Kohlberg's formulation of the "post-conventional" stages). There is no doubt that there are people who argue about moral dilemmas in line with one or other approach (or both), but that is not to the point. As meta-ethical and normative theories, they can be argued about, for or against, on their own merits. In these circumstances, the view that they mark out natural and culturally universal stages of development in moral reasoning must appear particularly bold.

Kohlberg himself makes clear that his ideas regarding levels and stages of moral development were drawn from Dewey and Piaget, each of whom proposed a pattern of three levels, pre-conventional, conventional, and post-conventional (autonomous or principled). Similar patterns were proposed, as Kohlberg points out, by W. McDougall, L. Hobhouse, and J. M. Baldwin.[30] In broad terms, the pattern commends itself as normatively inevitable. But it would be wrong to think that the Deweyian and Piagetian influences on Kohlberg form a seamless whole. Kohlberg's three levels of moral reasoning follow the general pattern of Dewey's schema; like Dewey furthermore, he seeks to place cognitive elements in a context of social interaction and affective growth. But as William Sullivan suggests in *Reconstructing Public Philosophy*, Kohlberg appears to have had misgivings about the philosophical adequacy of Dewey's ethical naturalism and the adequacy of his epistemological views as scientific psychology. He thus turned to Piaget's structuralist psychology to supply a scientific account of cognitive development with which moral development could be aligned, and in the same spirit, he turned from Dewey's ethical naturalism to Kantian deontological ethics in philosophy to supply the desired formal characterization of the highest stage of moral reasoning. In Sullivan's words:

> The logical and epistemological commitments of Piaget's structuralism turn out to have close affinities to the liberal-Kantian metaphor of moral reasoning as legislating. The Deweyan, operational sources of Kohl-

berg's theory, press in the opposite direction, towards a situational, prudential understanding of moral reasoning that includes an interpretative aspect in strong contrast to the Kantian or the structuralist paradigm.[31]

Having taken his stand with Kantian ethical theory, Kohlberg hoped to see it confirmed by psychological data relating to the stages.

In a complex blend of philosophical and psychological theory such as Kohlberg has elaborated, problems predictably arise in regard to each body of theory and to the way in which they are brought together. In psychology, a good deal of questioning surrounds the general validity of Piaget's cognitive-developmental stages. There is the additional question whether the Kohlbergian moral stages meet the criteria of Piagetian cognitive stages in a clear or plausible way, and whether they meet more general scientific criteria for theories. Related difficulties also surround the Kohlbergian research methodology. These are large questions which do not permit ready pronouncement on either side, but the existence of serious problems in Kohlberg's research program is well known. My intention is to focus rather on problems which concern the more philosophical aspects of Kohlberg's views, but in this way, the theory as a whole can be brought under critical consideration.

JUSTICE AND MORALITY

In the 1983 formulation of the theory and reply to critics, Kohlberg and his associates took up the question of the choice of justice:

> Following Piaget's lead, Kohlberg thought that justice reasoning would be the cognitive factor most amenable to structural developmental stage analysis insofar as it would clearly provide reasoning material where structuring and equilibrating operations (e.g. reversibility) could be seen.[32]

One might add that the choice of justice could draw on the resonances of Greek ethical thought while being readily fitted into the formalized character of Kantian ethical theory. The bearing of this choice on the character of the program and the whole theory of moral stages needs closer attention.

Kohlberg acknowledged in later writings that justice is not the whole of morality. This acknowledgment has not always been so clear, however. In pressing the superiority of the moral stages approach in moral education, Kohlberg aligned it in a number of essays with the Socratic view of justice. In the argument, the stage theory — the putative "Socratic" account — is set against a view of morality and moral education which was prevalent in schools, and supposedly derived from Aristotle, which Kohlberg calls the "bag of virtues" view.[33] In the crude account of this alternative, the theorist or educator is imagined as picking a list of virtues (and vices), apparently without reference to any clear principle, which are then treated as constitutive of moral character. The Socratic view, by contrast, holds that virtue is one, not many, and that it is the same for all; it consists, in short, of knowledge of the good.

Kohlberg takes up this Socratic idea but restates it in the significantly different form: "Virtue is not many, but one, and its name is justice"! This assertion carries the clear implication that justice and morality are one. The rhetorical force of the move is to place a claim on the whole domain of morality. In fact, Kohlberg's reading of Plato rests on a wild interpretation of a Socratic thesis which is questionable in the first place, viz., the Socratic conception of the unity of the virtues. But even if the Socratic conception were accepted, the accompanying thesis is that the unity of the virtues is realized in the *knowledge of the good*. The knowledge of the good in its turn is the notion of something which embraces qualities such as courage, self-control, justice, and so on. In other words, Socrates does not offer any escape from the need for a "bag of virtues." What Kohlberg does is to identify the Socratic idea of the knowledge of the good with one specific virtue, justice. This is a misreading of Socratic thought which quickly generates absurdities.

Another example of the way in which Kohlberg's idea of justice spreads across morality as a whole can be found in the following passage:

> When we move from role taking to the resolution of conflicting roles, we arrive at the "principle" of justice. *A moral conflict is a conflict between completing claims of men*; you versus me; you versus a third person. The precondition for a moral conflict is man's capacity for role taking. *Most social situations are not moral, because there is no conflict between the role-taking expectations of one person and another.*[34]

Whatever is to be said for the importance of role-taking in moral learning, moral conflicts are not confined to conflicts in the domain of justice or even to conflicts between people (individuals or groups). Again, it is symptomatic of a particular and limited way of thinking about morality to suggest that social situations, in the absence of conflict, are not moral. Justice conceived on a conflictual model has expanded to fill the domain of morality, or rather, morality has been contracted into a specific and limited field.

Kohlberg's later acknowledgment that justice is not the whole of morality or the only field of moral judgment has been made without any corresponding revision of the way in which justice shapes the specifications of each of the six stages. For example, young children's thinking about morality is restricted to the way in which they respond to certain hypothetical dilemmas in relation to justice. Their moral thinking — verbal and behavioral — is clearly much wider than this perspective allows. Consider, for example, behavior such as expressing and responding to affection, helping others, looking after things, putting up with illness, showing trust, sharing things, and so on. It is not simply that in focusing on one specific dimension, the Kohlbergian emphasis simply leaves the other aspects out of consideration: the specifications of Stages 1 and 2 are put in quite general moral terms. Or again, Stage 4 is counted as morally more adequate than Stage 3 since it is taken to involve a more general, and presumably more integrated, level of thinking connected with a person's adopting a general societal point of view in dealing with the dilemmas. This may be defensible in its chosen terms, but the ranking begs questions in supposing that moral reasoning is better for being more general since other factors are filtered out of consideration. The more general reasoning may in fact be less sensitive to situation and less inclined to take account of relevant circumstances; it would then be less flexible and less competent in interpreting moral situations in their complexity. In this way, Kohlberg's model of adequacy in moral reasoning is likely to come into conflict with an Aristotelian-type account of the sort espoused, for example, by Dewey. (Issues of the sort I have just been considering are central to Gilligan's critique of Kohlberg's stages; I will return to the topic more fully in the next section.)

The idea of justice at Stage 5 also spreads across the moral field as a whole through its association with Utilitarian moral theory. In this case, the idea is guided by a theory in which all values are reduced to the one value of happiness as pleasure. Again, it is additionally shaped by the particular social and political thought of the early modern period, especially in the attempt to legitimize the authority of the state on the hypothesis of an original social contract. Finally, the idea of justice in Stage 6 is allied with the full panoply of Kantian ethical theory. At this point, the principle of utility leads on (somewhat mysteriously) to a conception of enlightened rationality in which the individual intuits ethical principles (that is, the formal principle of justice). In summary, the Kohlbergian idea of justice pretends to draw in the whole of morality at each level; alternatively, it constructs it in its own likeness.

PROBLEMS OF THE HIGHER STAGES

In response to criticism of this sort, Kohlberg's work has been developed in two main ways. First, the emphasis came to be placed, more clearly than before, on the attempt to uncover levels of reasoning about justice in a relatively pure form. This has not shown up, however, in a revision of the way in which the stages are identified and described. In a second line of response, Kohlberg took up wider research concerns in regard to morality. Thus, more attention has been given to the question of the relationship of moral reasoning to behavior.[35] In response to Gilligan's work in particular, Kohlberg and some associates began to consider ways of thinking about justice as related to "issues of care and response in real life dilemmas as well as . . . a concern about the issue of how such dilemmas are resolved in practice." On these lines, Kohlberg was prepared to accept adult forms of development which are clearly not derivable from the Piagetian structural stage model. These are described accordingly as "soft stages"; they are specified as "levels of existential and reflective awareness" and could presumably be counted as candidates for moral maturity.[36] On the other hand, Kohlberg continued to maintain that justice as defined by the post-conventional level, specifically Stage 6, constitutes the core of morality. The status of the post-conventional stages clearly remains crucial to Kohlberg's whole program.

Philosophical criticism, as I have already indicated, is addressed particularly to the notions of justice in Stages 5 and 6. This is especially true of justice in Stage 6, given its supreme status. Kohlberg might have hoped to disarm this criticism on the strength of empirical evidence. But the evidence was not forthcoming. On the revised scoring system in particular, very few subjects, and no one from outside the educated circles of Western culture, attained Stage 6. Faced with mounting criticism, Kohlberg withdrew the stage from the sequence of stages in the early 1980s. In its changed status, Stage 6 was now designated as a "theoretical construct in the realm of philosophical speculation," to be used as an interpretative principle in relation to the other stages.[37] With this retrenchment, the strong claim to a culturally universal invariant sequence was restricted to Stages 1 to 5. It was thus assumed that the withdrawal of Stage 6 would leave everything else as it was. The question arises immediately whether Stage 5 can survive the change unscathed.

In connection with the claim to a culturally universal sequence, Stages 5 and 6 provided the site of an evolutionary thesis in which the principles of Western liberalism are identified with the universal ethical principles of reason. According to this thesis, "the prevailing moral standards in the United States and in other societies are gradually evolving towards higher developmental stages and thus towards more adequate conceptions of justice."[38] Kohlberg's original claims regarding cultural universality up to the early 1970s rested on limited cross-cultural studies and were extremely bold:

> The same basic ways of moral valuing are found in every culture and develop in the same order. There is a universal set of moral principles held by people in various cultures, Stage 6.

These bold claims were placed under immediate strain with the accompanying acknowledgment that Stages 5 and 6 are not found in preliterate or semi-literate village cultures; and Stage 5, it was agreed, was "much more salient in the United States than in Mexico or Taiwan at age sixteen."[39] Indeed, later evidence would suggest that the two stages are hardly found at all other than among people with an articulate commitment to the liberal-democratic moral ethos.

In the account of the moral stages offered in 1983, Kohlberg stepped away quite generally from cross-cultural comparison in the sphere of moral development:

> We do not believe that comparison of one culture to another in terms of moral development is a theoretically useful strategy for the growth of scientific knowledge. . . . It is difficult to understand what a valid concept of "comparative moral worth of culture" might be, but in any case such a concept could not be established on the basis of a comparison of means on our moral judgment assessment scale. There is no direct way in which group average can be translated into statements of the relative moral worth of groups.

At the same time, Kohlberg and his fellow authors go on to claim, on the basis of more recent cross-cultural research, that Stage 5 reasoning has been found in a fairly large number of non-Western cultures; and they propose that its absence in village societies is to be explained by their comparatively simple social structure and the relative absence of formal education.[40]

These claims on behalf of Stage 5 are less than conclusive. In a survey of the studies cited by Kohlberg, Ian Vine has shown that there is very little unambiguous evidence of Stage 5 subjects in other cultures. The study in India, working with an upper-middle-class sample, yielded only one Stage 5 subject (a male parent); and the study in Turkey failed to uncover any clear Stage 5 subjects — and it is acknowledged in the report that the data does not necessarily support "a strong claim of universality . . . that the structures described by Kohlberg exhaust more or less the whole domain of morality in every culture."[41] The study in Israel showed results more comparable with those in the United States, as might be expected; but in fact the emergence of Stage 5 subjects even in the United States has been very low. On the evidence, Vine's conclusion seems to be well-founded: "It therefore appears that Kohlberg has not yet established definitively that *purely* postconventional reasoning is more than another idealization for any group so far studied." Similarly, Carolyn Pope Edwards, who is highly experienced in the field and sympathetic to Kohlberg's general program, makes no claim for evidence in support of Stages 5 or 6. This is in contrast to her view that there is some empirical evidence, though not yet enough, to support the cultural universality of "hard" moral Stages 1 to 3 or 4.[42]

All this suggests that, for Kohlberg, Stage 5 should be bracketed with Stage 6 as a theoretical construct in the realm of philosophical speculation. With this conclusion, Stages 5 and 6 constitute a way of thinking which is discontinuous with the earlier stages. The theory can no longer claim to provide an integrated typology across the range of moral development; Stages 1 to 4 alone carry the aspiration to scientific status; and within the account as a whole, the conception of forms of moral maturity, beyond Stage 4, is particularly problematic.

The need to go beyond the normative ethics of Stage 4, as Kohlberg saw it, arises from the inherent limitations of its thinking. This level of thinking provides no guide, he supposes, to the treatment of people outside the social order which defines its perspective, and it fails to provide a rational

guide for social change in the form of new norms or laws. From such
considerations, the Kohlbergian theory leaps to the postulation of Stage 5
which, in Kohlberg's words, "clearly has a perspective necessary for
rationally creating laws *ex nihilo*.[43] The idea of the rational creation of laws
ex nihilo is a Kantian or Rawlsian element in Kohlberg's account. It does not
fit properly with the emphasis which he had earlier placed on social
interaction in his account of development; but against his own convictions,
as it appears, he is drawn to an essentially individualistic and ahistorical
framework in specifying the perspectives and character of Stages 5 and 6 as
lying beyond the social order.

On reflection, neither of Kohlberg's comments about the inherent limitations of Stage 4 thinking is straightforwardly true. Social conventions may
contain definite specifications in regard to the treatment of outsiders
(varying from detailed obligations of hospitality to expressions of extreme
hostility). Secondly, a system of social conventions, even one that is quite
conservative, may embody provisions for social change or maintain itself,
by and large, on principles of collective wisdom. It is true that socio-moral
conventions may be maintained in a largely unthinking way, simply "to
keep the social order going" as the description of Stage 4 subjects puts it.
But to a degree, and in a variety of ways, conventions may offer scope for
the development of general moral principles and hence for principled
moral thinking. It is not necessary, therefore, to turn to a supposed
perspective from which laws are rationally created *ex nihilo* or from which
social arrangements may be derived. Indeed, this invocation has all the
appearance of a philosophical invention. The lesson is that ethical principles need to be found within the framework of the social order, though
they may run across societies generally.

In re-thinking his theory at its highest level, Kohlberg began to draw
support latterly from the social theorist Jürgen Habermas.[44] This was
connected with the fact that Habermas had already drawn on Kohlberg's
schema of stages in his own large projects of giving a structural account of
the development of moral and legal systems and working out a general
theory of communicative competence. Kohlberg, on his part, was brought
back by Habermas's work to the need to recognize social interaction in the
construction of the stages (including the higher stages). Habermas is also
the main source of the idea of interpreting the stages as a rational reconstruction of the ontogenesis of justice-reasoning. A rational reconstruction
in this context starts with a competence exhibited in performance and
seeks to make explicit the structures and rules which underlie it. This
procedure appears feasible, even promising, in the case of something like
linguistic competence. It might run on to include the Habermasian investigation of communicative social action. It appears somewhat more problematic, however, when the competence in question relates to deontological
ethics (which, apart from not being widely manifested, is highly specula-

tive in its own domain). There is also the problem of what appears to be discontinuity between the lower and higher stages; that is, there is a gap between stages for which a scientific status is claimed in the context of normal cognitive development and stages which are drawn from philosophical reflection. Kohlberg's response is that his guiding meta-ethical assumptions "have helped us to orient ourselves to the empirical study of moral development as justice-reasoning," and he goes on immediately to note that,

> at the philosophical level these assumptions remain controversial, but their use has led to the discovery of empirical findings which seem to justify their continued use.[45]

The appeal to empirical fruitfulness in connection with the philosophical assumptions appears deeply problematic. In some respects, the "findings" at lower levels are governed by the assumptions, most generally by the way in which attention is focused on moral reasoning of a particular sort (reasoning about conflicts of justice in response to hypothetical dilemmas to the exclusions of other contexts). In other respects, the empirical findings seem to be compatible with different meta-ethical assumptions. Piaget and Dewey, for example, recognize levels of development which correspond to Kohlberg's, but do not share his meta-ethical assumptions. Specifically, it is not necessary to assume a deontological standpoint to be able to recognize the sorts of moral reasoning associated with Stages 1 to 4 or to see them as inadequate. Finally, there are other matters on which the philosophical assumptions have no bearing — whether the lower stages are Piagetian "hard" stages or whether the sequence of development is invariant, for example. The attempt to justify the meta-ethical assumptions on the grounds of empirical fruitfulness thus appears dubious. The further assumption that nothing else changes with the changed status of the higher stages is also brought into question. One definite consequence concerns the relevance of the theory in moral education.

Kohlberg's argument that moral education should be based on the stages is seriously weakened by the problems of the higher level. In the first place, there is no longer any definite point toward which development proceeds. The higher stages in their specific forms are at best possible ideals, to be considered along with other ideas of moral maturity. Secondly, there is the acknowledgment that the program is concerned specifically with reasoning about justice, along with the admission that justice is not all-sufficient in accounting for morality and moral development. Finally, there is the enlarged scope of the program, especially the concern with the relationship between moral judgment and moral behavior and the need to deal more fully with affective aspects of moral experience and the topic of motivation. Concern of this sort also points to the need to pay attention to a wider range of dispositions for behavior — in other words, the whole question of the moral virtues, which Kohlberg had hoped to have eliminated, has to be brought back into consideration.

Following discussion of the problematic status of the higher stages, it is necessary to give some brief consideration to the earlier stages of the schema. The first two Kohlberg stages appear to have been comparatively neglected in research and related literature.[46] That children begin from a pre-conventional situation, whatever else is true of them, appears unchallengeable. It is possible that the two stages at this level constitute Piagetian "hard" stages, distinct and qualitatively different ways of thinking, structured wholes hierarchically ordered. But it is not clear that this has been established. There is also the question of how a stage, determined on the basis of reasoning about justice in response to hypothetical dilemmas, would relate to an account of children's moral thinking which draws on wider and more adequate criteria in more realistic situations. The designated Stage 1, with its emphasis on obedience and punishment, seems particularly narrow even with respect to young children's thinking about justice and fairness.

Evidence drawn mainly from a widely based approach is presented in a report by Martin Packer et al., "Moral Action of Four-Year-Olds."[47] This study focused on the participation of 40 pre-school children in a simplified version of a Prisoner's Dilemma game. What emerges most significantly, given the range of possible outcomes in the game, is the evidence of cooperation and concern for others, linked with a sense of the related moral issues, especially fairness. This study is far from exhaustive or conclusive, of course, but at the very least, it points to ways in which the cognitive-developmental approach in Kohlberg's program fails to deal with the complexity of children's moral thinking and experience.

Stage 3 outstrips Stage 2 in its enlarged conception of reciprocity — taking reciprocity beyond mere exchange to an ideal level — and in its conception of equity and concern for others. But thinking at this level belongs characteristically to dyadic interpersonal relationships. There is no general guide as to whose role to take in arriving at a just solution to moral conflict. Stage 4, the "morality of law, order and government," solves this problem systematically by reference to a social order of roles and rules which are accepted in the community (and which are constitutive of it). It thus marks a stage of moral thinking beyond Stage 3 in the terms chosen, to be accounted for, in the hypothesis, by a subject's advance to a further stage of cognitive formal operations and the opportunity for wider social experience. But as we considered earlier, the ranking of Stages 3 and 4 is question-begging in relation to moral adequacy: in other words, the matter should not be restricted to the criterion of generality. Specifically, there is question whether Kohlberg's emphasis on formal justice and respect for individual rights in framing the stages might not downgrade the importance of care and responsibility and other values in human relationships and whether, in turn, it builds in a significant degree of sexual bias. This is the criticism of Kohlberg which Carol Gilligan makes in her book, *In a Different Voice* (hereafter *DV*).

3. Gilligan: The Ethic of Care

GILLIGAN VS KOHLBERG: CARE BEFORE JUSTICE

In discovering that women have a different view of morality than men, Carol Gilligan revives an old theme. She is clearly aware of this since, early in her study, she refers to Freud's claim that "for women the level of what is ethically normal is different from what it is in men," and to his view that women "show less sense of justice than men, that they are less ready to submit to the great exigencies of life, that they are more influenced in their judgements by feelings of affection or hostility."[48] What she sets out to do is to ring the changes on this theme. Faced with the problem which women constituted for his theory of psychosexual development, Freud located the problem in women themselves. Gilligan's counter-argument is to transfer the problem back into the theory. With reference to Kohlberg's account of moral development in particular, her objection focuses on the way in which women have been excluded from the construction of the theory and misinterpreted or otherwise disadvantaged in its application.

Philosophers, who have mostly been male, have commonly believed that women are different in being less endowed with reason than men. They have commonly held that women's place is in the household, not in the political or public domain, and that women should always be subject to male authority. This view of the philosophers, while it might be presented in Olympian tones, is itself the echo of the common view of the philosophers' times.[49] Aristotle presents it in one way in the city-state of Athens in the fourth century B.C., Rousseau in another in eighteenth-century Europe. Notwithstanding the considerable differences between these two thinkers and their respective times and social orders, one finds in each case a version of the ideas just noted, that women are less endowed with reason than men and more subject to emotion, that their place is in the family, that they should be subject to male authority, and that, within a common morality that embraces men and women alike, moral virtue in women takes its own specific form. Virtue in this context is generally understood as other-related; the common specific difference in the case of women is that their courage or justice or self-control, etc, is thought properly to involve reference to a *male* other — husband or father as a rule — and to be subject to male guidance.

Kohlberg's philosophical assumptions are drawn, as we have seen, from social contract theory, Utilitarianism, and Kantian ethics. These approaches might be thought to escape sexual bias because of the common emphasis on equality: the parties to the social contract are individuals who are taken to be equal in all respects, their sex being treated as a matter of indifference; the individual whose happiness is to count in Utilitarian theory is everyman and everywoman; and the Kantian moral agent is the autonomous rational individual characterized only by a capacity to grasp the imperatives of the moral law. Appearances may be misleading. In fact, social contract theory is marked by a strong undercurrent of an essentially male world, and part of the not very hidden agenda of the scheme, whether in Hobbes, Locke, or Rousseau, is that the parties to the contract are men.[50] Kant's ethical theory, too, for all its air of detachment, is closely related to the public world of civil society which is the world of men (which is also a primary focus of Utilitarianism). Furthermore, Kant subscribed to a version of the thesis that women are less cognitively developed than men and stand in need of male guidance.

These elements in the background theories do not flow on automatically to Kohlberg's use of them in relation to moral stages. On the other hand, the background theories are implicitly assumed to be free of sexual bias when it is clear that they are not. Again, cognitive attainment and range of social experience, the very issues of ancient philosophical bias concerning women, are taken to constitute the primary conditions of development along Kohlberg's sequence of stages. More directly, the subjects of Kohlberg's original cross-sectional study and the subsequent major longitudinal study were all male, though the conclusions were readily put forward as universal across sex, culture, and time. There is also some evidence that, on average, women are assigned to a lower stage of development than men on the Kohlberg scale, both on the earlier and the revised scoring systems.

Women's moral judgments, Gilligan notes, are typically allocated to Stage 3, the stage of "personal concordance morality," which Kohlberg spoke of in an early study as "a functional morality for housewives and mothers," but not for professionals and businessmen.[51] Gilligan does not refer to statistical data in her book, however, and does not press this point. One reason for this may be that the difference, as she acknowledged in an earlier study, is not statistically significant. Subsequent studies have tended to confirm this and have been taken by Kohlberg and others to show that the charge of bias was unfounded.[52] But Gilligan might respond that there is *some* difference nonetheless which is to women's disadvantage. Moreover, studies related to the Kohlberg scale give a very incomplete moral profile of men and women, and, in any case, the question of bias remains open in other respects. Gilligan's major objection to Kohlberg's theory does not rest, in fact, on the matter of comparative ranking.

Kohlberg's stages — especially Stages 4, 5, and 6 — are seen as telling a story which relates to a psychology and a conception of morality (an ethic of justice and rights) which are characteristically male. What is offered, then, under the guise of universality, is a male standard of moral judgment. Women, it is argued, have a different path of development relating to a different moral psychology and a different conception of morality (an ethic of care and responsibility). In this light, the exclusion of women and of their moral point of view means that Kohlberg's theory is seriously impoverished. But this is not recognized, and in terms of the theory, the divergence of women from a masculine standard can only be seen as a failure of development on their part (*DV* 69–70). In taking up this point, however, Gilligan fails to explore a different puzzle, viz., why women who are disadvantaged in this way are nevertheless statistically very close to male subjects when measured on the Kohlberg male standard. Perhaps part of the explanation could be that women learn to conform to male standards in a male world. But there are two other points which could be relevant. One is the consideration that Gilligan draws the lines between male and female paths of development and conceptions of morality in an extreme way, to the exclusion of common ground. There is also the possibility that Kohlberg's male standard is not the standard of many males.

Gilligan acknowledges these two considerations to an extent in a comment in the Introduction:

> The different voice I describe is characterized not by gender but theme. Its association with women is an empirical observation, and it is primarily through women's voices that I trace its development. But this association is not absolute, and the contrasts between male and female voices are presented here to highlight a distinction between two modes of thought and to focus a problem of interpretation rather than to represent a generalization about either sex. (*DV* 2)

She also disavows generalizations of her claims to a wider population or across cultures or times. It is difficult, however, to hear the voice of the book in this highly qualified way. What is presented is the story of a sharp difference between men and women reaching across their respective experiences from early childhood, a story that is almost totally unrelieved by what Gilligan calls in the Introduction "the interplay of these voices within each sex." But when the qualification is brought back in, the idea that there are two voices which reflect different paths of development and different conceptions of morality remains for consideration; and so far as Kohlberg's theory is concerned, the other voice to which Gilligan drew attention was unquestionably the voice of women.

The primary site of Gilligan's critique is Kohlberg's post-conventional level, the "vortex of maturity: from which his developmental theory hangs."[53] The ethic of justice, with its emphasis on autonomy, individual rights, equality, and the authoritatively rational resolution of conflict, is conceived as casting its shadow back over the sequence of stages, marking points in the (male) individual's quest for identity, independence, separation from the other, autonomy. Alongside this, Gilligan places the ethic of care as marking, in effect, a different vortex of maturity. This ethic, with its emphasis on nurturance, concern for the other, equity, and the recognition of different points of view, would cast its shadow back in turn over a different sequence, marking points in the (female) individual's quest for attachment and intimacy, and a sense of self, in early childhood, adolescence, and adulthood. She will argue that the two ethics must be seen as complementary and as needing to be integrated in the end. In the meantime, they are presented as the end-points of distinctive male and female paths of progress.

In keeping with the twin-paths doctrine, Gilligan accepts the Kohlberg stages as valid for the male line (however unsatisfactory it might be). Her contribution at this point is to re-locate the cognitive-developmental emphasis within a framework of psychoanalytic theory drawn from Nancy Chodorow, according to which boys, "in defining themselves as masculine, separate their mothers from themselves, thus curtailing 'their primary love and sense of empathic tie'."[54] The inadequacies of the male line of development can be brought back to this point. Gilligan allows that women may be allocated to one or another Kohlberg stage in a loose sense, but her idea is that, from an early age, women's responses to hypothetical dilemmas typically relate to themes of care and concern for relationships which fall through the sieve of formal systems of logic and law. In other words, their voice is not heard or it is misinterpreted. For women, then, Kohlberg's cognitive-developmental scheme is inappropriate.[55]

Once again, Nancy Chodorow's psychoanalytic theory provides the primary framework within which women's experience is formed: "Girls in identifying themselves as female, experience themselves as like their mothers, thus fusing the experience of attachment with the process of identity formation."[56] Parallel with the Kohlberg line, women may be seen as following a broad path from pre-conventional to conventional to post-conventional levels of outlooks. But the moral domain is defined differently from the beginning: the central moral problem for women is the problem of care and responsibility in relationships, not the problem of rights and rules. What underlies their ethic, even initially, is the psychological logic of relations, not the formal logic of fairness associated with the ethic of justice. The perspectives are also different at each level. At the alternative pre-conventional level, egocentrism is not so significant because of the way in which identity is formed in empathic relations with others; the conventional level, by comparison, is more problematic since the individual's concern for others can be pushed by social forces toward excessive dependence on the opinions and expectations of others to the point at which goodness for women is equated with self-sacrifice. At the post-conventional level, however, the ethic of care takes a reflective form in which concern for others is integrated with awareness of self-worth (*DV* 72ff).

The setting up of two distinct lines of development leads on to comparative evaluation (of course, it also presupposes it). Given the key ideas of attachment as against separation, and intimacy as against independence, the primary contrast can be stated succinctly. The central insight of the ethic of care is that self and other are interdependent, while the ethic of justice responds to a world in which connections are fragmented. The one is associated with networks and webs of relationship, the other with hierarchical order and problems of domination and subordination. In situations of conflict, the one is concerned with mending broken relationships, the other with the determination of the rights and claims of individuals.

With the case set out in these terms, the ethical superiority of care over justice is overwhelmingly obvious, and the corresponding superiority of one line of development over the other is equally obvious. Gilligan speaks of the complementarity of the two ethics and envisages their integration as marking the common ideal of moral maturity. If one sets aside qualms about fitting complementarity and integration together, it is clear that the complementary paths to integration are by no means equally favorable.[57] Against the view of some male psychologists, Gilligan makes a plausible case that separation and individuation do not lead readily to attachment and mutuality in adult relations. (Some of Kohlberg's famous Stage 6 identities — all male — were notoriously inadequate in their family and personal relationships.) The corresponding task on the other path is considerably more feasible: it consists in extending the ethic of care to include oneself more clearly, integrating concern for others with the commitment to be true to oneself (resolving the conflict between integrity and care and finding a way between selfishness and self-suppression). Similarly, an ethic of justice, when linked with care, would have to forego its basic claim to provide formal and absolute principles. An ethic of care, by contrast, is marked by tolerance and contextual relativism — it can remain whole, therefore, while embracing the considerations of rights in appropriate contexts.

CARE AND THE NEED FOR GENERALITY IN ETHICS

Gilligan's argument, I have indicated, exposes the inadequacy of Kohlberg's theory as a *general* account of moral development. But the problem is that it gets to this conclusion by the unnecessary and questionable path of treating the theory as an adequate account of male moral development. As my earlier critique makes clear, the Kohlberg scales, in the higher stages at least, are not properly a measure of *anyone's* moral development. The theory is even more inadequate than Gilligan allows. It is true that her acceptance of Kohlberg's ethic of justice as the male voice was the means by which the other voice came to be expressed. This can be seen primarily, however, as a development within the history of Kohlberg's research program (in which Gilligan has played a significant and critical part).

There is also something deeply artificial in the sharp contrast Gilligan draws between the two ethics, even allowing that they are to be seen as complementary. (One could say that a similar artificiality affects Kohlberg's attempt to treat justice in separation from other values.) Care for others in any ordinary sense includes a concern for justice in their regard, where justice is also taken in an ordinary sense of concern for what is fair. At the very least, care for others would exclude unjust action in their regard in any serious way. On these grounds alone, an ethic of care is more adequate since it embraces justice and other values such as good-will, sensitivity to others' needs, compassion, friendship, and so on. But in that case, the sharp contrast between care and justice collapses. In this vein, Aristotle suggested that friendship and justice are concerned with the same objects and are both basic to the well-being of a community; indeed, he observes that when people are friends "they have no need of justice, while when they are just they need friendship as well, and the truest form of justice is thought to be a friendly quality."[58] Again, it is not a matter of simply adding an emphasis on care to a formal account of justice and rights; what is needed is a more satisfactory account than Kohlberg supplies of justice as a moral virtue. On the other side, more attention needs to be given to the idea of an ethic of care, especially the need for generality in ethics.

Gilligan expresses a central problem for women in the development of an ethic of care as follows:

> The notion that virtue for women lies in self-sacrifice has complicated the course of women's development by pitting the moral issue of goodness against the adult questions of responsibility and choice. In addition, the ethic of self-sacrifice is directly in conflict with the concept of rights that has, in the past century, supported women's claim to a fair share of social justice. (*DV* 132)

What is needed in a reflective ethic of care is the discovery of space between selfishness and self-sacrifice, and the right to include oneself in the compass of a morality of responsibility, and the realization of virtue in which concern for oneself goes along with concern for others (*DV*, Chap. 5). Taken in broad terms, this proposal of the different voice echoes an ancient and familiar theme. It is a version of the Gospel injunction, "Love your neighbour as you love yourself." Or it could be seen in terms of Aristotle's distinction between a selfish love of self which seeks to outdo others in competition as against a true love of self which is a sort of friendship with oneself and which is seen as the basis of good relations and friendship with others. This is related in turn to the distinction which Rousseau made central to his moral psychology: the distinction between a love of self in the form of vanity which is born out of comparing oneself with others competitively and a love of self which is, in Rousseau's words, "a natural sentiment which prompts every animal to watch over its own conservation and which, directed in man by reason and modified by pity, produces humanity and virtue."[59]

The credentials of Gilligan's ethic of care are thus very strong. Her meta-ethical standpoint of contextual relativism could be more problematic, however, though it too picks up ancient and familiar themes especially in the Aristotelian and medieval tradition. It draws attention, for example, to the inadequacy of relying solely on formal principles or abstract rules in moral evaluation: good moral judgment involves a capacity to recognize detail and complexity; it requires attention to particular circumstances of behavior and good sense in knowing when and how to apply general rules or maxims. This connects with the recognition that there may be circumstances in which, contrary to the Kantian view which Kohlberg adopts, there is no final, unambiguous resolution of a moral conflict: one is faced in the end with competing values and a choice between evils.[60] This connects with a certain unwillingness to indulge in the moral judgment of others (which is also a Gospel theme). In these respects, Gilligan's contextual emphasis is on strong grounds in comparison with the Kohlbergian reliance on formal principles of justice or a calculus of utility. The contextual approach also points to the inadequacy of a methodology for the assessment of moral judgment which relies entirely on hypothetical dilemmas. The danger in this practice is that complexity is overlooked in favor of immediate resort to principles. Thus Gilligan puts particular weight in her own inquiries on responses to *concrete* moral dilemmas.

The genuinely problematic issue with contextual relativism is whether it also involves moral relativism — in summary terms, the incoherent but not uncommon view that all moralities, all moral opinions, are equally valid or correct. As a strong critic of moral relativism, Kohlberg appears to see Gilligan's position in these terms. In continuing to insist that "justice is the first virtue of a person or society," he argues that there is a central, minimum core of morality which consists "in striving for universal agreement in the face of more relativist conceptions of the good" of the sort Gilligan proposes.[61] This is not a conclusive comment, however. A concern with contextual issues in moral judgment and a disagreement with Kohlberg's version of the idea of a central, minimum core of morality does not necessarily embroil one in moral relativism. Nor does it follow from the fact that Gilligan is critical of moral absolutism. There are some vaguely relativist remarks in her book and many that are anti-absolutist; on the other hand, she also says that the post-conventional or mature ethic of care should not be seen as moral relativism.

The problem is that Gilligan does not work out in any detail the implications of an ethic of care in relation to other values and virtues. Her idea that the ethic of care and the Kohlbergian ethic of justice are complementary is symptomatic of this. As I suggested above, an account of justice as a moral virtue is integral to an ethic of care, not something to be added on at the end. Further thought about the implications of an ethic of care would lead to the idea that there are certain forms of behavior and ways of life which are incompatible with it in a clear and indefeasible sense — forms characterized by malevolence, cruelty, callousness, neglect, greed, selfish aggrandizement. Equally, there are general forms of behavior and ways of life which go with care, nurturance, and responsibility, and give this ethic further positive content — forms associated with benevolence, love, kindness, justice, courage, friendship, and so on. Along with an emphasis on context in moral judgment, an ethic of care would need to include a range of principles, generalizations, and maxims in association with a conception of virtue and vice. Moral reasoning in this context is a matter of knowing how to blend the general and the particular. But, for one reason or another, Gilligan fails to develop the necessary aspect of generality in her account. It may be instructive to look for reasons for this failure. I will explore two factors.

Gilligan's discussion is shaped significantly by the attention she gives to moral dilemmas — concrete dilemmas more importantly than hypothetical — and situations of crisis (see DV 72, 100–01; Chaps. 3 and 4). Dilemmas of their nature involve a clash of principles. Now, the Kantian view, which Kohlberg endorses, is that whatever the appearances, a conflict of duties is strictly inconceivable; consistency in the moral law ensures that there is one proper and principled solution in every instance. This common philosophical view finds its profoundest opposition in Greek tragedy. Tragedy characteristically turns on the idea that situations arise in human life in which a conflict involving moral elements is strictly insoluble, and the moral agent is faced with a choice between evils. Kohlberg in fact has written on tragedy in relation to the moral stages. Consistently, he holds that in Greek (and Shakespearean) tragedy,

> the tragic heroes' misguided struggles for justice are generated from a conventional morality. The fate that strikes them down, like the heroes' own demand for justice, is both just and unjust and, like the heroes', is expressive of the framework of a conventional morality of civic and cosmic order.

In Kohlberg's rankings, Creon, king of Thebes, in Sophocles' *Antigone*, is assigned to a Stage 4 version of civic morality (which Creon employs in a pursuit of vindictiveness). His niece Antigone, who defies his law by burying her dead brother (who had betrayed the city) "in the name of the gods' unwritten and unfailing laws," is also assigned to Stage 4 morality. Her morality, according to Kohlberg,

> is a morality of loyalty to kinship and to the gods who support the norms of kinship . . . [it] is not a morality of conscience or principle. The norms of the morality are not universal principles of human justice and welfare but respect for the dead, expressed in maintaining concrete and arbitrary rules. It is essentially a Stage 4 morality of divine order rather than civic order.[62]

In this view, tragedy is unable to resolve moral conflict satisfactorily because it lacks awareness of (universal) moral principles; so Antigone's concern for the responsibilities of kinship is described as a matter of maintaining "concrete and arbitrary rules"! But perhaps Antigone's voice has not been heard across the grid of the moral stages. Perhaps tragedy shows more insight into the human moral condition than is recognized in some philosophies. Aristotle arguably provides a more perceptive interpretation of Antigone's behavior, and her own understanding of it, in seeing it in terms of natural justice:

> For there really is, as everyone to some extent divines, a natural justice and injustice that is common to all, even to those who have no association or covenant with each other. It is this that Sophocles' Antigone clearly means when she says that the burial of Polynices was a just act in spite of the prohibition: she means that it was just by nature
>
> > Not of today or yesterday it is
> > But lives eternal: none can date its birth.[63]

Moral dilemmas of the sort tragedy portrays are not amenable to a unique decision by principle; they are resolved in the end by action. In that case, one's attention as observer may be focused more readily on the complexities of the situation, on the ways in which the participants see the problem, how they feel about it, how they come to a decision, what they do in the end, and how they live with their decision beyond the particular time of crisis (if, unlike Antigone's case, it does not end in death). These are in fact the sorts of issues which Gilligan discusses in her report of the *abortion study decision* (*DV*, Chaps. 3 and 4, 68ff). The focus on particularities in regard to moral dilemmas is perfectly legitimate and important. But there is the risk that it could obscure the idea that principles remain important even when there is no uniquely principled way of settling a conflict between them. This can be readily established: if it were not so, there would not be a moral dilemma in the first place.

Gilligan's emphasis on growth through crisis — especially in Chapter Four, "Crisis and Transition" — echoes the theme in Aeschylus' *Oresteia* trilogy that learning comes through suffering. Even more closely it is an expression of one of the main ideas of the central ode of the *Eumenides*, that it is good for human beings "to learn wisdom under pressure." This too is an important consideration. But again, there is the risk that attention to crisis situations and dilemmas, real or hypothetical, could obscure the fact that there are numerous situations in which the relevant moral principles, general rules, or maxims of an ethic of care are perfectly clear and not in dispute. In focusing on difficult moral dilemmas and the importance of particularities in trying to resolve them, Gilligan fails to give sufficient weight to the need for generality in an ethic of care.

A second consideration is the familiar point that Gilligan developed her idea of an ethic of care in opposition to Kohlberg's ethic of justice. In this context of separation and contrast, a difference of emphasis may tend to take an exaggerated form. The extreme point here would be the view that concerns for people and for general principles of justice are mutually exclusive. Gilligan does not espouse any such dichotomy, nor would Kohlberg, but there is the risk of less extreme distortion.

Gilligan shows how an evaluation of a person's moral reasoning or moral outlook involves the art of interpretation. In this connection, she shows how Kohlberg's theory, with its grid of moral stages and conception of justice, either fails to hear care-oriented responses to moral dilemmas or misinterprets them. A reverse possibility is that Gilligan fails to recognize elements of generality in the expression of an ethic of care. There is an instructive example of this at the beginning of *In a Different Voice*, in connection with the first report of an interview which is intended to illustrate the different conception of morality in an ethic of care (*DV* 19–22).

The report concerns a woman who was a participant in Gilligan's rights and responsibilities study; she was 25 years old and a third-year law student at the time. The first question and the woman's reply is as follows:

[Is there really some correct solution to moral problems or is everybody's opinion equally right?] No, I don't think everybody's opinion is equally right. I think that in some situations there may be opinions that are equally valid, and one could conscientiously adopt one of several courses of action. But there are other situations in which I think there are right and wrong answers, that sort of inhere in the nature of existence, of all individuals here who need to live with each other to live. We need to depend on each other, and hopefully it is not only a physical need but a need of fulfillment in ourselves, that a person's life is enriched by cooperating with other people and striving to live in harmony with everybody else, and to that end, there are right and wrong, there are things which promote that end and that move away from it, and in that way it is possible to choose in certain cases among different courses of action that obviously promote or harm that goal. (*DV* 20)

The woman begins by rejecting moral relativism, while acknowledging that there are situations in which different people may reasonably take different views and act differently. But in keeping with her rejection of relativism, she considers that there are other situations in which there are right and wrong answers (a view which clearly involves a commitment to ethical generality). She then offers an indication of the sorts of situation she has in mind and the grounds of her view: they relate essentially to the conditions of social existence. The primary consideration is the fact of mutual dependence, but her approach moves on to include the idea of human beings' living well, of their being enriched by cooperative relationships. Finally, good and bad are understood as what promotes and harms this outcome. The statement as a whole certainly expresses Gilligan's idea of an ethic of care and responsibility. But one could say quite appropriately that it is a good expression of major elements in an Aristotelian outlook.

In reply to further questions, the woman explains that she had taken a relativist view of moral questions in her high school years, but with more experience, she continues, she has come to recognize that "there are an awful lot of things that are common to people," that there are things that are true about our nature and the world we live in which are relevant to making things go well for human beings, individually and socially, and which constitute, in turn, criteria for speaking of what is morally right.

In the text, the woman's reply is set alongside the response of a 25-year-old man in Kohlberg's study, whose replies exemplify Kohlberg's principled stages, with talk of morality in terms of individual rights, especially the right to life, respect for individual rights, and so on (*DV* 19–20). Gilligan's major comment is that the woman has arrived at a reconstructed moral understanding, not on the basis of the primacy and universality of individual rights, but through a sense of responsibility to others. This is a very fair comment. But in a framework of contrast with the Kohlberg approach, the dominant theme of generality in the woman's thinking about morality is passed over in total silence.

I have argued that the different moral voice which Gilligan has found in women reaches back across the period of modern liberalism and the Enlightenment, to pick up again some important features of Greek ethical thought, especially in Greek tragedy and the Aristotelian tradition. But this connection is not recognized in the study itself. The likely reason for this is that the voice is muffled by the way in which Gilligan's whole account is shaped by its unhappy relationship of separation from and complementarity to Kohlberg's ethic of justice. Freed from that relationship, the ethic of care could be built into a plausibly adequate general account of ethics.

The return to themes in Aristotle and tragedy is not a case of antiquarianism. The Aristotelian ethical tradition has continued to be a living voice in a variety of ways.[64] Where Kohlberg turned to Piagetian cognitive structures and Utilitarian and Kantian ethics, Gilligan might have turned to Dewey, for example, for a different, more Aristotelian conception of morality and moral reasoning. There is, in any case, a major common matrix between Gilligan's ethic of care and the ancient sources. The primary notion in the moral and political thought of the Greek tradition is the idea of community. This is in contrast to most modern theory: in the major theories of justice and the state over recent centuries, the idea of community has at best an uneasy place. (The major exception is in the ethics of Hegel — see chapter nine below.) In adopting the modern, individualist outlook, Kohlberg sees an ethic of care as supplementary to an emphasis on justice: justice relates significantly to the public sphere, while care and benevolence go with the more private world of family and special relationships.[65] From the point of view of an approach in which community occupies a central place, however, this whole contrast is misconceived. One could not expect that the idea of community could have exactly the same meaning and force over the long path of history from the Greek city-states to modern societies. Nevertheless, the quest for community is a deep and persistent theme in Gilligan's account of the moral voice of women. It is not surprising, then, that the ethic of care should share common ground with Greek ethical experience and thought.

PART TWO
Historical Studies

Introduction

The discussion of contemporary views about moral development in Part One has involved frequent reference to past philosophical ideas. Some of the broad connections with Utilitarianism and Kantian ethical theory were set out at the beginning of chapter two; other connections, especially with ideas in Greek tragedy and in the writings of Plato and Aristotle, have been noted in the discussion. Past philosophical views about morality thus provide important reference points for the understanding and assessment of contemporary theories of moral development.

There is an even closer connection between past and present concerns inasmuch as the major philosophers of the past ordinarily treated the topic of moral development as an integral part of their ethical theory. The history of an undertaking which is now pursued mainly by psychologists is embedded in the writings of the philosophers. The uncovering of this history is directly relevant to contemporary developmental inquiry and research in psychology. But it also has relevance for a philosophical recovery of neglected aspects of past ethical inquiry. My aim in both these regards is to examine some major accounts of ethics, from the Greeks to the nineteenth century, mainly from a developmental point of view. This will involve discussion of the range of ideas concerning moral development which can be found in these accounts. In addition, developmental considerations will be invoked in assessing the adequacy of the accounts.

The locus of philosophical concern with moral development was traditionally found in the consideration of education. This concern began with the Sophists in the latter half of the fifth century B.C., and it was taken up by Plato in the following generation, in critical response to the views of the Sophists and in the hope of finding a way of resolving the social and political problems of his time. A generation later, Plato's pupil, Aristotle, gave the topic of moral development an important place in his own treatment of ethical and political questions. The centrality of the theme was thus established at an early stage in Western philosophy; and the study of education, and of moral formation conceived as the major aim and point of education, remained a central philosophical concern until comparatively recent times.

The present situation in which accounts of morality and theories of moral development are presented largely in separate disciplines, and without much reference to one another, is itself a historical development. It reflects the growth of specialization in forms of inquiry and branches of knowledge which has gathered pace since the second half of the nineteenth century. In the English-speaking world in particular, it has been tied to a positivist separation of philosophy from the social sciences, a near obsession in philosophy with questions of demarcation, and the conviction that philosophy is concerned strictly with the world of ideas and their relations and not directly with the world of empirical reality. In the ensuing fragmentation of knowledge, philosophy tended to withdraw even from the domain of morality, confining itself to meta-ethical issues treated in a self-conceived, ahistorical way. The topic of moral development, as a first-order question involving empirical concerns, came to be placed outside its sphere of legitimate interest and competence.

At the same time, the social sciences, in aspiring to the status of value-free science, set aside the conceptual complexities of the philosophical traditions within which they had originally developed as forms of inquiry. Philosophy and psychology chose to go largely separate ways. In this development, ethics tended to cut itself off from empirical content and problems, and the study of moral development in psychology has usually proceeded on the basis of a conceptually impoverished understanding of morality in its historical forms.

The historical studies presented here are concerned with ethical and developmental ideas in Aristotle, Locke, Rousseau, Kant, the line of mainly English and Scottish thinkers from Hobbes to Mill associated with Utilitarianism, and Hegel. At this point we are brought reasonably close to contemporary issues and the discussion of Marx, Nietzsche, and Freud which was undertaken at the beginning of the inquiry. There are notable omissions from the studies: Plato above all, Stoic and Epicurean philosophy, Augustine, Abelard, and Thomas Aquinas in connection with Christian ethical thought; Spinoza in the seventeenth century, the Encyclopaedists and French Utilitarians in the eighteenth century; and, among more contemporary figures of importance, John Dewey. But the omissions are not total. In important respects, Plato's moral psychology and developmental views were taken up by Aristotle, and some other themes in Plato's writings are discussed at various points. This applies, albeit to a lesser extent, to the other sources just noted: Stoic themes have an important place in Hobbes and Rousseau, for example (and in modern ethics as a whole); Thomas Aquinas' ethical views were greatly influenced by Aristotle; the ideas of freedom and reason which Spinoza stressed in his ethics were to be of major significance for Rousseau, Kant, and Hegel; and some of Dewey's ideas are taken up at points, especially in the concluding chapter in connection with the theme of community in relation to moral life and development. The following chapters, it is clear, do not cover everything of importance; at the same time, each inquiry has direct bearing on the theme of moral development. Taken together, the studies provide a reasonably complete historical background to the topic.

The inquiry as a whole is significantly incomplete in a different way since it is restricted to ethical thought and experience in the Western tradition. Typically, accounts of ethics in our tradition, from Plato onwards, have had universalist aspirations (or pretensions). Typically, they have incorporated large preconceptions and biases in respect of gender, race, and class. More often than not, a similar outlook is characteristic of the major contemporary accounts of moral development in psychology. For all that, one could argue that the recognition of certain universal values is defensible, and indeed, is a condition for overcoming exclusivist prejudices. One could also note with caution that this ethical tradition includes among its resources a willingness to learn from others, a concern with fairness, and a sensitivity to relevant differences and similarities in that context. Moral awareness, however, is not a guarantee of corresponding behavior.

4. Aristotle:
Reason and the Passions

1. The Aristotelian Context

Morality, as Aristotle conceives it, is concerned with promoting human good. It is concerned with promoting the conditions in which human beings act well and live well, the conditions of well-being or happiness.[1] Ethics, the study of moral questions, is accorded the same character: it deals with human good and seeks to promote it. Aristotle's account of morality is thus practical in intent.[2] Furthermore, with its emphasis on a conception of human well-being, it is closely tied to what could be called his anthropology, his views about human beings and the nature and conditions of human life.

Many of Aristotle's ideas and metaphors in this connection, and the dominant framework, reflect his deep interest in biology: the human being as a living body with characteristic patterns of growth and forms of behavior, an emphasis on form and structure and goals of development, the individual as the member of a species and as a social animal by nature, a conception of natural orders and hierarchies within and across species, the family and society as organic or systematic wholes, and human well-being as a harmony of elements within the individual and in a society as a whole. In a wide sense, Aristotle's ethics incorporates a conception of the universe as a whole and of the place human beings occupy in it; but the idea of an eternal or total destiny for human beings had no place in his thought: well-being has to be attainable within the natural conditions of human existence. More particularly, his ethical ideas were presented in conjunction with a developed psychology and an extended inquiry into the social and political domains in which human life is realized. Ethics and politics are presented as component parts of the same inquiry, the study which has for its object and aim the good for human beings.

As part of this study, Aristotle provided an account of education and specifically of moral development, that is, an account of the way in which the individual, over time, succeeds or fails in the task of becoming a morally mature person. An interest in this topic fits very closely with the biological character of Aristotle's conception of ethics. In any case, questions about moral development had long been raised in Greek thought and literature, and from the time of the Sophists, the issue had come to occupy a specific place in moral inquiry. Thus, at the beginning of Plato's dialogue, the *Meno*, Socrates is asked by the Sophist-educated Meno: "Can you tell me, Socrates, whether virtue is acquired by teaching or by practice; or if neither by teaching nor by practice, then whether it comes to man by nature, or in what other way?"[3] Aristotle is witness to the continuation of the debate on this topic in his discussion of virtue in Books 1 and 2 of the *Nicomachean Ethics* (hereafter *NE*) and in the summary of views which he gives in Book 10: "Now some think that we are made good by nature, others by habituation, others by teaching" (*NE* 10, 9: 1179b20f).

In the *Meno*, Socrates puts Meno's question aside, at first, on the grounds that it must wait on our knowing what virtue is. Stalemate ensues when it appears that no secure knowledge of virtue is available, but then the discussion is resumed in the form of a hypothetical inquiry, the hypothesis being that if virtue is a form of knowledge it will be something that can be taught. This leads to a very interesting discussion of what knowledge is and what virtue might be in this connection, and of where one would look to find teachers of virtue. The dialogue ends, however, without a firm resolution of the questions with which it began.

Socrates, it could be agreed, was right in his primary insistence that an account of how virtue or moral goodness is realized depends critically on an understanding of virtue. But the Socratic version of this request needs to be qualified in at least two ways. In the first place, Socrates sets unrealistically high conditions on what could count as having the requisite knowledge: he insists that Meno should be able to produce a strict and complete definition (as might be available in mathematical inquiry). More specifically, the acquisition of an understanding of moral virtue does not occur in a vacuum; it takes place in one or another definite social and historical context and goes along with a fund of experience and insight which is itself acquired only in the process of growing up in a moral climate of some sort and coming to be involved in some complex set of moral beliefs, attitudes, and practices. The philosopher (or anyone else) cannot pluck an account of virtue out of the sky. This suggests that there is a relationship of mutual dependence between the provision of theories of morality and of moral development. An adequate account of moral development depends on a reasonably developed conception of morality. At the same time, the elaboration of an account of morality rests on a degree of concrete experience and a grasp of what is involved in the process of entering into social relations, learning about morality, and coming to be involved in moral practices.

Aristotle undertook to deal with both of these dimensions in his ethical and social inquiries. He sought to answer Socrates' request for an account of virtue and Meno's question of how virtue is acquired. In keeping with his naturalist approach in ethics, Aristotle rejected Plato's quest for a universal or eternal conception of the good divorced from the specific human situation. His view was that the good for human beings has to be worked out in relation to goods that are achievable by human activity or in terms of goals at which human beings are able to aim. On the other hand, Aristotle drew considerably on Plato's later discussion of moral psychology and education and developmental questions, especially in the *Phaedrus*, the *Republic*, and the *Laws*.

2. The Nature of Moral Maturity

Aristotle says in the *Politics*:

> What each thing is when fully developed we call its nature, whether we are speaking of a man, a horse, or a family. (I,2: 1252b32f)

The nature of a thing in this conception is its fulfilment or goal (*telos*), the realization of what is best in its regard. It conveys the idea of a thing with the structure and powers characteristic of its sort in full maturity. One approach to Aristotle's views about morality and moral development is to begin with an account of the morally mature person. (This fits in with Piaget's idea that a developmental theory hangs from its "vortex of maturity.") From this point one can mark the ways in which the immature, specifically the young, are thought both to approach and fall short of the standard, and consider how moral growth is envisaged.

Aristotle speaks of a nature and goal for human beings quite generally (the "human good"), and clearly intends his ideas to have general application. But in keeping with a point already touched on, we have to note immediately that his account of the morally mature person has a very definite, historically shaped cultural setting. Aristotle's morally mature human being is Greek rather than barbarian, male, not female, a free man, not a slave, a man who is at once the head of a household and a citizen in a city-state (Athens by preference) with a part to play in government, and a man well enough off to enjoy a degree of cultivated leisure, hence not a craftsman or manual laborer.[4] Those who are excluded from the privileged group are not thereby excluded from the sphere of morality or their own level of moral maturity, but in one sense or another, they are held to fall short of the standard of completeness. Inclusion in the privileged group, on the other hand, was certainly no guarantee of moral achievement. Aristotle was critical of the conventional mores of his social class, the well born and the well to do; in any case, he considered that it is "no easy task to be good . . . goodness is both rare and laudable and noble" (*NE* 2, 9: 1109a24f).

Virtues. The Aristotelian account of moral maturity turns centrally on the idea of a life lived according to a complex (and complete) set of excellences or virtues, certain dispositions for action and feeling, exercised in choice and responsibility. The designated virtues are primarily moral virtues, or virtues of character, under the guidance of certain qualities of mind, especially the intellectual virtue of *practical wisdom* (*phronesis*). This latter is the virtue of being able to work out what to do in order to act well in any given situation, allied with an effective commitment to acting well — a combination of knowledge and desire which sums up the Aristotelian conception of moral maturity. Aristotle's list of moral virtues is drawn, not surprisingly, from his own society and class. Even so, a core of the values he picks out could reasonably be seen as desirable quite generally in any society: courage, self-control, generosity, a spirit of good-will and coopera-tiveness, truthfulness, justice as fairness, and a capacity for love and friendship. The virtues are the primary conditions of happiness; more deeply they are constitutive elements of a good life, intrinsic to the sort of life in which human powers and capacities (or rather, a fair range of them) can best be developed and the best values realized. But while the posses-sion of the moral excellences makes a person good, it cannot ensure happiness: *eudaimonia* depends on other things as well, the sort of society and times one lives in, for example, and on one's having a degree of luck in matters over which one has no control.[5]

The life which exhibits the virtues is summed up most generally by Aristotle as life "according to reason." Life of this sort is to be contrasted with living "by the passions." These two forms of life divide the Aristot-elian moral field between them. But the contrast proposed between reason and the passions is misleading in a number of ways. Life as ruled by the passions may indicate mere immaturity, the condition of very young children. But it is also used to characterize sustained moral badness on the part of adults. From a different point of view, life according to reason does not exclude the passions and is not in opposition to them, for the passions are an integral and, in any case, inexpungible part of the human psyche: "The irrational passions are thought not less human than reason is, and therefore also the actions which proceed from anger or appetite are the man's actions" (*NE* 3, 1: 1111b1–3). It is a question, rather, of how they are to be incorporated in a person's life.

Passions. The passions are feelings in the sense of emotions, feelings which in general are accompanied by pleasure or pain — typically, the feelings of anger, fear, hope, joy, love, hatred (*NE* 2, 5: 1105b21f; cf. *Eudemian Ethics* 2, 2: 1220b13f). They are associated in turn with the possibility of desire, in virtue of which they constitute motivation for action on the part of human beings. The passions, then, are precisely the field of operation of the moral virtues: a moral virtue is a state of character on the basis of which we act and stand well with reference to the passions, and hence with reference to pleasures and pains (*NE* 2, 4: 1105b25f; 1104b14f). The morally mature person is the one who loves and hates in the right way, who experiences pleasure and pain rightly. In the discussion of moral virtue, especially in Book 2 of *NE*, Aristotle makes the point insistently that the virtues are concerned with actions and passions, with how we act and feel. Moral excellence is a matter of acting and being emotionally affected in the right ways. But what is the measure of rightness? Aristotle's view is that it is to be found in reason and that it is realized in general in the situation in which the passions are guided by reason. This proposal draws on an appropriate psychology.

The soul (*psyche*), in Aristotle's biological approach, is thought of as the actuality or form of the body, not a separate (or separable) reality, but the body as realized as a living body with its associated powers.[6] One element of the psyche is the power of nutrition and growth, common to plants and animals, embryos and fully grown specimens alike. In the ethical writings, Aristotle goes on to concentrate on just two other psychological elements in the specifically human context, the power of reasoning and an appetitive or desiring element which incorporates the passions (*NE* 1, 13; *Eudemian Ethics* 2, 1; for a more complete account, Aristotle refers his readers to other sources in his writings). Reason in turn is either theoretical (the capacity for speculative inquiry and understanding) or practical, reason which is directed to behavior. In reference to practical reason, Aristotle speaks typically of deliberation about means to desired ends, but he also makes clear that reasoning includes attention to what is to count as an end or with consideration of what goals are worth pursuing.[7]

Aristotle is drawn to include the appetitive element in the rational dimension of the psyche as well, provided that it is seen as subject to the guidance of reason. He also observes in *NE* that the appetitive element might equally be classified as non-rational, albeit as having a share in rationality in being able to respond to reason. This is suggestive of a certain ambivalence about the passions as forces which might be deaf to reason (as in the life ruled by the passions). But his considered view is that emotions in their developed form, and desire related to emotions, involve cognitive elements of belief and judgment (see *Rhetoric* II).

In speaking of the passions as subject to the guidance of reason, Aristotle is presenting a normative view in which he clearly has in mind the morally mature person. The relationship is expressed in an image of speech in which the appetitive and desiring element is said "to listen and obey" reason (*NE* 1, 13: 1102b31); this is the sense, he says, in which "we speak of paying heed to one's father or one's friends." The metaphor of reason as parent or wise friend is fully compatible with the idea that reason is itself importantly shaped by desire and the emotions. This is connected in part with their direct motivational role. But it also arises from the conception of the emotions as integral elements of human experience and as ways of seeing situations and responding to them. Appropriate emotional response to situations, as we have noted, is treated as an essential part of moral excellence of virtue, and reason endowed with practical wisdom, for its part, is engaged reason, not a disembodied mind: intelligent choice of action involves both knowledge and desire (Aristotle describes it both as "deliberative desire" and as "desiderative thinking" — *NE* 1113a9; 1139a23; b4–5). All of this presupposes that the passions can be trained and educated, and that they enrich human life to the extent that they can be brought into harmony with the measure of goodness provided by reason.

The Measure of Goodness. Something of the character and content of Aristotle's idea of the rational measure of goodness can be suggested as follows. The objects of the passions, what human beings desire and strive for in general, are such things as sensual pleasure, wealth, honor, physical and mental skills, health, and power.[8] The morally bad person seeks such goods in an uncontrolled way, in a way as to do harm to himself and others. The morally immature person either does not know the measure in which to seek them, or does not know how to go about seeking them properly. Such people are at a disadvantage in promoting their own good or in helping others. Morally mature persons seek them in the right measure, neither too little nor too much, in a way as to benefit themselves and others. (This is not very informative, in part because it is circular, but it could be filled out best by reference to examples.)

This illustration could suggest that moral development is mainly a matter of acquiring knowledge (perhaps through teaching and experience). In fact, Aristotle puts the major emphasis on habit formation. His view, as we shall see, is that moral instruction can be effective only on this basis. But assuming the effective outcome of the process, the moral virtues can be seen as states of character by which the individual is disposed to seek a distribution of natural goods which benefits others no less than himself. Justice occupies a central place in this regard; so too do courage and moderation, generosity, and the qualities associated with friendship. The morally mature person is characterized by a concern for others which shows up in the exercise of these dispositions. But the capacity to relate to others in this way presupposes, Aristotle argues, love for oneself (*NE* 9, 8: 1167b28ff) — though not self-love in the sense of self-indulgence or in competition with others for wealth, honors, and bodily pleasures (*NE* 1167b14ff). The treatment of virtue in terms of the sharing of goods points to the need to consider moral maturity (and its development) in a community setting.[9] The Aristotelian moral agent exists as a member of inter-related communities (family and household, village, and a self-sufficient society or state, properly a city-state, a *polis*). This supposes most generally that involvement in a common life is a central human need and value, and that the family and the state, for their part, are ethical communities. What makes a family and a state is precisely the association of living beings who characteristically have "a sense of good and evil, or just and unjust and the like" (*Politics* 1, 2: 1253a15–17). At the same time, the emphasis on community goes along with an affirmation of a certain self-sufficiency or independence as a feature of adult moral agency.

No individual is strictly self-sufficient, as Aristotle insists at the beginning of the *Politics*: family and society are natural conditions of human life (1, 2; *NE* 1, 7). Self-sufficiency in the relevant sense is explicated in terms of an individual being one among equals and as being able to take part in the government of the community: political association is an association of equals which is marked by justice and scope for friendship. But self-sufficiency for some in this sense rests on the exclusion of others: the self-sufficiency of the adult male citizen is manifested as master in relation to slaves and as head of the family with authority in relation to wife and children. These socio-political rankings are given an ethical rationale in Aristotle's teaching in connection with the capacity for deliberation and the exercise of practical wisdom (*Politics* 1, 13: 1260a5ff). Members of the subordinate groups are accorded a capacity for moral virtue in keeping with their status. Slaves, held to lack the deliberative faculty entirely, are made entirely dependent on their master for guidance. Women are said to have the deliberative faculty but "without authority" (where the likely implication is that their emotions are overly dominant: in a different way, then, women are held to need male guidance); and children also have the faculty but in an immature way, so that they too are in need of guidance.[10] All should have a share in the excellences of character, Aristotle concludes, "but only in such manner and degree as is required by each for the fulfilment of his function" (*Politics* 1260a15–17).

Practical Wisdom. Practical wisdom, in its developed and flawless sense, is the capacity to deliberate well about human affairs and to work out effectively what is "the best for man of things attainable by action" (*NE* 6, 7: 1141b12f). In this sense it embraces knowledge of what is good for oneself and the members of one's community and what is best in particular situations. It is concerned, in other words, with the grasp of the relevant general truths — things "true for the most part" in human affairs — knowledge about human beings, of connections between actions and their outcomes, especially in their bearing on good and harm for individuals and the community. This general knowledge is to go along with the capacity to appreciate particular circumstances and situations in the choice of suitable action (*NE* 1141b14–16). Moral maturity in this account is not a matter of living by fixed rules or precepts. Life according to reason imposes certain absolute prohibitions and obligations (which relate to behavior incompatible with the moral excellences, prohibitions which are often enshrined in the law of the State). But moral wisdom, to use Aristotle's favorite analogies, is like medical skill or navigation: there are general guidelines, and procedures which should definitely be avoided, but the individual must know how to exercise judgment and arrive at appropriate choice in relation to particular situations. Finally, practical wisdom cannot exist in separation from the moral virtues, ensuring that the appropriate knowledge is tied to concomitant desire.

Motivation. The whole question of the moral quality of our actions and feelings in Aristotle's view revolves around our response to pleasures and pains. There are, he proposes in Book 2 of *NE*, three general objects of choice (or pursuit) and three of avoidance:

There being three objects of choice and three of avoidance, the noble, the advantageous, the pleasant, and their contraries, the base, the injurious, the painful, about all of these the good man tends to go right and the bad man to go wrong, and especially about pleasure; for this is common to the animals, and also it accompanies all objects of choice; for even the noble and the advantageous appear pleasant. Again, it has grown up with us all from our infancy; this is why it is difficult to rub off this passion, engrained as it is in our life. (*NE* 2, 3: 1104b30ff)

The basic opposition of pleasures and pains has to do with the satisfaction (or otherwise) of physiologically based appetites. The noble and the base point to the idea of a code of honor and the question of conformity of behavior to standards set by a group or community which have regard to interests beyond the individual. The probable reference here is to forms of behavior endorsed by the community in relation to the moral virtues. Finally, the opposition of the "advantageous and the injurious" very probably refers to the notion of human good (and evil) as specified by practical wisdom — a reinforcement of the idea of the noble by an internal criterion, viz., whether a course of action is such as to promote good or harm for oneself and others.

The three pairs of contraries then yield graded types of motivation. The basic motivation for behavior, common to human beings and animals alike, is the desire to secure pleasure and avoid pain. The morally immature and the bad are credited in general with no other form of motivation; for them, everything turns on this scale and their behavior, left unchecked, is thereby drawn to what is base and injurious. For the morally mature, however, the noble and the good constitute distinct and overriding attractions. The morally virtuous person must act, as Aristotle frequently says, "for the sake of the noble." In the same spirit, the person of practical wisdom has to aim at "goodness of action itself."[11]

In the person who chooses to act for the noble and the good, pleasure has been modified as the principle of action. Bodily pleasures associated with human needs for food and drink, sexual satisfaction, and physical comfort nevertheless remain as basic and integral in this conception of human well-being (see *NE* 1119a6–10). Aristotle argues, in addition, that with the pursuit of the noble and the good, a person's conception and experience of pleasure are in fact enlarged. The noble and good life, as he portrays it, harmonizes basic appetitive pleasure with pleasures of the mind and the pleasure which is characteristic of virtuous activity (the genuinely virtuous person being one who actually enjoys acting well). In this lies the best and most genuine form of human pleasure, for pleasure is found in what one loves: hence the best pleasure lies in loving what is best (cf. *NE* 10, 5: 1176a3ff; 1099a6f). With the passions under the guidance of reason, the morally mature person enjoys psychic harmony and unity, and this unity is further expressed in the assumption of responsibility for one's behavior in an overall pattern of life.[12]

Aristotle resists the view that, on this account of the virtuous life, the ideas of the noble and the good emerge simply as re-defined versions of the basic motivation of pleasure. One reason he would give is that pleasure cannot be reasonably understood as a single thing: there are different kinds of pleasure associated with different activities, not all of them worthwhile or even desirable; in addition, pleasure cannot be intelligently separated from the activities in which it is realized. (Aristotle discusses pleasure in Book 7 in *NE* and in a somewhat different way in Book 10.) Furthermore, while pleasure accompanies the exercise of virtue, it is not the primary reason for which the virtuous person acts; if it were, one would have to say that the person had not really succeeded in acquiring the virtue or had lost it. Some of these points are suggested in the following passage:

> No one would choose to live with the intellect of a child throughout his life, however much he were to be pleased at the things that children are pleased at, nor to get enjoyment by doing some most disgraceful deed, though he were never to feel any pain in consequence. And there are many things we should be keen about even if they brought no pleasure, e.g. seeing, remembering, knowing, possessing the excellences. If pleasures necessarily do accompany these, that makes no odds; we should choose these even if no pleasure resulted. (*NE*, 10, 3; 1174a1–7)

The pattern of the graded objects of choice, the pleasant, the noble, and the good, is suggestive of an order of moral development. I will take them up again later in that context. In the meantime, the general Aristotelian conception of moral maturity is now reasonably clear.

Aristotle observes on a number of occasions that most people fail to achieve moral goodness. Most fall short of the level of virtue, choosing to live a life ruled by passion rather than reason: "Those who are grasping with regard to these things [natural goods] gratify their appetites and in general their feelings and the irrational element of the soul; and most men are of this nature" (*NE* 9, 8: 1168b19). One factor which contributes to this sense of near universal failure is connected with Aristotle's list of exclusions — women and slaves (and, in a sense, non-Greeks). Failure of a sort is guaranteed in these cases since one or another condition for mature virtue is missing by an accident of nature, so to speak, in each case. They are accorded instead the possibility of lesser degrees of excellence linked with the assessment of their capacities and roles. There is a case for saying that failure is underwritten in other respects too in the account, especially in connection with the very high degree of knowledge which goes with the idea of practical wisdom. In any case, the distinction between two types of life, one guided by magisterial reason, the other by the passions, is obviously too sharp and simple. On the other hand, setting aside Aristotelian exclusions of whole classes of people, one is still likely to agree with his view that the achievement of moral goodness in any full sense is both difficult and rare, and that human beings "may be ruined and spoilt in many ways" (*NE* 10, 5: 1176a20).

3. Primary Educational Themes

What is needed for things to go right in achieving moral goodness, and how might things go wrong? It is time to consider Aristotle's views about children and the process of moral development. Children lack the moral virtues and the knowledge, insight, and experience necessary for practical wisdom. They are not fully moral agents, they are not capable of reasoned deliberation and choice in any full sense, and hence they fall short of the conditions for *eudaimonia* (which involves the idea of completeness).

Although Aristotle speaks on occasions of natural virtues, his view is that none of the virtues is innate in us; we are fitted by nature to receive the virtues, but we have to learn to take pleasure in the right things (*NE* 2, 1: 1103a14f; 1104b8ff). The sanguine conviction that we are fitted by nature to receive the virtues is tempered by the idea that we are born incomplete and that, in the absence of education, we will be drawn to take pleasure in the wrong things: "The deficiencies of nature are what art and education seek to fill up," Aristotle observes in his discussion of education in the *Politics* (7, 17: 1337a1–2). Taking his cue from Plato, he proposes in his ethics that the right education is one in which we "have been brought up from our very youth . . . so as both to delight in and be pained by the things that we ought" (*NE* 2, 3: 1104b11f; see Plato, *Laws* 653A; *Republic* 401E–402A). What is required, in brief, is teaching and experience over time in the case of intellectual virtue, and in the case of moral virtue, habituation (*NE* 2, 1: 1103a15ff).

BASIC EDUCATION AND HABIT-FORMATION

Young children live, in Aristotle's words, "at the beck and call of appetite, and it is in them that the desire for what is pleasant is strongest" (*NE* 3, 12: 1119b5f). The young child, with a limited grasp of its immediate situation, innocent of reflection and self-awareness, is motivated entirely by the inborn desire for pleasure, specifically pleasure as the feeling of well-being, especially in the forms of nourishment, warmth, and affection. Aristotle's view, as noted earlier, is that the desire for pleasure is innate and that it remains the basic human motivation; it grows up with us all from our infancy and is engrained in our life, as he puts it. But with reference to pleasure beyond the primary stage, he is drawn to the idea that the satisfaction of feelings in its pursuit is likely to be harmful unless it is modified by other systems of desire. The capacity for deliberation and rational choice lies undeveloped in the child. In this immature stage, therefore, if appetite is not to grow uncontrolled, the rational and guiding principle must be supplied by someone else, specifically the child's father, and its tutor or teacher (*NE* 3, 12: 1119b12ff). Being imperfect or incomplete, the child is not capable of achieving virtue of itself: it has to be referred to what is complete, the parent or teacher (*Politics* 1260a31f). In other words, the parent supplies the rational principle for the child: the father as embodiment of reason is legislator of the child's behavior, and as embodiment of virtue, he teaches by example (*NE* 10, 9: 1180bf).

In Aristotelian thought, the proper order of education is set by reference to its intended outcome, the cultivation of reason as exhibited in moral excellence. To this end, it needs to follow the order and conditions of natural growth: the generation of the body first, and then the psyche; and within the psyche, emotions and desire first since they are implanted from birth and most immediately active, and later reason and understanding. Education takes three forms, therefore, corresponding to these developmental stages: education of the body, education of the passions, and finally education in and through rational powers.[13] In the first two stages, the process is envisaged fundamentally as habit-formation, in keeping with the idea that in education practice goes before theory (*Politics* 8, 3: 1338b5): movement, physical exercise, and gymnastics to develop "the proper habit of body"; then practices in the domain of the passions to develop moral character, the proper habits of soul having to be laid down before the child is able to grasp their point. Fundamental importance is placed on this process: "It makes no small difference, then, whether we form habits of one kind or of another from our very youth; it makes a very great difference, or rather *all* the difference" (*NE* 2, 1: 1103b23–5). The insistence on the need for habituation as the prerequisite for instruction and understanding in morality is a recurrent theme in Aristotle's writings (see *NE* 1, 3: 1095a2–4; 1, 4: 1095b2–8; 10, 9: 1179b24–6; *Politics* 7, 15: 1334b6; 8, 3: 1338b4).

Aristotle supposes that these developments properly need a scheme of public or common education in addition to education in the family. The latter has the advantage of taking place in a context of natural affection, and it caters for individual attention and care. But it also opens the way to the dangers of arbitrariness and division in which "each man lives as he pleases, Cyclops-fashion, 'to his own wife and children dealing law'" (*NE* 10, 9: 1180a27, quoting *Odyssey* IX, 114). It is best, he thinks, that there should be public care for the way in which children are brought up, which has an eye to the common life of the society. This relates especially to the need for good laws in regard to childcare and in the state generally: "It is difficult to get from youth up a right training for excellence if one has not been brought up under right laws" (*NE* 10, 9: 1180a31–2). The desired outcome cannot be achieved within the authority of the individual family:

> The paternal command indeed has not the required force or compulsive power (nor in general has the command of one man, unless he be a king or something similar), but the law *has* compulsive power, while it is at the same time an account proceeding from a sort of practical wisdom and intellect. (*NE* 10, 9: 1180a19–22)

A scheme of public education, in short, is more likely to be effective, less given to arbitrariness, and more in keeping with practical wisdom. These considerations reflect a general Aristotelian principle which could be called the "collective wisdom argument" (and which Aristotle used in defense of a modified form of democracy):

> For the many, of whom each individual is not a good man, when they meet together may be better than the few good, if regarded not individually but collectively, just as a feast to which many contribute is better than a dinner provided out of a single purse. For each individual among the many has a share of excellence and practical wisdom, and when they meet together, just as they become in a manner one man, who has many feet, and hands, and senses, so too with regard to their character and thought. (*Politics* 3, 11: 1281b1ff)

But Aristotle's overriding argument for common education is that members of a society need to share common values — hence "the training in things which are of common interest should be the same for all" (*Politics* 8, 1: 1337a26–7). This is connected with the view that the individual does not exist as an individual alone but as part of the state or the society as a whole, in which case "the care of each part is inseparable from the care of the whole" (*Politics* 1337a30).

The insistence on habit-formation as primary in education involves more than a progression set by the natural order of physical, emotional, and mental development. It is connected more profoundly with the nature of its goal in the development of practical wisdom. The thesis (to be considered more fully later) is that the acquisition of moral wisdom and the capacity for reasoned choice are possible only if a person has already acquired the moral habits. Since practical wisdom involves both knowledge and desire, it is likely that two sub-claims are involved, viz., that without the moral virtues, (a) a person's capacity for knowledge and judgment is affected in such a way that moral teaching or instruction is ineffectual; and (b) the effective desire for right action is negated or blunted. Habit-formation would then be necessary in both respects. In what does it consist? Allowing that practice is not enough by itself to make perfect, the question is, how does habituation contribute to the development of the requisite understanding and motivation?

The division of education, corresponding to divisions of body and psyche, is likely to suggest that habituation is essentially non-cognitive in character. This is the way the notion has regularly been interpreted.[14] Passions, appetite, and desire, on the one side, are contrasted sharply with reason, on the other. First there is education of the passions (as conditioning), and when this is complete, education in and through reason can follow. But against this, we have already seen reasons in Aristotle's own thought for rejecting a sharp division between reason and the passions. More generally, it would be absurd if forms of rationality did not enter extensively into the first two stages of education. It should be enough in this regard to note that in the education curriculum of the *Politics*, the first stage (physical education) extends to age seven, and the second stage runs in two seven-year periods to the age of twenty-one (*Politics* 7, 17: 1336a4ff)! The stages of education — physical, sentimental, and rational — have to be seen as named by their dominant emphasis without being exhausted by it.

A further Aristotelian consideration is the idea that children begin to engage in voluntary behavior from a quite early stage. Behavior takes on an intentional character, an engagement with situations which is at once cognitive and appetitive. On this basis, the idea of responsibility on the part of the child and the related notions of praise and blame begin to make sense.[15] In a variety of ways, then, the idea of moral habituation as non-cognitive is clearly implausible. Part of the blame for the currency of this interpretation arises perhaps from the tendency to build watertight compartments on the basis of a distinction (in this case, the distinction between reason and the passions). Another consideration is that Aristotle did not discuss the notion of habituation in detail in spite of the importance he attached to it. He invokes it frequently in Books 2 and 10 of *NE* and in the discussion of education, conceived fundamentally as moral *paideia*, in Books 7 and 8 of the *Politics*, but the notion itself is not examined directly. In the *Politics*, however, he does discuss at length the way in which the education of the passions and moral education should proceed. In Aristotle's prescription, the primary if not quite entire emphasis is placed on the role of the musical paideia, education in music.

MUSIC AND MORAL VIRTUE: THE EDUCATION OF THE PASSIONS

There is a good case for thinking that Aristotle included poetry, epic poetry and tragedy in particular, in the proper scope of musical education; certainly in the context of education, he thinks of music as normally and properly accompanied by words.[16] Another consideration is that Aristotle put particular stress on the importance of learning to sing and to play a musical instrument, as distinct from simply learning to appreciate music by listening to it.

The importance of music in education is placed in the perceived link it has with virtue (though not in this alone). Music is accorded power to form our minds and habituate us to true pleasures (*Politics* 8, 5: 1339a22–4). The argument can be summarized as follows (allowing for some obscurity in the text). Music is pleasurable, and the pleasure it gives is natural; on that ground alone it has an important place in education and life. But in addition, music in song, rhythm, and melody is credited with a special power to supply likenesses of the passions and the virtues: enthusiasm, anger, gentleness, courage and temperance, and so on, as well as contrary qualities. The experience of music evokes feelings in us — our souls undergo a change as Aristotle says — in a way as to bring us into sympathy with the moral qualities. Our characters are formed in the process since the feelings we experience are genuine feelings of joy, peace, sadness, and so on. It is then an easy step for the same feelings (which relate to representations) to flow on to good moral qualities in actuality. Music thus helps to cultivate the power of "forming right judgments, and of taking delight in good dispositions and noble actions" (*Politics* 8, 5: 1340a18–20). Thus it rightly occupies a central place, along with gymnastics, reading, writing, and drawing, in the education of the young.[17]

Whatever the large question marks which hang over this argument, it points to a significant contrast between habituation and the ordinary sense of teaching. No amount of teaching about the passions and moral qualities can evoke them with anything like the immediacy and force of music, poetry, and dramatic story; the process in which the child becomes accustomed to feeling the feelings includes cognitive elements and imparts its own form of direct knowledge. It is clear, however, that the quest for moral habituation through music would have to be accompanied by a great deal of teaching in the ordinary sense. To feel enthusiasm in listening to a piece of stirring music in the Phrygian mode is one thing, but the experience can convey no idea of how much enthusiasm is appropriate or anything about other circumstances in which it might or might not be appropriate. In the education of the young, Aristotle particularly favored the Dorian mode on the grounds that it was the gravest and manliest and most balanced, calculated to produce a moderate and settled temper (*Politics* 1340b4–5; 1342b14f). But even if this were so, the regular experience of this music would not help to determine, for example, when gravity is in or out of place.

Together with the feelings, the child in Aristotle's school would have to be helped to see the connections between the music and the feelings it evokes and the moral qualities it is held to resemble. The child would have to learn how to recognize the moral qualities outside the music or the drama as well as within it, and learn something about which responses in action and feeling are appropriate beyond the music and to what degree; in other words, the child would be involved in acquiring a grasp of particular situations from a moral point of view in the light of general ideas.

These aspects of moral education through music, poetry, and drama are further underlined by the insistence on the need for children to be taught to sing and play an instrument. Aristotle indicates that he thinks that listening to music (of the appropriate sorts) helps to form moral character. He allows that appreciation of music in these ways is sufficient for its place in the life of cultivated leisure of adults (that is, of his educated and well-off class). Having canvassed the question at some length, he concludes abruptly that education in music must include the learning of musical skills on the grounds that it is otherwise difficult, if not impossible, to become a good judge of musical performance. Then he adds without elaboration that, "clearly there is a considerable difference made in the character by the actual practice of the arts" (*Politics* 1340b20ff).

Perhaps Aristotle's idea is that actual participation in music-making gives one more direct experience of the character of the music and evokes more readily the feelings correlated with forms of the passions and moral qualities. On that basis, the practitioner of the art becomes a better judge of pleasure and of the noble and the good. Whatever of this, the process involves the same combination of direct experience of emotions (which cannot be taught) together with the need for considerable teaching if connections are to be made from the music and song to the appreciation and acquisition of the moral qualities. In addition to the more immediate involvement with music and poetry, the task of learning to sing and play calls for practice. This is a form of habituation in its own right. What practice suggests is a parallel instance and illustration of the way in which Aristotle envisages moral habituation. The parallel is suggested in his remark that learning music "is not with a view to amusement, for learning is no amusement, but is accompanied by pain" (*Politics* 1339a29–30) — which is consistent with the idea that the exercise of the skills, once they are acquired, is a source of pleasure. One could then say that moral habituation as practice has the same structure: the child is diverted from immediate pleasures (associated with untutored appetite) and got to act in keeping with virtue, a process involving a degree of pain; then gradually as the virtue is acquired, its exercise comes to be enjoyed.

The emphasis on practice is the best known feature of Aristotle's remarks on moral habituation:

> Excellences we get by first exercising them, as also happens in the case of the arts as well. For the things we have to learn before we can do, we learn by doing, e.g. men become builders by building and lyre-players by playing the lyre; so too, we become just by doing just acts, temperate by doing temperate acts, brave by doing brave acts. (*NE* 2, 1: 1103a31ff)

But as we have now seen, practice in regard to the virtues is placed in a rich educational context. In summary, the whole educational process connecting music and poetry and drama with virtue is presented as a form of induction into attitudes and feelings and dispositions for action that also imparts knowledge and skill: to the goddess Athene, Aristotle says, we ascribe both knowledge and art (*Politics* 1341b8). The relevant moral knowledge, however incomplete, arises in part through teaching and in part through direct experience; both are linked with the cultivation of desire in the education of the passions.

4. Moral Stages

THE PLACE OF MORAL INSTRUCTION

In a discussion which is particularly relevant to moral development, in Book 10 of the *Nicomachean Ethics*, Aristotle summarizes the competing views as follows:

Now some think that we are made good by nature, others by habituation, others by teaching. (1179b201)

Setting aside nature's part as something that does not depend on us, he
argues that moral argument and teaching is likely to be effective only with
young people who have been prepared for it by habituation:

> Argument and teaching, we may suspect, are not powerful with all men,
> but the soul of the student must first have been cultivated by means of
> habits for noble joy and noble hatred, like earth which is to nourish the
> seed. (NE 1179b25–26)

Just prior to this he had proposed that arguments "are not able to encourage the many to nobility and goodness," on the grounds that "the many"
live by *passion*. About them he says:

> For these do not by nature obey the sense of shame, but only fear, and
> do not abstain from bad acts because of their baseness but through fear
> of punishment; living by passion they pursue their own pleasures and
> the means to them, and avoid the opposite pains, and have not even a
> conception of what is noble and truly pleasant, since they have never
> tasted it. (NE 1179b9–15)

The conclusion that moral argument is of no avail against these contrary
ingrained character traits follows. More strongly, Aristotle contends that
the person who lives by passion is insensible to argument:

> For he who lives as passion directs will not hear argument that dissuades
> him, nor understand it if he does; and how can we persuade one in such
> a state to change his ways? And in general passion seems to yield not to
> argument but to force. The character, then, must somehow be there
> already with a kinship to excellence, loving what is noble and hating
> what is base. (NE 1179b26–30)

A first comment on this argument is that Aristotle works with an overly
sharp contrast between the few among the young who are lovers of what is
noble, who can therefore be helped to understanding and goodness by
instruction, and the many who have no conception of the noble and who
are in no immediate position to learn about it. There is the suggestion of
elitism in this contrast, especially as it can be readily connected with the
insistence in Book I (no doubt with an eye to his own courses) that "anyone
who is to listen intelligently to lectures about what is noble and just and,
generally, about the subjects of political science must have been brought
up in good habits" (NE 1095b4–5). This is not a major criticism of the
argument itself, however, for the insistence on the prior need for the
formation of character through good habits could be accommodated to the
idea that many people fall between the ideal and the worst possible case.

A second comment, drawn from our earlier discussion, is that habituation itself necessarily includes a good deal of moral teaching. The present

claim could accommodate this on the grounds that the teaching which goes with habituation rests on learning of a different sort, viz., the experience of emotions by which the child is attracted to moral qualities, and the experience of pleasure which eventually goes with the exercise of virtue. Aristotle's argument would then be that this emotional development of the child (accompanied by primary teaching) is the necessary basis for more advanced moral instruction and understanding. Someone who has not been brought up in this way (who therefore lives "by passion") has not had the passional experience of "what is noble and truly pleasant," and hence is unprepared to appreciate argument and teaching in regard to it.

The underlying idea of this significant argument is that the key to *moral* understanding is found in what a person loves. What we first love (or are helped to love) on some basis other than knowledge, we come to know; and what we love we find pleasant. Those who live by passion love and know, are familiar with, the corresponding level of pleasure; they do not love what is noble and have no conception of its pleasures; hence they do not hear or do not understand argument in connection with it. But through habituation, the child comes to love what is noble, becomes familiar with it, finds enjoyment in it, and can go on then to deeper understanding.

The idea of levels or types of pleasure in this argument relates to a consideration in an earlier chapter in Book 10. In the course of remarking that each animal species has its characteristic forms of pleasure, Aristotle proposes that the morally good and bad have different pleasures or, where pleasures are common, enjoy them differently. Adapting Protagoras' dictum, "man is the measure of all things," he proposes:

> In all such matters that which appears to the good man is thought to be really so. If this is correct, as it seems to be, and excellence and the good man as such are the measure of each thing, these also will be pleasures which appear so to him, and those things pleasant which he enjoys. (*NE* 10, 5: 1176a17–20)

Here, as elsewhere, Aristotle invokes a medical analogy: "The same things do not seem sweet to a man in fever and a healthy man — nor hot to a weak man and one in good condition" (*NE* 1176a12–14). The lovers of virtue alone are healthy and they alone can properly judge what is natural and true; the incapacity for understanding on the part of those who live as passion directs is a sickness (associated with a deprived childhood).

The argument in *NE* 10, 9 allows that the sickness can be cured. But not by argument. The primary locus of treatment has to be in what people love; and passion, Aristotle says, "seems to yield not to argument but to force." The idea of force in this context needs to be considered, suggestive as it is of a violent and non-cognitive process. Aristotle cannot mean the sort of force which renders action completely involuntary, as if people could be shaken into virtue. It is also clear from what he says elsewhere in the passage that he does not mean the sort of compulsion which the law exercises and which a person obeys out of fear of punishment, for in that case, the person's feelings remain unchanged. Almost certainly, the idea of "passion yielding to force" is a reference to the process of habituation in which one is made to perform a type of action against one's inclinations until one comes to act willingly and to enjoy acting in this way.[18] But Aristotle's view is that little can be done with adults who are set in contrary ways other than to invoke the force of law; habituation to virtue needs to begin in early childhood. The way is then open — eventually — for fruitful moral instruction.

TRUE LOVERS OF WHAT IS NOBLE, READY TO BE POSSESSED BY EXCELLENCE

Drawing on earlier discussion, we can now set out an Aristotelian view of moral stages. The primary, pre-moral stage, in which the young child lives "at the beck and call of appetite," has been covered in enough detail already at the beginning of section 3. Gradually, and especially with the acquisition of language, the child starts to become a moral agent. At the beginning, and for a long time, it is told what to do or how to respond in a range of situations which recur in a broadly similar form: to share things with others, to be truthful, to be patient, to put up with some pain, not to eat too much or too little, not to be cruel, and the like, and most generally, to be obedient. What the child is told and got to do is action in accordance with the virtues — as judged by parents or teachers. In the process the child learns a moral vocabulary in a lived context. But for a long time it has no conception of action as action in accordance with virtue; nor does it have any possible motive for acting in this way *for this reason*.

The guidance by parent or teacher depends to a considerable extent on example. It takes place best and most naturally, in Aristotle's view, in an atmosphere of mutual love and friendship between parents and children (see *NE* 8, 12: 1161b17ff). In this setting, the child's primary motive for conforming to the guidance can be supposed to be a desire to win parental affection, or not to lose it — or the fear of some other punishment; there is likely to be a mixture of factors. The specified motives for action arise before the child has any rational grasp of morality. At the same time, these motives are in conflict, in Aristotle's psychology, with the inclination of the passions in general: the desire for affection draws the child to do what it finds painful or not immediately pleasant, whereas the inclination of passion is to immediate pleasure.

The power of habituation is that it changes this situation over time, changing the passions by bringing them under a form of control. Appetite is always the measure of what one finds pleasant, but in Aristotle's words,

> things familiar and things habitual belong to the class of pleasant things;
> for there are many actions not naturally pleasant which men perform

with pleasure, once they have become used to them. (*Rhetoric* 1, 10: 1369b 15–19; cf. *NE* 10, 9: 1179b356)

The idea, as we have seen, is that action in accordance with virtue ceases to be difficult or painful as it becomes customary. Given proper training, the stage will arrive when the child comes to enjoy such action as pleasant and worthy of choice "for the sake of the noble." But that is still far in the future. The first step is that the natural desire for pleasure is modified by the responsive desire for parental affection and approval or by the fear of punishment.

The further move toward the "love of the noble" is particularly tied in Aristotle's account to the development of a sense of shame in the face of transgression, and the gradual acquisition of temperance in the control of the original passions (*NE* 3, 10–12; 4, 9). Temperance can be seen in this context as the anticipation of moral reason or practical wisdom in the child. In the first stage, and to an extent throughout childhood, the father or tutor is the embodiment of reason for the child and the legislator of the child's desire; but with a share in temperance, the child begins to move toward self-guidance.

Shame is also associated with the assumption of an internal principle of behavior.[19] Shame, Aristotle proposes, is not a virtue since it is more like a feeling or passion than a state of character. He thus defines it as a form of fear, the "fear of disrepute," of being disgraced (*NE* 4, 9: 1128b10f), and treats it as linked appropriately only with the young:

> The passion [of shame] is not becoming to every age, but only to youth. For we think young people should be prone to shame because they live by passion and therefore commit many errors, but are restrained by shame; and we praise young people who are prone to this passion, but an older person no one would praise for being prone to the sense of disgrace, since we think he should not do anything that need cause this sense. (*NE* 4, 9: 1128b16–22)

Frequent failure is to be expected on the path to moral virtue, but, then, in the case of failure, shame supplies a motivational support system toward the love of the noble.

How does the system work? The emphasis on shame points to a difficulty in the Aristotelian idea of the noble. The noble, with its contrast in the base or the dishonorable, carried with it in Greek culture something of the idea of a traditional code of honor upheld by the leading social class. But more than this, Aristotle intends it to be linked with a sense of failure in respect to the moral virtues as having overriding value in themselves. Shame in his ethics is contrasted with shamelessness, which is contempt or indifference in regard to bad things. It is also contrasted with concern for obedience to law merely from fear of punishment, which is the only operative factor in those who live by the passions (*NE* 1179b10–12). The fear felt in connection with shame is not fear of punishment, but fear of disrepute; it goes with the desire to be well thought of by others. The same elements are present in the account in the *Rhetoric*:

> Shame may be defined as pain or disturbance in regard to bad things, whether present, past, or future, which seem likely to involve us in discredit; and shamelessness as contempt or indifference in regard to these same bad things. (*Rhetoric* 2, 6: 1383b15–17)

Shame would appear to be linked, therefore, with the desire to secure parental approval, extended perhaps to figures of authority in a kinship group or in the wider community. It shows up as a sense of disgrace or discredit if one is disloyal to the tradition they represent and of which one is now a part. This motivation could go with commitment to a code of honor, obedience to a tradition mediated by a family, party, religion, or political community. But in these terms, it could be more concerned with the desire to please others and to enjoy a good reputation in their eyes than with virtuous action in its own right.

What is missing from the Aristotelian picture at this point is precisely the need for a growing understanding of morality beyond mere willing obedience on the part of the young. This is missing, however, only if one forgets that habituation also involves growth in knowledge in the child; not full or adult understanding, but the first stages of understanding, or what Aristotle calls a starting point (see *NE* 1, 4: 1095b6).

In talking of habituation as the basis for moral understanding in the passage just cited, Aristotle goes on to quote Hesiod:

> Far best is he who knows all things himself;
> Good, he that hearkens when men counsel right;
> But he who neither knows, nor lays to heart
> Another's wisdom, is a useless wight.
> (Hesiod, *Works and Days*.293–7; *NE* 1, 4: 1095b10ff)

The child is told what to do, or not to do, in a range of identifiable situations. Its knowledge rests, entirely at first, on the word of others, in the manner of one who "hearkens to counsel" rather than one who knows. But Aristotle's view, in the *Politics* especially, is that what begins in this way is enlarged through education, especially in connection with music and poetry. In experiencing the emotions and moral qualities and learning about them in a wide range of circumstances in song and story, and in getting practice in acting as virtue requires and then experiencing shame in relation to failure, the child begins to acquire a grasp of morality which is at once more its own and more general, less tied to routine situations and to personal loyalties. The child needs to be given good advice and guidance all along, but in addition, it needs to appropriate what it is told if only to be able to recognize the recurrence of a given situation. Perceptual understanding, imagination, memory, and a degree of experience and judgment are all involved in this development. The baseline of development lies in what the child comes to love. The Aristotelian view is that, for moral development, this has to be significantly fixed at a relatively early stage to form the basis for later understanding; but elements of understanding, as I have argued, need to be brought into the picture from an early stage.

The concluding stage of development begins when one who has been brought up in good habits is "ready to be possessed by excellence" and is able "to listen intelligently to lectures about what is noble and just" (*NE* 1, 4: 1095b4; cf. 1179b9). Aristotle supposes that this stage equally involves cognitive and affective dimensions. To be endowed with practical wisdom, the outcome of the process, is to have a good general grasp of what is best for the well-being of the community and oneself, and to know how to take a responsible part in political life and household management. It is to know how to arrive at the truth of what to do to act well. It is also to have an effective desire or commitment to this end, which has the form of love of virtue and good for its own sake as of supreme value. (But goodness here is not an abstract or purely formal notion: it relates to the concrete conditions in which individuals and human communities flourish.) The state of practical wisdom is "truth in agreement with desire," and for this, Aristotle argues, the reasoning must be correct and the desire right, the desire pursuing what the reasoning asserts (*NE* 6, 2: 1139a24–31).

The account allows that things may go wrong for the morally wise person since there is much that lies beyond control, and it recognizes that circumstances may arise, as in time of war or great personal suffering, in which the character of such a person changes for the worse.[20] But Aristotle's portrayal of practical wisdom and the morally wise man (the *phronimos*) is best seen as the projection of an ideal type. Endowed with the necessary general and particular knowledge and concomitant desire, he cannot fail: "Nor can the same man have practical wisdom and be incontinent; for it has been shown that a man is at the same time practically wise, and good in respect of character" (*NE* 7, 10: 1152a7–9). But types always have their place in a social context. Significantly, Pericles is the one explicit example Aristotle gives of a *phronimos*, and the relevant passage is revealing in a more general way:

> It is for this reason that we think Pericles and men like him have practical wisdom, viz. because they can see what is good for themselves and what is good for men in general; we consider that those can do this who are good at managing households or states. (*NE* 6, 5: 1140b8–10)

This connects with some of the exclusions in Aristotle's ethical thought. It is clear in the *Politics* in particular that his moral community embraces everyone: membership of one or another social group — free male citizens, women citizens, children, artisans and manual workers, slaves, and so on

— entails characteristic virtues and a related capacity for virtue in general. Specifically, in reference to the education of women and children, he says:

> For, inasmuch as every family is part of a state . . . and the excellence of the part must have regard to the excellence of the whole, women and children must be trained by education with an eye to the constitution, if the excellences of either of them are supposed to make any difference in the excellences of the state. And they must make a difference: for the children grow up to be citizens, and half the free persons in a state are women. (*Politics* 1, 13: 1260b12–17)

But women (in Athens in particular) were free persons and citizens only in a limited sense: some cults were reserved to them and they were citizens for purposes of marriage and procreation, but they otherwise lacked independent status and were always subject to male authority.[21] Aristotle's contribution at this point was to provide an "ethical" basis for these arrangements on the grounds that women could attain no more than an incomplete form of practical wisdom. Thus, in the given historical and cultural setting, Aristotle's projection of an ideal moral type could also serve to enhance the position of a definite and limited social group.

MORAL FAILURE AND RESPONSIBILITY

Aristotle's account of moral development, it can be readily seen, yields a map of exclusions amounting to near universal failure. Apart from exclusions "by nature," individuals may fail to get proper example, right advice, and enough sustained practice in their upbringing. They will be drawn into bad habits, vices of various kinds, brought about by the natural desire for pleasure running on without control and the bad example of others.

At the same time, Aristotle wants to hold that virtue and vice are voluntary, that the good and the bad are, in general, responsible for their states of character and their behavior. It can be seen that the emphasis on habituation in early development creates a problem in this regard, especially if it were thought to exclude cognitive elements. The objection would be that the morally bad are victims of their upbringing: having failed to acquire good moral habits as children, at a time when they could not be held responsible, they lack the necessary motivation and knowledge for choosing moral good as adults. Being ruined with regard to pleasure and pain, they fail to see what is good for themselves or others and hence aim at wrong ends. Appeals to reason carry no weight with them since they live by their passions and cannot understand such arguments.

Against this, however, Aristotle argues in Book 3 of *NE* that virtue and vice are both within our power; the bad are therefore blameworthy. This is not at all a blanket doctrine of responsibility. Apart from being well aware of particular excusing conditions which diminish responsibility, he recognized that there are disabilities and extreme environmental pressures which rule it out or render it problematic; his description of the brutish state of character in Book 7 points to a person who is at most marginally responsible. But the bad and the weak-willed, two other groups in Aristotle's taxonomy of flawed character, are held responsible for their failings.

The major contention in the argument in Book 3 is that the bad have made themselves bad by their choice of actions; even if they cannot now change their state, the fault lies with them. Comparing them to a person who becomes ill "through living incontinently and disobeying his doctors," he argues:

> In that case it was *then* open to him not to be ill, but not now, when he has thrown away his chance, just as when you have let a stone go it is too late to recover it; but yet it was in your power to throw it, since the moving principle was in you. So, too, to the unjust and the self-indulgent man it was open at the beginning not to become men of this kind, and so they are such voluntarily; but now that they have become so it is not possible for them not to be so. (*NE* 3, 5: 1114a16–20)

In this insistence, Aristotle appears to have set aside his view about the sequential character of moral development. The phrase, "it was open at the beginning not to become men of this kind," has the force of something within a person's own active power. If the *beginning* in question is a stage in childhood when the moral habits begin to be laid down, the proposal would fly in the face of the insistence elsewhere on the priority of affective development and the child's limited understanding. In any case, that is entirely implausible. Responsibility for having a bad character, for being unjust or self-indulgent or whatever, cannot be fixed so early. The teaching about responsibility in Book 3 needs to be modified to take account of developmental considerations; on the other hand, emphasis needs to be given to cognitive elements in habituation (and the sharp contrast between the few and the many in Book 10, 9 needs to be modified).

There is a case for distinguishing between the level of responsibility of which children are capable and full-fledged responsibility exercised with full awareness and choice.[22] But full-fledged responsibility needs to grow out of the former. If there is to be responsibility in this basic sense for one's character, Aristotle must allow that just about everyone acquires some grasp of moral values in conjunction with their affective formation in their upbringing, enough for them to have some idea of "the noble and the good," and for them to have a part in deciding what sort of person they want to be and in building their own characters before good or bad habits as a whole are firmly entrenched. The "beginning at which it is open to people" to take on this responsibility can hardly be determined very definitely: it has to concern a period before everything is fixed, but a time at which much has already been settled or taken shape in their character and moral outlook. In that sense, Aristotle's account of agency and responsibility can allow for a type of continuing "underground" element, consisting of pre-rational components which arise out of the original attachment to pleasure and early affective formation toward the noble and the good. Furthermore, people whose early moral formation is poor may, on this account, always fall short of full-fledged responsibility.

M. F. Burnyeat has shown how developmental considerations are particularly relevant to the problem of weakness of will.[23] The weak-willed or incontinent are distinguished from the bad (including the self-indulgent), in Aristotle's treatment of the topic (*NE*, Book 7), in being credited with a clear grasp of the good, equivalent even to that of the *phronimos*; but while knowing what to do in a situation, they succumb on occasions to the contrary sway of passion. The climate of thought which Aristotle inherited from Socrates and Plato challenged this possibility in arguing that wrongdoing is always due to ignorance. In throwing light on Aristotle's view that it is possible to act wrongly in spite of knowledge, Burnyeat suggests that an account of the conflict manifested in weakness of will needs to take note of the person's earlier history. Reasoned desire for the good comes later in time than the primary motivational factors, and may remain unstable in the face of knowledge. In this case, he suggests, the onus of explanation is turned around: "What needs explanation is not so much why some people succumb to temptation as why others do not. What calls for explanation is how some people acquire continence or, even better, full virtue, rather than why most of us are liable to be led astray by our bodily appetites or unreasoned evaluative responses."[24] Aristotle's explanation of both matters lies, of course, in his account of moral development.

The Aristotelian stages of moral development follow his three-tiered pattern of motivational levels (which is not affected by the need for modification in what he says about responsibility): the desire to secure pleasure and avoid pain as original and basic; conformity with a code of behavior and honor linked first with securing kinship approval; then a reasoned conception of the good as supremely worthwhile. The first level relates to a largely unreflective (and pre-conventional) individual point of view; the second level, focused on basic education and habituation, extends to one's kinship group and perhaps more widely (depending on community structures and traditions), and begins to incorporate the first stages of a reasoned conception of and commitment to the good; the idea of the good in the third level is grounded in the basic communities of social and political life, but it runs on, in Aristotle's phrase, to embrace universal law or the law of nature, a "natural justice . . . common to all, even to those who have no association or covenant with each other" (*Rhetoric* 1, 13: 1373b7–8).

Allowing that most people, good and bad, have some cognitive grasp of the good and some affective involvement with virtue, the model could be used to classify dominant types. One could then speak in Aristotelian terms of three forms of moral life as linked predominantly either with the pleasure principle, or a principle of honor, or a principle of seeking the good of self and others in a life according to reason.

5. Locke: The Character of Modern Virtue

1. White Paper, or Wax, to Be Molded as One Pleases

At the beginning of the modern era, Locke proclaimed a belief in the value and power of education, characteristic of his age and of his own thought. In his immensely influential treatise, *Some Thoughts Concerning Education*, he announced in the opening paragraph:

> I think I may say, that of all the Men we meet with, Nine Parts of Ten are what they are, Good or Evil, useful or not, by their Education. 'Tis that which makes the great Difference in Mankind.[1]

He repeats the claim in § 32 when he begins his discussion of the "general method of educating a young gentleman." The final paragraph of the book strikes the same note as the first: Locke writes of the boy, for whose education the book was originally written (as a series of letters), that since he was then very little, "I considered [him] only as white Paper, or Wax, to be moulded and fashioned as one pleases." Some exaggeration has to be allowed for in this echo of his best-known work, the *Essay Concerning Human Understanding*,[2] inasmuch as the child in question was already eight years old when Locke began the letters which led to the treatise on education. But the substantive point is unaffected. Locke proclaims a doctrine of human malleability.

It can be seen that Locke's expression of this idea — the child as wax to be molded and fashioned as one pleases — is nevertheless marked by a mild degree of caution. Almost, but not quite, everything is made to rest on education. A more substantial qualification, to which he returns four or five times, is the idea that each person has an innate temperament, natural aptitudes and inclinations, a natural genius — a characteristic disposition, happy or grave, sportive or melancholy, confident, modest, tractable, obstinate, and so on. He says, in the treatise on education, for example:

> God has stampt certain Characters upon Men's Minds, which like their Shapes, may perhaps be a little mended; but can hardly be totally alter'd, and transform'd into the contrary. (§ 66)

The characters alluded to here are not to be understood as cognitive principles in any sense. In Book I of the *Essay Concerning Human Understanding*, Locke set himself against the "received Doctrine, that Men have native ideas, and original Characters stamped upon their Minds, in their very first Being."[3] The treatise on education makes little or no reference to this question. But we should assume that the teaching of Book I of the *Essay* is taken for granted in its argument. All our knowledge, theoretical and practical, and all our ideas are derived from experience: this is the fundamental tenet of Locke's empiricism, and it is linked with his insistence on the importance of education. Thus the characters stamped on the mind, behavioral dispositions, in effect, have to be thought of as originally non-cognitive. They constitute in some sense a fixed and given element in an individual nature. But it would be a mistake to make too much of this point in connection with Locke. It is witness to the fact that a version of the longstanding nature-versus-nurture dispute was current in the late seventeenth century. Locke makes a concession to nature, but clearly accords the major role to nurture.

The major focus of the treatise on education is provided by Locke's conception of the primary aim and end of education. Time and again he insists that the chief business of education is the acquisition of virtue, the formation of moral character. In § 134 Locke lists virtue, wisdom, breeding, and learning as the aims of education, and he goes to proclaim:

I place *Vertue* as the first and most necessary of those endowments that belong to a Man or Gentleman. (§ 135)

Learning must be had, but in the second place, as subservient only to greater Qualities. (§ 147)

Tis Vertue, then, direct Vertue, which is the hard and valuable part to be aimed at in Education. (§ 70)

In keeping with Plato and Aristotle (and the Christian tradition), education for Locke is fundamentally moral education.

Given that virtue is held to depend almost entirely on education, Locke holds that human beings are not born good or evil. This is broadly what he says in § 1 of the treatise. Human nature is neither good nor evil in some essential or universal sense. In regard to virtue we are malleable: our being good or evil depends on how things go in our upbringing, the product of nurture not nature.

The context in which Locke subscribes to this view is a world apart from Aristotle and traditional Greek confidence in the powers of human achievement. Between Aristotle and Locke lies Christianity and the doctrine of original sin. In essence, this is the idea that human beings have a "fallen nature," that in some sense we inherit a state of sinfulness or enmity with God (who is all good and all holy) arising from a deep primeval rupture, and that we are capable of moral goodness only with the special help of God which is called grace (help which is therefore undeserved and *super*-natural or beyond human powers). The original "original sin" is conceived as Adam's repudiation of God, manifested as the desire to have God's power. Its consequences then flow on to all human beings and are realized in the phenomenon of human evil and in every instance of moral badness and wrongdoing. Locke makes no mention of original sin in the treatise on education, but this absence, in the context of his confidence in the power of education to produce virtue, is highly significant. Thus J. A. Passmore suggests that the crucial importance of *Some Thoughts Concerning Education* "lies not so much in its rejection of innate ideas as in its rejection of original sin."[4]

Locke's view of the doctrine of original sin is set out in his work, *The Reasonableness of Christianity* (1695).[5] That he rejected the common doctrine as upheld in one form or another by the Catholic and Protestant churches is clear. Locke naturalized the doctrine. For more than a thousand years the issue of sin and grace and human powers had been argued about in terms of a fiery dispute between Augustine, the renowned bishop of Hippo, and an otherwise little known Irish monk living in Rome, Pelagius. For Augustine, the central consideration is human sin and weakness and the necessity of grace, based on the idea that everyone is inculpated in the postulated sin of Adam; for Pelagius, by contrast, the power to act for good or ill is fixed in the human will. On the matter of Adam's sin and fall, Locke considered that there were two extremes to be avoided: one, the view that all human beings have sinned "in Adam" and are born corrupt and subject to eternal punishment but for God's forgiveness and grace (an Augustinian-type view); the other, that salvation does not strictly require any special divine grace or redemption in Christ since it is attainable through the natural — albeit God-given — powers of human will, provided we make enough personal effort (a Pelagian-type view). In Locke's compromise proposal, the sole general consequence of Adam's sin is taken to be human mortality, the fact that we are subject to death. Correspondingly, divine grace and redemption in Christ are treated as necessary, precisely for the overcoming of death which is to be effected through the resurrection of the dead. In adopting a position that was significantly closer to Pelagius than Augustine, Locke found himself at odds with orthodox Christian teaching (and especially Calvinist teaching). Unlike Pelagius, he finds a necessary place for special divine action, though he has a naturalized conception of its effect, but with Pelagius he shares the view that sin cannot be inherited, that no one can be fairly blamed for another's sin, that we are neither morally good nor evil at birth. Given a clean slate and human malleability, everything turns on education.

Locke's doctrine of malleability has been subjected to considerable criticism in recent years. There is an argument to the effect that the empiricism on which it rests is linked historically, and in some sense conceptually, with oppressive social doctrines. Versions of this argument, with explicit reference to Locke, can be found in Noam Chomsky, *Reflections on Lan-*

guage, H. M. Bracken, *Berkeley*, and Ellen Wood, *Mind and Politics*.[6] Chomsky allows that empiricism served as a doctrine of progress and enlightenment for a time; but drawing on Bracken's study, he points to its rise to ascendancy in association with the development of "possessive individualism," imperial expansion, and the concomitant growth of racist ideology. The mere association of empiricism with these developments in the time scale of modern history would not establish very much: the same association can be made out for rationalism and any number of other movements. The case would need to rest on some more internal link between empiricism and oppression. Chomsky suggests such a connection in the following way:

> The [empiricist] concept of the "empty organism," plastic and unstructured, apart from being false, serves naturally as the support for the most reactionary social doctrines. If people are, in fact, malleable and plastic-beings with no essential psychological nature, then why should they not be controlled and coerced by those who claim authority, special knowledge, and a unique insight into what is best for those less enlightened? (*Reflections on Language* 132)

This indictment of empiricism turns on its notion of human malleability and the associated view that there is no essential human nature. This general position, Chomsky believes, is characteristic of contemporary thought, occurring in one form or another in the prevalent positivist outlook in science, in behaviorism and psychoanalysis, as well as in Marxist and existentialist philosophy. Furthermore, the origin of this outlook in modern thought is to be traced importantly to Locke. Passmore's account of Locke's rejection of the orthodox doctrine of original sin effectively supports the same line of criticism.

In his rejection of the orthodox doctrine, Locke is held to have excluded even the idea that there is a natural tendency to good or evil in human beings: that is why he sees the possibilities of education as boundless. This account of Locke's view is not entirely justified, however. It is true that Locke was critical of the idea, which was beginning to gain ground in some quarters in the seventeenth century (in reaction to Hobbes for example), that human beings are born with a natural tendency to goodness. It is also true that he rejected the Augustinian view of an inborn tendency to evil, as well as Hobbes' more generalized pessimism about human nature and human social relations. Against both poles, his general contention is that we acquire virtue or vice through a process of habituation. But in the treatise on education Locke speaks of the importance of acquiring genuinely virtuous habits which are "woven into the very principles of [human] nature" (§ 42). Such talk does not involve any claim to an innate tendency to goodness. It is suggestive, however, of the idea of an inbuilt basis for the acquisition of virtue as well as the idea of fixed standards by which genuine virtue might be judged. (This could be compared with Aristotle's view that while we are fitted by nature to acquire the virtues, we have to learn to take pleasure in the right things.)

It is also clear that, whatever his account of original sin, Locke thought that human beings ordinarily have certain inborn inclinations away from virtue. He comments cautiously that "few of Adam's children are so happy, as not to be born with some Byass in their natural Temper, which it is the Business of Education either to take off, or counterbalance" (§ 139). He considers that our first actions "are guided more by Self-love, than Reason or Reflection," so that children are apt to deviate from the just measures of Right and Wrong" (§ 110). More generally, he thinks that virtue and wisdom consist in the acquisition of mastery over one's inclinations and the submission of appetite and passion to reason (§ 200; cf. 108). Locke's "empty organism" is rather less empty than either Chomsky's or Passmore's account would suggest.

There is a further relevant consideration. Passmore claims that Locke rejects Pelagius' teaching that the basic, innate human power and gift of God is the freedom of the will, which gives us the power to act for good or ill. Locke is credited rather with the view that, "we become free . . . by habituation, we are not born free by nature." Pelagius' claims, reflected in his polemical exchanges with Augustine, are far from clear, but he could hardly have thought that we are born with the active power of exercising freedom. In any case, Locke observes in *The Second Treatise of Government* that, "we are *born Free*, as we are born Rational; not that we have actually the Exercise of either; Age, that brings one, brings with it the other too."[7] He goes on to argue that freedom is grounded in rationality. Contrary to Passmore's claim, therefore, Locke does not treat it as a matter of habituation alone. On two matters, then, Passmore exaggerates the extent to which Locke rejects the idea of a determinate human nature. Accordingly, there is exaggeration in his suggestion that, for Locke, custom or habit constitutes "first nature" inasmuch as there is no given nature on which it might be built. Locke's ideas need to be seen in the climate of thought in which they originated. Against an extreme Augustinian view, revived by Jansenists and others, according to which human nature is essentially and irremediably corrupt, Locke asserts that the acquisition of virtue is possible. Against a more moderate, but more generally entrenched, religious view, he holds that the acquisition of virtue is possible without the need of special divine grace — that is, it is possible by human powers. This possibility has to reside in human nature, and its realization through education needs to follow principles of human nature. Along with this, Locke rejects the view that human beings are naturally virtuous: virtue has to be acquired, he maintains, by a demanding process. The claim that habit or custom constitutes "first nature" in his account is not properly justified.

Locke denies that we are born virtuous or vicious. Does he also deny that we have any innate passions as Passmore supposes? His discussion of this matter, as with his moral inquiry generally, is thin. However, there is one passage in the treatise on education of considerable interest:

> I told you before that Children love Liberty. . . . I now tell you, they love something more; and that is *Dominion*: and this is the first Original of most vicious Habits, that are ordinary and natural. (§ 103)

Locke goes on to claim that the love of power and domination associated with dominion shows up very early in two forms of behavior, the desire of the child to have its own way in all matters and the desire to possess things, that is, to have property.

It is clear from the context that Locke considers that these desires or tendencies precede any process of habituation, being original sources of forms of behavior. Although he does not offer any account of their provenance, it is clear that he considers that they are general features of human nature: he suggests that anyone who has not observed them working in children could not have given much attention to infant behavior. The attribution of these tendencies to children is compatible with holding that we are born without virtue or vice, but not with the view that we have no inborn tendencies in this respect. Of course, we might reasonably object that Locke has arrived at his generalization on very thin inductive evidence and that his observation is guided by theory. It could be claimed, for example, that he makes the mistake of attributing to the very young child attitudes of wilfulness and acquisitiveness which are appropriate only to certain forms of adult behavior. The behavior of children may be more opaque than he supposes. But these queries do not affect the immediate question, whether Locke recognizes any passions as innate. It could be noted that, of the two original loves, Locke holds that the love of liberty is to be encouraged to the extent that it fits with appropriate (virtuous) behavior; by contrast, the love of power and possession is to be weeded out as the major source of injustice and strife.[8]

Granted that Locke's discussion of the love of liberty and dominion does not go very deeply into the topic of the passions, he nevertheless fixes them at a radical level in human nature. This is linked with the more general view espoused in the treatise that human beings have a "natural Propensity to indulge Corporal and present Pleasure, and to avoid Pain at any rate" (§ 48). A similar point is made in Book I of Locke's *Essay Concerning Human Understanding*, in the argument against the prevalent thesis that the mind is furnished from birth with certain truths of understanding, innate speculative and practical ideas. He grants that there are innate practical principles, specifically a desire for happiness and an aversion to misery, but these, he insists, are inclinations of appetite, not truths laid down in the understanding:

> Nature, I confess, has put into Man a desire of Happiness, and an aversion to Misery: These indeed are innate practical Principles . . . ; but these are Inclinations of the Appetite to good, not Impressions of truth on the Understanding. I deny not that there are natural tendencies imprinted on the Minds of Men. . . . (*Essay* I, III, 3)

At the same time, Locke would say that the natural inclinations of the appetite to good are not, as such, desires for the morally good. This is brought out in a more recondite passage in Locke's writings, a marginal note written in his copy of Thomas Burnet's third series of *Remarks* (on his *Essay*):

> Men have a natural tendency to what delights and from what pains them. This, universal observation has established beyond doubt. That the soul has such a tendency to what is morally good and from what is morally evil has not fallen under my observation, and therefore I cannot grant it for as being.[9]

Before returning to this passage, it is worth noting that Locke distinguishes between what he calls wants of nature and wants of fancy. Parents, he argues, should supply the former and turn children's desires away from the latter as much as possible. Natural wants are specified as those which "reason alone, without some other Help, is not able to fence against, nor keep from disturbing us" (§ 107). He has in mind, in particular, the need for relief from pain, hunger and thirst, the need for shelter, for sleep, and for rest and relaxation after work, needs which arise inescapably. Once again, the Lockean version of malleability acknowledges constraints arising from factors rooted in the conditions of human existence.

In *The Perfectibility of Man*, Passmore cites the passage from the *Marginalia Lockeana* quoted above as indicating that Locke holds that, "men are born with one, and only one natural impulse — the morally neutral impulse to pursue what gives them pleasure and avoid what gives them pain. Apart from that one natural tendency their minds are entirely devoid of any impulses whatever."[10] It is not clear that Locke's starting point in this domain is greatly different from the Aristotelian view. But even if it is conceded that everything Locke says on the matter can be brought under this general umbrella, it is misleading to say that the impulse is treated as morally neutral. The context of Locke's denial of a natural tendency to what is morally good and from what is morally evil in this source is provided by Burnet's view of conscience as a "natural Sagacity to distinguish Moral Good and Evil . . . [anticipating] all External Laws and all Ratiocination."[11] Locke's position rests on his rejection of the view that we have an innate and innately effective source of moral *knowledge* of the sort Burnet supposes. Locke's view (like Aristotle's) is that such knowledge has to be acquired by habituation and teaching. But the natural impulses of the desire for happiness and aversion to misery, being "inclinations of the appetite to good," are treated as relevant to moral considerations. In the treatise on education, Locke claims explicitly that the natural propensity to seek immediate physical gratification is "the Root from whence spring all Vitious Actions, and the Irregularities of Life" (§ 48). Thus, Passmore's account distorts Locke's views by simplification and exaggeration.

The points I have assembled do not constitute anything like a strong view about innate characteristics. But they provoke the question as to how Locke became the rallying point for the proponents of nurture over nature which developed in the eighteenth century, a secular echo, as Passmore suggests, of the Pelagian versus Augustinian dispute of the previous thousand years. Part of an answer is that Locke himself engaged in a degree of simplification and exaggeration in presenting his views (as in the phrase at the head of this section). Locke's writings, and notably the treatise on education, attracted a wide readership. Even so, the conception of him as the champion of malleability emerged strongly only in the second half of the eighteenth century. By then, the idea of malleability was promoted by writers who pushed his position considerably further than he himself had gone (writers such as John Gay, David Hartley, and Joseph Priestley in England, or de Condillac and Helvetius in France). I will return to the question of the context in regard to this issue in section 3, and take up larger aspects of eighteenth-century moral thought in later chapters.

Locke looked to earlier traditions to a considerable extent in his moral and political thought (in connection with natural law theory and in his account of the idea of the state of nature and the social contract, for example). But he was in most things a powerful critic of reliance on authority and secondhand opinion and a major defender of the modern way of thinking and the new science. He stands to the eighteenth century as the chief proponent of the power of education, especially in the moral sphere. Furthermore, although the trappings of the Christian moral outlook remain, the education in question is predominantly secular. With Locke, a view of education as the source of human growth and improvement took the place, as Passmore observes, of doctrines of divine grace. It is not simply that original sin no longer poses an obstacle to moral development — after all, the Jesuit educationists of the seventeeth century had made that clear; just as importantly, Locke sees no need for a doctrine of grace at all. He does not deny that there are obstacles to the process of education, some of them inborn, but he proclaims that education can overcome them. Nor is he required to deny the existence of innate dispositions and powers, for he has only to hold (as he does) that education is needed to develop them or, where appropriate, curb them.

2. Themes in Moral Education

Lockean confidence in the power of education is to be contrasted with attitudes engendered in some sources in the seventeenth century by versions of Augustinian pessimism or religious abasement and resignation. In stressing the power of education, Locke was also reacting to the sustained attacks on learning and the value of education which had characterized the Civil War period in England. His conviction about what education can achieve is not accompanied by a vision splendid of some great end to be realized or the promise of indefinite progress and human achievement (such as Descartes could envisage). This perspective in the context of a doctrine of malleability was to be supplied by subsequent thinkers and activists in later generations. Locke's own presentation of the case is sober and prosaic, singularly lacking in the rhetoric which is characteristic of writing on education. He takes the view that education can make human beings virtuous (as well as wise, well-mannered, and learned), or at least, that it is the only hope of attaining these ends since they are not gifts of nature or divine grace. Along with this, he claims to provide a guide to the necessary method or technique for achieving the goals.

THE GENTLEMAN'S CALLING AND MORAL FORMATION

Before examining Locke's proposals concerning the technique of moral education, note should be taken of the provenance and precise scope of his concern. The treatise on education grew out of a series of letters, beginning in 1684, which Locke wrote from Holland to his close friend, Mr Edward Clarke, and his wife concerning the education of their son, then eight years old. Clarke, a member of the landed gentry in Somerset and a distant relative of Locke's by marriage, had requested advice; Locke, absent from England for reasons of health and politics, clearly warmed to the idea. Over the next several years he wrote regularly to the Clarkes on the topic. The letters formed the basis of *Some Thoughts Concerning Education*, which he published (though not at first in his own name) in 1693, in the conviction that the views espoused with reference to a child in one family could have more general application and value.[12] At the same time, Locke explicitly conceived his undertaking as having a definite class and gender orientation. He wrote with a view to the education of the sons of gentlemen, holding that, "a Prince, a Nobleman, and an ordinary Gentleman's Son, should have different ways of Breeding" (§ 216).

Locke, like Aristotle, albeit in a very different age and social order, subscribed to a stratified conception of society, marked out by distinct and given "callings." In this connection, he held that the calling "most to be taken care of is the Gentleman's Calling. For if those of that Rank are by their Education once set right, they will quickly bring all the rest into order."[13] Concerning the education of classes other than the rank of gentleman and the education of women as a whole, he says nothing in the treatise, nor was he concerned very directly with the education proper for a scholar. What belongs to a gentleman's calling, as Locke expounds it, is "to have the Knowledge of a Man of Business, a Carriage suitable to his Rank, and to be Eminent and Useful in his Country according to his Station"

(§ 94). The emphasis in education thus falls on the acquisition of what is of "most and frequentest use to him in the World," on public bearing, and a corresponding moral formation. Latin and Greek, which were so important in the education of elites before Locke's time (and were to be again in the age of empire), are played down in this curriculum for the man of property; knowledge of the sciences is supposed only to a broad level, fit for a gentleman.

Locke's primary concern in the treatise, therefore, was with a very small class of men, 4 to 5 percent of the population at most, it is calculated. As J. L. Axtell observes, "this tiny minority owned most of the wealth, wielded the power, and made all the decisions — political, social, economic — for the whole nation."[14] The social order, as Locke willingly acknowledged, guaranteed the general significance of the education of the chosen group. Apart from this general influence, the idea of universal formal education could hardly have occurred to Locke and would certainly have been considered inappropriate. On the evidence of his report to the Board of Trade in 1697 (as one the commissioners), education for the children of the poor would consist essentially in the use of the Bible for the inculcation of appropriate moral attitudes (obedience, industriousness, thrift, gratitude, and the like).[15]

Locke was also drawn to comment on the upbringing of daughters of gentlemen in a letter of February 1685 in reply to a request from Mrs Clarke concerning her daughter.[16] The letter contains less detail than one might expect. For girls, hardly less than for boys, Locke puts considerable emphasis on robust physical well-being, to be acquired through plain diet and exercise in the open air; emphasis is placed too on the development of physical grace in bearing and movement, to be developed by dancing lessons. Education in regard to truth, virtue, and obedience is held not to involve any difference of sex, except that the "governing and correcting [of daughters] . . . properly belongs to the mother" (346); otherwise, the same principles apply as for boys. This difference, it is worth noting, is significant enough, being linked with the transmission of different attitudes between men and women, associated with differences of place in the family and civil society (in which men alone are members of the body politic). The primary explicit difference Locke points to in regard to the education of girls derives from the assumption that girls, unlike most boys of this class, will not be sent away to school. Remaining in the domestic sphere, girls do not become part of the public order of the world. Locke says nothing in the letter to Mrs Clarke about an appropriate curriculum for girls. It is clear, if implicit in what he says, that they should acquire the skills and knowledge and social and moral attitudes in keeping with their essentially domestic role as the future wives of gentlemen and mothers of children.

Notwithstanding its initially limited concern, Locke's treatise on education clearly belonged to the period in which childhood had been discovered (or re-discovered).[17] It quickly ran through four editions in the last decade of the century, and a definitive text was ready shortly before Locke's death in 1704 for the fifth edition which appeared the following year. A French translation appeared as early as 1695, to be followed by translations in all the major European languages and by numerous editions as the eighteenth century unfolded. Pierre Coste, the French translator of this text as well as of Locke's *Essay Concerning Human Understanding* and some of his other writings, was convinced that the work would (and should) have quite general application (see note below). Beginning with letters concerning the education of one child, Locke became the universal educationist for much of Europe during much of the eighteenth century.

The technique of moral education which Locke offers is fundamentally a process of habituation, the inculcation of specified behavioral habits from the earliest possible stage. This was hardly new in itself, but it was put forward by a thinker who was independently well known for his views on the origin, certainty, and extent of knowledge, and for his teaching about the power of custom and the "association of ideas" in the *Essay Concerning Human Understanding*, and who, as a medical practitioner, spoke with a ring of authority on child-rearing in general. Apart from a natural correspondence of some ideas (to be discerned by reason), most combinations of ideas, so Locke proposed in the *Essay*, arise from decision, chance or custom, depending commonly in turn on a person's education (II, XXXIII, 5 and 6). In this lies the importance of education, a consideration which Locke emphasized again in the same chapter of the *Essay* (8ff) as well as in the treatise on education.

The domain of moral formation as Locke portrays it is the experience of pleasure and pain, to be modified through regular practice and the use of rewards and punishments. If we assume that the child is conceived initially as an "empty organism," the model of habituation we are offered could be quite similar to one or another version of moral development put forward in twentieth-century behaviorist psychology or empiricist learning theory. If the account is filled out in somewhat different ways, it may be closer to the sort of account given by Plato or Aristotle, or the imaginative rethinking of Aristotle's ethics in a Christian setting by Thomas Aquinas in the thirteenth century. For a just appraisal, we need to consider more fully the method, content, and idea of motivation which make up Locke's account of moral education.

As regards moral knowledge, Locke proposed that a science of morals, comparable to mathematics, is possible; but he did not make any proper start toward providing such a systematic account.[18] In *Concerning Education*, as elsewhere, he claims that it is enough for practical purposes to follow the moral teaching of the Gospels, which contain all we need to know.[19] More generally, his consideration of moral beliefs and practices in this source and in other writings is thin and not entirely consistent. In contrast to Thomas Aquinas and the Greek philosophers, he does not offer any detailed consideration of the role of reason and the passions in morality; nor does he provide any treatment of the moral virtues except in the most general way. Thus the idea of ethics as the fruit of rational understanding and inquiry is regularly invoked in his writings. Virtue consists in the right ordering of desires to reason: the "right improvement and exercise of our Reason, [is] the highest perfection, that a Man can attain in this life" (§ 122). Custom, it is declared, needs to be based on reason, not mere tradition, and in the background, there is the concept of a natural moral law discernible by reason or identified as reason: "the *State of Nature* has a Law of Nature to govern it, which obliges every one; and reason, which is that Law, teaches all Mankind, who will but consult it, that being all equal and independent, no one ought to harm another in his Life, health, Liberty, or Possessions."[20] But in the end, morality is made to rest on authority. The content of morality, Locke supposes, can be drawn from the Bible (§ 185), and its foundation is placed in the possession of a true notion of God whose will constitutes the true ground of morality. In making this proposal, Locke was subscribing, unselfconsciously, to the position which had been subjected to powerful criticism long before in Plato's *Euthyphro* (see chapter one above). One could suppose that Locke, if he were pressed, would hold that the grounds of morality are to be found in the proper use of reason and that this would be found to correspond to the biblical teaching. But these are questions which he does not pursue.[21]

The Lockean account of the role of reason in the moral development of children is similarly clouded. In various passages Locke emphasizes the importance of reasoning with children in ways adapted to their understanding, and speaks of the need for a grasp of good principles. But the major emphasis by far falls on the inculcation of habits which, he says, work "more constantly and with greater facility than Reason" (§ 110). This picks up a central theme of the *Essay Concerning Human Understanding*, that "custom settles Habits of Thinking in the Understanding, as well as of Determining in the Will, and of Motions in the Body" (II, XXXIII, 6). Locke's emphasis on habit leads Passmore to conclude that the only essential requirement for Lockean moral education is habit-formation and that, for Locke, *true* virtue consists in the possession of habits without need of knowledge or understanding. In this way, Passmore is able to present a straightforward transition from Locke to the moral developmental theories of twentieth-century behaviorists such as J. B. Watson or B. F. Skinner. This transition is smoothed by the neglect of aspects of Locke's ideas on the matter, but is made more plausible in being able to trade on Locke's failure to provide a consistently worked out account of morality.

Locke speaks glowingly of the place of reason in ethics and of the need to develop understanding along with the formation of good habits, but he fails to show how the components fit together in a unified structure. Worse than that, he fails to acknowledge the problems involved in working out a rational account of ethics and the further problems of communicating that understanding to children in their development. It is possible, then, though not entirely fair, to conclude that Locke's appeal to reason in this context is an idle wheel in the mechanism: the real work is done by the power of authority (the authority of the Bible, of the State, of parents, or of fashion) together with the human susceptibility to conditioning which builds on the force of the association of ideas.

Plato and Aristotle and long centuries of Christian reflection and practice had similarly emphasized the centrality of habit-formation in moral development. None of these sources would allow, of course, that acquired habit alone is sufficient for moral virtue; as we saw in connection with Aristotle, virtue presupposes understanding and right motive. In spite of Passmore's suggestion to the contrary, Locke did not think that acquired habit is sufficient for virtue either. This is sufficiently clear from his insistence on the rational component of virtue and his attention to the need for reasoning with children. It is made even clearer by Locke's special use of the term person (or self) which is elaborated in Book II of the *Essay Concerning Human Understanding*. "Person" is used to connote the human being as fully developed, as one capable of intelligent action and as fully responsible for one's behavior.[22] J. W. Yolton expresses its import as follows:

> "Person" refers to a man who can take responsibility for his actions and who is concerned with those actions and their consequences, a man who is vitally interested in his moral worth and his happiness, and who recognises he is God's workmanship. It is the concern — the moral, responsible concern — taken for what he does which Locke stresses in his depiction of a person. . . . A moral man becomes a person when he learns to act intentionally, out of deliberation over right and good, in respect of moral laws which are or are ultimately based upon God's law. Another way to bring out what Locke is saying is to remark that one cannot act responsibly and morally by chance, unconsciously, or just out of habit.[23]

This captures Locke's best thoughts and intentions, but his account of the matter is underdeveloped and subject to a degree of unclarity. He thus leaves his position open to the sort of interpretation which Passmore reads into it. His account of morality and moral development is particularly vulnerable in regard to motivation.

IN LOVE WITH THE PLEASURE OF BEING WELL THOUGHT OF

The end to be achieved in moral development, as Locke conceives it, is the situation in which a person is able to resist his or her desires, inclination or appetite, whenever these clash with the guidance of reason (mediated, it is to be remembered, by the voice of authority). This is the principle and foundation of all virtue. To act well, therefore, is to act according to reason (authority). At the same time, the nature of moral good and evil lies in relation to the domain of pleasure and pain. Good and evil are taken to be productive of pleasure and pain respectively, though they are not to be *equated* with the pleasant and the painful. Our natural propensity, Locke holds, is to seek physical and present pleasure and always to avoid pain. In a range of cases, however, this propensity will clash with the guidance of reason. One must then learn to recognize what reason requires, and have developed the corresponding habits. At this point Locke follows Plato and Aristotle once again in holding that the formation of habits has to precede understanding. Habits in turn are to be acquired through practice rather than the learning of rules — reinforced by appropriate motivation. The emphasis on practice rather than rule-learning again echoes an Aristotelian idea. It also fits in with Locke's pedagogical views in other domains, notably in regard to language-learning in which he emphasizes practice in speaking as against learning rules of grammar (§ 168). But the problem for Locke in the domain of moral learning is twofold: the goal of understanding appears to give way in the end to rule by authority; and he is unable to give a satisfactory account of motivational development.

Locke holds that the only possible motives for a rational being are reward and punishment, experienced respectively as good and evil. This principle is to be applied to children: they are rational beings, moved by the idea of rewards and punishments. At the same time, their capacity for thought and understanding is limited: it is effected best, Locke suggests, by reasons "such as may (if I may say so) be felt, and touched" (§ 81; cf. 54). The task of moral education is to bring the child to the point where it has mastery over its inclinations and willingly submits appetite to reason, and the first step to this outcome is the use of rewards and punishments to establish the requisite habits. The art of moral education, then, is to provide the right sort of reward and punishment in the right setting.

The general setting for moral formation, it is assumed, is the family relationship of parent and child. The recommended setting, more specifically, is one which elicits fear and awe and respect as the basis of absolute obedience to the father's authority in the early years, to be followed in later years by increasing familiarity and friendship: "Fear and Awe ought to give you the first Power over their Minds, and Love and Friendship in riper years to hold it" (§ 42). To be fair, Locke puts considerable stress on familial affection and on making children's lives as pleasant and agreeable as possible where things are "not injurious to their Health and Vertue" (§ 53). And he holds that correction should be kept to a minimum.

In the matter of correction, Locke took a particularly strong stand against corporal punishment, countenancing it only in extreme cases of insubordination (§§ 47–52; 78). His argument is that corporal punishment, by an association of ideas, breeds in children a hatred for things they should be encouraged to like. Either it creates a slavish temper in which a person

obeys only for fear of punishment without any change in natural inclination, or it ruins the child for life by breaking its spirit. In any case, the use
of corporal punishment is self-defeating in overcoming our natural tendencies in regard to pleasure and pain — "our Natural Propensity to indulge
Corporal and present Pleasure, and to avoid Pain at any rate" — since it
reinforces those same tendencies, viz., to prefer the greater corporal
pleasure or avoid the greater corporal pain. For the same reason, Locke is
critical of rewards such as sweets, new clothes, or money, which provide
immediate physical gratification or otherwise satisfy the child's natural
inclination to pleasure. Rewards of this sort cater to natural inclination and
desire, he suggests, and provide a basis for the vices of luxury, pride,
covetousness, and so on: "What Principle of Vertue do you lay in a Child,
if you will redeem his Desires of one Pleasure, by the proposal of another?"
(§ 55; cf. 52).

The great secret of education, Locke proposes, is to "get into Children a
Love of Credit, and an Apprehension of Shame and Disgrace," on which
basis they become subject to *esteem* and *disgrace* (§ 56). These motives, the
most powerful incentives of the mind once they are developed, rest
respectively on the love of credit and the apprehension of shame, the love
of praise and commendation and reputation and the dislike of criticism and
blame and ill-repute. The first stage of development is accorded a natural
basis: from an early age "children are very sensible of Praise and Commendation. They find a pleasure in being esteemed, and valued, especially by
their Parents, and those whom they depend on" (§ 57). The desire for
praise, then, is to be used as a lever against the immediate inclinations of
self-love (as in conflict with reason). The immediate and obvious requirement is for a show of parental affection when the child acts well and cold
reproof when it acts badly. Along with this, parents are to see to it that
"other agreeable or disagreeable Things should constantly accompany
these different States." They are encouraged to orchestrate a situation in
which things go well quite generally for the child who acts well and badly
for the one who does not, with the aim of shaming children out of their
faults and making them in love with the pleasure of being well thought of.
Thus the objects of desire help toward virtue: the child comes to learn that
the things it delights in can be enjoyed only by one in a state of reputation;
in making children in love with the pleasure of being well thought of, "you
may turn them as you please, and they will be in Love with all the Ways of
vertue" (§ 58). In this manner, so Locke proposes, the pleasures of the
mind supplant physical and immediate pleasures as the foundation of true
moral virtue.

It is not possible to treat this teaching merely as a piece of pragmatic
advice in the matter of child-rearing. Notwithstanding the parallels with
Aristotle's treatment of these issues *up to a point* (the role of parental
affection and the early stage of shame), Locke's proposals mark a dramatic

shift in the history of moral thought. In a word, Locke makes self-esteem and concern with reputation the foundation of moral development and morality. Simultaneously, and without any apparent sense of strain, he recommends the moral teaching of the Gospel. By way of concession he grants that reputation "is not the true Principle of Measure of Vertue," which is given as knowledge of the will of God through the light of reason (§ 61). Nevertheless, the sense of credit and shame, linked with praise and blame, is specified as the stock on which "to graft the true Principles of Morality and Religion" (§ 200). Nor does Locke make any attempt to explain how this motivation is to be modified by moral understanding or how the latter is to be acquired. He takes reward and punishment as the only possible motives for a rational being; there is no hint in his account of the Socratic — and Aristotelian — idea of the reward of virtue being internal to its practice, nor of the Christian conception of morality as presupposing *caritas*, the non-self-interested love of God, as the primary love even though he appeals to the morality of the Gospel. (One could argue, on the other hand, that Locke is influenced by a religious outlook in which morality is linked with a conception of eternal reward and punishment.)

The criticism of Locke's account of moral motivation is not that praise and blame are taken as natural and reasonable in the moral education of children and as a proper dimension of human relations. Moral views which object to such practice (not uncommon in some seventeenth-century religious circles) breathe an air of self-denying narrowness and unreality. The objection concerns rather the centrality of the motivation in Locke's account, its effective exclusiveness, the externality of its relationship to moral values, the idea that behavior is essentially tied to the promotion of pleasurable feelings, and the easy assumption that the established practices of praise and blame in a society in association with reputation can be taken as fair guides to moral goodness and badness.

Though Locke might protest, his idea of the love of the pleasure of being well thought of is akin to the notion of *amour-propre* which, in common use in French moral thought in the seventeenth century, had meant vainglory, an addiction to seeking one's honor, or more simply, vanity.[24] In a stronger and more technical sense, Jansenist writers in this period had treated it precisely as the negation of charity (the love of God) and the root of evil. It would seem that Locke chose a singularly inappropriate basis for morality and moral development (and religion). Yet, as Anthony Levi points out, *amour-propre* came to be widely accepted in the eighteenth century as the entirely proper basis of virtuous behavior, as for example in the writings of Fontenelle, de Mandeville, Voltaire, d'Holbach, and Bayle.[25] By this stage, the notion had become associated with the idea of reasonable self-interest from which it had previously been distinguished. Locke reflects this partial change of sense, blurring the distinction between *amour de soi* and *amour-*

propre which was to be revived in an amended form by Rousseau in the second half of the eighteenth century. He was also probably an important influence on the emergence of this account of moral motivation since his writings were widely read on the Continent as well as in England.

Locke presumes to redeem vanity by linking it to morally good behavior and advantage generally: "Since we are all, even from our Cradles, vain and proud Creatures, let [children's] vanity be flattered with Things, that will do them good; and let their Pride set them on work on something which may turn to their Advantage" (§ 119). Self-interest is similarly incorporated into morality, as can be seen in Locke's discussion of "the Law of Opinion or Reputation" as the common measure of virtue and vice in the *Essay Concerning Human Understanding* (II, XXVIII, 10–12). Locke does not equate reputation or the "law of fashion" with the law of nature or the law of God, which he treats as the *true* rule of right and wrong, but he is confident that the former everywhere corresponds substantially with the latter since "men without renouncing all Sense and Reason, and their own Interest, which they are so constantly true to, could not generally mistake, in placing their Commendation and Blame on that side, that really deserved it not" (II, XXXVIII, 11). In Locke's treatment, the love of the pleasure of being well thought of has become respectable, as respectability itself has become central. This love would not be identified with vanity or vainglory, but its character is hardly different. There is a telling contrast, to which Passmore draws attention, between Locke's proposal and a theme in one of the essays of P. Nicole in his *Essais de Morale* (1671–78). In an essay "On Charity and Self-Love," Nicole had written:

> Entirely to reform the world, that is to banish from it all vices and all the grosser disorders . . . one would need, given the absence of charity, that men should possess an enlightened self-interest [un amour propre éclairé]. . . . However corrupted such a society might be within and to the eyes of God, there need be nothing lacking to it in the way of being well regulated . . . and what is even more wonderful is that although it would be entirely animated and moved by self-love [amour-propre], self-love would nowhere appear in it; and although it is entirely devoid of charity, one would see everywhere only the form and characteristics of charity.[26]

Nicole's thought-experiment has its basis in the fairly implausible suggestion in Augustine's much-studied commentary on the first epistle of John that, "vanity so nearly imitates the works of charity, that there is almost no difference between their effects." Thus a person, moved by the desire to be well thought of by others, might generally do what the virtuous do on the basis of the love of God and neighbor. Nicole suggests that those charged with the education of the aristocracy, if they cannot inspire in their pupils a sense of charity, might try at least to develop their *amour-propre* along the requisite lines: their behavior would then have the semblance of moral goodness and would be advantageous to others. Nicole's proposal is rich in irony since he goes on to argue that behavior based on *amour-propre* constitutes the way of death and is directly at odds with the way of life to which genuine morality, inspired by the love of God, is held to lead. Locke was certainly familiar with Nicole's essays (he had translated them into English, as Passmore points out). One is tempted to think that he must have read Nicole's advice regarding the education of the aristocracy and passed it on as his own prescription for moral development. But unlike Nicole, or Augustine, Locke is ensared by the idea that the love of praise and commendation can be brought within the ambit of virtue as its true foundation.

In an instructive example, which Rousseau was to seize upon in criticism, Locke proposes that children be encouraged in generosity to overcome the tendency to acquisitiveness:

> As to the having and possessing of Things, teach them to part with what they have easily and freely to their Friends; and let them find by Experience, that the most *Liberal* has always most plenty, with Esteem and Commendation to boot, and they will quickly learn to practice it. (§ 110)

Thus generosity is recommended in place of greed in keeping with Locke's view that covetousness, or the desire to possess more than we have need of, is the root of all evil, but generosity is recommended on a basis likely to encourage greed. Furthermore, the envisaged happy outcome — that the most liberal has always most plenty — indirectly confers the accolade of virtue on property-holders. And it relates to his view in the *Second Treatise of Government* that "God gave the World to the use of the Industrious and Rational" (§ 34); and that "he that incloses Land and has a greater plenty of the conveniencys of life from ten acres, than he could have from an hundred left to Nature, may truly be said to give ninety acres to Mankind" (§ 37). The problem in Locke's recommendation of generosity is symptomatic of internal inconsistency in his moral and educational theory and tensions between moral claims and approved social reality. In this case, the method he espouses for the promotion of virtue subverts its own subject. That must be accounted a major weakness in his view of the basis of moral development.

3. Doctrines of Malleability in Context

Locke's epistemology, it is generally agreed, is an uneasy mixture of empiricist and rationalist elements. His moral and educational theory similarly reflects the confluence of different sources whose relationships remain ill-defined in his writings: moral rationalism (morality as demonstrative science), morality as the expression of the will of God, natural law theory, and elements of Platonism, Aristotelianism, Stoicism, and Epicureanism which were current in the seventeenth century. Locke placed morality "amongst the Sciences capable of Demonstration" (with mathematics and geometry), but in the absence of any contribution to showing the place of reason in morality, the vacuum is filled by custom and authority, and his account of motivation is effectively subversive of virtue. But these criticisms, however valid, do not capture the full extent or character of his thought. It is not possible to present a fully consistent position which would be characteristic of the "real" Locke. An important part of his significance in the history of modern thought is that he reflects different and sometimes contending traditions. Part of his great influence on child-rearing and education in the eighteenth century is connected with this factor. At the domestic level, Dr. Locke's proposals for bringing up children are generally enlightened and humane, but could be invoked nonetheless in a harsh parental regime. More generally, Locke argues against "Old Custom" while leaving ample scope for moral traditionalism. In speaking for individual judgment against received opinion, he was lending support to the authority of the new social forces with which he himself was linked.

The character of Locke's ideas on moral development may appear quite different in different settings. As indicated earlier, it is not difficult to find terminological and structural connections between his account and what various twentieth-century behaviorists have to say on the matter. On the other hand, the discontinuities are also considerable. In contrast to the empiricism of the last one hundred years, for example, Locke did not subscribe to scientific determinism and he did not allow that mind and nature form a unitary law-governed system. Indeed, his belief in the power of education has to be set against Hobbesian mechanism, an idea of human nature fixed by metaphysical necessity. Against this background and other views of human nature as irremediably corrupted by sin, the Lockean belief in human malleability has inbuilt potential for liberation. This dimension of Locke's enterprise can easily be exaggerated, but should not be neglected. Attention to it throws light on a central element of his thought about education; in addition, it can provide a basis for reflection on the social and ethico-political ramifications of doctrines of malleability. This is part of the long-running and vexed set of questions concerning the roles of nature and nurture in human development.

In the context of late seventeenth-century conservatism — in religion and elsewhere — Locke's rejection of innate ideas and an Augustinian view of original sin can be seen as part of a case for social change, albeit of a limited sort. This is precisely the concluding message of *Some Thoughts Concerning Education*, where the possibility of change is predicated on our rational capacity to break free to some extent from dead tradition. Clearly, Locke believed that the changes to be effected through right educational ideas and practice were both *possible* and *desirable*. Furthermore, this belief — about what was possible and desirable in this sphere — obviously incorporated views about human beings and their powers and needs as part of a general view about human nature. Here we have the main elements for reflection on the ramifications of doctrines of malleability.

Etymologically, "malleability" carries a sense of passivity — something able to be hammered out of one shape into another. So Locke speaks of the child as "white paper, or wax, to be moulded and fashioned as one pleases" (§ 16). But the scope for molding here (hammering would hardly sound right in the context in question) is hedged in, in part, by given factors, in part, by moral and political considerations. It is action carried out by one set of people on others, but action which increasingly involves the active participation of the others. Furthermore, it draws its character from its general aim, which is the development of the powers of rationality and freedom exercised in morally good choice (allowing that this is a regulative ideal which is subject to all sorts of defects in any realized interpretation). Malleability in this context then becomes a question in general about what is fixed and unalterable and what is subject to development and change in the conditions of human life (including the ways in which we think about human nature). Such a question makes proper sense and can be assessed only in relation to specific historical situations and with reference to one or another philosophical anthropology (which brings in moral and political views about individuals and society). But a little more can be said about the question in general.

We need to distinguish between beliefs about malleability in general and beliefs which involve a commitment to trying to bring about change in human life. Clearly, one might think that change of a certain sort is possible without considering it desirable. A belief about malleability, then, could be treated as a function of the extent to which one thinks that genuine and significant change can be effected in individual and social life by human action (such as education, conditioning, medical procedures, revolution). Commitment to effecting change in practice depends, I suggest, on the extent to which one thinks the means are acceptable and the goals desirable. Locke spoke on occasions of unlimited possibilities; but on each of these measures — the possibility and desirability of change — his position was fairly limited. Beliefs about malleability and commitment to social action became vastly more pronounced some generations after Locke, in the late eighteenth and early nineteenth centuries — as with Helvetius, or William Godwin, or Robert Owen, to take three different examples. Why was this? Locke certainly contributed to the development, for one general reason was a growing belief in the power of techniques to effect change based, for example, on the associationist psychology which Locke had fostered. There was a growing sense that change in the conditions of human life (in the form of improvement) was possible. But with many social thinkers it was likely that a belief in the need for change, and hence its desirability, was the more powerful factor.

It might appear logical to try to work out first what sort of changes are possible independently of questions about their desirability. After all, it is stupid to desire what is not possible. But a generalized procedure of this sort would presuppose that we could settle on an account of human nature, in the form of "the facts" about human beings, without resort to moral or political ideas and historical context ("values"). Perhaps the belief that this can be done provides a way of specifying part of the character of modern positivist social science with its insistence on the separability of facts and values. A positivist standpoint is often associated with a belief in malleability. But it is instructive to recognize that this need not be so. Thus La Mettrie, the author of *L'Homme Machine*, originally criticized the Lockean malleability view for failing to appreciate the innate characteristics of human beings (which La Mettrie conceived mechanistically). Along with this, La Mettrie espoused naturalism and determinism, major preconditions of empiricist social science, and he held that inequalities among human beings in skill, knowledge, or virtue are due largely to inborn constitutional differences (a contention which is regularly associated in the twentieth century with the espousal of reactionary social views). Admittedly, the association of positivism with a doctrine of malleability is more familiar, accompanied by a belief in the power of scientific techniques to produce change. In theory, science would be held to establish what is fixed and the scope of possible change in value-free terms. But even if this were possible, a commitment to seeking change would reflect more than a belief about malleability — it would reflect convictions about the *desirability* of the change and an endorsement of the means science provides. In any case, the positivist program founders on the belief that an adequate account of human nature is possible independent of value beliefs.

A doctrine of malleability has an entirely different character in the hands of someone whose effective starting point is a belief in the desirability of social change along definite lines. A belief of this sort may be based on an immediate practical concern over the conditions of existence in some specific context or may reflect some broad moral and political (or even religious) point of view. Malleability, conceived as the possibility of change, is then invoked at least to the extent of making sense of the degree of change thought desirable. Of course, the beliefs of reformers or revolutionaries about what is desirable may be hopelessly utopian or contravene in some other way any realistic appraisal of what is possible for human beings (as in the once popular talk in the Soviet Union about "new socialist man"). Or the commitment may include features which many people would consider morally objectionable and undesirable whatever their possibility. Contrary to Chomsky's suppositions that the espousal of malleability goes with the repudiation of an essential human nature, versions of malleability along the lines just noted are not necessarily opposed to essentialist theories of human nature.

A belief in malleability in this context may well involve a fairly explicit view of a true human essence as something to be achieved or uncovered through rituals, education, legislation, social reform, or revolution, for example, rather than as something already given. The theory may also include an account of history (as in some major religions and in some versions of Marxism for example) designed to explain how the development of this essence was lost, frustrated, or simply set (by God or "History") as a goal to be achieved. And it may provide a blueprint for recovering it or bringing it into existence or else a predictive account of how change of the appropriate sort will occur without reliance on human will. In short, a malleability doctrine may go along with a strong theory of an essential human nature. There are numerous examples of this sort in the religions and philosophies and social movements of both East and West. In other words, there is no reason for thinking that there is any deep conceptual tension between belief in malleability and belief in an essential psychological nature. Nor is there any good reason for thinking, in advance of actual inspection, that a belief in malleability provides natural support for reactionary social doctrines. On the contrary, such a belief is a condition (though not sufficient of itself) for intelligent commitment to social change.

From a different perspective, consider the transition from belief in a fixed human essence, specified by what is natural or innate, to belief about the desirability or otherwise of change. Convictions about what is natural or innate can obviously serve to support the belief that change is undesirable or undesirable in a particular area, and it often serves as a basis for moral opposition to social reform, especially in fundamentalist circles, the assumption being that it is wrong even to try to change what is natural. There is a good case for thinking that the doctrine of innate moral principles to which Locke objected in the *Essay Concerning Human Understanding* (I, III) had this conservative character among some of the bishops and theologians of the time. Should we conclude that belief in a fixed human essence serves naturally as a support for reactionary social doctrines? That too would be mistaken.

There is no way of deciding these questions without reference to the content of the beliefs and the circumstances in which they are held; even where claims enjoy a *prima facie* plausibility, there is no substitute for actual inspection. Consider, for example, the idea of a natural human right of free association. An appeal to such a right may be part of an attempt to resist restrictive change threatened by a repressive government or to restore a freedom in law already lost; or it may operate as a way of escaping responsibility for helping others or as an excuse for complicity in crime. In general, appeals to essential human characteristics may be linked with promoting change as much as resisting it. They may be linked with oppressive and reactionary social policies as much as with liberating policies. The general conclusion to be drawn from this is the now familiar point that it is a mistake to take a stand for or against theories about the human essence, or about malleability, independently of their specific content and historical context. This is compatible with holding that there are features of human nature, human needs and powers which, so far as we know, are universal and constant across cultures and history, basic characteristics of the species. These features provide part of a guide to a realistic account of malleability and a reasonable commitment to bringing about changes in the human condition. There are also possibilities which only make sense in a given culture or period of history, and there are needs and possibilities which have their basis in specific moral and political theories. A doctrine of malleability can be properly assessed only against a complex background of the possible and the desirable in a range of contexts.

To return now to Locke. The terms of the question, as I have suggested, have to do with attitudes to change on the basis of beliefs about what is possible and desirable. Consider now the main aspects of the Lockean context. The doctrine of original sin, in the strong form it took in many quarters in the seventeenth century, ruled out certain human possibilities: in particular, human beings were seen as irremediably corrupt and incapable of acquiring genuine virtue. In rejecting this doctrine in all but a residual form, Locke enlarged the accepted understanding of the scope of human possibility; specifically, genuine moral development by accessible means could now be seen as radically possible. This perspective dominates Locke's thought about education. His standpoint might have arisen from a predominantly scientific outlook on human nature in opposition to one based on religious belief — a transition which was becoming increasingly widespread. But in Locke's own argument, moral convictions, associated with his own religious beliefs, played the major role: he considered that the orthodox doctrine of original sin was morally offensive since it involved the idea of human beings being punished by an all-good God for wrongdoing which they had not committed. In addition, he was convinced that the acquisition of virtue along traditional lines was individually and socially desirable.

A similar diagnosis applies to Locke's relationship to Hobbesianism in the same context. A generation before Locke, in the period following the Civil War, Hobbes had presented a powerful and supposedly scientific model according to which human beings, conceived as essentially selfish machines, are locked by nature into universal enmity. Locke certainly rejected Hobbes' mechanistic materialism as an unacceptable science of human nature. Yet his argument against Hobbes proceeded, to a major degree, on broadly moral and political grounds. Thus he confronted the Hobbesian account of the state of nature with a version of the natural-law tradition of morality in which human beings are portrayed as naturally disposed to a degree of cooperation (without the need for an absolutist authority as postulated by Hobbes). As in the argument with the church-men concerning original sin (and their claims about innate moral knowl-edge), Locke's appeal to malleability is to be linked with his moral convictions and desires in opposition to the fixed constraints set by the Hobbesian view. This applies also to his confrontation with the patriar-chalist and absolutist views of Sir Robert Filmer with which he was most directly concerned in the *Two Treatises of Government*.[27]

In fact, Locke's inadequate account of morality could not match even the modest idea of human development he envisaged. In any case, the scope for applying the idea was restricted in his political thought and policy to a very small group of men in his society. His political thought in particular, with its unthought out moral implications, could then serve as a bastion of support for privilege and acquisitiveness. At the same time, the idea spread quickly in the eighteenth century that Locke's thoughts on edu-cation and moral upbringing could be applied quite generally without regard to class.[28] And by the end of the century, some early socialists appealed to Locke's political thought (especially the thesis relating prop-erty to labor in Chapter 5 of *The Second Treatise of Government*) in support of egalitarian moral values and social reform opposed to class divisions. Distinct from this, Locke enjoyed an established reputation as an impor-tant figure (albeit an underlaborer) in the new age of science. Specifically, his account of the origin of ideas in experience and his emphasis on the scope for the association of ideas and habit-formation generally lent sup-port to the program for a scientific psychology and, in the long course of time, to the values of positivist social engineering.

Locke's fairly modest idea of malleability reflected a liberating moral stance against certain religious and philosophical constraints on human development. It was accompanied by a traditional but theoretically impov-erished conception of virtue which was undermined by its associated motivational basis and which was directed, in any case, to the interests of a particular class. Then, as we have just noted, the Lockean idea of mallea-bility, suitably recast, was to keep company in the modern era with a variety of different moral and political stances.

6. Rousseau: Natural Goodness and Virtue

1. The Return to Origins

Rousseau's moral thought is marked by a profound concern in regard to the character of modern society. He believed that, for all its dazzling achievements, eighteenth-century culture was fundamentally corrupt:

> In the midst of so much philosophy, humanity, politeness, and sublime maxims, we have only a deceitful and frivolous exterior, honour without virtue, reason without wisdom, and pleasure without happiness.[1]

In this situation, social ties are based on illusion: beneath the veneer of politeness, society is driven by lust for power, egotism, and vanity. The individual "knows only how to live in the opinions of others"; the social bond enforces an abject and deceptive uniformity:

> Incessantly politeness requires, propriety demands; incessantly usage is followed, never one's own inclinations. We no longer dare seem what we are; and in this perpetual constraint the men who form this herd which we call society will all do the same things under the same circumstances.[2]

Rousseau's strictures, addressed immediately to his own time, are criticisms in particular of Parisian society in the mid-eighteenth century. But like Nietzsche's critique of European culture a century later, Rousseau's diagnosis of the evils of the day portends a world-historical thesis. In his inquiries, the whole nature of human society is placed in question. The path to this level of generality was smoothed by the adoption of a developmental approach, that is to say, an approach based on the idea that the understanding of social phenomena lies in the discovery — or construction — of their growth from an original state.

The "return to origins" was not at all a new approach. A model for it could be found in as familiar a source as Genesis or in other ancient accounts of the human condition such as Protagoras' speech in Plato's *Protagoras*.[3] But in the seventeenth and eighteenth centuries it had acquired the status of a scientific methodology, due in large measure to Hobbes. In elaborating his "civil science," a science of morals and politics to rank with geometry and physics, Hobbes had taken over ideas which were commonplace in late medieval political theory, notably the idea of a pre-political state of nature and the hypothesis that political authority rested in some sense on the agreement of the people. Interpreting these ideas in his own fashion, Hobbes brought them forward in the framework of a dynamic and highly elaborated genetic definition of civil society. Rousseau, as heir to the established methodology, adopted the same ideas, but no less than Hobbes he placed his own stamp on the common tradition.

Rousseau's primary conviction was that human beings are everywhere corrupt and degraded, a conviction which he elaborated with all the force of a Calvinist or Jansenist preacher. But in seeking to account for the human condition, Rousseau had no place for Calvinist or Jansenist ideas of original sin and divine wrath; in fact, he had no place even for a benign version of the doctrine of original sin.[4] Nature as coming from the hand of God, and as found in the human individual, is declared good. The problem lies rather in the forms of social relationship into which human beings have stumbled over the long history of development in our becoming moral and political beings.

For an assessment of Rousseau's account of morality and its development, one must try to fix the points at which the moral being is seen to emerge and then falter. This gives rise to the questions, (a) whether, in the given terms, different and more satisfactory forms of social relationships might have been possible; (b) whether the character of natural goodness might even now be developed, notwithstanding the prevalence of a corrupt social order; and (c) whether the corrupt social order itself might be turned around so that moral virtue could flourish naturally in civil society.

Rousseau deals with matters relating to the broad question of moral development — bearing on the possibility of a different human history — in the *Discourse on the Origins of Inequality* (the *Second Discourse*). This is the primary source for his account of the imagined transition from a healthy state of human existence to the broken forms of relationship in which civil society became established. The second of the questions noted above is taken up most fully in *Emile*, Rousseau's treatise on education which he described as being, more properly, a "rather philosophical work on the principle that *man is naturally good*."[5] In a remark which has bearing on the third of the questions, Rousseau observed in the *Confessions* that following his study of the history of morals:

> I had seen that everything is rooted in politics and that, whatever might be attempted, no people would ever be other than the nature of their government made them. So the great question of the best possible form of government seemed to me to reduce itself to this: "What is the nature of the government best fitted to create the most virtuous, the most enlightened, the wisest, and, in fact, the best people, taking the word 'best' in its highest sense?"[6]

His attempt to answer this question is given most fully in *The Social Contract*.[7]

My inquiry, bearing on Rousseau's views regarding morality and moral development, will take *Emile* as its primary focus.[8] *Emile* has important links with each of the other works. The development of Emile from child to adult follows loosely the general path of the development of mankind in the state of nature which is set out in the *Second Discourse*; the story of the race is re-told in the individual. Again, Emile, as adult moral being, is free, independent, and naturally good. He has a will which, in a virtuous society, would be in harmony with the General Will, the expression of which in law is in the true and morally enlightened interests of the community and all its members (as set out in the *Social Contract*). But he must live in the sort of corrupt social world which is depicted in the *First and Second Discourses*.[9]

2. The Age of Nature in the (Male) Child (*Emile*, II and III)

One of Rousseau's guiding ideas is the thought that we become moral beings only by entering into developed social relationships. He thus envisages the entirely reasonable idea of a primary, pre-moral stage of development in the child. But what is special in Rousseau's case is that this stage is thought of as extending, ideally, through childhood up to puberty. This is the stage of nature in the child, corresponding to his idea of the long pre-social childhood of mankind. It soon becomes clear, however, that the stage of nature can be maintained only by a high degree of artifice. The art takes the form of shielding the child as far as possible from what is corrupt and artificial in the social world, while fostering certain normative dispositions and conditions which are specified as natural. The pre-moral or natural stage is thus marked by a very definite regime of moral formation and growth.

In espousing natural forms of development in infancy, Rousseau begins from the consideration that the child is by nature helpless, dependent, and in need of affection. This reasonable observation is followed quickly, however, by a problematic claim. For Rousseau insists that nurture and the earliest education of the child rest naturally (and hence properly) with its mother; they are undoubtedly *woman's work*, he argues, because men are not equipped by nature to feed children. This argument, which appears at the beginning of *Emile*, would be unconvincing even if nature were identified with biology, but for all its weakness, it points to a significant general feature in Rousseau's account of moral development. *Emile* is concerned with the education of a male child. As the work unfolds, it becomes clear that, for women, the path of development and the corresponding ideal of morality is different in important respects. It is different insofar as women are assigned an essentially supportive role as contributors to male development (specifically as wives and mothers).

The ideal of Rousseauian natural development for men is self-sufficiency and independence from others as the condition of liberty:

Each of us, unable to dispense with the help of others, becomes so far weak and wretched. We were meant to be men, laws and customs thrust us back into infancy. (*Emile*, II, 49)

The condition of dependence and need for affection, which is natural in childhood, is thus tied specifically to a relationship to women. The ideal of self-sufficiency is defined, at its base, in terms of the overcoming of this relationship. This is highlighted in *Emile* by the insistence that the education of the male child beyond infancy rests naturally (and hence properly) with its father — or with a good tutor who takes his place. The question of Emile's relationship to women is set aside at this point until he arrives at puberty or, more properly, at a suitable age for marriage. In the meantime, Emile's future wife, Sophy, will have been educated primarily by her mother in a context of dependence, in preparation for her role as the dependable guardian of Emile's well-being and the mother of his children.

Rousseau holds in *Emile* that there is only one natural passion in human beings, self-love, *amour de soi*, an inborn inclination to self-preservation which, being natural, is deemed naturally good. Self-love in the infant takes the form of an instinct. But then in the context of dependence on others, the child's sentiment of self-love gives rise to a feeling of love for those who care for him, especially as he comes to recognize their desire to help him. The experience of being surrounded by kindly feelings in this way leads on to "the habit of a kindly feeling towards his species" (IV, 174).

At this point, the path of development lies open to a dramatic and radical shift. Rousseau continues:

But with the expansion of his relations, his needs, his dependence, active or passive, the consciousness of his relations to others is awakened, and leads to the sense of duties and preferences. Then the child becomes masterful, jealous, deceitful, vindictive. . . . Self-love which concerns itself only with ourselves, is content to satisfy our own needs; but selfishness, which is always comparing self with others, is never satisfied and never can be; for this feeling, which prefers ourselves to others, requires that they should prefer us to themselves, which is impossible. (IV, 174)

The radical shift is marked by the replacement of the natural sentiment of self-love, *amour de soi*, by a relative and artificial love of self, *amour-propre* (selfishness), which Rousseau sees as inspiring in men "all the harm they do to one another" (*Discourse on Inequality*, note [o], 222). This is the path to egotism and the wish to dominate others which is characteristic of social relations across human history. The path of natural progress by contrast lies in learning to be independent of others. Paradoxically, however, Emile can become independent only by a type of largely unrecognized dependence on his tutor. Later on, his independence will rely on the role of his wife, Sophy, as his guide, counsellor, and guardian.

One might conclude that no sooner is the child aware of social relationships than it is caught up in the web of *amour-propre*. It is likely that
Rousseau thinks that something of this sort happens, albeit by degrees, as
the common lot. But he also thinks that the pre-social and pre-moral stage
of nature can be prolonged by art. The art of the tutor is to hold off the
critical point at which the question of *amour-propre* becomes inescapable.
This point, Rousseau believes, comes with the onset of sexual desire and
love:

> As soon as a man needs a companion he is no longer an isolated
> creature, his heart is no longer alone. All his relations with his species,
> all the affections of his heart, come into being along with this. (IV, 175)

In the meantime, Rousseau sees himself as having opened up space
between the love of the other in infancy and the love of the other in early
manhood (the "other" being designated as woman in each case).

The regime of moral formation in the natural stage turns on the development of virtues which are thought to concern the self (as opposed to social
virtues, so-called). Thus, Emile in his fifteenth year is imagined as industrious, temperate, patient; steadfast, and full of courage. All that is needed to
acquire the social virtues, it is said, is knowledge of the relations which
make these virtues necessary, knowledge which Emile is deemed ready to
acquire. Furthermore, the conditions in which *amour-propre* might manifest
itself have been kept at bay (III, 170–71).

A look at these proposals suggests that it is questionable whether virtues
which concern the self are not also social virtues. Specifically, it is questionable whether the virtues in Rousseau's list could be acquired independently of a social context and in such a way that the social dimension enters
into the nature of the virtue. Indeed, it is doubtful whether a criterion
could be found for dividing up virtues in this way at all. And, if the
division did obtain, it is doubtful if the acquisition of social virtues, on the
basis of the other virtues, could simply be a matter of acquiring relevant
knowledge.

These questions come to a head in the consideration that the whole idea
of a pre-social natural stage following infancy is illusory. Emile's infancy
has been spent in dependence on others; he has learned to respond to
affection, he has learned a language and a complex range of behavioral
skills which involve social elements and belong to a social form. Rousseau
presents the natural stage — the age of childhood — in Books II and III of
Emile. What is offered in these books is the picture rather of a restricted,
highly controlled social environment — a life in the country — which is a
social space ("far from the vile morals of the town, whose gilded surface
makes them seductive and contagious to children" (II, 59); a life in the
immediate care of the tutor, without any other close personal relationships, but with occasional access to aspects of village life.

In this setting, the regime of moral formation is concerned especially with the development of self-reliance. This is connected with a certain conception of happiness and liberty as interrelated human (and moral) values. Happiness consists in the enjoyment of liberty. The scope of liberty rests on one's power of action in relation to one's desires. In this light, happiness consists in securing a perfect balance between desire and power. Liberty and happiness together therefore require that one be self-sufficing, able to do what one wants to do, in other words, self-reliant and independent of others. In speaking of the ideal of a balance between power and desire, Rousseau envisages that desire be restricted to basic needs:

> So it is the fewness of his needs, the narrow limits within which he can compare himself with others, that makes a man really good. (IV, 175)

With reference to powers, the other side of the equation, there is the idea of making use of all the forces of the soul. But Rousseau immediately sounds a warning about the power of imagination and its expansive effects on desire. Again, he takes the view that "childhood is the sleep of reason," and on this basis he rejects Locke's maxim, "reason with children," as wrongheaded and morally harmful (II, 55). In its place he recommends: "Use force with children and reasoning with men; this is the natural order" (II, 55). In other words, the way of learning for the (male) child is for him to be brought into contact with the limits set by nature (the natural environment) rather than by reason or society. Emile is to learn to be dependent on things (i.e., on nature) and independent of fellow human beings. (Sophy by contrast is to be brought up in a context which is marked by social requirements throughout its course.)

The regime excludes words such as *obey, command, duty,* and *obligation,* terms which belong to a context of social relations. Nor does it incorporate punishment for wrongdoing other than the price nature itself exacts when it is flouted. Nevertheless, it is a regime of artful control: in Rousseau's words, it is "the art of controlling without precepts" — an art which rests on deception, as he recognizes (II, 84). In any case, social relations are accorded a more open part in Emile's formation according to nature.

In his encounter with the gardener, Emile begins to learn from an early age "how the notion of property goes back naturally to the right of the first occupier to the results of his work" (II, 63). He is to be encouraged in generosity (and not by way of rewards, as Locke recommended, which, as Rousseau comments, begets greed and the liberality of the moneylender) (II, 67–68). Furthermore, there is one moral lesson which the child is definitely to be taught: "Never hurt anybody" (II, 69). Finally, the idea of social relations has to be developed gradually in the child's mind. He has to realize that he is not in fact "an isolated individual, self-sufficing and independent of others" (III, 156). He has to learn about the necessity of cooperation as the foundation of human institutions.

In a variety of ways, therefore, Rousseau undercuts his own rhetoric concerning the development of independence in a pre-social setting. What can be salvaged from this is an emphasis on the value of self-reliance (and hence on the value of helping children to acquire it). But there is no reason to think that self-reliance could be developed as a human quality except in a context of relations with others. (Nor has any reason been given for thinking of it as a peculiarly male virtue.)

3. The Origin and Grounds of Moral Knowledge (*Emile* IV)

With the approach of adulthood, Emile is deemed to enter the social order and to become aware of himself as a moral being; at this point too, he attains the age of reason. The focus of this "second birth," which Rousseau considers in Book IV, is directed especially to the passions which, in connection with sexual desire, now come into full expression.

More generally, Books IV and V are concerned with Emile's moral education. He is now to be introduced to the study of human relationships; the study is accompanied by extended moral instruction and guidance on the part of his tutor. The process as a whole is directed immediately to preparing Emile for marriage and adult life. Rousseau thus concerns himself in Book V with the question of the education and character of the naturally good woman. Book V nevertheless remains centrally concerned with Emile's development, for the whole discussion under the title "Sophy, or Woman" is a portrait of woman as occupying, by nature, the role of helpmate to man.

Rousseau is primarily concerned with developmental aspects of morality in *Emile*. But in this connection, Books IV and V in particular provide an important source for his views about the nature of morality and about the origin and grounds of moral knowledge. It would be useful to consider some main aspects of these views first. Rousseau's moral theory can then be seen at work in the developmental account which is given in relation to Emile and Sophy. It could be argued that reference to moral theory is out of place in connection with Rousseau. As Robert Derathé has pointed out, Rousseau was not concerned with the primary philosophical question of how we know what is good; the question for him was how we are to achieve the good.[10] But as Derathé's work itself indicates, the very choice of this emphasis reflects a certain understanding of moral theory and morality.

CONSCIENCE: NATURAL FEELINGS AND REASON
Rousseau's approach to moral questions puts particular stress on the idea of conscience, and specifically on conscience as a feeling or sentiment. One could be led to think, furthermore, that conscience as a sentiment is a natural and infallible guide to good and evil, without reference to reason or understanding. Some well-known passages concerning conscience in the

Creed of the Savoyard Priest (*Profession de Foi du Vicaire Savoyard*, contained in Book IV of *Emile*)[11] would appear to indicate that this is indeed Rousseau's view:

> Too often does reason deceive us; we have only too good a right to doubt her; but conscience never deceives us; she is the true guide of man; it is to the soul what instinct is to the body; he who obeys his conscience is following nature and he need not fear that he will go astray. (IV, 249–50)

> Conscience! Conscience! Divine instinct, immortal voice from heaven; sure guide for a creature ignorant and finite indeed, yet intelligent and free; infallible judge of good and evil, making man like to God. (IV, 254)

Rousseau's exaltation of conscience appears both excessive and obviously vulnerable, especially as he insists in this context that the same ideas of right and justice, the same principles of morality, the same ideas of good and evil, are to be found everywhere. It has only to be pointed out that different people arrive at different views in conscience and that it is not difficult to find execrable things being done in its name. But perhaps Rousseau's idea of conscience is more subtle — and less vulnerable — than it appears.

The first step to a more satisfactory appraisal is to recognize that Rousseau does not think that conscience is a source of knowledge at all. More generally, he does not allow that there is innate knowledge of good (or of anything else). In his view, the only source of knowledge of good and evil is the exercise of reason in an experiential context. But prior to reason, and underpinning it, are our natural feelings. It is here, in the domain of feelings, that the Rousseauian conception of conscience is located: "The decrees of conscience are not judgments but feelings" (IV, 253). But which feelings are envisaged? And how are they related to conscience?

The suggestion in the *Creed* or *Profession of Faith* is that there are two sets of innate feelings relevant to conscience, feelings concerned with the self in the first place, viz., self-love (*amour de soi*), fear of pain, dread of death, and the desire for comfort; and secondly, innate feelings related to one's kind such as fit us by nature to be or to become sociable. The twofold relation of feelings is then thought of as setting up a (pre-conscious) moral system which provides the motive power of conscience. The system of feelings specifies the scope of good and evil, and conscience consists especially in the feeling by which the individual is moved to love the one and hate the other. Taken in this sense, conscience is innate, and the claim that it is infallible is also plausible for the pre-rational phase since the natural feelings associated with self-love and sociability *define* the scope of the good.

Beyond the pre-rational phase, however, conscience can develop only in conjunction with reason. Rousseau makes this clear in a passage in Book I of *Emile*:

Reason alone teaches us how to know good and evil. Therefore, conscience, which makes us love the one and hate the other, though it is independent of reason, cannot develop without it. (I, 34)

At the developed stage, reason supplies understanding or knowledge in regard to moral questions. Thus the pre-conscious moral system is now imagined as filled out by rational understanding. But reason in this context is treated as purely theoretical and hence as lacking motivational force. Motivation is to be supplied by the original set of feelings, enhanced by development, that is to say, by conscience. Thus in the *Profession of Faith*, Rousseau portrays reason and conscience as working together to constitute the developed moral system:

To know good is not to love it; this knowledge is not innate in man; but as soon as his reason leads him to perceive it, his conscience impels him to love it; it is this feeling which is innate. (IV, 253)

It can be seen that, so far as the individual is concerned, the developed moral system of feelings enlightened by reason is far from being a guaranteed source of moral knowledge. The original feelings, beginning with self-love, are subject to distortion and corruption, and effective moral understanding depends on the proper development of the passions as well as suitable instruction. Thus the passages in which Rousseau exalts conscience are quite misleading as they stand. His considered teaching is that no one has an immediate or intuitive source of good moral judgment; moral claims always stand in need of grounds in support of their title to be genuinely expressive of natural passion enlightened by reason.

THE GROUND OF MORALITY AND THE PROBLEM OF SOCIAL RELATIONS
With reference to the general question of the foundations of ethics, Ernst Cassirer says that, "Rousseau's ethics is not an ethics of feeling but the most categorical form of a pure ethics of obligation that was established before Kant."[12] Given what Rousseau says about the role of reason in ethics, there is good reason to conclude that he does not subscribe to a pure ethics of feeling. But Cassirer's Kantian categorization of his ethics is questionable. Rousseau's primary position can be seen more properly as a version of ethical naturalism. But in his insistence on the foundational role of feelings, Rousseau takes a stand against the overly intellectual emphasis which had become characteristic of natural-law theory. In this approach, reason alone is thought of as providing access to the laws of nature; or, more strongly, reason is identified with natural law. This can be seen, for example, in Locke's appeal to natural law in *The Second Treatise of Government*:

The *State of Nature* has a law of Nature to govern it, which obliges every one: And Reason which is that Law, teaches all Mankind, who will but consult it that being all equal and independent, no one ought to harm another in his Life, Health, Liberty, or Possessions. (§ 6)

Rousseau does not dispute the role of reason in morality. But in his account, what reason understands regarding good and evil is the developed product of the moral system formed by the original, twofold relation of feelings. Justice and kindness, then, are "no mere abstract terms, no mere moral conceptions formed by the understanding, but true affections of the heart enlightened by reason, the natural outcome of our primitive affections" (*Emile*, 196).

On this basis, Rousseau parts company with theorists who place the foundation of natural law in reason alone.[13] His alternative version of naturalism is expressed succinctly in a comment on the "Golden Rule":

> The precept "Do unto others as you would have them unto you" has no true foundation but that of conscience and feeling; for what valid reason is there why I, being myself, should do what I do if I were some one else, especially when I am morally certain that I shall never find myself in exactly the same case; and who will answer for it that if I faithfully follow out this maxim I shall get others to follow it with regard to me? . . . But if the enthusiasm of an overflowing heart identifies me with my fellow-creature, if I feel, so to speak, that I will not let him suffer lest I should suffer too, I care for him because I care for myself, and the reason of the precept is found in nature herself, which inspires me with the desire for my own welfare wherever I may be. From this I conclude that it is false to say that the precepts of the natural law are based on reason only; they have a firmer and more solid foundation. The love of others, springing from self-love, is the source of human justice. The whole of morality is summed up in the gospel in this summary of the law. (IV, 196, note)

In forging an alliance between reason and feeling, Rousseau was reviving an older medieval tradition of natural law; in the thought of Thomas Aquinas, in particular, the desire for the good plays an essential part in moral inquiry.[14] Rousseau, however, was less confident than many of his predecessors and contemporaries in the power of reason to harmonize the interests of individuals in society. According to the standard, traditional view, society arises on the basis of the individual's dependence on others; given an assumption of natural sociability, the social order can be thought of, ideally, as embodying a complex set of cooperative undertakings involving relations of dependence which work to the advantage of each individual.

Rousseau, as we have seen, refers on occasions to the idea of natural sociability and of concern for others as arising out of self-love. But then the whole character of his thought is shaped by concern about the way in which passion becomes disordered in social relationships and overpowers reason and the natural passions alike. He thus has no confidence in a utilitarian system in which each man would be advantaged by serving others: that would be all very well, he retorts, but for the fact that he would gain even more by harming them.[15] On these grounds, he is critical of the

optimistic utilitarianism of the Encyclopedists. In its place, he seeks an
order in which, so far as *men* are concerned, there is as little dependence on
others as possible. What is then envisaged is a social order in which law
takes the place of individuals and in which the General Will is supreme
over individual interests:

> Dependence on men, being out of order, gives rise to every kind of vice,
> and through this master and slave become mutually depraved. If there is
> any cure for this social evil, it is to be found in the substitution of law for
> the individual; in arming the general will with a real strength beyond the
> power of any individual will. (II, 49)

The notion of law, and the accompanying idea of duty, clearly occupies a
central place in Rousseau's moral thought. But this emphasis does not
make it a pure ethics of obligation as Cassirer claims. For Rousseau, the
principles of conduct of the moral law rest on the initial system of natural
feelings enlightened by understanding; they are, in short, precepts of the
natural law. Furthermore, the whole purpose of morality is the promotion
of happiness: to be happy "is the end of every feeling creature; it is the first
desire taught us by nature, and the only one that never leaves us" (V, 406).
But Rousseau's ethical naturalism is thrown into question by his conception of the social problem. Happiness, which consists in the enjoyment of
liberty, draws the individual away from human association; it turns on
making oneself independent of others, limiting one's wants so that they
can be met out of one's own resources:

> Where then is human wisdom? Where is the path of true happiness? . . .
> True happiness consists in decreasing the difference between our desires
> and our powers, in establishing a perfect equilibrium between the power
> and the will. (II, 44)

The profound problem in this approach can be seen clearly in what
Rousseau says about virtue, which is the fulfilment of natural goodness
and the condition of happiness.

Rousseau holds that virtue consists in part of a rational component — an
understanding of moral relations and related laws and duties, the knowledge of good and evil; more deeply, it has the form of a love of order in
which one's life is shaped around concern for others on the basis of love of
one's own well-being (IV, 255). In this case, virtue is the outcome of our
primitive affections. It consists in the development of the natural passions
and affections in relation to others, a natural growth which nonetheless
requires effort and struggle. Justice, with its concerns for the common
good, to take a central example, is presented as springing from the love of
others with its origins in the natural love of self. In this case, virtue is
manifested in the bonds of human affection. But then the problem of social
relations reasserts itself in Rousseau's mind. The one who loves desires to

be loved; affection for others sets up chains of dependence; in forming ties with others, one becomes a slave of one's desire.

On the basis of such considerations, Rousseau is led to embrace a Stoic conception of emotional detachment according to which the wise man lives within himself alone:

> What is meant by a virtuous man? He who can conquer his affections; for then he follows his reason, his conscience; he does his duty; he is his own master and nothing can turn him from the right way. So far you have had only the semblance of liberty. . . . Now is the time for real freedom; learn to be your own master; control your heart, my Emile, and you will be virtuous. (V, 408)

In this setting, reason is charged with delivering the individual from the tyranny of the passions (which are now thought of as immoderate, specifically in the context of social relationships). Freedom in the form of mastery of one's life, subject to rational law, takes the place of bonds of association and affection as the essence of virtue.

Rousseau did not solve the problem set by his divergent conceptions of moral virtue. The problem, as we shall see, arises in connection with Emile rather than Sophy. His account of woman's virtue, while deeply problematic in other ways, is defined consistently (albeit excessively) in relational terms. In dealing with virtue in male life, however, Rousseau is torn between two models. According to one model, virtue is essentially the extension of natural human feelings and is manifested in forms of affection and association. According to the other, virtue consists in detachment from others and the overcoming of passion by reason. Both can be seen at work in the story of Emile's moral development to which I now turn.

4. Social Relations and (Male) Virtue (*Emile* IV)

TWO FORMS OF LOVE IN RELATION TO THE OTHER

Rousseau's account of Emile's moral education, taken up explicitly in Book IV, is indicated in a passage toward the end of Book III. Emile's childhood is now over; the tutor's task at this point, in connection with his becoming a man, is "to make him loving and tenderhearted, to perfect reason through feeling" (III, 165). The focus of attention thus falls on the education of the feelings.

In Rousseau's genealogy of the passions, everything turns on self-love:

> The origin of our passions, the root and spring of all the rest, the only one which is born with man, which never leaves him as long as he lives, is self-love; this passion is primitive, instinctive, it precedes all the rest, which are in a sense only modifications of it. (IV, 173)

This leads, as we saw, to a love of those about one and thence to a more generalized feeling of good will. In the common conditions of human suffering, good will shows up characteristically as pity, "the first relative sentiment which touches the human heart according to the order of nature" (IV, 184). From this point, but with the scene now moved forward to the age of sexual awareness, two divergent forms of love are envisaged.

Rousseau's approved path of development is expressed clearly, albeit generally, in the maxim:

> Extend self-love to others and it is transformed into virtue, a virtue which has its roots in the heart of every one of us. (IV, 215)[16]

The opposing path is the transformation of *amour de soi* into *amour-propre*, the transition from a healthy love of self to a vain and competitive selfishness which Rousseau presents as endemic in social relations. Along each path there is a characteristic cluster of other-related passions (and virtues or vices): tender and gentle passions springing from self-love — benevolence, pity, kindness, goodness, peacefulness, love of mankind which is "nothing but the love of justice within us." Hateful and angry passions springing from selfishness — envy, covetousness, deceitfulness, injustice, vindictiveness. In recommending the extension of self-love to others, Rousseau set himself against the growing eighteenth-century idea that social virtue and public good could be assured by the individual pursuit of self-interest. The self-love which he commends obviously involves an interest in the self, but the need for its extension to others points to the view that it becomes a virtue only when account is also taken of the interests of others — in other words, the proper guide to virtue is to seek the common interest or the General Will (within which the interest of the self is included). Society and the individual, morals and politics are thus brought together according to Rousseau's dictum:

> Society must be studied in the individual and the individual in society; those who desire to treat politics and morals apart from one another will never understand either. (IV, 197)

We have now seen Rousseau's general account of the way in which natural passions and natural goodness take on the form of moral virtue in the context of social relations. Emile as natural man is not intended to live in a pre-social situation; on the other hand, the idea of a society governed by law and reason expressed in the General Will is far from being realized. Within a sea of social evil, the individual is called on to constitute an island of moral virtue:

> But remember, in the first place that when I want to train a natural man, I do not want to make him a savage and to send him back to the woods, but that living in the whirl of social life it is enough that he should not let himself be carried away by the passions and prejudices of men; let him see with his eyes and feel with his heart, let him own no sway but that of reason. (IV, 217)

There is a deep and unresolved tension in Rousseau's thought which is suggested in this passage. Moral virtue arises only on the basis of social relations, but given that social relations constitute the site of everything that is wrong in the human condition, the man of virtue is to be conceived as self-sufficient. On the one hand, Emile, the paragon of virtue, is said to love everyone and to wish to please them and to be loved in return (IV, 302). On the other hand, human sociability is a consequence of weakness:

> Every affection is a sign of insufficiency; if each of us had no need of others, we should hardly think of associating with them. (IV, 182)

Emile's virtue could thus appear as weakness. Our needs drive us together, we are then led to compare ourselves with others, and a struggle for power and preference ensues. Rousseau's ideal in this situation is for the man of virtue to be dependent on but few people, hence to have but few needs and wants. In this case, the whole question of the possibility of moral (social) virtue becomes acute.

SEXUAL LOVE AND THE LOVE OF MANKIND

Rousseau, as we saw at the beginning of the chapter, raises this question in his developmental critique of society in the *Discourse on the Origins of Inequality*. The long descent into hellish social relations portrayed there is marked by the institution of property, large-scale division of labor, growing inequality, struggle between a rich minority and the impoverished mass of people, and the establishment of political order on the basis of a fraudulent social contract which, accepted unwittingly by the poor at the insinuation of the rich, "changed a clever usurpation into an irrevocable right, and for the profit of a few ambitious men henceforth subjected the whole human race to work, servitude and misery" (*Discourse*, 160). All this is obviously relevant to an analysis of Rousseau's social and political thought. But the seeds of the problem of sociability are sown more deeply at an earlier stage of development.

With the emergence of an elementary form of social life such as a small community of family groups, the problem is linked with sexual desire, love, and ordinary types of human play (and display) such as singing and dancing, "true children of love and leisure" (*Discourse*, 149). Desire, love and play, in the setting of growing relationships, are held to give rise to practices of comparison, ideas of merit and beauty and public esteem, and feelings of preference; and "from these first preferences were born on the one hand vanity and contempt, on the other shame and envy." The treatment of sexual desire and love is taken up in a related way early in Book IV of *Emile* (at the point at which the hero is imagined as entering upon the social and moral world).

Rousseau's primary insistence in *Emile* is that sexual love, as the love of a particular person, is the child of reason, not nature. What is of nature is the general desire, impulse, or instinct by which one sex is attracted to the

other without distinction of partners. Love, however, involves comparison, preference, and the choice of one person over others; it is an exercise
of judgment and reason (whether good or bad) which can occur only in a
social setting.

Furthermore, the "logic" of love carries it inexorably toward forms of
amour-propre:

> We wish to inspire the preference we feel; love must be mutual. To be
> loved we must be worthy of love; to be preferred we must be more
> worthy than the rest, at least in the eyes of our beloved. Hence we begin
> to look around among our fellows; we begin to compare ourselves with
> them, there is emulation, rivalry, and jealousy. . . . He who feels how
> sweet it is to be loved, desires to be loved by everybody; and there could
> be no preferences if there were not many that fail to find satisfaction.
> With love and friendship there begin dissensions, enmity, and hatred. I
> behold deference to other people's opinions enthroned among all these
> diverse passions, and foolish mortals, enslaved by her power, base their
> very existence merely on what other people think. (IV, 175–76)

In this understanding, sexual love sets in motion a bond of mutual and
utterly precarious dependence between lover and beloved. It makes each
of them subject to the judgment of the other as worthy of love and hence as
excelling all others in worth. It thus sets up the conditions for the mutually
false presentation of the self; at the same time, it proceeds by way of
divisive rivalries with others and paves the way to the generalized form of
social relations governed by *amour-propre*.[17]

The problem of sexual love is emphasized all the more when it is
contrasted with Rousseau's conception of virtuous love as the extension of
self-love to others:

> Extend self-love to others and it is transformed into virtue, a virtue
> which has its roots in the heart of every one of us. The less the object of
> our care is directly dependent on ourselves, the less we have to fear from
> the illusion of self-interest; the more general this interest becomes, the
> juster it is; and the love of the human race is nothing but the love of
> justice within us. If therefore we desire Emile to be a lover of truth, if we
> desire that he should indeed perceive it, let us keep him far from
> self-interest in all his business. The more care he bestows upon the
> happiness of others the wiser and better he is, and the fewer mistakes he
> will make between good and evil; but never allow him any blind prefer-
> ence founded merely on personal predilection or unfair prejudice. . . .
> this care for the general wellbeing is the first concern of the wise man, for
> each of us forms part of the human race and not part of any individual
> member of that race. (IV, 215)

The problem here, however, is that Rousseau's generalized love of others
appears to work insofar as it is withdrawn from actual relationships with
them. In a revealing amendment of the Gospel injunction, he observes that

"reason and self-love compel us to love mankind even more than our neighbour" (IV, 215). The problem is how one could love mankind *other* than through love of one's neighbor; for Rousseau, the problem is how virtuous love of one's neighbor is possible at all. Love is inseparable from a degree of dependence on the other: "He who loves desires to be loved" (IV, 302). In the nature of the case, therefore, love threatens the postulated ideal (for males) of self-sufficiency.

MARRIED LOVE AND THE (MALE) IDEAL OF DETACHMENT

Rousseau in fact does not follow through the logic of his argument concerning sexual love in the rest of *Emile*. At the beginning of Book IV, sexual love is presented as central to the syndrome of *amour-propre*. But the rest of the book is concerned substantially with a love story in which the theme of *amour-propre* plays a muted role. For the most part, the relationship of Emile and Sophy is seen in glowing light as a manifestation of nature and virtue alike. It is as if a different and traditional set of moral reference points, turning on love, marriage, and the family, have now been assumed (for the most part). Preference and choice, properly exercised, are now redeemed, and marriage and justice (the care for the general well-being) are seen as the basis for a moral social order. At the same time, marriage is saved insofar as it is presented as a relationship based on natural inequality between men and women. In exercising an essentially supportive role, Sophy is deemed to be fulfilling her nature in virtuous activity. Emile can draw on this support without threat to his independence, again presumably because it is based in nature.

There are clear indications in *Emile*, however, that Rousseau had serious misgivings about this proposal. One element of doubt is that Emile and Sophy, either as a couple or as individuals, could fail to achieve the ideal status to which they are assigned. *Emile* ends on a note of wedded and expectant paternal bliss, but it is clear that the status of virtue, wisdom and happiness, is a task to be achieved, not a *fait accompli*.[18] More deeply, there is a question of the ideal status itself so far as it concerns Emile. While Rousseau does not appear to have had any doubts regarding the subordinate and complementary role assigned to woman, the problem of male self-sufficiency continued to trouble him.

At the height of the courtship, the tutor shocks Emile with the (false) suggestion that Sophy is dead. When calm is restored, a long speech of "pure reason" follows on the theme of detachment as the condition of happiness. Emile is imagined as having been left free by nature and fortune, "dependent on nothing but [his] position as a human being." As for Emile in love: "Now you depend on all the ties you have formed for yourself, you have learnt to desire, and you are now the slave of your desires" (V, 407). What is needed is a discipline for acquiring mastery of one's affections, the art of living with few wants, detached from others and from life itself, with one's heart fixed on eternal beauty. In such mastery, one possesses true freedom, that is, freedom which is subject only to natural necessity and rational law. In Emile's case, the discipline of detachment is underlined by an enforced absence for foreign travel. This is also the period of Emile's political education in which he is made ready for a public life separate from the domestic sphere. Notwithstanding the advice concerning detachment, Emile returns to marry Sophy and to take his place as a member of civil society. But Emile is left in the end with the impossible task of living in accordance with divergent patterns of moral virtue.

5. Woman's Virtue (*Emile*, V)

THE OTHER-RELATED NEEDS AND DUTIES OF WOMAN

The natural goodness and virtue prescribed for Sophy is problematic in a different way. Rousseau's account of woman and woman's virtue is marked by a wilful essentialism. Women are designated as childbearers, "their proper business" (V, 325); nature has entrusted them with the care of children and the preservation of the unity of the family. On Rousseau's understanding, the difference between men and women is fixed entirely in their sex. They are credited with a relationship of mutual dependence and complementarity which is, however, asymmetrical in form:

> Men and women are made for each other, but their mutual dependence differs in degree; man is dependent on woman through his desires; woman is dependent on man through her desires and also through her needs, he could do without her better than she can do without him. She cannot fulfil her purpose in life without his aid, without his goodwill, without his respect; she is dependent on our feelings, on the price we put upon her virtue, and the opinion we have of her charms and her deserts. Nature herself has decreed that woman, both for herself and her children, should be at the mercy of man's judgment. (V, 328)

Everything concerning the specific character of woman's morality and her education follows from the supposed asymmetry regarding needs; paradoxically, it is underlined by the fact that men are so utterly dependent on women in infancy. Woman's education, in a word, must be planned in relation to man; woman's virtues and primary duties are not merely other-related, they are *man-related*:

> A woman's education must therefore be planned in relation to man. To be pleasing in his sight, to win his respect and love, to train him in childhood, to tend him in manhood, to counsel and console, to make his life pleasant and happy, these are the duties of women for all time, and this is what she should be taught while she is young. (V, 328)

A natural education for women, on this basis, concerns the knowledge, skills, and attitudes involved in being a mother and wife. This supposes that a woman's mind is to be cultivated to a degree: she could not otherwise provide suitable companionship for man. Again, to be in a position to please her husband, to justify his choice of her, and to do him honor, she must know something of man's judgment and the passions by which it is swayed (V, 346).

With reference to moral formation in particular, Rousseau recommends that girls should be accustomed early to restraint since they are to live under the lifelong restraint of propriety and be subject to male authority. The marked contrast with the recommendations for Emile's education finds its rationale in the supposed asymmetry regarding needs. Women are made to be dependent on men by nature, whereas men are to be dependent (ideally) only on things (on nature). With Emile, therefore, the emphasis falls on the absence of imposed restraints with a view to his developing self-reliance (though the tutor must engage in a good deal of covert restraint and manipulation to this end).

Restraint in woman's education is associated especially with docility and gentleness, again in the context of submission to man. In woman, the common moral virtues are to be suffused with the overall quality of charm. "Woman is especially made for man's delight" (V, 322); even her happiness, the goal of moral virtue, is to be found in the happiness of a good man (V, 362).

MODESTY AND ITS RAMIFICATIONS

The relentless consistency of Rousseau's account of woman's morality, based in restraint, finds particular expression in the virtue of modesty. This is identified as woman's virtue par excellence, the very idea of womanly propriety, expressed especially in unimpeachable chastity. Men and women alike are endowed with boundless passions; in controlling passion, man has his reason, woman her modesty:

> The Most High . . . has endowed man with boundless passions . . . ; though swayed by these passions man is endowed with reason to control them. Woman is also endowed with boundless passions; God has given her modesty to restrain them. (V, 323)

The contrast portrayed in this passage clearly involves, on the male side, the Stoic (and more "Kantian") strand in Rousseau's moral theory. His more general view is that immoderate passions are checked importantly by the growth of the natural and gentle passions. The contrast on its other side is not meant to imply that reason is not involved in woman's modesty at all. The point, once again, is that woman's reason is made subject to male judgment.

Modesty is linked with three further elements in the Rousseauian conception of natural goodness and virtue for women: woman's "place" as being in the household, removed from direct participation in civil society; the subjection of women to public opinion with respect to their moral status; and the idea that women, though made for obedience to men, nevertheless exercise a natural and therefore proper form of control over them.

(a) Woman's "Place." With respect to woman's "place," there is the idea that the home, as a miniature fatherland, constitutes the natural foundation without which the artificial bonds of the State could not hold firm. Woman's natural task is to secure this foundation. In Rousseau's thinking, then, it is political promiscuity for women to be assigned occupations beyond this sphere in the manner of men (V, 326). Secondly, the State is ideally conceived as a union of autonomous individuals. Since women are deemed to be subject to man's authority by nature, they lack the requisite autonomy. Rousseau, it is true, does not explicitly say in *The Social Contract* that men alone can properly be parties to the social contract, but it is clear from *Emile* that it would be an act of impropriety — an offense against modesty for a woman to assume this status.[19]

(b) Subjection to Public Opinion. The idea that women are subject to public opinion with respect to their virtue, while men are not, is another aspect of the general thesis of asymmetry. Modesty is specifically connected with the claim inasmuch as this virtue involves reference in a particular way to public standards of propriety. Rousseau's general claim is put as follows:

> Worth alone will not suffice, a woman must be thought worthy; . . . . A woman's honour does not depend on her conduct alone, but on her reputation. . . . A man has no one but himself to consider and so long as he does right he may defy public opinion; but when a woman does right her task is only half finished, and what people think of her matters as much as what she really is. Hence her education must, in this respect, be different from man's education. "What will people think" is the grave of a man's virtue and the throne of a woman's. (V, 328)

This passage — and others in which Rousseau pursues the theme — does not actually say why reputation is so important in the one case and irrelevant (or worse) in the other. It is not important for woman's virtue, for it is explicitly treated as additional to virtue. For what then? The only plausible conclusion is that it is an arm of male authority.

The claim regarding public opinion has an air of exaggeration on both sides of the contrast; there is also an element of equivocation. So far as men are concerned, Rousseau reasonably rejects the emphasis which moralists such as Locke placed on reputation and public esteem as the touchstone of virtue. But the complete dismissal of its relevance is extreme: it points to a radically atomized conception of virtue and a world of isolated, autonomous wills in which the mutual acknowledgment of good social relations has no place. Such a picture is inconsistent in fact with Rousseau's primary insistence on the tender and gentle passions and on social virtues. In short, the good opinion of others is a proper consideration in regard to male virtue. The importance placed on public opinion in regard to women is no less extreme in the other direction; among other things, there is no reference to whether the opinion is well- or ill-formed, or whether there is the least entitlement to its expression and propagation. The exaggeration on each side of the contrast suggests that there is an element of equivocation in Rousseau's use of "reputation," "public opinion," and especially the phrase, "What will people think." Insofar as "what will people think" is the grave of a man's virtue, the phrase is suggestive of the whole complex of social relations driven by *amour-propre* in which the individual "knows only how to live in the opinions of others." But *amour-propre* subverts virtue; "what will people think" could not be the throne of anyone's virtue in this sense. If the phrase is to have an acceptable moral significance it needs to have the normative force of something like "public opinion for which there is reasonable ground and entitlement." But public opinion in this sense is unrelated to *amour-propre*, on the one hand, and it is applicable to men no less than women, on the other. In fact, when Rousseau comes to speak of the need for women's reason to be cultivated, he undercuts the emphasis on women's subjection to public opinion, though the framework of subordination is maintained:

> Since she depends both on her own conscience and on public opinion, she must learn to know and reconcile these two laws, and to put her own conscience first only when the two are opposed to each other. She becomes the judge of her own judges, she decides when she should obey and when she should refuse her obedience. (V, 346)

(c) *Woman as Guardian.* The theme of woman's "managerial" role, based on yet another "law" which Rousseau discovers in nature, runs throughout Book V of *Emile.* The law — according to which the weaker rules the stronger — is manifested in woman's power to stimulate man's passions beyond his power to satisfy them. In respect of his desire, man is thus dependent on woman's good will and compelled to try to please her. But then woman's modesty reins in male desire. Woman's control arises, therefore, from the combination of two powers in response to male strength: the power to stimulate male passion by a sort of conquetry, which is then balanced by the power of modesty. Rousseau is anxious to insist that he does not mean false or foolish coquetry! The coquetry he has in mind is declared genuine on the grounds that it is in accord with nature in its means and aims. It calls especially on woman's wit and charm and cunning, conceived as natural gifts for securing influence; furthermore, it is "coquetry on behalf of virtue" (V, 346). Art and modesty thus combine to constitute a law of right conduct and the basis of woman's influence and control:

> The more modest a woman is, the more art she needs, even with her husband. Yes, I maintain that coquetry, kept within bounds, becomes modest and true, and out of it springs a law of right conduct. (V, 348)

Once again, everything that concerns woman is given its rationale in relation to man.[20]

Rousseau returns to this theme toward the end of *Emile*, following the marriage of Emile and Sophy. First, a balance of power is declared. By one law of nature, the woman owes obedience to her husband; by another, it is good for the man to be led by a good wife (who employs "coquetry on behalf of virtue and love on behalf of reason") (V, 443). But at the last, the tutor yields the authority, which Emile has allowed him, to Sophy; henceforth, she is to be Emile's guide and counsellor and his guardian (V, 444). In becoming Emile's guardian, Sophy continues to be constituted by her relations to the other. Emile, for his part, appears no longer destined for the role of the detached, autonomous man of reason; rather, he is confirmed in his long-established position as he-who-is-to-be-cared-for.

I have had occasion to note the extent to which the tutor's art in *Emile* rests on deception and manipulative control exercised in the name of nature. It can be seen that woman's art, with its idea of a coquetry on behalf of virtue, is endowed with the same characteristics. This is in keeping, no doubt, with the proposal that Sophy is to assume the mantle of the tutor. But it means that Rousseau's idea of natural goodness and virtue rests on an unsatisfactory moral basis, for men and women alike, from beginning to end.

AN ETHIC OF CARE?

Taken very generally, Rousseau's account of woman's virtue has the form of an ethic of care. What it lacks profoundly is any sense of woman's status as a person in her own right.[21] In connection with male development, Rousseau drew an overly sharp and artificial distinction between virtues which concern the self and social virtues. In the case of women, he goes to the different extreme of treating all their virtues (and their being) in terms of relations to the other, specifically relations to men. The primary account he gives of male virtue begins with the natural passion of self-love (*amour de soi*); bonds of affection and the requirements of justice are constructed on this basis. It is significant that the account of woman's virtue does not start from *amour de soi*, but from an essentialist claim regarding woman's responsibilities for others. The space in which woman could exist naturally in her own right is thus closed off. Had Rousseau taken *amour de soi* as his starting point in this case (as his psychology requires), his version of ethical naturalism might have been developed as common to both sexes. In this case, it would have been an ethic of care in which women are accorded value in themselves no less than men, and in which concern for the other falls equally on both sexes.

Rousseau's ethical naturalism would nevertheless remain deeply problematic even if it had been developed along the lines just indicated. Apart from the tendency to identify various contingent social practices as natural, the main general weakness concerns the narrow basis of the account in (male) individual psychology. The logic of Rousseau's views about the corrupt nature of social relationships took him in this direction. Genuine social reform, he believed, presupposed radical moral change on the part of individuals. A natural basis for ethical and social reform had to be found from within individuals. The account of Emile's education according to nature draws on social considerations (and an implicit social order) far more than it acknowledges. But the emphasis on individual nature exacts its toll. Emile's eventual entry into bonds of association and affection is imagined as the extension of his natural passions. The problem is that Rousseau says very little about the social forms and practices which provide the necessary and natural basis for this extension. He says nothing about Emile's relations to others as he lives in "the whirl of social life" in such manner that "he owns no sway but that of reason." In comparison with Aristotle, Rousseau's conception of nature relevant to ethics is narrow and impoverished. The neglect of the social conditions of moral development is not an accident: it arises in a context in which there is a strong inclination to think of bonds of association and affection as debilitating and corrupting forms of dependence. What Rousseau seeks, therefore, is a way of developing communal-social passions in the individual without having to depend on the formative influence of social conditions. This task, if it could be done at all, would have to be done by reason; that is, reason thought of as having the power to overcome immoderate passions, grasp the moral law, and lead the individual to the performance of duty in respect of himself and others. Rousseau did not arrive at a fully consistent position on these matters. But in thinking along these lines, he was being drawn toward a Kantian solution to moral and social problems.

7. Kant: The Sovereignty of Reason

1. The Educational Task and the Science of Ethics

Kant wrote that "the prospect of a *theory of education* is a great ideal; it does not matter if we are not able to realise it at once. But we must not look upon the idea as chimerical or decry it as a beautiful dream, notwithstanding the difficulties which stand in the way of its realisation." No less than John Locke at the end of the seventeenth century, he emphasized the role of education in the making of the human being: "Man can only become human by education. He is merely what education makes of him."[1]

The broad character of the Kantian conception of education is indicated in the idea of a transition from animal nature, in which we are born, to the development of human nature. More specifically, it is a transition from "the tyrannical propensities of sense" to "a sovereignty in which reason alone shall have sway."[2] The first major stage of the development is from nature to culture, where culture is understood as the realization of natural human endowments, on the one hand, and the overcoming of natural (animal) inclinations, on the other. But the major goal of the process, the ultimate aim with reference to the individual, is the formation of moral character — that is, the development of a disposition according to which a person chooses nothing but good ends.

Kant's conceptions of these transitions — from animal nature to culture and from culture to morality — concern the human race as a whole as well as the individual: "With education is involved the great secret of the perfection of human nature"; at stake is the "realisation of the ultimate destiny of the human race."[3] While Kant admired Rousseau greatly, he did not share his pessimism regarding the human future. His Enlightenment optimism was tempered by the conviction that the human race was still far from the desired and destined age of morality. But he was equally convinced that there was the prospect of continual progress toward the moral goal and the guarantee of ultimate success in achieving it. The path to this end depended fundamentally on the great and difficult art of education.

The basic problem of education is thought of as the problem of history, viz., how to establish a political order founded on morality and freedom. In the *Lectures on Ethics*, Kant asks: "How then is perfection to be sought? Wherein lies our hope? In education and nothing else" (252). Education, which is thus recognized as profoundly political, is charged with solving the riddle of history. As an art, it has a twofold task: within a given generation it is the means by which individuals develop to become moral agents; over generations yet to come, it is the means of bringing about a genuinely moral social order in the fullness of time. The theory needed to go with the practice of education thus includes an understanding of human nature, ethical and political theory, and a philosophy of history. It is not surprising that Kant treats the prospect of a theory of education as a great but difficult ideal. In the meantime, the art of education as a practice cannot wait until we have a proper science of human development. Kant's hope, rather, was that the practice of the art would help to produce the science.[4]

Whatever of education, Kant did not doubt that a science of ethics as such was already available. The goal of individual development, and of humanity as a whole, is seen therefore as clear and beyond doubt. The Kantian science of ethics is conceived as a body of ordered knowledge relating to absolute and universally binding laws which constitute grounds of obligation for all rational beings. Such knowledge, he argues, is derived, not from experience of any sort, but from reason alone:

> Everyone must admit that a law, if it is to hold morally, i.e., as a ground of obligation, must imply absolute necessity; he must admit that the command, "Thou shalt not lie," does not apply to men only, as if other rational beings had no need to observe it. The same is true for all other moral laws properly so called. He must concede that the ground of obligation here must not be sought in the nature of man or in the circumstances in which he is placed, but sought a priori solely in the concepts of pure reason.[5]

In rejecting ethical naturalism and all attempts to ground ethics in relation to the condition of happiness (or any other condition), Kant concedes that moral philosophy has an empirical part — practical anthropology — which is concerned in particular with questions relating to the application and implementation of the moral law. But moral philosophy proper, in being concerned with a priori laws, rests solely on reason. At the same time, Kant insists that it is not remote from ordinary experience. He holds that the science of ethics is in harmony with common moral understanding, specifically that it supplies the supreme principle which lies behind ordinary moral knowledge.

This conviction is connected with Kant's vagueness in regard to the actual content of morality. His prima facie claim is that all imperatives of duty can be derived from a single, essentially formal, principle of reason, the categorical imperative. While he seeks to demonstrate this claim by reference to a basic set of examples, for the most part he treats the content of morality as a matter of common knowledge and not in need of serious argument. *His* task is the more general one of uncovering the nature and ground of the moral law and providing an account of the general conditions of moral goodness and worth.

Kant's moral philosophy, and especially its tone, is influenced considerably by elements in his pietist (Lutheran) upbringing and by a range of more general intellectual and social influences operative in eighteenth-century thought. Against this background, Kantian ethics is universal in scope, yet is focused on the individual as endowed with rational will and capable of developing the principles of morality out of his own resources. It proclaims the freedom of the individual as inherent in rationality, and his autonomy as subject only to a law of which he is the lawgiver. Morality has the form of *law* insofar as reason and inclination are thought of as characteristically in conflict — it is in itself the expression of freedom. The duty it imposes is unconditional and has nothing to do with happiness or any other condition (though the desire for happiness is natural and proper). It is traditional and conservative in content and character, yet is free of the traditional authority in morals exercised by religion and society. It invokes, rather, an ideal of society in which virtuous, rational beings, each of whom is an end in himself, together constitute a universal kingdom of ends. It is non-discriminatory and altruistic in intent and proclaims a fundamental principle of respect for persons. Finally, it is an ethics which is established on the basis of an austere and enlightened appeal to reason, marked by sustained rational argument in support of bold and highminded moral contentions. Yet for all its embodiment of ideals and forms of rational argument in ethics, and its immense influence, Kant's moral philosophy is less than rationally compelling in many of its major claims.

What reason shows, according to Kant's argument in the *Foundations of the Metaphysics of Morals* (hereafter *FMM*), is that there is nothing that could be called good without qualification except a *good will*. Reason itself is a practical as well as a speculative faculty, i.e., it has the effective role of producing a will that is good in itself. Further, an action has moral worth only if it is done from duty, not from inclination. Moral worth itself rests entirely on the will to act according to duty and has nothing to do with what is aimed at in action, and duty is purely "the necessity of an action executed from respect for law" (*FMM* 16). The principle of the will consists, therefore, of nothing except "universal conformity of its action to law as such. That is, I should never act in such a way that I could not also will that my maxim should be a universal law" (*FMM* 18). The moral law, since it binds unconditionally, irrespective of the individual's wishes or inclinations, takes the form of a categorical imperative, viz., "act only according to that maxim by which you can at the same time will that it should become universal law" (*FMM* 39). The test of acceptability for a moral maxim — i.e., a subjective principle governing behavior — is thus placed in its universalizability. The test is whether one could consistently will that everyone should always act on it (or could will, in a different formulation, that it be a universal law of nature).

Kant does not make especially clear what he means by the requirement for universality though the general idea is built into the notion of rationality. Furthermore, his attempt to show how a sample of moral maxims passes the test of universalizability is far from conclusive. (The chosen maxims relate to the duties not to commit suicide, not to make false promises, to develop one's talents, and to help others.) What is worse, the test does not properly serve to distinguish moral from non-moral maxims. It fails to rule out pointless maxims or examples which would generally be classed as immoral; for example, principles which advocate the persecution of one or other group or arbitrary discrimination between people can be put in appropriate universal form. R. C. S. Walker observes in this connection that the maxim "'Always treat black people like animals' contains no singular terms, and someone — a 'fanatic' — might accept that if he were black he should be treated as an animal too."[6] What is needed here, as Walker continues, is a requirement that moral principles enjoin equality of respect. But then, equality of respect, if it is taken as a purely formal requirement, is unable to ensure maxims that are morally satisfactory: a recommendation that everyone be treated badly is compatible with a pure principle of equality of respect. One would need to know in what way equality of respect is being proposed. In the same way, the related idea of a universal requirement of impartiality needs to be given content.

That Kant subscribes to a principle of impartiality is clear from a further formulation which he offers of the categorical imperative: "Act so that you treat humanity, whether in your own person or in that of another, always as an end and never as a means only" (*FMM* 47). This formulation embodies the characteristic Kantian emphasis on respect for all rational beings as persons, beings who are able to possess a good will, autonomous agents with value and dignity in themselves. The argument for this principle turns on the necessity of extending to other rational beings what one holds necessarily of oneself. In fact, it is not clear that this consideration can ground the conclusion Kant wishes to draw from it. Richard Norman brings out the problem he faces here in the following way: "If I treat myself as a person, I may be logically committed to accepting that others have good reason to treat themselves as persons, but I am not logically committed to the principle that *I* should treat *them* as persons. A world of self-respecting egoists is not an irrational world."[7]

At a more general level, it is puzzling that Kant holds that the formula about treating everyone as ends is equivalent to the original version of the categorical imperative. Universality is a formal requirement of maxims; respect for persons as ends presupposes content. This is all the more puzzling inasmuch as Kant goes on to say that in addition to form (which consists of universality) all maxims have a material element (*FMM* 54–55), that is, the moral law has content as well as formal characteristics. In referring to matter or content in the *Foundations of the Metaphysics of Morals*, Kant speaks only of the formula according to which the rational being is an end in itself and says nothing of what would be involved in detail. Elsewhere, the proposal is made somewhat more specific in terms of a requirement to promote one's own perfection and the happiness of others.[8] The principle for inclusion in regard to content, as Walker suggests, turns on the range of appropriate objectives of rational beings: "The law must itself be rational, and can hardly therefore involve self-contradiction, or conflict with those objectives which every rational being must, in virtue of his rationality, have."[9] The problem once again is that Kant has very little to say on this matter. One objective which a rational being will certainly have is its own happiness; Kant recognizes this but fails to give the notion content. What he actually does, as Walker concludes, "is tacitly to build into the conception of rationality all his substantive moral views."[10]

The point of major significance is that Kant's moral philosophy moves beyond reliance on formal principles or rationality alone. It incorporates content which relates to the nature and ends of rational beings specifically as realized in human nature. Yet he characteristically writes as if formal principles were sufficient of themselves; and he invokes substantive moral views, in the name of rationality and nature, without providing the specific argument of which they stand in need.[11] There is good reason, then, to conclude that Kant fails to meet his own claim (in the Preface of the *Foundations*) that moral philosophy "applied to man . . . borrows nothing from knowledge of him (anthropology) but gives him, as a rational being, a priori laws" (*FMM* 5). Apart from the substantive elements which find their way into the "pure" ethic, there is a good deal of concern with more empirical questions in Kant's moral thought. He attached particular importance to questions concerned with the moral development of the individual and of humanity as a whole. Furthermore, he was greatly taken up with methodological issues in general, and he considered that a science or domain of inquiry demands its corresponding pedagogy, that is, an account of the relevant method of instruction in the field. There is good reason, then, to take account of his moral theory in the light of his views about education and moral development.

2. Themes in Education

Kant was involved, as publicist and financial supporter, with an experimental school at Dessau, set up on lines inspired by Rousseau's *Emile*.[12] But he was concerned more directly with the practice and theory of education in his work as a university teacher. As professor of philosophy in the University of Königsberg, he delivered the annual series of university lectures on pedagogy on four occasions in the 1770s and 1780s. Kant did not publish these lectures. But then a text appeared in 1803, not long before his death, with the title *Immanuel Kant über Pädagogik*, edited by F. T. Rink, a former pupil of Kant's and editor of some of his other writings. In a short editorial foreword, Rink gives the reader to understand that he had access to Kant's own lecture notes on pedagogy or to reliable student copies. The text is presented as if it were an edited version of these sources, modestly, though not inaccurately described by Rink as "remarks on pedagogy."

Kant's remarks on pedagogy, as edited by Rink, deal with the need for education and its general character in an introductory section. In the first of two main sections, there is material relating to basic childcare and nurture, the development of mental powers, and aspects of moral development. The second section deals more extensively with moral education; finally, there is a brief concluding section in which there is discussion of education in relation to religion and sex.[13] There is rather less unity to the text than a summary of its contents might suggest. Within the span of a hundred pages, there are incompatible schematic divisions, a number of odd beginnings and endings, repetitions, and curious juxtapositions. There are also quite a few passages taken without acknowledgment from Rousseau's *Emile*. Furthermore, there is a notable lack of argumentation throughout.

It has now been established with reasonable authority that the text on education is not based on Kant's lectures on pedagogy at all, at least not in any direct sense. Rather, it is a compilation of passages cobbled together by the editor from other sources in Kant's writings (for the most part): in particular from the *Lectures on Ethics*, the *Anthropology from a Pragmatic Point of View*, the section on methodology in the *Critique of Practical Reason*, the essay *Religion within the Limits of Reason Alone*, and, importantly, the *Doctrine of Virtue* (Part Two of the *Metaphysics of Morals*). Finally, a number of passages are taken from quotations and notes made by Kant in his study of Rousseau's *Emile* (a book for which he had a high regard). The argument for these conclusions is presented in T. Weisskopf's study of Kant on education, *Immanuel Kant und die Pädagogik* (1970). Weisskopf's view is that the text should be removed from the Academy edition of Kant's works on the grounds that it cannot be treated as an authentic work by Kant.[14] Weisskopf's argument that Kant was not responsible for the construction and shape of the work is entirely convincing. It follows that Rink's account of its provenance — with the implication of a close connection between the text and the lectures on pedagogy — is no longer tenable.

At the same time, Weisskopf's own work has shown that the greater part of the text can be traced to one or another source in Kant's writings. As a compilation of remarks on education drawn from these writings, the text is substantially authentic. But, in the light of Weisskopf's study, it would be foolish to criticize Kant himself for failing to deal with various questions in this text, or for failing to provide argument in the text in support of his views, or for adopting inconsistent divisions in the treatment of the subject matter. Such criticisms miss the mark, insofar as they apply to the text, for it is not Kant's work.

Immanuel Kant über Pädagogik can still be used as a sourcebook of Kant's views where passages can be checked against their original source;[15] given that it consists of an extensive compilation of passages, the work allows for some speculation and conclusions about the character and scope of Kant's educational thought. But it is a major consequence of Weisskopf's investigations that we now know that there is no sustained study of educational questions in Kant's writings. He gave considerable attention to the topic, but the material is scattered in different sources — the anthropological reflections, the teaching on method in the three *Critiques*, the *Lectures on Ethics* and other ethical and political writings, and the writings on history.

THE IDEA OF CULTURE

The two major concepts in Kant's educational thought are culture and character. Of these two notions, character, more specifically moral character, occupies the supreme position in the order of ends. The ultimate point of education is conceived as the development of moral character in the individual and in the human race as a whole. But the idea of culture — *Bildung* — is the more pervasive, the more generic, and the more critical notion. It embraces the whole conception of education as the process of development — in both individual and race — which culminates ideally in the formation of character and the emergence of an ethical society. The two ideas are thus closely associated in Kant's understanding, the one constituting the process of which the other is the outcome.

In speaking of culture, Kant commonly uses the general term, *Kultur*. But he uses as much, or even more, the more specialized word, *Bildung*, especially in educational contexts. The significance of this is that *Bildung* was just then coming to be a standard German word for education itself. *Bildung*, as the dictionary attests, is education *or* culture; more generally, it connotes shape, form, structure, creation, growth, formation. With its etymological basis in the word for image or likeness (*Bild*), it originally conveyed a religious dimension: the formation of the human being as bearing the likeness of God, the *imago Dei*. In a more secularized setting, "formation" — *Bildung* — came to be thought of as the development of "germs lying undeveloped in man," to use Kant's words — that is to say, *Bildung* was thought of as the process of education.[16] From the end of the eighteenth century, the notion has continued to occupy a prominent place in philosophical thought in Germany, specifically in philosophical anthropology. Appropriately, perhaps, it exhibits a particular cultural character for there is no immediately equivalent term in English, French, or Italian.

Bildung as education/culture is broadly taken to encompass the complete formation of human beings in intellectual, volitional, and emotional terms. But how such formation is to be understood is a matter of dispute: it differs with different philosophical anthropologies. Its importance for Kant can be seen in the pivotal role it holds in relation to other basic notions. Culture, for Kant, has to be understood in relation to all of the following notions: nature; discipline; instruction and guidance in basic skills, and pre-eminently in fine arts and the sciences; work and play; prudence in one's dealings with others; human history and destiny; freedom and purpose; duty, character, and morality.

Kant's philosophical thought typically consists in the drawing of boundaries and the setting up of apparently sharp divisions — as between the phenomenal and the noumenal, the empirical and the intelligible, the sensuous and the rational, the prudential and the moral, nature and morality, civil society and ethical society. The science of ethics, as we saw, is presented as a non-empirical body of knowledge grounded in reason; moral psychology, by contrast, is necessarily empirical. The human being as moral agent, a self in possession of free will, belongs both to the noumenal world of "things in themselves" and the phenomenal world of "appearances." Morality, it can be seen, crosses the boundaries just noted, and the focus on pedagogical concerns in particular brings the divisions into question. Education and culture constitute, for the individual and society, the link between the realm of nature and the realm of morality. Education is fundamentally *moral* education, education for the development of moral character and preparation for the establishment of a morality-based culture. In the meantime, the culture within which moral education proceeds is based not on morality, but on prudence (i.e., on people's interest in their own happiness and well-being). The problem for Kant, in terms of his dichotomies, is to show how moral education is possible in the given conditions, and how a culture based on prudence could give rise to one based on morality.

The Kantian idea of culture begins in a contrast with nature, more specifically, animal nature. The intended contrast is between a nature which is complete and effectively closed with one that is significantly incomplete but open to development. In the *Conjectural Beginning of Human History*, Kant imagines an original state in which human beings were guided essentially by instinct. But the power of reason made development beyond that state inevitable.[17] Human beings, endowed with reason and freedom, are alone among animals in having a future, but the future is precisely what has to be made to be, not something that unfolds according to ironclad laws of nature. The condition of freedom grounds the need for education and, in that connection, establishes the possibility of culture. Human beings are distinguished from animals in being free, in having a future; animality is typically presented by Kant as something to be overcome. In what sense, and how?

Animality as a condition to be overcome points to a Kantian conception of the state of nature, which he refers to on occasions as the state of savagery. It signifies a condition "in which freedom and independence from all coercive law holds sway"; more succinctly, it is a state of independence from law as a state of *injustice*. Animal impulses, as associated with human animal nature, are treated as lawless and anti-human, whereas the impulses of animals are governed by instinct and the laws of nature. The transition from animal nature to humanity and culture consists, in the first place, therefore, in our becoming subject to rules; it is the conquest of lawlessness. Thus culture in its original form is discipline; as subjection to rules, it marks the emergence of the human from the state of savagery.

In the *Critique of Pure Reason*, Kant specifies discipline as "the compulsion, by which the constant tendency to disobey certain rules is restrained and finally extirpated," and he distinguishes discipline from culture on the grounds that one is negative in form, the other positive.[18] The grounds offered for an unqualified distinction between discipline and culture are not compelling. There is no reason why discipline could not be linked with positive forms of behavior and be specified by positive commands as much as with restraints and prohibitions. In any case, discipline clearly falls under the wider notion of culture as the formation of human nature, for subjection to rules is indubitably a feature of the Kantian conception of human nature.

What the distinction between discipline and culture properly marks are two senses or two aspects of nature in relation to culture. There is nature which is to be overcome, nature thought of as animal impulses or feelings or passions which, as such, are independent of and inimical to laws. Secondly, there is nature which is to be developed, nature thought of as a set of inherently good powers — gifts of nature — present in germ form from the beginning of human life. Kant means, in particular, reason and the capacity for free action according to reason. Culture, as the transition from animality to humanity, embraces both processes. In forming a being who has learned to be subject to rules, culture in its first stage gives rise to the major condition for the development of morality. In its second stage, however — the development of reason and the capacity for free action — culture appears to have run on already into morality proper. The idea of the development of natural human gifts thus threatens to undermine the Kantian division between nature and morality. Kant's response to the threatened collapse is to draw attention to a stage of human development which he calls *civilization*, viz., a form of life involving subjection to rules and the development of rational skills in which behavior is based on prudence, outward decorum, and the love of honor. This constitutes the age of culture. Individuals may transcend this level of development in becoming moral agents, in which case their behavior is properly based purely on respect for law and duty for its own sake. But at the level of social existence, the human race remains at the pre-moral stage of civilization:

To a high degree we are, through art and science, *cultured*. We are *civilized* — perhaps too much for our own good — in all sorts of social grace and decorum. But to consider ourselves as having reached *morality* — for that, much is lacking.[19]

AESTHETIC EDUCATION

Kant emphasizes the role of discipline in restraining the impulses of animal nature and thereby civilizing us. Apart from this concern with the negative education of the passions, however, there is very little in *Immanuel Kant über Pädagogik* about the education of the feelings. This could suggest that the educational writings reflect the negative view of the passions which is characteristic of Kant's ethical theory. But this would be misleading. What this text entirely excludes is the treatment of the development of feelings and taste which can be found in Kant's *Critique of Judgement* (specifically in Book II). Why did the editor exclude this material? The following hypothesis deserves consideration.

The writings on education are concerned almost exclusively with the education of males, specifically of boys up to the age of sixteen — the age at which the pupil is to take full responsibility for his behavior, when the instinct of sex has developed and he is capable of fatherhood.[20] As regards the education of women, Kant's broad conviction was that it should be concerned primarily with the formation of taste and the cultivation of feelings, with a view to developing good morals (and not merely good manners). The education in question could allow for a little instruction in such inquiries as history and geography and an acquaintance with expression and music, to be treated more in the manner of feeling than knowledge of an art. But in general, instruction and the study of books was treated as out of keeping with "feminine nature." Woman's understanding is described as *beautiful* in contrast with male understanding which is *deep*. The latter is developed properly through formal instruction and study, while the former grows through personal guidance and direct experience of concrete examples in appropriate domains of feeling and taste.[21] In this light, it is not surprising that Kant's remarks about the development of feelings, taste, or artistic appreciation in its various forms are not included in a study which is concerned with the education of males. To talk of the cultivation of feelings in this context might have suggested to Kant (or rather, to the editor of his writings) the danger of "feminizing" education and thereby threatening the hoped-for science of pedagogy.[22]

This consideration provides a plausible hypothesis. Nevertheless, Kant's account of the formation of feelings and taste in aesthetics in the *Critique of Judgement* is put forward in quite general terms. In the *Critique*, there is the sense that the capacity to appreciate fine art and the works of the imagination generally (and to contribute to them) is one of the germs lying undeveloped in human beings at birth. There is the sense that such formation is a proper aspect of acquiring human nature and, indeed, that it is central to the growth of culture. But if it is part of human nature in Kant's understanding, then he would certainly have intended that male human beings should be included in its scope.

There could be a related formal reason on Kant's part, however, for hesitation in regard to aesthetic education. In the preface to *The Critique of Judgement* (hereafter *CJ*), he insists that his inquiry is restricted to transcendental aspects of taste as a faculty of aesthetic judgment, and that it is not being undertaken "with a view to the formation of culture and taste (which will pursue its course in the future, as in the past, independently of such inquiries)" (*CJ* 6). Then in an appendix to Part One of the *Critique*, entitled "The Methodology of Taste," he proposes that "the division of a Critique into Elementary and Methodology — a division which is introductory to science — is one inapplicable to the Critique of Taste. For there neither is, nor can be, a science of the beautiful, and the judgment of taste is not determinable by principles" (*CJ* 225).

In aesthetics, in contrast with ethics, Kant does not subscribe to absolute objectivism: there is no science of the beautiful; there are no rules of a universal sort governing the production of art; there are no principles, therefore, which could be used for teaching purposes in the art of developing critical taste. The abandonment of high objectivism, however, does not trigger a collapse into subjectivism. Kant's view is that there are appropriate ways of teaching fine art even if there is no formal general method. ("Fine Art . . . has only got a *manner* [*modus*], and not a *method* of teaching [*methodus*]" [*CJ* 226].) There is still scope for generality, but teaching in the domain has to proceed by the particular rather than the general, by way of examples, by concrete instances, by the presentation of ideals which excite the imagination and awaken a sense of general validity. These forms of teaching, it can be seen, Kant associates with feminine nature. But the appropriateness of the forms is determined in this case by the subject matter rather than the envisaged recipients. The lack of a fully developed *method* of teaching in aesthetics, therefore, does not tell against its importance for the education of men as well as for women. This would suggest that, by the time at which he wrote *The Critique of Judgement* (1790), Kant had modified the view of his essay of 1764 (*Observations on the Feeling of the Beautiful and the Sublime*) about what is appropriate for the development of "male" understanding.

Kant's developed views could also suggest that he saw in art a way of moving beyond the dualism which is characteristic of his thought. In René Wellek's words:

> [Kant] glimpses in art a possibility of bridging the gulf between necessity and freedom, between the world of deterministic nature and the world of moral action. . . .

The significance of art for him is that

> [art] accomplishes a union of the general and the particular, of intuition and thought, of imagination and reason.[23]

What is attributed to art in this way could be applied with no less force to the "world of moral action" itself — except that that world is inexplicably placed on one side of a dichotomy! Kant's own feelings for art were connected in fact with his conviction that "the beautiful is the symbol of the morally good" (*CJ* 223), and that the fostering of a regard for beauty will strengthen respect for moral good and the moral law. He would not claim that it could have direct effect on moral improvement any more than could the search for truth in the sciences; but art, together with science, is treated as a proper preparation for the moral order:

> Fine Art and sciences, if they do not make man morally better, yet, by conveying a pleasure that admits of universal communication and by introducing polish and refinement into society, make him civilized. Thus they do much to overcome the tyrannical propensities of sense, and so prepare man for a sovereignty in which reason alone shall have sway. (*CJ* II, 97)

It is clear, then, that any adequate account of the Kantian conception of moral education would need to acknowledge his recognition of the formative value of art and the sciences. It is also clear that Kant is at a considerable remove from the Rousseau of the *First Discourse* in his positive attitude to the arts and sciences. At the same time, the Kantian idea of the transition from animality to culture and from culture to moral maturity is fraught with problems.

Each individual in each generation starts at the beginning stage of animality as the condition to be overcome. Kant pinpoints the difficulty which this involves in his essay, *Idea for a Universal History from a Cosmopolitan Point of View* (1784):

> Man is an animal which . . . requires a master. . . . But whence does he get this master? Only from the human race. But then the master is himself an animal, and needs a master.[24]

The problem is the familiar one of who is to teach the teachers. The regular need for new beginnings before advances have been secured is invoked to explain why humanity has had such difficulty in approaching its postulated destiny. Kant believed that progress was possible over successive generations and that it was beginning to occur at a quickening pace: while we do not yet live in an enlightened age, we are advancing toward the light. But it is also true to say that he saw the educational task as infinitely precarious.

With reference to moral formation, there is a tension in Kant's thought regarding what can be achieved by the individual and what is possible for the race at a given time. The individual is obliged to become a moral agent, and one must assume that the outcome is attainable in a lifetime. But if the outcome is attainable for each human being, why is society as a whole still far off from the realization of morality? Kant's conception of civil society as an age of culture which falls short of morality is in question here. So too is the idea that there is a destiny of the human race as a whole, marked out by enlightenment and moral maturity.

A different tension arises from the fact that the individual is called upon to become a moral agent and to live at the same time as a member of civil society. The problem is that the appropriate pattern of motivation and the corresponding character traits are different in each case and are not easily reconcilable.

3. From Culture to Morality

To judge from the *Critique of Judgement*, one would think that there is a smooth transition from civil society to the moral order. Fine art and the sciences, though they do not make us morally better, contribute to overcoming the "tyrannical propensities of sense," and prepare the way for "a sovereignty in which reason alone shall have sway." The idea of the transition from nature to morality in the third *Critique* is based importantly on the analogical association of art and organic nature in Kant's thought, and especially on the teleological thesis which he developed in this context.

The analogy between art and organic nature is grounded on the idea that each points to a union of worlds which Kant holds as distinct. Organic nature is presented in the manner of art *as if* it acted purposely; it is portrayed as seeking an overall unity and harmony of parts in creation for the benefit of mankind. This assumption yields Kant's doctrine of the essential ends of humanity. Among such ends, happiness is the end toward which all the desires of the agent tend. As such, happiness constitutes the natural motivation of all action: "All material practical principles are, as such, of one and the same kind and belong under the general principle of self-love or one's own happiness" (*Critique of Practical Reason*, 20). But because of various internal and external factors which affect human beings, the attainment of this ideal outcome is impossible. Happiness, on this argument, cannot be treated as the ultimate end of nature in respect of human beings. The Kantian proposal is that nature, understood teleologically, has as its ultimate aim not happiness, but the production of culture. The ultimate end in formal terms is that the human being be constituted as able to choose his own ends in freedom. This is precisely what is involved in culture in a formal sense. In Kant's words:

The production in a rational being of an aptitude for any ends whatever of his own choosing, consequently of the aptitude of a being in his freedom, is *culture*. Hence it is only culture that can be the ultimate end which we have cause to attribute to nature in respect of the human race. (*CJ* II, 94)

The task which is set by nature's goal is educational in character. The process of culture, as we have seen, embraces discipline to strengthen the will by overcoming the despotism of desires and "the rudeness and violence of inclinations that belong more to the animal part of our nature." It includes the development of the skills necessary to make choice possible; it requires life in a civil community — and ideally in a cosmopolitan order — to provide a lawful authority to oppose the abuse of freedom. More completely, the goal of nature is achieved in humanistic education and the flowering of the fine arts and sciences. We are thus led to the threshold of the moral sphere. Indeed, the Kantian specification of culture in the *Critique of Judgement* takes one from nature to freedom in what appears to be an entirely harmonious resolution of the two orders.[25] And yet, the whole idea of a transition from nature to morality is problematic in the terms of Kant's thought.

The first great problem is that the requisite character traits and the pattern of motivation which are appropriate for the cultural sphere run counter in important respects to the demands of morality. How can human beings be educated to live in conflicting orders? The moral sphere, furthermore, is presented as discontinuous with the world of nature. In what sense, then, can it be approached from the non-moral natural order in which education takes place? I propose to consider each of these problems in turn. In terms of Kant's developmental schema, they relate to his notions of *pragmatic education* and *moral education* respectively.

PRAGMATIC EDUCATION

In the sphere of culture, Kant gives special prominence to formation in prudence (*Klugheit*). This is treated as the primary motivational force in the pre-moral stage of civil society; it is accorded its place in the education of the individual under the name of *pragmatic education*.

Prudence is connected with the practical or pragmatic natural disposition of human beings, flanked, on the one hand, by the technical disposition which it presupposes and, on the other, by the moral disposition from which it is sharply distinguished, but for which it is a presupposition. Again, it occupies a middle place in Kant's threefold order of imperatives. The counsels of prudence are described as assertoric, falling between the merely hypothetical imperatives which relate to the use of skills, on the one hand, and the categorical imperatives which govern moral behavior, on the other. Particular individuals may or may not be concerned to acquire or exercise a particular skill; rules regarding their employment are therefore hypothetical. But counsels of prudence — to look after one's health, for example, apply to everyone and relate to matters in which everyone *in fact* has an interest. At the same time, they do not oblige anyone unconditionally as the moral law does (*FMM* 31ff).

Prudence in the Kantian sense clearly has some connections with the Aristotelian (intellectual) virtue of practical wisdom, but when account is taken of the very different conceptions of happiness in each system and the different ways in which practical skill is related to moral virtue, the differences are significant. We might understand Kantian prudence in William Frankena's words as "the art of being happy in the world, the art of using our skills and knowledge in such a way as to be happy in the long run as individuals."[26] This formulation could disguise, however, the coincidence for Kant of one's own happiness with self-love, which he takes to be the natural motivation of all behavior. One also needs to keep in mind the sharp distinction which Kant makes between prudence and morality. In the *Anthropology*, the pragmatic disposition is linked specifically with the ability for "using other men skilfully for [one's own] purposes." The rule of prudence is associated with "the inclination for power to exercise influence over other men," which is, so Kant writes,

> the inclination which comes closest to technically practical reason, that is, to the maxim of prudence. For getting other men's inclinations into our power, so that we can direct and determine them according to our purposes, is almost the same as *possessing* other men as mere tools of our will. (*Anthropology*, 238)

Prudence as the art of turning our skills to account is essentially the art of using our fellow human beings for our own ends, where the ends are to our lasting advantage. Kant's most authoritative statement of the matter is in the *Foundations of the Metaphysics of Morals*:

> The word "prudence" may be taken in two senses, and it may bear the name of prudence with reference to the things of the world and private prudence. The former sense means the skill of a man in having an influence on others so as to use them for his own purposes. The latter is the ability to unite all these purposes to his own lasting advantage. The worth of the first is finally reduced to the latter, and of one who is prudent in the former sense but not in the latter we might better say that he is clever and cunning yet, on the whole, imprudent. (33, note)

Prudence, in short, is the art of using others to promote our own happiness. It requires that, along with learning to read the characters of others, we should disguise our own feelings and learn to be reserved, concealing our faults and keeping up outward appearances as constituted by good manners. In speaking of such character traits in the *Critique of Pure Reason*, Kant explains:

> There is in human nature a certain falseness [*Unlauterkeit*] which, like everything that comes from nature, must finally contribute to good ends,

namely, a disposition to conceal our real sentiments, and to make show of certain assumed sentiments which are regarded as good and creditable. This tendency to conceal ourselves and to assume the appearance of what contributes to our advantage, has undoubtedly, not only *civilised* us, but gradually, in a certain measure, *moralised* us. (599; A748/B776)

A few sentences later, Kant insists that the recommended practice of duplicity has to be seen as a merely provisional arrangement: from the standpoint of morality it must be combatted, he says, for its continuance would be a source of corruption. On this basis, it might be suggested that formation in prudence is equally to be treated as provisional, at least as it involves using others for our own ends, possessing them as "tools of our will." From the standpoint of morality achieved, prudence will have served its purpose and could remain only as a source of corruption.

This proposal seems to capture Kant's intentions, but it is subject to a number of serious difficulties. In the first place, there is a pedagogical problem concerning the moral development of the individual. The pupil is to be guided first in the ways of prudence (and the accompanying duplicity). At a later stage, the true principles of morality are to be instilled, and from this vantage point, action is to be taken against the earlier practices. But when is the teacher supposed to stop inculcating one set of practical principles and turn to the recommendation of the new and opposing moral set? How is the old set of principles to be unlearned or transmuted?

The dynamics of the account holds that the assumption of sentiments which "are regarded as good and creditable" will lead to the adoption of true moral principles in time. The motivation for assuming the appearance of virtue arises specifically from the two natural impulses which Kant attributes to human beings: the longings to be esteemed and to be loved. Thus self-love, which is expressed in the natural impulses, becomes the foundation of moral development. In giving this account, Kant was aligning himself with John Locke, who was the first modern philosopher to account the pleasure of being well-thought of, and, more generally, self-interest, a respectable and proper motivation in the development of morality in the individual. That he would strongly repudiate self-interest as a proper motivation of virtuous behavior is not to the point.[27]

This particular attempt to provide a transition from Kantian prudence to morality is in any case irrelevant. It holds that the assumption of what are regarded as good and creditable sentiments will lead to the adoption of true moral principles. But the rules according to which one treats others as means to one's own ends and dissembles one's real sentiments are not generally regarded as good and creditable in the first place. The proposal that prudence be treated as a (merely) provisional arrangement on the way to morality gives rise to a further problem in connection with the different time scales applicable to individual human beings and the human race more generally. Individuals, under the dictates of practical reason, are obliged to seek to act as moral agents and to base their behavior on the motive of duty. But the same individuals will live out their lives in a civil society, in a culture marked by technico-practical rationality, as Kant puts it, far removed from a genuine moral culture. The destiny of the race in coming to perfection lies far into the future. At the same time, the emergence of a culture based on morality is presented as the outcome of a prudence-based culture developing according to its own proper principles. According to what set of rules, then, should individuals live? As individual moral agents, they fall under the categorical imperatives of the moral law. As members of civil society, however, they are to be guided presumably by the pragmatic imperatives of prudence, with the added reflection that action of this form will ultimately lead to the advent of the kingdom of ends, that is, a culture based on morality. Kantian individuals are thereby placed in an impossible situation.

One relevant strand in Kant's conception of the developmental nature of history is connected with the idea of the sense of decency, as Kant calls it, viz., "the inclination to inspire others to respect by proper manners, i.e. by concealing all which might arouse low esteem."[28] The sense of decency, it is claimed, is the real basis of human sociability and carries the promise of our development as moral beings.

A second strand in the account gives higher-order approval to forms of motivation which, on the face of it, appear forthrightly questionable. The argument is that cultural development also depends on motivating forces of an unsociable sort, in particular, vainglory, lust for power, and avarice. The competitive strivings which are involved in these egoistic desires are credited with taking us from barbarism to culture, and to the progressive development of talents and the refinement of taste toward the emergence of a "moral whole." Kant exclaims in this connection:

> Thanks be to Nature, then, for the incompatibility, for heartless competitive vanity, for the insatiable desire to possess and rule! Without them, all the excellent natural capacities of humanity would forever sleep, undeveloped.

The natural urges in question, though they result in considerable evil, are held to reflect the ordering of a wise creator. In this light Kant concludes:

> All culture, art which adorns mankind, and the finest social order are fruits of unsociableness, which forces itself to discipline itself and so, by a contrived art, to develop the natural seeds to perfection.[29]

Kant is thus placed in the position of approving motivations such as vanity and the desire for power as they are thought to constitute the dynamic forces of history. But in his central moral teaching, notably in regard to virtue and vice, these dynamic forces of human progress must fall under condemnation. What is treated as objectionable in the morality which pertains to individuals is accorded approbation in the higher order of the historical process. But the historical process is itself conceived as being, in large measure, the product of individual action. The impossible situation of Kantian individuals is rendered even more impossible. Which order of principles is to be chosen and which will ensure the morally preferable outcome? There is a conflict for the individual between the immediate demands of morality and the imperatives of historical progress.[30]

More generally, Kant's whole attempt to find a place for pragmatic education and for a culture based on prudence as preparatory to morality ends in failure. The root of the problem lies, as I have indicated, in the initial determination to set prudence and concern with one's happiness outside the moral sphere, in terms that are opposed to morality though they are supposed to contribute to it in the end. The irony of this is that the moral philosophy proper does find a place for happiness, as we have seen, albeit in a way that is not fully acknowledged. But this is problematic in a different way inasmuch as happiness is construed within the limited framework of self-love. The problem of the supposed discontinuity of the moral and non-moral spheres — or rather, the narrowness of the strict Kantian conception of the moral sphere — is especially acute in connection with the topic of moral education and development.

MORAL EDUCATION

The final stage of Kant's developmental schema is moral education proper. In the writings on education, this topic occupies the central place; indeed, all education is treated as ultimately concerned in one way or another with moral formation.

Kant's concern with pedagogical aspects of moral growth is entirely consistent with his general view that a domain of inquiry needs to be supplied with its corresponding methodology. On the other hand, it does not appear to be at all consistent with his moral philosophy strictly understood. In blunt terms, Kant's insistence on the discontinuity of the moral and the non-moral spheres, and his conception of the moral agent as the noumenal self standing outside the empirical order, renders moral education impossible. Consistently enough, perhaps, Kant ordinarily holds that there is no duty on anyone even to try to promote the (moral) perfection of others, children included. The basic argument for this implausible claim is that the promotion of a person's perfection lies solely in the power of the individual concerned; it would be self-contradictory, therefore, "to demand that I do (make it my duty to do) what only the other person himself can do" (*Doctrine of Virtue*, 44–45). There would appear to be no possibility, then, for a charter for moral education.

Whatever may be said about the logic of the situation, there is the contrary evidence of Kant's writing on the topic. He takes it for granted that it *is* possible to contribute to the moral formation of others and that there is a duty to do so, specifically in regard to children.[31] At this point, some writers are drawn to say that in the context of education Kant is prepared to relax his customary rigor. It should be clear that this tactic of "double standards," if it did pertain, would be entirely unsatisfactory. The question, How is moral education possible? is a serious one for Kant, with bearing on his whole moral theory.

Moral education in this setting is concerned fundamentally with the development of moral character. In what does this consist? The *Anthropology* specifies character as relating to "that property of the will by which the subject has tied himself to certain practical principles which he has unalterably prescribed for himself by his own reason" (203). Established moral character in these terms consists in knowledge of the moral law and an aptitude for acting in accordance with its maxims: "a consistent practical habit of mind according to unchangeable maxims," as it is put in the *Critique of Practical Reason* (156). Ideally, it would consist in perfect virtue, the disposition always to act according to duty and always to choose good ends. The acquisition of character is properly understood as self-formation, a consideration which points once again to the problem of moral education. The problem emerges more acutely, in fact, in the discussion of character in the *Critique of Pure Reason*, where, in the case of human agents, Kant distinguishes between empirical and intelligible character (468; A539/B567).

Character involves the idea of a regular or consistent pattern of behavior. Empirical character is attributed to a subject as belonging to the sensible world in which its actions, as appearances, conform to laws of causal determinism. Intelligible character, by contrast, belongs to the subject as thing in itself, standing outside all conditions of sensibility, and existing as cause of its actions as appearances (and hence as cause of empirical character). Clearly, the free moral agent must be understood as the subject under the aspect of intelligible character and hence as noumenon outside space and time. Moral action, on the other hand, takes place in the empirical world. Furthermore, the character developed through moral education (beginning with discipline) must have an empirical dimension. As source of moral action, it cannot be identified with empirical character, but neither can it be treated as intelligible character.

If one sets aside the problem of showing how moral education is linked with its specified outcome, the Kantian account of the educative process itself is straightforward. It consists, in a word, in the transmission of appropriate information regarding moral duties and virtues within a framework of Kant's own ethical theory (as the "Fragments of a Moral Catechism" in the *Doctrine of Virtue* would suggest) (153ff). Attention is also given to the need to foster appropriate dispositions. As regards method, Kant suggests that the requisite information may be taught directly by lectures or, more indirectly, by the use of questions in the form of dialogue or catechism, supplemented by some practice in casuistry. But Kant is wary about appealing to examples of moral virtues since this would link principles too closely, in his view, to particular cases and the arousal of feelings. His conviction is that, in the proper circumstances, the pupil will see the truth of the relevant duties by rational grasp "from within," and see that duty itself is the only proper motive for morally good action. Methods for fostering the appropriate dispositions begin with discipline, with practices intended to develop self-restraint and fortitude, progressively structured by the need to develop the subject's autonomy in choosing freely to submit to laws. In its highest form, education of this sort consists in the cultivation of virtue or what Kant calls moral asceticism.

Kant clearly thinks that the practices which constitute moral formation are important and that they would ordinarily be necessary conditions of the acquisition of virtue. In his moral anthropology, virtue has to be learned, and the learning needs to include practice on the basis of appropriate information. In this respect, Kant is in agreement with Aristotle or Locke (or Rousseau, for that matter) that we are not born either virtuous or vicious (see *Doctrine of Virtue*, 149). But given this, there is no reason to accept his claim that an obligation to promote the moral perfection of another person is self-contradictory. Virtue has to be learned, and the learning is impossible without the assistance of others. It follows that others may be of help (or hindrance) in the process, and hence some (parents, for example) may reasonably fall under a particular obligation in this regard. It is true that virtue, as achievement, depends necessarily in the end on the individual subject, but it is no different in this respect than any number of skills, capacities, or habits which a person may acquire. Having recognized the general conditions for the acquisition of virtue, Kant seeks to separate virtue as the product of pure practical reason. But the attempt to separate virtue in this way from its grounds in human life is no more successful than the attempt to portray the moral law in purely formal terms.

The account of moral education which Kant provides belies the thesis of the discontinuity of the moral and non-moral spheres. Given that he is forced to recognize considerable exchange and interaction, one might be inclined to suggest that the claim to discontinuity is no more than a defense of moral autonomy, an insistence on the idea that the moral subject in its freedom lies in some way beyond the conditions of empirical determinism. In Kant's system of idealized sharp divisions, however, the thesis of individual autonomy itself takes a very strong form. The free moral subject is placed in the noumenal world, beyond space and time. In an unexplained way, the noumenal order gives rise to the phenomenal order and is expressed in it while remaining untouched and untouchable. The problem of moral education therefore returns. Since there is no transition from the phenomenal to the noumenal, the process of moral formation must appear ineffectual. Furthermore, the noumenal self, outside space and time, exists in isolation from other noumenal selves, with the consequence that there cannot be a community of moral agents. It is not a matter for surprise, then, that Kant sought to show that morality could be spun out of the resources of the individual as such (each individual being treated as the representative of humanity). These considerations are set aside, however, in the context of education. Should we say that Kant is simply relaxing his customary rigor in view of the fact that in talking of education and moral development, he has left the realm of pure philosophy? One might say, rather, that the problem lies in the pure philosophy and its dream of reason.

In the discussion of pragmatic education, I drew attention to problems in Kant's idea of the emergence from civil society of a culture based on morality. Just now I have been concerned to argue that there is a conflict between his commitment to moral education and the strict terms of his moral philosophy. The problem arises in each case from the postulation of utopian ideals of reason.

Kant's views about the emergence of a culture based on morality constitute, as F. E. and F. P. Manuel propose in their book, *Utopian Thought in the Western World*, a doctrine of *euchronia*. A *euchronia* is a utopia in which perfection, social and personal, is located in the historical future; the term thus means "a future good time," a future golden age. Euchronic visions burgeoned in the second half of the eighteenth century and found their primary systematic expression in different ways in the writings of Turgot and Condorcet in France and of Kant in Germany. Kant's version of euchronia, in the words of the Manuels, was "a German version of the dream of reason and of the triumph of instinctual repression as the only ideal worthy of man."[32]

The task in hand, "the realisation of the ultimate destiny of the human race," as Kant puts it at the end of the *Lectures on Ethics*, is conceived as essentially educational. My argument has been that, quite apart from the general implausibility of utopian doctrines, Kant's conception of the task, in regard to individuals and the human community alike, runs into specific insoluble difficulties of its own making.

The doctrine of euchronia, with its vision of future perfection, is fundamentally social in character and time-oriented. It is the idea of an ethical society in the historical future. By contrast, Kant's strict moral philosophy, arising out of pure reason, has no reference to the future and is essentially individualist in character. At its heart stands the moral agent as noumenal self, outside space and time, with access through reason to the eternal moral law. This suggests the idea of a utopia of a different sort: a utopia in which each individual self is an island and which is properly to be found nowhere.

8. From Hobbes to Mill: The General Happiness

1. Hobbes: Felicity and the Quest for Peace and Unity

A version of the idea of happiness stands at the heart of Utilitarian ethical theory. In the words of John Stuart Mill, "the creed which accepts as the foundation of morals, Utility, or the Greatest Happiness Principle, holds that actions are right in proportion as they tend to promote happiness, wrong as they tend to promote the reverse of happiness. By happiness is intended pleasure, and the absence of pain; by unhappiness, pain and the privation of pleasure."[1] In assessing behavior, or policies, institutions, or practices and the like, Utilitarianism looks to a collectivity; it is concerned with the community of people whose interests are affected (more strictly, it is concerned with their feelings). Within this framework, individuals are assumed to be fundamentally concerned with their own happiness. It is also assumed that the interest of the community is, in Jeremy Bentham's words, "the sum of the interests of the several members who compose it"; general happiness is treated as the product of the happiness of individuals.[2] One large problem here, among others, is that there is no obvious guarantee of a harmony of interests among the relevant parties. Indeed, there has been a persistent view from the beginning of the modern era that individuals, in quest of their own happiness, are locked into conflict with one another. There is no natural or moral ground on which a harmony of interests could be based.

A view of this sort is associated especially with the moral and political philosophy of Thomas Hobbes. There is serious question whether Hobbes's writings have been rightly interpreted in this vein, but from an early stage he was taken to have put forward an egoistic theory of motivation and to have dissolved morality into nothing more than obedience to civil law, which is secured on grounds of pure self-interest.[3] According to the account, every individual has a natural and overriding desire for self-preservation in a situation in which, by nature, every other individual is seen as constituting a threat to his life. What is needed in the situation is peace. Each individual must want peace, if he comes to think about it, to escape the fear of death. The only way to ensure peace, however, is to have a common power with such authority over life that everyone recognizes that it is in their interests to obey its laws.

On the basis of a broad interpretation of this sort, Hobbes can be seen as setting the terms of the moral question for subsequent Utilitarian theory (and for modern ethical theory more generally). This is connected importantly with the ways in which Hobbes's writings reflected and responded to the great political, social, and ideological crises in which the modern era was born. His ideas were worked out against the immediate background of the Puritan Revolution and the Civil War. He wrote, therefore, in a situation of immediate crisis and breakdown in regard to political and religious authority and the claims of law. More generally, he wrote against the background of the collapse of the Christian-Aristotelian world view of the Middle Ages, the transition from feudalism to capitalism in economic and social relations, the breakdown of religious unity in the Reformation and the associated questioning of the whole nature of law and authority in society, the emergence of nation-states, and the revolutionary developments in science in which the Greek and medieval conception of the cosmos was replaced by the idea of the universe as a mechanical system governed by mechanistic laws, specifically by laws of motion.

Two ideas in particular dominated Hobbes's moral and political thought. He wanted to see a moral and political order in which civil authority would be powerful enough to resist rebellion and to ensure the conditions of peace at home and abroad; and he considered that the basis of such an order could be found in a study of human beings and their relationships according to the principles of the new science.

The significance of the background issues and the subtlety of Hobbes's own thought make the task of interpretation immensely difficult and fascinating. His philosophy is the harbinger of tough-minded reductionist accounts of human beings — whether in science or literature — in which morality vanishes or takes the form of considerations of what is technically possible in relation to desired ends. But Hobbes incorporated a good deal of the natural-law tradition from Greek and Christian thinking, perhaps more than he was aware of or would have wished; in any case, he was genuinely concerned with the substance of the traditional moral issues and their significance in the turbulent conditions of his time. This concern comes out especially in what he says about reason as a source of moral knowledge and influence on moral motivation. But this has to be balanced against Hobbes's more "scientific" teaching concerning the passions as the primary system of motivation and his argument, on this basis, that human beings are by nature locked into conflict with one another. In treading a way through some aspects of his thought, I will be particularly concerned with his views about moral motivation and human sociability.

INDIVIDUAL MOTIVATION

Happiness, according to the definition which Hobbes gives in Chapter VI of *Leviathan* (hereafter *Lev.*), consists in sustained success in getting what one wants:

Continual success in obtaining those things which a man from time to time desireth, that is to say, continual prospering, is that men call FELICITY.[4]

This definition, which says nothing about the specific character or content of a person's desires, is presented as part of a general account of human motivation. As it stands, there is nothing essentially egoistic in the proposal: after all, a person's desires may include the wish to help others. More obvious weaknesses concern the formalism of the account and the limited, albeit ambitious, scope of Hobbes's basic theory of motivation.

Hobbes tells a story of motivation which is supposedly scientific. The idea is that sensory experience, as when we see or hear something, characteristically sets off internal motions toward or away from the object of sensation. These internal motions are held to constitute the passions. That is to say, the passions, for all their variety, take one of two basic forms: the beginnings of movement toward a perceived object (appetite or desire) or the beginnings of movement away from it (aversion). The individual is conceived as a field on which at any given time different passions (different forms and forces of appetite or aversion) contend until one or other prevails, giving rise to appropriate appetitive or evasive behavior (voluntary behavior or, in physiological terms, "animal motions").

Desire and aversion, which are equated with love and hate respectively, go with an individual-related system of evaluation. Hobbes supposes that while a few appetites and aversions are innate, most are learned "by trial of their effects"; and he further supposes that what people learn to pursue and avoid, and hence what they think of as good and evil, varies considerably:

But whatsoever is the object of any man's appetite or desire, that is it which he for his part calleth *good*: and the object of his hate and aversion, *evil*. (*Lev.* VI, 32)

Finally, appetite or desire or love is accompanied always by a degree of pleasure, and aversion or hatred by displeasure (the one being the "appearance, or sense of good," the other the "appearance, or sense of evil"). All voluntary behavior, in short, is undertaken in the pursuit of pleasure, whether pleasures of sense or of the mind.

This account, as I noted earlier, is not egoistic, but it is excessively individualistic. Hobbes writes as if the development of the passions and the concomitant acquisition of behavioral tendencies could be effected in the individual without reference to others. It would be a mistake, however, to treat the basic formal account as complete in itself, as if it exhausted Hobbes's views regarding motivation, morality, and the idea of happiness. The physiological character of the account is entirely promissory and is belied in fact by the whole manner of presentation. It becomes clear that Hobbes thinks that, in addition to the system of the passions, reason supplies a distinct and controlling source of knowledge and motivation.

The topic of morality is taken up again in Chapter XI of *Leviathan* under the term manners, understood as "those qualities of mankind, that concern living together in peace, and unity" (63). Having introduced the topic, Hobbes proceeds immediately to speak of happiness, for it emerges that he thinks that the pursuit of happiness by individuals stands in the way of the moral goal of peace and unity. Happiness now is specified as follows:

> Felicity is a continual progress of the desire, from one object to another; the attaining of the former, being still but the way to the latter. The cause whereof is, that the object of man's desire, is not to enjoy once only, and for an instance of time; but to assure for ever, the way of future desire. And therefore the voluntary actions, and inclinations of all men, tend, not only to the procuring, but also to the assuring of a contented life. (*Lev.* XI, 63)

But the assurance of the way of future desire to the end of assuring for oneself a contented life is possible only if one has power, that is, in Hobbes's definition, "present means, to obtain some future good" (*Lev.* X, 56).

Moreover, this desire for power, given awareness of the future, can have no limit. All mankind is thus credited with "a perpetual and restless desire of power after power, that ceaseth only in death." To ensure his own life, each person must seek power over the life of the other; each therefore constitutes a threat to the life of others. The starkly competitive character of the model emerges even more sharply in the well-known passage in *The Elements* in which Hobbes employs the image of life as a race and characterizes happiness as the beating of others:

> Continually to be outgone is *misery*.
> Continually to out-go the one before is *felicity*.
> And to forsake the course is to die.[5]

The upshot is that the pursuit of happiness takes the form of a competitive struggle for survival. In seeking contentment, human beings find themselves faced with misery and the threat of violent death.

Hobbes's hard-headed argument is that this outcome is the natural condition of mankind. In the absence of the restraining force of civil law, everyone is taken to have unrestricted liberty. In such a situation, assuming that everyone is broadly equal in power, and setting aside other real conditions of existence, human passion, geared to the pursuit of individual happiness, ensures general conflict and the misery of all. There is, however, the possibility of an escape from nature. The general experience of misery and fear of violent death gives everyone the desire for peace; then, human reason is at hand to work out peace terms (to be enforced by a common power).

Many of Hobbes's readers conclude that he portrays human beings as radically egoistic, incapable of giving weight to interests other than their own. The argument from the passions (in *Lev.* XIII) is taken to imply that there is no place for benevolence or any other regarding virtue in human relations. In this interpretation, the institution of civil authority, with power to ensure conformity to law, does nothing to change the underlying conditions. Law ensures peace only by the power of the sword; people are moved to act justly in accordance with law, not for moral reasons, but merely on the basis of self-interest.

Bishop Butler, in the first of his *Fifteen Sermons Preached at the Rolls Chapel* (1726), provides an early and well-known interpretation of Hobbes's teaching along these lines. In Butler's view, Hobbes is committed to a general hypothesis which has no place for benevolence or good will. He must therefore treat the appearance of good will among human beings as *mere* appearance; specifically, according to Butler, he treats it as being "only the love of power, and the delight in the exercise of it."[6] Butler refers in this connection to Hobbes's work, *Of Human Nature*, where he probably has in mind a passage in which Hobbes explains what he means by *love*, or more properly, *good will* or *charity*: "There can be no greater argument to a man, of his own power, than to find himself able not only to accomplish his own desires, but also to assist other men in theirs: and this is that conception wherein consisteth *charity*."[7] This passage appears to say less than Bishop Butler thought to find in it: it proposes that charity is evidence of a person's power (and there is the implication that the exercise of charity presupposes power); but charity is not identified with the love of power or with delight in it. Elsewhere, Hobbes defines benevolence more succinctly (and clearly) as the "*desire* of good to another" (*Lev.* VI, 34), without any suggestion that it is really the manifestation of a desire of a different sort.

A conclusive argument on this topic would need to consider other passages in Hobbes's writings and other more general aspects of his views. But a number of recent studies have provided strong grounds for thinking that Hobbes was not committed to a doctrine of psychological egoism.[8] His position unequivocally is that for each individual the desire for self-preservation is overriding: "The greatest of goods for each is his own preservation"; furthermore, "nature is so arranged that all desire good for themselves,"[9] more specifically, "of the voluntary acts of every man, the object is some *good to himself*" (*Lev.* XIV, 86). It does not follow from this, however, that Hobbes thought, or was required to think, that a person can act *only* for his own benefit. Benevolence as the desire of good to another is not excluded by concern for one's own good. Hobbes's position, rather, is that benevolence does not go very far: it is hedged in by considerations of self-interest and extends only to a limited circle. This limit is then pushed to an extreme in the abstract depiction of the state of nature: in the terms allowed, benevolent action would put one's life at risk and would count as contrary to reason.

THE BONDS OF THE SOCIAL ORDER AND MORAL DEVELOPMENT

The general question at issue concerns the bonds of the social order. In the first chapter of *De Cive*, Hobbes explains why he rejects the traditional view that "man is a creature born fit for society."[10] The argument turns on the facts of human infancy and the nature of (civil) society; specifically, Hobbes argues that "all men because they are born in infancy, are born unapt for society." The argument allows that, by nature, infants need the company and help of others:

> To man by nature, or as man, that is, as soon as he is born, solitude is an enemy; for infants have need of others to help them to live, and those of riper years to help them to live well. (*De Cive*, 110, note)

On this basis, furthermore, Hobbes allows that human beings have a desire, a natural compulsion even, to come together. But infants, as infants, lack any (immediate) capacity for engaging in the sorts of agreements the social order involves. They cannot enter society, Hobbes argues, since they do not even know what it is:

> But civil societies are not mere meetings, but bonds, to the making whereof faith and compacts are necessary; . . . [children,] because they know not what society is, cannot enter into it; . . . Manifest therefore it is, that all men, because they are born in infancy, are born unapt for society. (*De Cive*, 110, note)

In this argument, Hobbes asserts what no one would deny. Who would think that *being born fit for society* means that infants have an immediate capacity to make contracts, for example, or know anything about society?[11] Hobbes's own view is that "man is made fit for society not by nature, but by education" (*De Cive*, 110, note). Once again, no major thinker in the "born fit for society" tradition would disagree about the necessity and utter importance of education in preparing children for social life. In the passage quoted above, Hobbes draws a distinction between civil society, with its bonds which rest on faith and compacts, and mere meetings. Where do the natural relations of infants and those who care for them stand? They could hardly be described as "mere meetings," but they fall short of social status as Hobbes depicts it. One is drawn to the conclusion that Hobbes is able to push the case against the idea of a natural bond in social relations only by his determination to insist on practices which involve conventions or agreements. He acknowledges the relations surrounding infancy, but then sets them aside because they do not meet the chosen requirement. When he goes on to consider the conditions under which people seek to enter social relations, he confidently locates the basis of society in mutual fear, the cause of which "consists partly in the natural equality of men, partly in their mutual will of hurting" (*De Cive*, 113). In other words, he now ignores the original and universal relations surrounding infancy: relations which, in fact, involve inequality and which are normally constituted by the will to care for the life and well-being of another. This criticism of Hobbes's argument regarding the nature of social bonds does not affect his view about the general lack of good will among human beings, but it suggests that the whole attempt to mount an argument about the *nature* of human relations (the "inference from the passions" in *Lev.* XIII) in abstraction from the basic general conditions in which these relations develop is mistaken in principle.

In accounting for the social formation of the individual, Hobbes puts all the emphasis on education: "Man is made fit for society not by nature, but by education" (*De Cive*, 110). This emphasis serves to draw attention to his conception of the role of reason in the process of development, and it points to the presence of a notion of moral development in his thought.

When the passions would condemn us to the misery of war with one another, reason shows the way to peace. According to Hobbes's official account, reason is essentially a power of reckoning associated with awareness of the future, a capacity for calculating possible effects from known causes. Put in this way, reason is accommodated to Hobbes's scientific image of the human being, and it serves to point the way to the maximum gratification of desire (or the least worst situation in this regard) through the institution of civil authority with power to keep the peace. In fact, Hobbes's writings point to a much more substantive conception of reason in relation to morality and to social and moral development.

According to this larger conception, the passions or emotions are liable to come into conflict with right reasoning:

> [The emotions] obstruct right reasoning in this, that they militate against the real good and in favour of the apparent and most immediate good which turns out frequently to be evil when everything associated with it hath been considered. (*On Man*, XII, 1, 55)

The *real good* in this context is not a matter of the determination of maximal gratification of desire in the long run. It relates rather to the idea of something which is determined by the *law of nature*. The law of nature in this context is conceived as the expression of dictates of reason regarding moral behavior, viz., what, so far as reason in general can determine, is to be done or omitted for the preservation of life and for peace and unity (matters of common good). What this yields in detail, in Hobbes's several accounts of the laws of nature, is a summary of traditional Greek and Christian teaching concerning moral precepts and the virtues, with a particular focus on justice and charity (as subsuming other virtues).[12]

While Hobbes puts all the emphasis on education, he insists that the power of reason, specifically in regard to moral knowledge, is "no less a part of human nature than any other faculty of the mind" (*De Cive*, 122). *Right reason* is not an infallible faculty, but as a power of the individual it consists in "the peculiar and true ratiocination of every man concerning those actions of his, which may either redound to the damage or benefit of his neighbours" (*De Cive*, 123, note). To this end, however, education is required, especially as reason develops later in the individual than the basic system of the passions. Hobbes does not discuss in any detail how

the relevant knowledge and dispositions are to be acquired. But he supposes that good teaching and, more importantly, good example are basic:

> Whence it must be understood . . . not only how much fathers, teach-
> ers, and tutors of youths must imbue the minds of youths with precepts
> which are good and true, but also how much they must bear themselves
> justly and in a righteous manner in their presence, for the dispositions of
> youths are not less, but much more disposed to bad habits by example
> than they are to good ones by precept. (*On Man*, XIII, 67)

The account allows that many people — perhaps most — fail to get the
necessary education or to profit from it (*De Cive*, 110). In their case,
inclinations to infringe the conditions of peace and unity are restrained
principally by the force of civil law. Their actions in conformity with law
are just, but they themselves are said to lack justice inasmuch as they act
out of fear. The will of such a person, Hobbes says, "is not framed by the
justice, but by the apparent benefit of what he is to do" (*Lev.* XV, 97).[13] But
equally, Hobbes supposes that there are others whose moral education has
been satisfactory. Such people have acquired a knowledge of right and
wrong on grounds of reason (as opposed, e.g., to mere custom), and they
have acquired the corresponding moral qualities, justice and charity in
particular, as effective dispositions for behavior. Hobbes's account of the
laws of nature thus points to a moral theory (and an account of moral
development) which is broadly in keeping with Aristotelian and medieval
views. But he tells the story of the passions and reason separately and does
not explain how the two systems fit together. Reason conveys a knowledge
of right and wrong which corrects the subjective and relativist system of
valuation associated with the passions. Again, reason is associated with
the development of dispositions for behavior (manners or virtues). Reason,
it appears, must operate through the passions; presumably, a connection
might be made through those passions which are related to the primary
moral goals of peace and unity.[14] But Hobbes does not offer enlightenment. Another problem is that in the account of motivation which concerns
the passions alone, the agent effectively disappears, being hardly more
than a field on which forces contend. But with a substantive conception of
reason and the moral virtues, the agent is brought back in. Again, Hobbes
would need to give consideration to the place of pleasure in the new
context. In connection with the passions, the pursuit of maximum pleasure
is built into the idea of voluntary behavior. In relation to the virtues, by
contrast, pleasure is one consideration among others.

At this point Hobbes would also need to provide a revised account of
happiness. His treatment of happiness, in *Leviathan* and elsewhere, relates
it to the satisfaction of desire (the feeling of contentment and security)
without reference to considerations of reason. But now, as we know, he
puts forward an account in which reason is connected centrally with social
and moral development and hence with the conditions for preserving

human life. What is needed is an account of happiness which would link it with the exercise of reason manifested in the qualities and forms of behavior encompassed in the laws of nature. The pursuit of happiness in this sense obviously incorporates a concern for one's own well-being, but in the exercise of moral virtue, such concern is properly caught up with concern for others and for matters of common good.

Hobbes said that the science of the laws of nature is "the true and only moral philosophy" (*Lev.* XV, 104). But it can be seen that he did not follow the logic of his account. The focus of *Leviathan* (and other writings in moral and political philosophy) turns quickly from the laws of nature to civil authority and civil law. The whole weight of his argument now falls on civil law and the authority of the sovereign power. Hobbes assumes that the laws of nature are properly contained in the civil law; whereas everyone educated for social life is credited with moral knowledge, the determination of the law is made to rest with the sovereign alone.

Hobbes's moral philosophy proper is beset by unanswered questions. In this situation, the focus of attention has subsequently tended to fall on the apparently self-contained system of the passions in the individual, the dramatic picture of the "natural conditions of mankind," the denial of natural sociability, and the espousal of an absolutist conception of civil authority for the maintenance of peace and unity. Approaches which take their inspiration from these Hobbesian themes have continued as an apparently permanent strand in modern consciousness. More generally, and from an early stage, the Hobbesian version of the themes was rejected.

2. The Eighteenth-Century Debate: Benevolence and Self-Love

Locke, as we have seen, sought to repudiate Hobbes by returning to a natural-law tradition which postulated a degree of natural sociability among human beings and which appealed (overambitiously) to reason. Versions of the appeal to reason were to continue, but the idea of a natural basis for sociability in the emotions became particularly significant in the eighteenth century. Writer after writer (and numerous preachers) questioned Hobbes's account of the affective basis of human relations. A good deal of moral thought was taken up with the conviction that benevolence, or something like it, is part of human nature, sufficient to serve as a bridge to account for the general acceptance of moral precepts and concern for the happiness of others. But the different attempts to account for moral motivation along these lines were in fact shaped in significant ways by a Hobbesian outlook. The most important of these influences concern the individualist framework within which the moral question is raised and the associated conception of happiness.

THE IDEA OF PRIVATE HAPPINESS

Hobbes, of course, was not the begetter of modern individualism; rather, he reflected a major current of the time and gave it dramatic expression in his writings. This embodies, importantly, the idea that it makes sense to think of human nature as complete within a single individual or as adequately specifiable without reference to social context. On this basis, social relations, and specifically moral relations, are treated as something that have to be added on (however important the addition might be). Hobbes, in the light of his account of the passions, was understood to have made the addition particularly problematic. But if human beings are seen as naturally sociable and benevolent (to some extent), the problem could be solved or, at least, made more manageable. In other words, concern with the happiness of others, expressed in moral rules, could be drawn into harmony with the individual's undoubted concern with self.

Both Hobbes and his eighteenth-century critics, it is clear, attempt to say what human nature is like in advance of moral considerations. In each case, moreover, the argument falls back on a conception of the psychology of the individual, primarily with reference to the passions. Different things are said about them, but the passions function in each case as the given (as indicating what human beings are "really" like, or can become, or can be made to be).

The idea of happiness is brought into this framework at both stages. In connection with the passions, the happiness of the individual is the focus of attention; in connection with morality, it is a question of the individual's contribution to the happiness of others and hence to the general happiness. But the idea of happiness itself is characteristically fixed at the primary level of the individual: it consists in the satisfaction of the appetites or desires associated with the passions. Its primary definition is thus expounded independently of moral considerations. Furthermore, happiness in the framework of the passions is understood fundamentally in terms of feelings or a state of mind. The focus on happiness at this level points to a significant shift in moral thinking.

The idea of happiness in terms of the acquisition of power or the experience of pleasurable feelings was not new. Callicles in Plato's *Gorgias*, for example, is made to express a view of this sort in a particularly strong (but vulnerable) way, and there were other, more moderate, defenses of the approach in Greek thought. There was a general conviction among the Greeks, at the same time, that happiness was properly linked with moral goodness and the practice of virtue. Plato and Aristotle, albeit in different ways, espoused this view. In the Aristotelian account in particular, happiness is associated with the exercise of virtue through one's actions in the variety of communities by which the life of the individual is structured (household and family, locality, religious, educational, and recreational associations, friendships, the *polis* or general political community). Moral goodness is acquired through the acquisition and practice of virtue, and virtue is realized centrally in behavior and emotional response in one's spheres of social relationship.

The idea that happiness is properly linked with moral goodness was no less strong in Christianity (which in any case gradually began to incorporate Greek conceptions of the virtues into its own emphasis on the love of God and one's neighbor). In the early and medieval Christian order, as in the Greek and Roman, the individual was identified significantly in terms of relationships and roles within a range of relevant communities. Alasdair MacIntyre puts this point as follows:

> In much of the ancient and medieval worlds, as in many other pre-modern societies, the individual is identified and constituted in and through certain of his or her roles, those roles which bind the individual to the communities in and through which alone specifically human goods are to be attained; I confront the world as a member of this family, this household, this clan, this tribe, this city, this nation, this kingdom.[15]

Happiness as a human possibility is based on one's activities and satisfactions within such a context. The setting is one in which the pursuit of happiness *is* the pursuit of moral goodness and virtue.

To turn from this perspective to the Hobbesian account of happiness is to enter a completely different climate of thought. What has gone on in the meantime is the breakdown of the basic forms of the ancient and medieval worlds in the immense economic, social, political, and ideological changes associated with the emergence of the modern world and the rise of individualism. In the changed setting, the idea of happiness as the pursuit of moral goodness through the responsibilities and opportunities constituted by one's communal relationships is rendered problematic. In Alasdair MacIntyre's words again, with reference to the new situation in which the links between duty and happiness were gradually broken:

> Happiness is no longer defined in terms of satisfactions which are understood in the light of criteria governing a form of social life; it is defined in terms of individual psychology.[16]

In a word, the focus of attention turned to the passions and affections of the individual to provide the primary and controlling idea of happiness. Such happiness is private and individual. The question is how to harmonize private happiness with moral virtue and public good.

The characterization of both earlier and later approaches to happiness is, of course, a matter of emphasis; the change in a climate of thought is rarely absolute or clearcut. For example, elements of individualism were clearly present in medieval thought in connection with the idea of eternal or perfect happiness. On the other side, eighteenth-century writers (and preachers) were familiar with the earlier traditions in classical Greek thought and Christianity, and, in a variety of ways, they continued to make use of ideas and terminology from the past. There is no doubt, however, that from around Hobbes's time, the climate of thought in regard to morality and human nature had changed deeply (along the lines indicated).

FRANCIS HUTCHESON: PUBLIC GOOD, OR UTILITY

Opposition to the Hobbesian account of human nature and motivation was expressed most eloquently in the early part of the eighteenth century by Francis Hutcheson. Nevertheless, in important respects, Hutcheson's thought reflects the new individualism and the desire for a scientific system of morals; it points forward in these and other respects to the emergence of Utilitarian ethics. Hutcheson interpreted Hobbes's teaching as a revival of Epicureanism, to the effect that "all the *Desires* of the *human Mind*, nay of all *thinking Natures*, are reducible to *Self-Love*, or *Desire of private Happiness*: that from this desire all Actions of any Agent do flow."[17] In the meantime, the thesis that human beings are moved entirely by considerations of self-interest had been given a particularly arresting formulation earlier in the century.

In a widely read poem, *The Grumbling Hive, or Knaves turn'd Honest* (1705), and later in a book, *The Fable of the Bees, or, Private Vices, Public Benefits* (1714)[18], Bernard de Mandeville proclaimed that, "bare Virtue can't make Nations live in splendor . . ."; prosperity and social benefit arise, rather, from the pursuit of wealth and luxury and enjoyment; money, maligned as the root of evil, is properly the source of progress. Human beings are moved not by benevolence, but by self-interest. This is all to the good, however, for private vice or the pursuit of selfish interests (and not benevolence) is the source of public benefit. It is possible that Mandeville's wit was directed primarily against cant in the form of virtuous-sounding hypocrisy. But the central idea (private vice, public benefit) came to be espoused widely in the eighteenth century, and had its place, as we have seen, in Kant's social thought. Certainly, Hutcheson and many others thought it important to combat Mandeville's opinions and arguments.[19] Indeed, Hutcheson opposed any view in which self-love (and "the prospect of private happiness") plays a major part in moral motivation.

Against all views in which self-love is made basic to motivation, Hutcheson presents an alternative schema in his *Essay on the Nature and Conduct of the Passions* (hereafter *Essay*), to the effect

> that we have not only *Self-Love*, but *benevolent Affections* also towards others, in various Degrees, making us desire their Happiness as an *ultimate End*, without any view to private Happiness. (211)

Self-love and benevolence, the primary springs of action, are each associated with the promotion of happiness: one's own, or private, the happiness of others in the case of self-love, the happiness of others in the case of benevolence. Hutcheson speaks everywhere of the happiness of others (anyone other than oneself) as *public good* or *public utility* (where public good, it is clear, is made up of a sum of individual instances of happiness).

Happiness itself is taken to consist in the gratification of desire, in securing pleasure and avoiding pain in a sustained way; succinctly, it denotes "pleasant *Sensation* of any kind, or a continued State of such *Sensations*; and *Misery* denotes the contrary *Sensations*" (*Essay*, 205).

Morality is brought into this picture with the proposal that virtue "consists in Benevolence, or Desire of the Public Good" (*Essay*, 115). Hutcheson supposes that everyone is endowed with an innate moral sense, viz., a natural determination of the mind to approve of benevolent affections and publicly useful actions (one's own or others) without any view to one's own happiness. The whole of moral goodness and virtue thus turns on the single idea of behavior which promotes the happiness of others ("public utility"). The promotion of public utility in this sense is assumed to arise necessarily from benevolence, to the exclusion of self-love.

The spirit of economy involved in this approach is connected with a desire for computational finality. In the words of Hutcheson's *Inquiry concerning the Original of our Ideas of Virtue or Moral Good* (hereafter *Inquiry*), self-love and benevolence "are to be considered as two Forces impelling the same Body to Motion" (186). Here is the input (allowing that the two forces may work in opposition to one another, or in harmony, or independently, in different situations). The relevant output consists in the degree of public utility (or hurt) produced by the action. Hutcheson's idea is that input and output can all be measured. In this hopeful spirit, moral sense is credited with the judgment that:

> Virtue is in a compound Ratio of the Quantity of Good [happiness or natural good], and Number of Enjoyers. In the same manner, the moral Evil, or Vice, is as the degree of Misery, and Number of Sufferers; so that, that Action is best, which procures the greatest Happiness of the greatest Numbers; and that, worst, which, in like manner, occasions misery. (*Inquiry*, 107)

The problem of what appears incalculable by nature, in the formulation of what was to become a famous formula, is compounded by incalculable qualifications in Hutcheson's more detailed discussion. (It is allowed, for example, that the dignity and moral importance of persons may compensate for numbers.)

The general scheme (leaving aside the difficulties of the computational dream) manifest clearly the individualist framework considered earlier in this section. This is particularly notable in connection with the idea of a moral sense. The postulate of a moral sense is invoked precisely to provide a ground for morality in nature in advance of social relations. Reason is deemed unsatisfactory for this task on the grounds that it is purely instrumental; since we have ideas of virtue and vice, the argument goes, it is necessary to postulate a specific power of perception and judgment in their regard.

Hutcheson does not suppose that human beings have innate ideas or knowledge in connection with the moral sense; it is conceived rather as a natural "Determination of our Minds to receive amiable or disagreeable Ideas of Actions, when they occur to our Observation" without reference to any advantage or loss to ourselves (*Inquiry*, 83). One would suppose that the moral sense waits on development, presumably through the course of a child's upbringing. But at this point, Hutcheson insists that the power to "apprehend Actions as amiable or odious, without any Consideration of our own advantage," could not be learned (*Inquiry*, 82–83). In this spirit, children, as soon as they understand language, are held to demonstrate a practical grasp of what is morally good and evil and a sure attachment to virtue in advance of instruction, and without ideas about God, laws, or the state. Education and example, and the like, appear to be excluded from having any bearing on its development. Hutcheson's view is that such influences bear rather on the development of ideas which relate to a capacity for perceiving actions as advantageous or detrimental to ourselves. With moral sense identified as a power within the individual, maturity in moral perception and judgment, it is clear, is deemed a remarkably early achievement!

Hutcheson, it should be said, is concerned to recognize the need for social relations in human existence. Specifically, his account of the passions and affections is intended to make sense of "the principal Actions of human Life: Such as the *Offices of Friendship, Gratitude, natural Affection, Generosity, public Spirit, Compassion*" (*Essay*, 209). Nevertheless his account of morality and the virtues is tied to the mental states of individuals. In the chosen framework, there is no place for consideration of the way in which virtues are realized in social relationships and forms of human life. Specifically, virtues are not dispositions for behavior acquired over time in anything like the Aristotelian sense; they are expressions rather of a natural power of the mind.

Happiness is similarly located within the passions and affections of individuals. Hutcheson speaks of public good in relation to moral behavior, but "public good" in this connection means only the happiness of individuals other than oneself. Of course, he does not suppose that happiness is limited to sense pleasure. Pleasures of the mind are envisaged, the love of beauty, and harmony, the enjoyment of company, friendship, and love. Indeed, Hutcheson goes on to propose that the highest pitch of happiness is found in the possession of virtue. Furthermore, the enjoyment of virtue is recognized as a major motivational force in leading a person to act virtuously. This proposal strengthens Hutcheson's account of motivation by closing the gap to some degree between concern with one's own happiness and the demands of morality, but it brings out the limited and questionable character of his conception of happiness in the first place. In focusing on states of mind within individuals, Hutcheson closes off the space in which a public and more general account of happiness might have been developed.

JOSEPH BUTLER: THE REASONABLE LOVE OF SELF

For Bishop Butler, a contemporary of Hutcheson's, the idea of happiness is equally central to his reflections on human nature and morality: "Our ideas of happiness and misery are of all our ideas the nearest and most important to us."[20] Butler also holds that human beings are characteristically marked by benevolence as well as self-love. But in contrast with Hutcheson, he argues that self-love and benevolence are not opposed to each other. His argument is that a due love of self is an important factor in our being able to love others; on the other side, our greatest satisfactions depend on our having a proper concern for others. On this basis, Butler insists at various points in his Rolls Chapel sermons that benevolence and self-love are perfectly coincident (for the most part).

This argument involves the idea that reasonable self-love is morally good. It appeals too to the idea that happiness is determined by conditions of nature:

> Happiness or satisfaction consists . . . in the enjoyment of those objects which are by nature suited to our several particular appetites, passions, and affections. (*Sermon* XI, 53)

Butler was writing at a time when prudence, or concern with one's own happiness, was coming to be set over against moral duty, but he was able to hold on to a standpoint which resisted this development. Reasonable self-love, in conjunction with benevolence and the other virtues, makes it possible for us to achieve our own good as constituted by nature and to contribute to the happiness of others; a lack of self-love, or an excess of it, by contrast, closes us off from this possibility.

Butler's defense of the view that self-love is a virtue reflects his interpretation of the New Testament saying, "Thou shalt love thy neighbor as thyself" (Rom. XIII: 9; text for *Sermons* XI, XII). There is also the echo of an Aristotelian approach in his drawing virtue and happiness together around the idea of the satisfaction of human needs and powers. In relation to both sources, his standpoint is plausible. The great weakness, however, is that his account of human nature is tied to individual psychology. Butler considered that human beings are made for society, but in the absence of attention to a social framework in connection with virtue and happiness, his remarks about human nature are narrowly conceived. This in turn put a strain on his central thesis regarding the coincidence of duty and interest. Butler always qualified the thesis with the telltale phrase "for the most part." He made it secure in the end only by an appeal to God as the guarantee that "all things shall be set right at the final distribution of things" (*Sermon* III, 49).

The appeal to God to ensure an eventual harmony between duty and interest was taken up by many theological writers on ethics in the eighteenth century. In the best known later versions, the natural association between self-love and morality, such as Butler had envisaged, was abandoned. Thus, in William Paley's *Principles of Moral and Political Philosophy* (1785), morality and self-love are seen as standing in opposition to one another: by nature, human beings seek their own satisfaction; according to moral duty, they must be concerned with the happiness of others. The supposed resolution lies in the prospect of divine favor and eternal happiness, as the ultimate satisfaction of individual desire, combined with the idea that God makes moral duty the condition of his favor. The sole motive for moral behavior is made to rest, therefore, in the prospect of divine reward (or punishment). This argument, it is clear, is subject to Plato's objection in the *Euthyphro* to the attempt to ground morality on the will of God. But not only does it vainly try to make morality dependent on God in this way, in its account of motivation it reduces virtue to the pursuit of self-interest. Thus Paley defines virtue as "the doing good to mankind, in obedience to the will of God, for the sake of everlasting happiness."[21]

DAVID HUME: SYMPATHY AND MORAL SENTIMENT

The most sustained and significant inquiry into moral subjects in this period is to be found in the writings of David Hume, who was a powerful critic of theological ethics.[22] Like his contemporary fellow Scotsman, Adam Smith, Hume was greatly influenced by Francis Hutcheson in his ethical thought. But in the scope and character of his inquiry, and the force of his arguments, he is a towering figure. In the context of the main topic of this chapter and the more general orientation of the study, however, my discussion will be very limited.

Like Hutcheson, Hume espoused a psychological theory of ethics. At the same time, his treatment of the virtues gives a particular emphasis to justice and hence to matters which have regard to social relations. Hume held that moral judgments are expressions of sentiment rather than of reason or understanding. The relevant general sentiment, he says in *An Enquiry Concerning the Principle of Morals* (hereafter *EPM*), "can be no other than a feeling for the happiness of mankind, and a resentment of their misery" (App. 1, 286). The idea of utility is thus placed at the center of his thought. Moral sentiment, in its concern for the happiness, pleasure, or good of mankind, relates to whatever is useful to the promotion of this end. Virtue and vice lie respectively in whatever qualities of mind have the tendency to promote or obstruct the end. Thus, virtue consists in "every quality of the mind, which is *useful* or *agreeable* to the *person himself* or to *others*" (*EPM* IX(i), 277). Whatever advantage virtue confers on its possessor, however, the special mark of *moral* sentiment is that it relates to these qualities *"without reference to our particular interest,"* as Hume notes in *A Treatise of Human Nature* (hereafter *Tr.*) (III, i, [2], 472). The sentiment is pleasing when it is a feeling of approbation (as bearing on virtue) and displeasing when it is a sentiment of blame (as bearing on vice).

Hume's main argument for characterizing moral beliefs and judgments as expressions of sentiment is that they are closely linked with action, whereas reason, as he understands it, is not. He allows that reason, properly developed, is "sufficient to instruct us in the pernicious or useful tendencies of qualities and actions," but awareness of the facts, such as reason provides, is unable to lead us to moral blame or approbation: reason, Hume says, is cool and disengaged and provides no motive to action (*EPM* App. 1, 286, 294). We are moved to act, according to this psychology, not by reason, but by the passions.

This view regarding a division of labor between reason and the passions has been fraught with significance in subsequent moral philosophy and social theory. Most generally, it has been connected with the view that there is an unbridgeable gap between facts and values, and the idea that moral judgments, as expressions of passion and desire, fall outside rational appraisal. Hume unquestionably considers that matters of fact, on the one hand, fall within the scope of reason, together with logical relations, and that moral judgments, on the other hand, are expressions of feeling. But whether his arguments establish the sorts of conclusions just noted, and whether Hume thought that they did, is far from clear. I will not take up this very large question other than to make some general remarks which are suggestive of a point of view. Let us suppose with Hume that the passions lead us to want to attain happiness and to avoid misery and that reason shows us the means to this end. In the first place, a being who acquires knowledge about all manner of things in a purely cool and disengaged and motiveless way appears unthinkable unless the being were entirely passive even in the acquisition of knowledge. The idea of a moral life, and the condition of rational agency that is part of it, presupposes beings in whom reason and desire are linked in a concrete way, such as to ground reasoning of a practical sort. Secondly, with regard to any end or goal specified by desire, it is possible (and makes sense) to ask whether it is a reasonable goal to pursue either in particular circumstances or as a general aim in life.

Hume traces moral sentiments back to the natural feelings of sympathy and benevolence. More exactly, these feelings are proposed as the origin of the natural or social virtues such as beneficence, generosity, equity. The origin of justice is located rather in selfishness and limited generosity: Hume supposes that human beings, educated by the experience of unrestrained self-interest, are led to establish rules regarding property the better to ensure their interest, but then, sympathy with the public interest which the rules promote becomes the basis of moral approval (cf. *Tr.* III, ii, [6], 529).

In the *Treatise*, Hume rejects the view that there is any such passion "as the love of mankind, merely as such" (*Tr.* III, ii, [1], 481). He appeals rather to *sympathy* as the source of our esteem and concern for the general happiness. Sympathy in this context is a general psychological process in which the experience of a feeling in someone else gives rise to the same feeling in oneself. On the grounds that "the minds of all men are similar in their feelings and operations" (*Tr.* III, iii, [1], 575), Hume proposes that sympathy is a universal phenomenon. The connection with the moral sentiments and the happiness and misery of mankind is that, in feeling pleased by the pleasures of others, we are led to approve of whatever contributes to happiness generally, even when our own interests are not concerned. Hume continues to invoke the idea of sympathy in the *Enquiry*, but in this text he also brings in reference to natural feelings of humanity and benevolence as the basis of moral judgment and action: "A tendency to public good, and to the promoting of peace, harmony and order in society, does always, by affecting the benevolent principles of our frame, engage us on the side of the social virtues" (*EPM* V [ii], 231; cf. 219).

Here as elsewhere, Hume rejects the view that moral sentiment can in some way be brought back to the principle of self-love. Dismissing the "vulgar dispute concerning the *degrees* of benevolence or self-love, which prevail in human nature," all that he insists on is that "there is some benevolence, however small, infused in our bosom" (*EPM* IX [i], 271), and with this bridgehead, he hopes to secure moral sentiment in its full force.

The idea that morality is connected with a capacity for sympathy in human beings is plausible, and the modest claim on behalf of benevolence also appears reasonable. But there is good reason to doubt that these considerations could support the weight Hume places on them. There is also reason to doubt whether Hume thought that they could. In his discussion of moral obligation he turns, in fact, to the consideration of one's own happiness as the critical factor:

> Having explained the moral *approbation* attending merit or virtue, there remains nothing but briefly to consider our interested *obligation* to it, and to inquire whether every man, who has any regard to his own happiness and welfare will not best find his account in the practice of every moral duty. (*EPM* IX [ii], 278)

Hume's affirmative answer to this question does not commit him to a thesis of crude self-interest. His standpoint can be treated perhaps as one with the Greek conception of the association of virtue and happiness. The great difference is that the terms of the association are now located primarily in a psychological framework.

In locating the criterion of moral judgment in feelings, Hume supposes that the sentiment is common to all mankind and that more or less universal agreement in regard to virtue can be expected on this basis. He is confident that one has only to look into one's own breast to find the proper catalogue of virtues, though he would certainly reject Hutcheson's faith in the powers of infants in this regard. This confidence might be embarrassed, however, by the well-known fact that different conceptions of what counts as virtue have flourished in different times and places. Hume himself is particularly critical of the "monkish virtues," such as penance, self-denial, humility and the like. But he "saves" his thesis on the grounds that such virtues are "everywhere rejected by men of good sense" inasmuch as they "neither advance a man's fortune in the world, nor render him a more valuable member of society" (*EPM* IX [i], 271).

This defense, it is clear, reflects a particular outlook in regard to beliefs about what is individually and socially worthwhile in human life. In Hume's account, however, background influences and specific social context are set aside, and the views are projected as universal. The particularity in his outlook is seen even more clearly in the treatment of justice: it is related essentially to property relations, and, within this limited domain, emphasis falls on the stability of established possession without reference to whether laws relating to property might themselves be unjust. In related vein, "the *modesty* and *chastity* which belong to the fair sex" are brought within the domain of justice and hence property relations: if *men* are to accept the fatigues and expenses to which marriage and the care of children subjects them, they must be assured that the children in question are their own! (*Tr.* III, [ii], 12, 570).

In dealing with the natural or social virtues, Hume says very little about the process of their development whether in general or in relation to individuals. On the grounds that these virtues are realizable outside a developed social system and without reference to custom or reason, he assumes too readily that natural sympathy and feelings of benevolence will secure the outcome. But even if the basic assumption were granted, it would not justify neglect of developmental and educational considerations in this context. Specifically, it would be necessary to show how the individual, on the basis of the experience of sympathy and affection in the limited community of a family or kinship group, arrives at the generalized, impartial standpoint required of moral sentiment. Hume allows that "sympathy . . . is much fainter than our concern for ourselves, and with persons remote from us much fainter than that with persons near and contiguous." As for the development of the impartial standpoint, he simply proposes that "the intercourse of sentiments . . . in society and conversation, makes us form some general unalterable standard, by which we may approve or disapprove of characters and manners" (*EPM* V [ii], 229).

Education is given a more central place, by contrast, in the case of justice and the other socially constructed virtues such as promise-keeping and chastity. Justice, as noted above, is imagined as arising out of self-love, the "avidity . . . of acquiring goods and possessions for ourselves and nearest friends" (*Tr.* III, ii, [2], 491). The first lesson — that the unrestrained exercise of this passion results in general violence and fear — leads to the reflection that the love of gain is best served by the institution of rules of restraint; then sympathy with the public interest, which is seen to be served by the rules, leads to *moral* approbation. Hume represents this progress of sentiments as natural. But, in an echo of de Mandeville, he appeals also to the "artifice of politicians" in securing esteem for justice and abhorrence for injustice, and to private education and instruction as providing secondary influences (along with "the interest of our reputation"):

> For as parents easily observe, that a man is that more useful, both to himself and others, the greater degree of probity and honour he is endow'd with; and that those principles have greater force, when custom and education assist interest and reflexion: For these reasons they are induc'd to inculcate on their children, from their earliest infancy, the principles of probity, and teach them to regard the observance of those rules, by which society is maintain'd, as worthy and honourable, and their violation as base and infamous. (*Tr.* III, ii, [2], 500)

Through education and political indoctrination, the sentiments of honor become so firmly established "that they may fall little short of those principles, which are the most essential to our natures, and the most deeply radicated in our internal constitution" (ibid.). But Hume did not explore the detailed implications of this claim himself nor the more general character of moral education and development. These are matters to which his younger contemporary, Adam Smith, gave closer attention.

ADAM SMITH: SYMPATHY AND THE GROWTH OF MORAL SENTIMENT

Adam Smith, in *The Theory of the Moral Sentiments* (hereafter *TMS*) (1759), followed Hume both in treating moral judgments as expressions of sentiment and in tracing moral sentiment back to feelings of sympathy.[23] But he went considerably further than Hume in attempting to give a developmental account of the process. My discussion will be restricted for the most part to this particular aspect of his thought.

By sympathy, Smith means "our fellow-feeling with any passion whatever" (*TMS* I, i, [1], 5). It is the sense of sharing the feelings of another in a given situation, a source of particular pleasure when sympathy is mutual. The primary focus concerns the response of a spectator to the emotions and behavior of an agent designated as "the person principally concerned." Where the spectator enters into the original feelings of the agent, he will judge them just and proper in their context; where he does not, he will think of them as unjust and improper. On the other hand, an agent who is aware of the sympathetic response of others is typically brought to modify his or her emotions to fit in with these others'. The efforts of the spectator to enter into the sentiments of the person principally concerned give rise, in Smith's words, to "the soft, the gentle, the amiable virtues";

the reverse procedure is the foundation of "the great, the awful, and respectable, the virtues of self-denial, of self-government . . ." (*TMS* I, i, [5], 26).

The propriety and merit of an action, and hence its virtue, depends on the sentiment or affection from which it proceeds, viz., whether the sentiment is in proportion or not to its cause or object (propriety); and whether the effects at which it aims are beneficial or hurtful (merit). But who is the judge in these matters? Smith's answer in a word is the *impartial spectator*, the well-informed and indifferent bystander (where indifferent has the sense of "fairminded"):

> But these [gratitude and resentment], as well as all the other passions of human nature, seem proper and are approved of, when the heart of every impartial spectator entirely sympathizes with them, when every indifferent bystander entirely enters into, and goes along with, them. (*TMS* II, i, [2], 97)

The procedures and rules which we, as impartial spectators, might apply in the approval or disapproval of the sentiments and conduct of others are to be applied equally in self-judgment. In other words, we need to become impartial spectators of our own character and conduct. Smith takes up this topic, with attention to its developmental aspects, in Part III of his study.

Human beings, he proposes, can think of themselves as selves and as moral beings only in virtue of being aware of others: others constitute a mirror without which we cannot see or appraise ourselves (*TMS* III, [1], 162). In this light, the development of conscience (the impartial spectator within) is an essentially social process which works on the conditions of individual psychology. Smith supposes that we are by nature selfishly concerned with our own pleasure and satisfaction. But there are natural conditions (such as "the feeble spark of benevolence which Nature has lighted up in the human heart") on the basis of which we come to take fair account of the interests of others (*TMS* III, [3], 193).

This developmental picture can be illustrated by reference to the very young child:

> A very young child has no self-command; but, whatever are its emotions, whether fear, or grief, or anger, it endeavours always by the violence of its outcries, to alarm, as much as it can, the attention of its nurse, or of its parents. (*TMS* III, [3], 203)

But human beings stand in need of others; by nature they want to be loved; thus they have an original desire to please others, to win their approval and avoid their censure. On this basis, and with a degree of parental discipline, the child begins to learn to take note of others, and to adapt its emotions and behavior in relation to their sympathetic responses. This is the beginning of conscience, but Smith also supposes that there is a natural and original desire, not only to be loved and to please others, but to be worthy of love and approbation. Conscience then develops on the basis of the latter desire. It is difficult to see, however, how the desire to be worthy of love could be original, or how this could possibly be shown.[24]

Within this general framework, the growth of conscience is marked by a movement toward impartiality and a sense of fairness. When the child is old enough to go to school and mix with its equals, it finds that it does not get favored treatment from them. In this situation,

> it naturally wishes to gain their favour, and to avoid their hatred or contempt. Regard even to its own safety teaches it to do so; and it soon finds that it can do so in no other way than by moderating, not only its anger, but all its other passions, to the degree which its playfellows and companions are likely to be pleased with. It thus enters into the great school of self-command. (*TMS* III, [3], 204)

Smith illustrates an important aspect of this development with an analogy that is suggestive of Piaget's idea of the move from an egocentric point of view to a "decentered" one. With perceptual experience, one learns to discount the relative proximity of objects to oneself in estimating their size; something similar takes place, Smith suggests, with the natural eye of the mind in regard to one's own interests and the interests of others. In the primary stage, our own immediate interests loom large; then we find ourselves faced with the opposite interests of another, and to make a proper comparison between us, we have to look "neither from our own place nor yet from his, neither with our own eyes nor yet with his, but from the place of the eyes of a third person . . . who judges with impartiality between us" (*TMS* III, [3], 191f).

Along these lines, Smith concludes that the natural inequality of our sentiments is corrected by the sense of propriety and justice which we learn in association with others. Our recognition of the way in which we are perceived by others, reinforced by the sense of shame (and remorse) in connection with wrongdoing, is accorded an important place in the development (*TMS* II, ii, [2]). In one of Smith's most characteristic images, life is portrayed as a competitive game in which everything is acceptable provided one observes the rules of fair play (ibid., 120). Through association with others, the strongest impulses of self-love are counteracted by "reason, principle, conscience, the inhabitant of the breast, the man within, the great judge and arbiter of our conduct. . . . . and the natural misrepresentations of self-love can be corrected only by the eye of this impartial spectator" (*TMS* III, [3], 194).[25] Smith, of course, is presenting an ideal projection in this account. In filling out the ideas, he gives particular attention to the power of self-deceit, "the source of half the world's disorders," in leading us to favor ourselves over others (*TMS* III, [4], 221ff). But then the remedy against partiality and the delusions of self-love is to be found in general rules.

At this point Smith's attention turns to the broader topic of the development of moral rules within a social group. His thesis is that the general rules or maxims of morality are formed from experience and induction: "We observe, in a great variety of particular cases, what pleases or displeases our moral faculties, what these approve or disapprove of; and by induction from this experience we establish these general rules" (*TMS* VII, iii, [2], 469; cf. 224f). We do not approve or condemn particular actions on the basis of a prior rule; on the contrary, the general rule is established on the basis of our finding that actions of a certain sort secure approval or disapproval.[26]

Smith's account of the origin of rules hardly describes the general situation at any given time, though it could plausibly apply to particular issues over a short stretch of time, such as changes over a generation regarding sexual morality or in views about the moral justification of a particular war. Perhaps, then, it could be applied to moral rules generally over a very long time. For the most part, however, there is a good deal of stability and continuity in the moral views of a society, and a good part of the early moral experience of children consists in their being told what to do or not do according to rules.

In his primary account of moral development, Smith concentrates on the role of sympathetic adjustment and the process by which a principle of guidance is internalized as conscience. But while he does not give attention to the role played by the transmission of rules at this stage, it would be a mistake to think that he was unaware of the matter. On the contrary, his view is that a sense of duty in regard to general rules of conduct is "the only principle by which the bulk of mankind are capable of directing their actions" (*TMS* III, [5], 229). He thus supposes that many people live decent lives merely out of respect for established rules "who yet, perhaps, never felt the sentiment upon the propriety of which we found our approbation of their conduct" (ibid.).[27] From this point, Smith goes on to place more and more weight on the idea of "sacred regard to general rules."

These rules — assuming that the true governing principles of human nature have been established — are to be considered laws of the Deity (*TMS* III, [5], 235). Smith was not a Utilitarian in a strict sense (though the promotion of happiness is given a central place in his ethical thought).[28] In the present perspective, however, he espouses a form of theological utilitarianism. The primary elements of this are that God intends the happiness of mankind and, on condition of reward or punishment, requires the observance of the moral law. Propriety in respect of God then becomes the major consideration, "well supported by the strongest motives of self-interest" (*TMS* III, [5], 241).

Smith's general account of moral development is of considerable interest and force (leaving aside the aspect just sketched). On the other hand, the emphasis on psychological factors, albeit in a general framework of social relations, is connected with a serious lacuna inasmuch as no proper attention is given to the nature or place of virtues. Smith discusses virtue in terms of character, and character under the aspect of its bearing on one's own happiness and the happiness of others (*TMS*, Part VI). The first consideration is restricted to prudence as the proper (hence virtuous) care for one's own preservation and health. So far as the happiness of others is concerned, there is justice, which Smith interprets as an essentially legal notion concerned with precise laws prohibiting the infliction of injury on others in their person or property. There is also benevolence, in such forms as generosity, kindness, and compassion, especially for those who are close to one, virtues "which please the indifferent spectator on almost every occasion." In the absence of any developed treatment of virtue, however, moral rules come to occupy the central place; alternatively, virtues come to be seen primarily as dispositions to obey rules. From a developmental point of view, as we have seen, Smith put particular emphasis on self-command as the basis on which the child becomes a moral agent. With ramifications in courage, fortitude, and temperance, self-command can be seen as a sort of military virtue of obedience to rules, a "manly" virtue (Smith speaks of the "manhood of self-command" — *TMS* III, [3], 213).

Smith thought that, apart from respect for moral rules or virtue, human beings are characterized by respect for wealth and greatness. He argues in *The Theory of the Moral Sentiments* that the disposition to admire the rich and great leads to the corruption of morality. But his thought on this matter involves complications. In a well-known passage in *The Wealth of Nations*, he proposed that

> in every civilized society, in every society where the distinction of ranks has once been completely established, there have been always two different schemes or systems of morality current at the same time; of which one may be called the strict or austere; the other the liberal, or, if you will, the loose system. The former is generally admired and revered by the common people: the latter is commonly more esteemed and adopted by what are called people of fashion.[29]

A distinction of the same sort appears in the earlier study on moral sentiments in terms of people "in the middling and inferior stations of life" as against those "in the superior stations of life" (*TMS* I, iii, [3], 86ff). The latter, because of their wealth, are likely to indulge in a degree of vanity, vice, and folly. The road of the "strict or austere morality" of *The Wealth of Nations* falls to the lot of the former. The character *they* need — their virtue — takes the form of "humble modesty and equitable justice"; they need application to work, honesty, and prudent, just, firm, and temperate conduct. But in what could be called Adam Smith's economy of the moral life, it turns out that these qualities are precisely what is needed for financial success:

> In the middling and inferior stations of life, the road to virtue and that to fortune, to such fortune, at least, as men in such stations can reasonably expect to acquire, are, happily, in most cases very nearly the same. (*TMS* I, iii, [3], 86)

It thus becomes clear that, no less than in the theological dimension of Smith's ethics, concern for propriety at the human level is "well supported by the strongest motives of self-interest" (*TMS* III, [5], 241). The final emphasis on self-interest reflects a more general theme in Smith's thought.

In *The Wealth of Nations* in particular, Smith espoused a version of Mandeville's theme that the pursuit of selfish interests by individuals is commonly the unintended source of public benefit: the capitalist, intent on money-making, is led "by an invisible hand to promote an end which was not part of his intention. . . . By pursuing his own interest he frequently promotes that of the society more effectually than when he really intends to promote it."[30]

In *The Theory of the Moral Sentiments*, Smith suggests that the self-interested person is deceived in thinking that the pursuit of the pleasures of wealth and greatness is worth the trouble it costs. Nevertheless, he continues, "it is this deception which rouses and keeps in continual motion the industry of mankind" (*TMS* IV, [1], 263f). The self-interested pursuit of wealth and greatness is the driving force in the development of the arts and sciences and every aspect of economic growth. In the earlier work, too, there is the idea that the rich are led "by an invisible hand" to advance the interest of society without intending it (*TMS* IV, [1], 265). At the same time, as we have seen, the attractiveness of virtue for people in the "middling and inferior stations of life" is that it is perceived as the road to comparative wealth and esteem. In short, in Smith's more developed account of the sentiments, self-interest is put forward as the driving force of human behavior, and self-interested activity (especially in barter and trade) is happily thought to serve the general utility.[31]

3. Utilitarianism: Bentham and Mill

JEREMY BENTHAM: THE SACRED TRUTH OF UTILITY

In a note in *A Fragment on Government* (1776), Bentham linked his conversion to the principle of utility to the influence of Hume; with reference to the third volume of *A Treatise of Human Nature*, he wrote:

> That the foundations of all *virtue* are laid in *utility*, is there demonstrated, after a few exceptions made, with the strongest force of evidence: but I see not, any more than Helvetius saw, what need there was for the exceptions. For my own part, I well remember, no sooner had I read that

part of the work which touches on this subject, than I felt as if scales had fallen from my eyes. I then, for the first time, learnt to call the cause of the people the cause of Virtue.[32]

Elsewhere Bentham wrote that, "Priestley was the first (unless it was Beccaria) who taught my lips to pronounce this sacred truth — that the greatest happiness of the greatest number is the foundation of morals and legislation."[33]

This profusion of possible sources is evidence of how widely the idea of utility had taken root in the eighteenth century (and incidentally of Hume's influence on European writers such as Helvetius and Beccaria). Bentham did not in fact contribute greatly to the underlying theory of "the sacred truth." Rather, he expressed the main ideas in robust and simple terms and made the approach appear workable and uniquely reasonable in the broad domains of legal and social reform. In time, he became the inspirational leader of a movement which made Utilitarianism a major force for social reform in England and elsewhere in the nineteenth century. Its critical development as a major theory of ethics was not effected until considerably later, notably in John Stuart Mill's essay, *Utilitarianism* (1861).

Bentham, it is commonly noted, was primarily concerned with the reform of the legal system. In this spirit, he turned to the principle of utility as the proper basis for good legislation. Traditional wisdom held that law exists for the common good. Bentham accepted this view, but in the framework of thought which he inherited, the community is "a fictitious body": common good, or the interest of the community, is in "the sum of the interests of the several members who compose it."[34] A concern with law, therefore, must turn to the good or happiness of individuals and, more specifically, the basis of happiness in individual psychology.

In Bentham's forthright account, in *An Introduction to the Principles of Morals and Legislation* (hereafter *Princ.*), human beings are placed by nature "under the governance of two sovereign masters, *pain* and *pleasure*" (I [ii], 1). Motives for action are uniformly pleasure-seeking (or pain-avoiding), and individuals act out of self-interest for the promotion of their own happiness. In this framework, pleasures of whatever sort fall under a single idea, along a single scale of evaluation based on the contention that pleasure can be measured mathematically. In this way, Bentham espoused the dream of computing a sum of happiness, for a collection of individuals in any given situation, as a matter of addition or subtraction.

Bentham supposes that a good deal of self-regarding action will in the natural course of events be of benefit to others. On the other hand, he acknowledges that individuals in pursuit of their own happiness are commonly in conflict. Given that the legislator is to have an eye to common interest, the art of law-making is to frame laws which get individuals to take account of the interests of others; more specifically, it is the art of effecting this to the highest possible degree (if it is allowed that this makes sense in quantitative terms). In short, the proper basis of legislation is utility or the greatest-happiness principle: "The happiness of individuals, of whom a community is composed, that is their pleasures and their security, is the end and the sole end which the legislator ought to have in view" (*Princ.* III [i], 14).

But what are the grounds on which the legislator *ought* to have this end in view? Given the original account of human psychology, it is not clear why people who make laws should be concerned with the common interest at all except where it fits with self-interest. The same problem arises in regard to individuals. While Bentham's primary focus concerns the law, utility is invoked as a universal moral principle, the single and sole measure of right and wrong. He observes that the principle takes our subjection to pleasure and pain as foundational. But the transition from the thesis regarding individual psychology to the moral principle relating to general happiness is left obscure.

Bentham's outlook supposes that there are people who are sufficiently enlightened to see that their own happiness is tied up with the recognition of the claims of others to *their* happiness. Allied with this is the hope that through law and education, and a system of rewards and punishments, which is the business of government (*Princ.* VII [i], 35), this belief would become general. The psychological thesis, it is clear, is accompanied by a strong belief in human malleability. Apart from holding that our subjection to pleasure and pain is unalterable, Bentham's account is one in which change in regard to objects of pleasure is entirely open-ended (especially as quantity of pleasure is the operative consideration). But an emphasis on malleability, as I argued in connection with Locke, is characteristically accompanied by the conviction that particular sorts of change are desirable. What was most generally desirable, so far as Bentham was concerned, was that everyone should act in accordance with the principle of utility. Once again, however, the question of the grounds of the proposed desirability can be raised. It cannot rest on the principle of utility itself, for that is what is in question. Yet, in Bentham's terms there is no other relevant standard.

In the meantime, there appears to be no limit in principle to activities designed to get people to implement the greatest-happiness principle (provided they feel happy). Nor is there any restriction on what sorts of pleasure individuals find satisfactory provided that their private happiness contributes to the general sum of happiness. These possible consequences do not fit with Bentham's own practice, inasmuch as he was concerned to bring about a more enlightened and humane legal system and did not think that the law should extend across the whole field of ethical conduct. At the same time, one has to remember that Bentham was the energetic designer of the Panopticon, a proposal for a prison in which the inmates could be observed at all times from a central lodge, subject to an all-seeing and invisible power. Furthermore, he thought that this scheme for the

reform of prisoners could be modified to apply to all sorts of establish-
ments, for example, to hospitals, asylums, workhouses, and schools, "a
great and new invented instrument of government. . . . Its great excellence consists in the great strength it is capable of giving to *any* institution it
may be thought proper to apply it to."[35]

Bentham commended the principle of utility for its power to settle
disputes in the assessment of laws. Its great strength in relation to any
other system, he considered, is that dispute is made to turn on a matter of
fact, specifically, "future fact — the probability of certain future contingen-
cies," namely, the amount of benefit or harm that would ensue (*A Fragment
on Government*, IV, 39, 291). Bentham's claim to give this idea mathematical
exactness was, of course, entirely promissory and spurious. Nevertheless,
the proposal to evaluate laws or policies on the way in which they affect
the happiness or welfare of interested parties seems reasonable. The
question, however, is whether this is the *only* criterion.

At a much earlier stage in the history of Utilitarian thought, Joseph
Butler had questioned Hutcheson's confidence (which was not unlike
Bentham's belief in utility) in the all-sufficiency of benevolence. Butler too
wished to recognize the pre-eminence of this virtue, but cautioned that
when it comes to the promotion of happiness, "we are not competent
judges what is upon the whole for the good of the world."[36] In other
words, Butler thought that, because we cannot be sure of future consequences in any complete way, we should not make this consideration the
sole basis of judgment. A reply on behalf of Bentham could argue that
judgment has to be based on what we can reasonably predict about the
future in relation to consequences, not on a requirement for complete
knowledge. This defense, however, does nothing to establish that the
appeal to an overall "sum" of happiness is the proper test, much less that it
is the sole basis of judgment. Perhaps consideration would need to be
given to *what* it is that gives rise to greater happiness; for example, whether
it is building hospitals for the treatment of the sick or labor camps for the
removal of a troublesome minority.

In relation to this matter, Butler argued that there are sorts of action
which are recognized as base and detestable in themselves — actions such
as treachery, injustice, murder, and persecution. Yet if utility were the sole
consideration, there would be many instances in which actions of these
sorts might be supposed to contribute more, on balance, to happiness than
to misery (the happiness and misery of different people). Butler's argument, one could say, still turns on the assessment of consequences,
specifically of the immediate or built-in consequences of the sorts of action
in question (betrayal, death, suffering, and so on). This touches on the
difficult question of the extent to which reference to consequences can be
drawn into action descriptions and of what constitutes action proper. But it
is not necessary to take up that question to agree that a distinction can be

made between the immediate and necessary outcome of actions of various types and further contingent consequences which might or might not follow on their performance. Butler's argument could then be re-phrased to hold that the built-in consequences of certain sorts of actions are so harmful that they could not be outweighed by the consideration of any other consequences, most pertinently, by the pleasure some parties might feel in their occurrence, as when, for example, a majority feels pleasure in the persecution of a minority group.[37]

Bentham's concern with broad questions of law and social policy, rather than particular actions, could be related to this issue, inasmuch as the lawmaker looks to classes of action regarding things to be done or not done; decisions are presumably based on the characteristic outcomes of sorts or types of behavior. But his Utilitarianism does not advert to the distinction I have drawn on the basis of Butler's argument. How then does he deal with the sort of example just noted in which the suffering of a small number of people is supposed to be weighed against the related pleasure experienced by many? There is the beginning of an answer in Bentham's proposal that the happiness of each individual is to be considered equally with that of others. This is a reasonable proposal, but it appears to involve a moral consideration which is not encompassed by the principle of utility itself. Bentham did not take the matter further, but his dictum, "everybody to count for one, nobody for more than one,"[38] was invoked again in John Stuart Mill's more developed and more critical account of Utilitarianism some seventy years later.

JOHN STUART MILL: PROBLEMS OF PROOF AND PEDAGOGY
In his essay, *Utilitarianism* (1861), John Stuart Mill remarked that the greatest-happiness principle "is a mere form of words without rational signification, unless one person's happiness, supposed equal in degree . . . is counted for exactly as much as another's."[39] Bentham's dictum, he added, "might be written under the principle of utility as an explanatory commentary." Interpreting the requirement of impartiality as supposing "that equal amounts of happiness are equally desirable, whether felt by the same or by different persons," Mill claims that this is the very principle of utility itself, not an independent principle on which it relies, "for what is the principle of utility, if it be not that 'happiness' and 'desirable' are synonymous terms?" (*Utilitarianism* V, 258, note). It is difficult to see how Mill's argument supports the claim about equal consideration in the principle of utility. He speaks of "equal amounts" of happiness as equally desirable, but what appears to be needed (and to be supposed by Bentham's dictum) is a prior requirement regarding the equal treatment of *individuals*.

In this vein, Henry Sidgwick argued in *The Methods of Ethics* (1874) that Utilitarianism needs the support of an "intuition of Rational Benevolence," associated, he proposed, with the following self-evident principle:

that the good of any one individual is of no more importance, from the point of view (if I may say so) of the Universe, than the good of any other. . . . And it is evident to me that as a rational being I am bound to aim at good generally, — so far as it is attainable by my efforts, — not merely at a particular part of it.[40]

In commenting that Sidgwick's self-evident principle is ethical in character, Bernard Williams adds that Utilitarianism needs a further principle (which is also an ethical intuition and subject to ethical disagreement), viz., "that there are no other basic ethical considerations besides that first one."[41]

Mill's starting point was the familiar contention that individuals desire their own happiness. So far as his moral theory was concerned, however, "the happiness which forms the utilitarian standard of what is right in conduct, is not the agent's own happiness, but that of all concerned" (*Utilitarianism* II, 218). Given the specified starting point, his primary task was the familiar one of showing how a concern with general happiness can be established. But while Mill understood happiness in terms of pleasure and the absence of pain, he was profoundly unhappy with Bentham's account of pleasure. He therefore undertook a defense of Utilitarianism on the basis of a revised conception of happiness.

Mill flatly rejected the Benthamite view according to which pleasures, however various in type, are judged on the basis of quantity alone. On the grounds that it would be absurd not to take account of quality as well, he proposed that "some *kinds* of pleasure are more desirable and more valuable than others" (*Utilitarianism* II, 211). Specifically, Mill argued that there are pleasures of the mind, the feelings and imagination, and the moral sentiments (higher pleasures) which are superior to, more valuable than, bodily pleasures (lower pleasures), whatever the quantity of the latter. The basis for this claim is placed in the judgment of those who have had experience of pleasures of both kinds and who alone, therefore, are judged competent to judge.

The character and force of Mill's argument concerning higher and lower pleasures is a matter of considerable dispute, which I shall not consider in any detail here.[42] At the level of dialectical debate, Mill was concerned to rescue Utilitarianism from the charge of being "a doctrine worthy only of swine"; by invoking the thesis that the higher pleasures are intrinsically more valuable, he could reclaim high ground on behalf of Utilitarian doctrine:

It is better to be a human being dissatisfied than a pig satisfied; better to be Socrates dissatisfied than a fool satisfied. And if the fool or the pig is of different opinion, it is because they only know their own side of the question. The other party to the comparison knows both sides. (*Utilitarianism* II, 212)

In particular, he could dissociate the doctrine from Bentham's bluff contention that, "prejudice apart, the game of push-pin is of equal value with the arts and sciences of music and poetry."[43]

In emphasizing quality in relation to pleasure, Mill effectively abandoned Bentham's vision of a calculus of pleasure, though he occasionally used some of the relevant terminology, such as "equal amounts of happiness" or the "sum total of happiness." More deeply, he placed in question the whole associated conception of happiness.

Mill's account of happiness, as many writers have pointed out, draws on themes from Greek philosophy. Chapter II of *Utilitarianism*, where he develops his argument regarding higher and lower pleasures, bears fairly close comparison with a related argument in Book IX of Plato's *Republic*, and there is a case for thinking that he derived the central idea from themes in Aristotle's discussion of pleasure in the *Nicomachean Ethics*.[44] More generally, Mill relates happiness to the satisfaction of the higher human faculties of mind, feeling and imagination. Although he put an excessive emphasis on the higher pleasures, there is the idea that happiness consists in a life marked by many and various pleasures and a plurality of interests and activities. In his essay, *On Liberty* (1859), happiness is associated especially with the idea of the development of creative human powers. This is linked with the view that a society needs to recognize the considerable differences among human beings and cater for different modes of life if people are to obtain a fair share of happiness and develop their different mental, moral, and aesthetic capacities to the full. In short, Mill's consideration of pleasure and value in human life placed him at odds with the whole conception of happiness which had developed in the wake of Hobbes and in which the Utilitarian outlook was at home. Nevertheless, he went on to espouse a Utilitarian standpoint and to consider aspects of moral formation in this context.

The conclusion which Mill-as-Utilitarian wished to establish was that the promotion of the general happiness is the test by which all human conduct is properly judged, that is, that it is the sole criterion of morality. His argument to this conclusion turned on the Utilitarian doctrine that happiness is desirable, and indeed the only thing desirable, as an ultimate end of behavior. From this it follows that, "each person's happiness is a good to that person, and the general happiness, therefore, a good to the aggregate of all persons" (*Utilitarianism* IV, 234). In setting out this argument, Mill was particularly concerned to establish the two elements of the Utilitarian doctrine just noted: (a) that happiness or pleasure is desirable as an end and (b) that happiness *alone* is desirable in this way.

The few paragraphs in which Mill argued for these claims in Chapter IV of *Utilitarianism* have been the subject of immense debate and criticism. Critical attention has been focused particularly on the argument in connection with (a) above, to the effect that happiness is desirable since people do in fact desire it and, more generally, that "the sole evidence it is possible to produce that anything is desirable, is that people do actually desire it." It is possible to agree with Mary Warnock that there is nothing wrong or fallacious in this proposal provided Mill is (reasonably) understood to be saying: "The question of proving what is an ultimate end does not arise; but you can find out what people recognize as ultimate ends by finding out what they desire."[45] In this case, Mill's point is similar to Aristotle's observation early in the *Nicomachean Ethics* that everyone agrees that happiness is the highest of all goods achievable by action (1.4, 1095a15ff). Aristotle, however, went on to point out that people have different views about happiness, and he sought to arbitrate between satisfactory and unsatisfactory conceptions of the notion. Mill might have been drawn to follow this example in the light of his distinction between higher and lower pleasures. But Mill-as-Utilitarian does not stop to raise this question: it is taken as enough that each person desires his or her own happiness, whatever its concrete form, and that this happiness is a good to that person.

The argument for the premise that happiness is the *only* thing desirable in itself begins with the concession that people appear to desire other things for their own sake — virtue notably, also music, health, money, power, or fame among "the great objects of life." Mill's response, in short, is that all these things may be desired as ends, but they are then ingredients or parts of happiness for the people concerned. This comes about on the following pattern. Virtue (to take Mill's primary example) begins as a *means* to happiness. In time, the individual comes to cherish it as a good in itself; in other words, it is experienced as pleasant for its own sake, as part of what counts as happiness for that person.

The idea that happiness is a concrete whole is plausible; so too is the recognition that virtue may be pleasurable and that happiness involves different things for different people. But a moment's reflection on virtue (or the other examples) shows that his focus of attention is excessively narrow and the account unsatisfactory. Virtue is presented, exhaustively, as a means to pleasant feelings or as a component in whatever it is a person finds immediately pleasant. But virtue, though it may be accompanied with pleasure, is not valued for that reason by the virtuous person. What is missing in this context is any consideration of such things as the way in which virtues fit within a person's life as a whole, mark out some forms of life as against others, open up possibilities for development, and constitute conditions of social relationships. More generally, Mill's argument that pleasure alone is desirable appears in the end to be definitional. He observes that the question is one of fact and experience, but, armed with the idea that more or less anything can come to be part of a person's happiness, he concludes with the conceptual remark, "that to desire anything, except in proportion as the idea of it is pleasant, is a physical and metaphysical impossibility" (*Utilitarianism* IV, 238).

The question of the general happiness remains. Mill says that no reason can be given why the general happiness is desirable, "except that each person, so far as he believes it to be attainable, desires his own happiness." The proof that happiness is a good, to the extent that proof is deemed possible, is "that each person's happiness is a good to that person, and the general happiness, therefore, a good to the aggregate of all persons" (*Utilitarianism* IV, 234). This argument, it is clear, does nothing to show that anyone desires the general happiness or hence that it can be counted, in Mill's terms, as desirable or good. In a letter written a few years later, Mill explained:

> When I said that the general happiness is a good to the aggregate of all persons I did not mean that every human being's happiness is a good to every other human being; though I think in a good state of society and education it would be so. I merely meant in this particular sentence to argue that since A's happiness is a good, B's a good, C's a good, &c., the sum of all these goods must be a good.[46]

While this clarification absolves Mill from an obvious fallacy, it does not make the argument any more satisfactory. In the end, therefore, it appears that Mill does not establish any connection between the doctrine that happiness alone is what everyone desires and the thesis that the promotion of the general happiness is the sole moral standard by which to judge human conduct. In connection with Mill's transition from individual to general good, Sidgwick argued:

> An aggregate of actual desires, each directed towards a different part of the general happiness, does not constitute an actual desire for the general happiness, existing in any individual; . . . There being, therefore no actual desire — so far as this reasoning goes — for the general happiness, the proposition that the general happiness is desirable cannot in this way be established. (*Methods of Ethics*, 388)

To make good this gap, Sidgwick proposed, as we have seen, that Utilitarianism needs to invoke a maxim of benevolence. Mill's attempt to avoid this demand (through a proof according to which the principle of utility embraces benevolence) is a failure.

There is nonetheless an interesting discussion of the question of obligation in regard to utility in Chapter III of Mill's essay (prior to the attempted proof of the principle). In the face of someone who asks, "Why am I bound to promote the general happiness?" Mill puts the primary emphasis on the role of education. The sense of obligation in regard to the principle is made to rest on improvement through education until "the feeling of unity with our fellow-creatures" becomes deeply rooted in our character as part of our nature.

External sanctions — "the hope of favour and the fear of displeasure, from our fellow-creatures or the Ruler of the Universe" (*Utilitarianism* III,

228) — are accorded a role in this development. But Mill puts the primary emphasis on the acquisition of the internal sanction of duty, the idea of conscience, a feeling in our minds regarding right and wrong grounded in "the conscientious feelings of mankind." For all the importance he attached to education, he did not deal with the process of moral development in any detail.

Mill was critical of the idea of an innate moral sense. Moral feelings are acquired, not innate, but the moral faculty, he proposes, "if not part of our nature, is a natural outgrowth from it" (*Utilitarianism* III, 230).[47] In this connection, he was sensitive to a problem which surrounds the acquisition of moral feelings in early childhood. To a considerable extent, the original acquisition of moral feelings depends on external sanctions. When this factor is added to the force of early childhood impressions, it becomes clear that moral feelings of almost any sort can come to take on the authority of conscience. Thus moral feelings generally lie under the threat of being the arbitrary impositions of authority. In this situation, what saves the principle of utility from arbitrariness is its basis in a powerful natural sentiment, viz., "the social feelings of mankind; the desire to be in unity with our fellow-creatures" (*Utilitarianism* III, 231). Utilitarian moral teaching can thus proceed on the basis of a natural affection. This is strengthened by appropriate education and social experience by which people are led (to some extent at least) to take account of the interests of others; further, they may become reflectively aware in time that "society between human beings . . . is manifestly impossible on any other footing than that the interests of all are to be consulted" (ibid.).

Mill's argument, in summary, is that Utilitarianism, like all moral outlooks, begins in the child in the form of imposed and unexamined behavioral procedures and continues on the basis of teaching and the formation of habits. But it has a natural basis in human affections, and as the child grows to maturity, its morality can be provided with a rational basis in terms of the conditions of its own happiness in relation to the happiness of others. As a major part of the educational process, Mill supposes (as we have seen) that the person who learns to desire the general happiness comes to find that this is a major ingredient in his or her own individual happiness.

Put in these broad terms, Mill's depiction of the desirable Utilitarian moral development is almost Aristotelian in character. A good part of the reason for this, however, is that Mill's treatment of the topic is suggestive of a moral formation precisely along the lines of Greek and Christian virtues and rules of behavior. He makes the connection with Christian teaching in a number of places in the essay, for example: "In the golden rule of Jesus of Nazareth, we read the complete spirit of the ethics of utility" (*Utilitarianism* III, 218). In that case, Utilitarianism would appear to be hardly other than a secular version of the New Testament proposal that all the commandments of the (moral) law can be summed up in the one rule, "Love your neighbor as you love yourself" (Rom. XIII, 9). Perhaps this is not surprising given Mill's effective abandonment of the Benthamite vision of a calculus of pleasure and his moves toward an enlarged, more "Greek," conception of happiness. But then there is reason to conclude that he did not think through the developmental implications of Utilitarianism in a thorough way. Attention to this consideration, I will argue, brings out a serious problem in the Utilitarian account of morality.

In his discussion of sanctions, Mill was concerned to insist that Utilitarianism is not subject to any special problems in comparison with other accounts of morality. It will emerge that this is in question. Given the emphasis Mill put on education, one would suppose that the principle of utility and the surrounding theory would be taught to children as openly as possible. That is to say, attention to the principle would be a major element in promoting the desired outcome. This idea was put in question, however, by Henry Sidgwick in his modified account of Utilitarianism. Bernard Williams expresses Sidgwick's thinking as follows:

> Sidgwick saw that it must be an empirical question what motivations lead to the greatest good; in particular, whether the practice of thinking about the greatest good is likely to lead to the greatest good. The utilitarian consciousness itself becomes an item about which it must think, and Sidgwick came to the conclusion that in many departments of life it should not be too encouraged.[48]

Like Mill, Sidgwick was concerned to argue that there is a broad coincidence between Utilitarian morality and traditional commonsense views regarding virtues and duties; commonsense morality, he proposed, might be seen as an "unconscious Utilitarianism." To this end, Sidgwick argued that the Utilitarian understanding of impartial benevolence can allow a proper place for natural affections such as loyalty to friends and the special concern of parents for their children; such things have utility. Similarly, he argued for the utility of justice, truth-telling, self-control, and other self-regarding virtues, and of chastity (including the utility of the common but anomalous difference as to what is expected of the two sexes in regard to this virtue).

It would clearly be an important part of moral development in this scheme for individuals to acquire the relevant habits or dispositions. But now a problem arises. From a utilitarian point of view, the dispositions are dispositions for actions which maximize pleasure; that is, their value is instrumental. But, as Bernard Williams points out, the virtues cannot have that appearance "from the inside," from the point of view of the person concerned:

> The dispositions help to form the character of an agent who has them, and they will do the job the [utilitarian] theory has given them only if the

agent does not see his character purely instrumentally, but sees the world from the point of view of that character.

Furthermore, the relevant dispositions are concerned with feelings and beliefs and judgments as well as actions: "They are expressed precisely in ascribing intrinsic and not instrumental value to such things as truthtelling, loyalty, and so on" (Ethics and the Limits of Philosophy, 108).

There is, in short, a clash between what the theory says about the role of virtue and what it requires of agents if the role is to be realized in practice. In application to the developmental situation, it would appear that if children are to acquire the virtues properly (as the theory supposes), they should not be taught to think about them in a Utilitarian way. Perhaps this knowledge can be imparted to them later. The risk is that, without a firm commitment to virtue, people may be drawn to interpret the principle too readily in their own favor. Nevertheless, there are those who do have the relevant knowledge. The general question Williams raises here concerns the kind of life, social or personal, which would be needed to embody such a theory.[49]

Sidgwick and others, as Williams notes, were drawn to distinguish between two classes of people, "a class of theorists who could responsibly handle the utilitarian justification of non-utilitarian dispositions, the other a class who unreflectively employed those dispositions." Sidgwick's preference, regarding the general goal of moral development, was for a society of enlightened Utilitarians. He did not deal with the problem that children must always constitute for this ideal, but he accepted in general terms that, on Utilitarian principles, there may be situations in which "it may be right to teach openly to one set of people what it would be wrong to teach to others." Even more generally, he observed that

> a Utilitarian may reasonably desire, on Utilitarian principles, that some of his conclusions should be rejected by mankind generally; or even that the vulgar should keep aloof from his system as a whole, in so far as the inevitable indefiniteness and complexity of its calculations render it likely to lead to bad results in their hands.[50]

Thus a very large gap is opened up between what the theory states and what it must recommend generally in regard to moral formation. The realization of Utilitarian theory, no less than Kantian ethics, is faced with a major pedagogical problem, stemming in different ways from their different conceptions about the place of happiness in morality.[51] This is a serious objection, given the practical character of ethical theory, though it is far from being the only problematic aspect of the attempt to ground ethics on the idea of the general happiness.

9. Hegel:
The Ethical Community

The themes which have emerged in the past three chapters all find their place in Hegel's philosophy. Hegel had read Rousseau's *Emile* — and Rousseau's writings generally — when he was still a student; he was steeped in the knowledge of Kant's philosophy, and he was acutely aware of the growth of Utilitarian ideas, notably in connection with French Enlightenment thinkers and the writings of Bentham. In major respects, Hegel's views concerning morality and moral development were worked out in critical response to these sources. But one should add immediately that Greek ethics, especially in relation to Greek tragedy and the writings of Plato and Aristotle, constitute his fundamental reference points. Stoicism, in both Greek and Roman thought, and the long history of the ethical consciousness of Christianity provide further major elements to which he responded critically in the development of his views.

1. Educational Themes: Family, School, and State

Hegel lived in an age in which the discussion of education had become intense, and although he did not publish a major work on the topic in a direct sense, educational themes run throughout his writings quite generally. His views on education were expressed in an occasional way in five prize-giving addresses which he made between 1808 and 1815 when he was Rector of the Nuremburg Gymnasium.[1] During these same years he wrote the *Philosophical Propaedeutic*, an introduction to philosophy, which included instruction in ethics, for school students.[2] As Bernard Bourgeois has said, the whole of Hegel's work underlines the basic importance of education in human development.[3]

The basic principle behind Hegel's Nuremburg addresses is related to the idea of self-education. This, in Karl Löwith's words, is "education by which the individual raises himself to the universal nature of the spirit."[4] This same pedagogical idea is a major theme in the preface and introduction in Hegel's *Phenomenology of Spirit*[5] (hereafter *PG*) and in his system of knowledge more generally. The concept of *Bildung* — education and culture, especially in a developmental sense — is central to his thought.[6] The Hegelian system, as Bourgeois suggests, can thus be characterized as a pedagogical philosophy, *the* pedagogical philosophy, and Hegel can be seen as the philosopher-pedagogue par excellence. But now the very scope of his thought must make a limited study appear problematic.

In the preface of the *Phenomenology of Spirit*, Hegel proposes that, in the course of education, the particular individual recapitulates the history of spirit or mind in general: "Past existence is the already acquired property of universal Spirit which constitutes the Substance of the individual." The individual traverses in microcosm the course of world history; for example, "in the child's progress through school, we shall recognize the history of the cultural development of the world traced, as it were, in a silhouette" (*PG* 28, 16). In this connection, Jean Hyppolite suggests that the *Phenomenology* can be seen as dealing fundamentally with the problem of the education of the particular individual in achieving consciousness of what Hegel calls his substance; this is a pedagogical task which is not unrelated to the one Rousseau had undertaken in *Emile*.[7] Measured in relation to these large claims, a short study of Hegel's ideas concerning ethics and ethical development must appear not so much daunting as absurd! Yet it is possible to make some sense of the ideas within these limits, albeit in a very general and incomplete way; and it should already be clear that the ideas are important in relation to the major themes of this study.

THE FAMILY

Education according to Hegel is the art of making human beings ethical, a task which finds its natural and original setting in the family.[8] The child lives originally at an instinctive and physical level. But the most basic consideration in regard to children is that they are potentially free. They do not exist, therefore, as the property of their parents or of anyone else, and they have rights, specifically the right to maintenance and education at the expense of the family. Educational (and hence ethical) development consists, in its turn, in the achievement of self-subsistence and freedom of personality. Hegel put particular emphasis on the idea of *self-education* in which the individual comes to share in a wider community, especially in its common language and customs, and becomes part of the universal spirit which is realized in the community. But the process of development begins with the parental role of instilling ethical principles in the form of immediate feeling, in a context of love, trust, and obedience, and it continues with the development of virtue in the individual character, until "the habitual practice of ethical living appears as a second nature" (*Philosophy of Right*, hereafter *PR*, 151, 108; see Add. 151, 260). Some of these ideas are expressed in an important paragraph in the Third Part of the *Philosophy of Right*:

> Children are potentially free and their life directly embodies nothing save potential freedom. Consequently they are not things and cannot be the property either of their parents or others. In respect of his relation to the family, the child's education has the positive aim of instilling ethical principles into him in the form of an immediate feeling for which

differences are not yet explicit, so that thus equipped with the foundation of an ethical life, his heart may live its early years in love, trust, and obedience. In respect of the same relation, this education has the negative aim of raising children out of the instinctive, physical level on which they are originally, to self-subsistence and freedom of personality and so to the level on which they have power to leave the natural unity of the family. (*PR* 175, 117)

This account of ethics and education within the family points beyond the family itself to civil society and the State. Marriage, Hegel says, is "but the ethical Idea in its *immediacy* and so has its objective actuality only in the inwardness of subjective feeling and disposition" (*PR* 176, 118). The family is an unreflecting unity based on feeling, specifically the feeling of love, i.e., "ethical life in the form of something natural" (*PR* Add. 158, 261). Ethical life is properly realized in the State, which in Hegel's conception is "the actuality of the ethical idea" (*PR* 257, 155); like the family, the State is an inward unity, but the unity is now mediated by reason. Education in its most complete form is realized in this sphere, but for reasons to be noted later, Hegel located education primarily in the sphere of civil society, the association of individuals related basically by economic ties, which lies between family and State.

It needs to be said that Hegel's projection of ethical development beyond the family relates directly only to men:

Man has his actual substantive life in the state, in learning, and so forth, as well as in labour and struggle with the external world and with himself so that it is only out of his diremption that he fights his way to self-subsistent unity with himself. In the family he has a tranquil intuition of this unity, and there he lives a subjective ethical life on the plane of feeling. Woman, on the other hand, has her substantive destiny in the family, and to be imbued with familial piety is her ethical frame of mind. (*PR* 166, 114)

Given this conviction (which needs further attention), it is not surprising that Hegel followed Rousseau in proposing that it is education by the mother which is especially important in the child's early years. This is connected with the idea, which is very interesting in itself, that love and trust provide the necessary ground for the development of practical rationality and the view that "ethical principles must be implanted in the child in the form of feeling" (*PR* Add. 175, 265). Hegel similarly allied himself with Rousseau (against Locke) in opposing early reliance on reasoning with children. On the other hand, he put considerable emphasis on discipline, and he was critical of the "play theory of education" which J. H. Basedow had popularized in Germany on Rousseauian principles (with support from Kant, as we have seen). More importantly, he pointed out that "the educational experiments, advocated by Rousseau in *Emile*, of withdrawing children from the common life of every day and bringing them up in the country have turned out to be futile" (*PR* Add. 153, 261). This relates to the major emphasis in Hegel's ethical thought: that individual freedom is possible only in an actual ethical community. He endorsed the Pythagorean (and Socratic) advice to the father who inquired about the best way of educating his son in ethical conduct: "Make him a citizen of a state with good laws" (*PR* 153, 109).

THE SCHOOL

In the more concrete focus of the prize-giving addresses in Nuremburg (hereafter *School Addresses*), Hegel would relate this Pythagorean advice to the need for good schooling. The ethical character of education, he proposes, is effected in three main ways in the school: directly through ethical instruction, indirectly through the teaching of the arts and sciences, and perhaps most importantly, by the fact that the school is an ethical community in which pupils become accustomed to principles in the form of ethical practice.[9] Hegel has interesting things to say about each of these aspects.

In rejecting an Enlightenment view that children should not be instructed in moral concepts and principles on the grounds that they are unable to understand them, Hegel observes that such instruction needs to be age-related (without waiting on full understanding):

> In considering the matter more closely, one readily sees that ethical concepts are grasped by the child, the boy, and the young man, in keeping with their age; indeed, it is the work of a lifetime to go on acquiring ever deeper understanding of their meaning and scope, seeing them reflected in examples and new instances, recognising their rich breadth of meaning and the specific conditions of their application in more and more developed ways. (*School Addresses*, 267)

One other consideration relating to ethical instruction is of importance. Hegel says that it is the privilege of consciousness, in contrast to the fixed character of animal instinct, to be open and contingent in its deliberations; it also has the power, through the will, to impose limits on what is open. Now, ethical considerations provide a fixed point in this shifting scene: "Without them, what is universally valid, what a person is required to do, and what is contingent, the pleasure of the moment, would collapse into one another under the form of something one is *able* to do" (ibid.).

With regard to scholarly formation in the arts and sciences, Hegel put particular emphasis on philosophy as embracing the formative stages of the development of mind or spirit. (He taught courses of this sort for high school students at the Nuremburg Gymnasium; the adaptation of his own philosophical system to this end is contained in the *The Philosophical Propaedeutic*.) But Hegel was drawn to put an even greater emphasis on the study of the literature of ancient Greece and Rome. The power of scholarly formation in general is that it separates a person from himself and his immediate inclinations and surroundings, installs in his thought a universal and ordered world, and thereby liberates him for the subsequent understanding of his own world. Such liberation, Hegel concludes, "constitutes the formal basis of ethical conduct in general" (268). But this liberating power is particularly present, he believes, in the study of classical Greek and Latin literature, for so long the basis of our culture, the "secular baptism" in which the soul acquires an indelible character in critical judgment and knowledge (237).

Finally, Hegel treats of the school as a specific sphere of ethical development:

> The school is not restricted to these general effects; it is a particular ethical milieu in which man lives and receives a practical formation in becoming accustomed to objective relations. It is a sphere with its own concerns and issues, its own rights and laws, and forms of reward and punishment; in truth, it is a sphere which constitutes an essential stage in the development of the complete ethical character. *The school is placed, in effect, between the family and the actual world*; it constitutes the middle term which assures the connection between them and the transition from the one to the other. (268–69; emphasis in original)

In keeping with this characteristic, Hegel portrays the school as exhibiting features of the two worlds it links: the personal, subjective life of the family, with its bonds of natural love and trust, and the objective being-in-common of the world with its rights and duties and practices which manifest a universal order. The school is accorded a particularly significant role in the development and practice of social virtues, and in preparing its members for independence, on the one hand, and for participation in public life, on the other.

These considerations, it is clear, relate in Hegel's terms only to male children. In contrast to his contemporary, Fichte, who proposed that "children of the two sexes should be educated in the same way," Hegel espoused a version of pedagogical difference in relation to the sexes.[10] This was based on his view that man has his "actual substantive life in the state, in learning, and so forth, as well as in labour and struggle with the external world," while "woman, on the other hand, has her substantive destiny in the family, and to be imbued with family piety is her ethical frame of mind" (*PR* 166, 114). This conviction about woman's place in the family, even if it were allowed without further question, would not settle the issue of woman's education. Hegel's contention is related also to an untried view, a prejudice in short, regarding women's capacities. He says in an additional remark in the *Philosophy of Right*:

> Women are capable of education, but they are not made for activities which demand a universal faculty such as the more advanced sciences, philosophy, and certain forms of artistic production. . . . Women are

educated — who knows how? — as it were by breathing in ideas, by living rather than by acquiring knowledge. (PR Add. 166, 263)

Hegel's views regarding woman's role were also influenced, as we shall see, by the weight we gave to precedents in Greek literature and practice.

The principle of education in the Hegelian account is that it should consist in the formation of individuals in the ethical milieu in which they are to live. On this basis, he was critical of a view, which had become current at the time, in later writings of Fichte and von Humboldt, for example, that authority in education should rest exclusively with the State.[11] In Hegel's thought, the State is the universal ground of education, the domain of reason in which the spirit of a people as a whole is expressed; as the basis of ethical life as a whole, it has supreme educational responsibility. But Hegel, as we have seen, treats the family as an ethical milieu in its own right, the "first ethical root of the state" (PR 255, 154). Again, the school is a further ethical milieu in which both family and state are accorded involvement. More strictly, however, Hegel identifies the school as an element of civil society, conceived as the sphere of culture which marks the transition from particularity to universality.

CIVIL SOCIETY AND THE STATE

Consideration of the school (or university) does not loom large in Hegel's major treatment of the progress of Spirit (family, civil society, State). This could be linked in part with the emphasis he places on self-education in connection with Bildung. Bourgeois plausibly suggests that it is connected with the fundamentally objective orientation of Hegel's thought: pedagogy is only one of the many functions of civil society and does not have any specific ontological significance; it relates particularly to the subjective history of the individual rather than to the objective content of universal development (La Pédagogie de Hegel, 31). There is, nonetheless, an important relevant passage in the Philosophy of Right:

> In its character as universal family, civil society has the right and duty of superintending and influencing education, inasmuch as education bears upon the child's capacity to become a member of society. Society's right here is paramount over the arbitrary and contingent preferences of parents, particularly in cases where education is to be completed not by the parents but by others. To the same end, society must provide public educational facilities so far as is practicable. (PR 239, 148)

It should be clear from earlier discussion that, in allocating authority to civil society (and ultimately the State), Hegel is sensitive to the educational role of the family. In this spirit, the comment on this passage proceeds: "The line which demarcates the rights of parents from those of civil society is very hard to draw here. Parents usually suppose that in the matter of education they have complete freedom and may arrange everything as they like. . . . None the less, society has a right to act on principles tested by its experience and to compel parents to send their children to school, to have them vaccinated, and so forth" (*PR* Add. 239, 277).

Hegel's argument rests on his view about the ethical character of the State. But the matter is given a specifically historical context in the *School Addresses*. In the last of the addresses, he proposes that most modern public institutions began as private enterprises designed to deal with a recognized general need such as help for the poor, the sick, matters of religious cult and justice. But as common life becomes more diverse and complex, reliance on isolated responses to needs becomes inadequate and no longer makes sense. In that situation, he continues:

> On the one hand, a sacred boundary must be maintained within which the government of the State must leave the private life of the citizen untouched; but it is no less necessary that matters which have a close connection with the purpose of the State should be taken up by the government and organised in a planned way. (*School Addresses*, 293)

Against this background, he affirms that the time has come for the State to take responsibility, as a matter of moral urgency, for the provision of education.

This proposal regarding the authority of the State in education is hedged in, as we have seen, by qualifications. The location of authority in civil society, rather than in the State as political authority, gives this point additional force. It means, as Bourgeois comments, that whatever interests the State has in education, it has no authority to determine the curriculum by reference to its political concerns (*La Pédagogie de Hegel*, 35). Hegel was deeply critical of a merely utilitarian approach to education; indeed, he argued that the attempt to ground education on its utility to the State, rather than as something with autonomous value, ends in disaster (*School Addresses*, 238). In relation to the State, education needs relative autonomy; or put in the slightly different terms of Karl Löwith, "for Hegel, the problem of a choice between humanistic and political goals was simply nonexistent; he still thought it obvious that 'humanistic' education was just what educated the individual for his life in the *polis*" (*From Hegel to Nietzsche*, 289).

The authority of Hegel's State, however, is less constrained than this account might suggest. The (true) State is "the rich inward articulation of ethical life . . . the architectonic of that life's rationality which sets determinate limits to the different circles of public life and their rights" (*PR* Preface, 6). In these terms, the State is empowered to determine the bounds of reason in all its domains.

Hegel considered that the ethical end of education (in the broad sense of *Bildung*) includes the happiness of human beings among its values (see *PR* 20, 29). On the other hand, he rejected "the feeling that needs, their satisfaction, the pleasures and comforts of private life, and so forth, are absolute ends," and the associated view that education is a "mere means to these ends." The final purpose of education, rather, is "liberation and the struggle for higher liberation still; education is the absolute transition from an ethical substantiality which is immediate and natural to the one which is intellectual and so both infinitely subjective and lofty enough to have attained universality of form." He notes that this liberation in the individual subject is "the hard struggle against pure subjectivity of demeanour, against the immediacy of desire, against the empty subjectivity of feeling and the caprice of inclination" (*PR* 187, 125). This is a lofty notion of subjective freedom defined by reason. Given the idea of the fully rational State, there is no theoretical problem in reconciling individual freedom in the specified sense with the authority of the State. Nevertheless, this remains a problem in the actual world.

2. The Greek Ethical World

Hegel's emphasis on ethical community, originating in the family and made actual in the State, draws attention to the centrality of the idea of the Greek *polis* in his thought. It also marks the standpoint from which he is critical of both Kantian ethics and Utilitarian thought and seeks to go beyond them.

Hegel saw the Greek *polis* in an idealized way as a type of organic unity in which individuals secured their particular interests and realized their potentialities through adherence to common laws and customs; the collective life of the city-state constituted the universal ground in which individuals found the essence and meaning of their lives. Hegel in fact reserved the term *Sittlichkeit*, which is the usual German word for ethics or morality, for situations of the Greek sort; that is to say, ethics or morality is found, in his understanding, only in a community, properly only in a self-sufficient community or state. So far as the individual is concerned in this setting, ethical life consists in carrying out "the well-known and explicit rules of [one's] own situation" (*PR* 150, 107), participating thereby in the (ethical) life of the community. There is in fact no way of expressing Hegel's use of *Sittlichkeit* simply and adequately in English because he uses it in explicit contrast with the word *Moralität*, which could also be translated as morality or ethics. Hegel reserves *Moralität* specifically for conceptions of ethics which are associated in a primary way with individuals and generalized conceptions of obligation; he thus speaks above all of Kantian ethics, with its basis in the autonomous rational individual, as *Moralität*. One could then say that *Sittlichkeit* is ethics (or morality) in an essentially communal setting. This conception points to the idea of objective spirit as transcending the individual. This, in the words of H-G. Gadamer, is the idea that "present in the customs, the legal order, and the political constitution of a land is a definite spirit that has no adequate reflection in the subjective consciousness of the individual."[12] I will try to acknowledge the communal (and objective) force of the term — though the acknowledgment is hardly adequate — by using "ethics," and such phrases as "ethical life," "ethical development," "ethical world," to refer to the Hegelian notion of *Sittlichkeit*.

FAMILY PIETY AND PUBLIC LAW

The Greek city-state, to take up the theme again, is presented as an actualization of *Sittlichkeit*, the only adequate instance of its kind in European history. But even the deep unity of Greek ethical life, as Hegel sees it, was subject to the possibility of tragic conflict between its component parts, notably between the demands of family piety and the law of the State. Hegel frequently refers to Sophocles' tragedy, *Antigone*, in this connection. On becoming king of Thebes, Creon had immediately decreed that the body of his nephew, Polynices, who had been killed in battle against his own city, must be left unburied. Antigone, sister of Polynices, defied the decree in the name of overriding and eternal laws of the gods (which bear on kinship obligations regarding the dead). She is sentenced to death, and with her death, there follows the death by suicide of Creon's son, Haemon (Antigone's promised husband), and, following Haemon's death, the suicide of Creon's wife, Eurydice.

In the *Philosophy of Right*, Hegel refers to *Antigone* in the context of his view that the two sexes belong to different ethical spheres. The tragedy thus marks a field of conflict between the family and state, between what is "principally the law of woman . . . the law of a substantiality at once subjective and on the plane of feeling, the law of the inward life, a life which has not yet attained its full actualization . . . the law of the ancient gods," on the one hand, and the "public law . . . the law of the land" (the world of men), on the other. In drawing attention to the conflict, Hegel says nothing at this point regarding possible resolution. He concludes with the remark that, "this is the supreme opposition in ethics and therefore in tragedy; and it is individualized in the same play in the opposing natures of man and woman" (PR 166, 115).

The more sustained discussion of the topic in the *Philosophy of Fine Art* turns on the same opposition between "ethical life in its social universality" and "the family as the natural ground of moral relations." The opposition is also expressed in ways that appear more obviously unequal: "Antigone reverences the ties of blood-relationship, the gods of the nether world. Creon alone recognizes Zeus, the paramount Power of public life and the commonwealth." Or again, the gods whom Antigone revered are "the *Dei inferi* of Hades, the instinctive Powers of feeling, Love and kinship, not the daylight gods of free and self-conscious, social, and political life." Hegel insists nevertheless that the two ethical principles in conflict — care for the well-being of the entire city and family love and obligation to one's dead — are of equal authority: each has validity in its own right.[13]

In the Hegelian interpretation of the tragedy, each of the protagonists takes a one-sided position. The real basis of the collision is placed in a one-sidedness which yields an opposition in which each side realizes only one of the moral powers. The moral power which is denied is, in each case, immanent in the life of each: Antigone lives under the political authority of Creon; Creon, as father and husband, is "under obligation to respect the sacred ties of relationship." In consequence of this refusal, "they are seized and broken by that very bond which is rooted in the compass of their own social existence." The tragedy thus points to the historical collapse of both state and family in the Greek ethical world. Hegel suggests, however, that Sophocles, in bringing out the one-sidedness of each protagonist, shows the way to a resolution of conflict:

> The final result, then, of the development of tragedy conducts us to this issue, and only this, namely, that the twofold vindication of the mutually conflicting aspects is no doubt retained, but the *one-sided* mode is cancelled. . . . The true course of dramatic development consists in the annulment of *contradictions* viewed as such, in the reconciliation of the forces of human action, which alternately strive to negate each other in their conflict.[14]

Martha Nussbaum argues that Hegel is correct is seeing both Creon and Antigone as one-sided in their respective view of what matters. (She allows that he might be criticized for not giving more attention to the superiority of Antigone's position.) But she is critical of his claim to find a basis for the resolution of conflict in the tragedy "in a synthesis that will do justice to both of the contending parties."[15] I would agree that the point concerning one-sidedness is well-taken in each case, but Hegel's portrayal of the nature of the conflict is itself touched by an element of one-sidedness, which in turn affects the question of a possible synthesis.

The principle of "social universality" on which Creon takes his stand is law in the form of a specific proclamation. His commitment to the decree does not have the support of the people of Thebes, and when this is pointed out by his son Haemon, he replies: "Am I to rule this land for others — or myself?" (line 735). Again, when he finally relents (though his change of heart comes too late), he says that "it's best to keep the established laws to the very day we die" (line 1113f). There must be question, then, of the extent to which Creon was concerned for the common weal in his original proclamation, even though he had insisted that the good of one's country and loyalty to the State were the supreme standards of behavior (line 180ff). Again, Hegel notes that Creon, as father and husband, is under obligation to respect the sacred ties of relationship. But one could argue that this obligation falls on him also *as ruler* of the State since matters regarding the burial of the dead, and the like, involve customs which concern the people as a whole. This is complicated by the fact that Polynices had betrayed his city. Custom would not suppose that he should be given burial in the manner of an honorable enemy, but it appears that Athenian practice would have allowed for burial outside the territory of the city.[16] In any case, even if Creon could claim authority to make the law, he could enact it only by neglecting his specific kinship obligations in regard to Polynices. Antigone is portrayed as acting in a one-sided way (a comparison with her sister Ismene is telling in this regard); nevertheless, the ethical commitment she defends (and dies for) has a universal character which grows out of the immediate context of the family and its responsibility to its dead.

The factors just noted point to an Aristotelian assessment of this tragedy, specifically that Antigone's action reflected a universal law which can be seen as a standard against which particular laws might be judged as unjust (*Rhetoric* I, 13, 1373b5ff). Creon was the political authority in Thebes; but it does not follow that he served the State wisely or well in proclaiming the prohibition and putting his authority to the test in the way that he chose. Hegel seizes on the general idea of the ethical value of political authority, but he fails to take account of relevant considerations in this particular exercise of the authority. For all that, his broad characterization of the play as a conflict between State and family values could still be defended. The conflict might have been avoided in *this* instance: Creon did not have to enact the law in the first place, or he might have heeded the warnings of the prophet Teiresias (as he did eventually) and changed his mind before it was too late. But one could still maintain that the seeds of conflict between the two spheres, and the inevitability of actual conflict on occasions, would remain as a permanent factor.

This raises a question about the thesis of "Hegelian optimism," that is, the idea of a synthesis that does justice to both sides of the opposition. Nussbaum interprets Hegel as saying that, "the very possibility of conflict or tension between different spheres of value will be altogether eliminated" (68). Drawing especially on the choral lyrics in *Antigone*, she makes out a strong case against this view. But there is a question whether Hegel is in fact committed to it. As A. C. Bradley says, he sees tragedy as portraying "a self-division and self-waste of spirit," and it is implied that there is a spiritual value on both sides of the conflict.[17] In this case, there is reason to affirm the value of both State and family. But then the *idea* of a possible reconciliation between the values seems both inevitable and necessary for an understanding of the tragedy. This, however, carries no promise of the elimination of all possibility of conflict or tension between different spheres of value. On the contrary, in affirming both family and State, Hegel affirms the possibility of "the supreme opposition in ethics and therefore in tragedy" (*PR* 166, 115).

SOCRATES AND THE INVENTION OF MORALITY

Hegel saw the occurrence of conflict between family and State in ancient Greece as an opposition *within* the ethical world (within *Sittlichkeit*). But with Socrates there arose an individual who, in the name of universal good, placed himself in opposition to the ethical life of his city as a whole. In speaking of the Greek ethical world, Hegel observed that, "the wisest men of antiquity have declared . . . that wisdom and virtue consist in living in accordance with the customs of one's nation" (PG 214). This conviction of the wise was brought into question in the period of educational expansion fostered by the Sophists in the latter half of the fifth century B.C.; and it came under pressures of a different sort in the social upheaval of the Peloponnesian War. Living at this time, Socrates was concerned to find fixed and universal standards, and to this end he took as his guide the saying of the Delphic oracle, "Know thyself." In *The Philosophy of History*, Hegel expresses the character of the Socratic standpoint as follows:

> [Socrates] taught that man has to discover and recognise in himself what is the Right and Good, and that this Right and Good is in its nature universal. Socrates is celebrated as a Teacher of Morality, but we should rather call him the *Inventor of Morality*. The Greeks had a *customary* morality; but Socrates undertook to teach them what moral virtues, duties, etc. were. The moral man is not he who merely wills and does what is right — not the merely innocent man — but he who has consciousness of what he is doing. Socrates — in assigning to insight, to conviction, the determination of men's actions — posited the Individual as capable of a final moral decision, in contra-position to Country and Customary Morality, and thus made himself an Oracle in the Greek sense.[18]

In Greek customary morality — in the idealized form in which Hegel portrays it — individuals identified themselves with the customs and laws of their city in an immediate and unreflective way. For them, virtue, freedom, and good consisted in being at home in this world; they realized through their lives, though not by conscious reflection, an objective expression of reason. What Socrates expresses, by contrast, is the principle of subjectivity and rational awareness: as an individual subject, he consciously steps back from the particular laws and customs of his city and reflects on morality in terms of universal reason. With the advent of universal consciousness and the idea of self-determination, the death of the Greek ethical world (and therefore the *polis*) is at hand.

Hegel, it is clear, uses Socrates to stand in part for complex developments in Greek ethical experience over a long period of time. The idea of laws and customs as reflecting a universal order — associated with the gods, or with nature and the cosmos as a rational and coherent harmony of ordered parts — had long been part of the Greek outlook. Indeed, a critical issue which the Sophists raised, as the age of agitated reflection set in, was whether justice is nothing more than a matter of purely conventional laws and customs. This question was raised, furthermore, in the context of a growing sense that the individual has interests and inclinations which exist independently of his social relationships. Socrates took up questions regarding individuality and the idea of universal moral standards in a distinctive way. He was, as Hegel saw it, a world-historical figure whose level of consciousness presaged the end of the Greek city-state.

In his *Lectures on the History of Philosophy*, Hegel argues that Socrates did indeed attack and destroy Athenian life in two fundamental respects, in public religion and family piety. The accusations brought against him at his trial are thus accorded a real basis. The kernel of the first charge is based on the idea that Socrates "is the hero who established in the place of the Delphic oracle, the principle that man must look within himself to know what is Truth."[19] He thus effected a revolution in Greek consciousness, in his awareness of himself as a moral being and in his claim to personal responsibility under the guidance of his own daemon or spirit. With the emergence of the individual as an oracle in his own right, one can speak of the introduction of a new god into Athenian life before whom the old gods are brought into question.

The question of Socrates' attack on family piety turns on the principle of respect for the feeling of unity between children and parents as "the first immediately moral relationship" and the basis of proper human development. Sons and daughters, Hegel notes, must eventually emerge from natural unity with the family and become independent, but "the separation must be one which is natural and unforced, and not defiant and disdainful." The basis of the charge that Socrates led youth astray was that he put himself forward as a better guide than parents in the search for virtue and the highest good. On some occasions, he was at odds with parental values and influence, and in some cases, his influence on the young, with its questioning of conventional wisdom and its emphasis on individual responsibility, turned out to be damaging. Family piety was "the substantial keynote of the Athenian State." In expounding a view in which moral authority is made to rest with individual consciousness with direct access to universal truth, Socrates brought the authority of both family and State into question.[20]

It is hardly surprising that Hegel portrays Socrates' fate as the enactment of a Greek tragedy. "In what is truly tragic," he maintained, "there must be valid moral powers on both sides which come into collision."[21] In the case of Socrates, there is the clash of objective freedom realized in the laws and customs of the Athenian state, on the one hand, and the right of consciousness, individual self-determination, or subjective freedom, on the other. The one principle destroys the other, yet both are mutually justified. Both principles were embodied furthermore in Socrates himself, for, while manifesting a new level of consciousness, he sought to live according to the laws of his native city. At the same time, the Socratic consciousness was beginning to take root more generally in the Greek ethical world. Socrates' tragedy, then, was the tragedy of Athens and of Greece.

The larger tragedy encompassed the eventual dissolution of the Greek *polis* and its ethical world. In the absence of a satisfactory ethical community, moral understanding and practice came to devolve primarily onto the individual. At this level, the Socratic principle of subjectivity and universal consciousness offered a high moral ideal, but since the individual cannot live a human life independently of social and ethical relationships, moral understanding and practice became problematic. The situation which now developed was one in which the moral power of individual consciousness was affirmed at the expense of the moral power of a genuine ethical community. What follows, in Hegel's portrayal, is a long and painful process of education (*Bildung*) over the centuries toward the formation of an ethical order — a new *Sittlichkeit* — in which the two powers would be fully realized in a proper relationship.

3. The Growth of Self-Consciousness and Ethical Relationships

In contrast to the spirit of modern individualism, Hegel's ethical thought was based on the Greek conviction that an isolated individual is not self-sufficient and that human values, including freedom, can be realized only in a social context. Hegel followed Aristotle in particular in emphasizing the role of the family as the natural basis of society, and in seeing the State as "a single complete community, large enough to be nearly or quite self-sufficing . . . originating in the bare needs of life, and continuing in existence for the sake of a good life" (Aristotle, *Politics*, I, 2).

In a fundamental argument bearing on the primacy of social relationships, Hegel sought to show that the attainment of self-consciousness can be effected only on the basis of awareness of others as selves. In this view, the development of self-consciousness beyond anything but the most primary level can proceed only with the setting up of social and therefore ethical bonds. We have already seen aspects of this standpoint in Hegel's views regarding the family and the development of the individual. The development of practical rationality and ethical life, he supposes, rests on the establishment of feelings of love and trust between children and parents. In his critique of Socrates, he insists that this feeling of unity is "the first immediately moral relationship" which every teacher needs to cultivate. Beginning at an instinctive level of awareness, children must subsequently achieve independence and freedom of personality through a long period of dependence, discipline, habit-formation, and education. But this growth is envisaged, ideally, as a natural, unforced, and cooperative undertaking. Hegel does not discuss in any detail, however, the child's transition from original consciousness to fully developed forms of self-consciousness.

The general development of self-consciousness in different social contexts and across history is a major theme in Hegel's writings. In this connection, his most celebrated discussion of the other-related character of self-consciousness (and of dependence and independence) is concerned not with relations in the family, but with the dialectic of master and slave.[22] What emerges in this inquiry, however, can be readily applied (albeit generally) to the relationship of parents and children.

MASTER AND SLAVE

In very general terms, Hegel proposes that self-consciousness arises with the desire for recognition as a conscious, free, and independent being. In the nature of the case, this can be achieved only by reciprocal acknowledgment on the part of another conscious being. The project of self-consciousness thus relates to the establishment of social relationships.

The master-slave dialectic, it should be noted, is associated primarily with an imagined pre-social situation or state of nature in which human beings exist only as separate individuals. The core of the account is that in conditions in which mutuality is absent, the project of self-consciousness necessarily arises as a struggle for life and death. Each party, in quest of recognition, seeks the death of the other and stakes his life on the outcome. But the death of either combatant undermines the project. What then develops, as "the emergence of man's social life and the commencement of political union,"[23] is the subordination of one party to the other: one emerges as lord or master, "the independent consciousness whose essential nature is to be for itself"; the other becomes his slave or bondsman, "the dependent consciousness, whose essential nature is simply to live or to be for another" (*PG* 189, 115).

Enslavement, it can be seen, fails to satisfy the project of self-consciousness in a different way. It fails so far as the slave is concerned since he is denied the status of free and independent being. But it fails also in the case of the master since there is now no other free self-conscious being able to accord him reciprocal recognition. The situation is not fixed at this point, however. Master and slave begin to be transformed through the dialectic of their social relationship. The master, in his independence, is cut off from the possibility of human acknowledgment. But in addition his relationship to the material world is mediated by the slave: he stands to things only in the relationship of one who desires and consumes them. He thus becomes locked in isolation and particularity. The slave in the meantime begins to move toward a more universal consciousness through work and discipline in conjunction with the experience of the fear of death. In his work for the master, he forms and shapes things; what he creates or produces becomes an expression of his being, a reflection in which he is able to find himself again: "Through this rediscovery of himself by himself, the bondsman realizes that it is precisely in his work wherein he seemed to have only an alienated existence that he acquires a mind of his own" (*PG* 196, 119).

The consciousness thus acquired has a universal character: the felt awareness of death breaks the bonds of particularity, and work involves the development of universally applicable skills and the transformation of things according to universal plans and rules of procedure. The worker finds in the things he makes a reflection of himself as a universal being. It is clear that this development does not solve the project of self-consciousness and the associated problem of social relationships. But the contrast of particularity and universality contains the germ of the Hegelian solution. The original opposition is a postulate based on the particularity of individuals as single and separate. Such individuals seek the recognition of the other as confirmation of their being, but since each is concerned only with his own interests, they are locked into conflict. With the development of a universal consciousness, however, the slave becomes capable of recognizing the interests of others and of entering into social relationships in which all would be recognized as free.

Hegel proposes a solution of this sort in the *Philosophy of Mind*.[24] He speaks there of universal self-consciousness as "the affirmative awareness of self in another self," a relationship in which each self is free without being set in opposition to the other, a reciprocal recognition involving a unity of "individuals mutually throwing light upon each other." He suggests furthermore that this level of recognition is realized in all true spiritual life, in family, homeland, and state, in love and friendship and other virtues. The master-slave relationship, as we noted, is placed more or less at the origin of social relations. This is now contrasted with modern civil society and the State where, he says, "the recognition for which the combatants fought already exists" — a society, in other words, in which all are recognized as free.

This contrast appears altogether too facile. The thesis of original conflict is secured by definition (given the postulated absence of mutuality between individuals). At the same time, the proposal gets some of its force from contemporary experience of the struggle for recognition on the part of individuals and groups. On this same basis, the claim that in modern society all are recognized as free appears absurdly naive in the face of deep and widespread forms of social oppression. Hegel, it should be said, applied the model more widely in his writings: in *The Phenomenology of Spirit*, elements of the master-slave relationship are invoked in the discussion of Stoicism, Skepticism, and the notion of the "unhappy consciousness" (which runs across much of the Christian era); he makes reference to it also in *The Philosophy of History* in dealing with the Oriental, the Greek, and the Roman worlds. It is clear, therefore, that the master-slave relationship is not restricted in the way the remarks in *The Philosophy of Mind* would suggest. On the other hand, it cannot be treated, in Hegel's view, as a completely universal or essential characterization of human relations. (Sartre, it can be noted, interprets the relationship in this way in his appropriation of Hegel in *Being and Nothingness*, Part 3.) Hegel insists plausibly that the emergence of self-consciousness, given the development of social forms beginning with the family, can be a non-oppressive process. But his suggestion that the conditions of reciprocal recognition had been established quite generally in modern society strains credulity. One could say, rather, that the master-slave relationship, while it takes different forms in different social and historical contexts, remains as a permanent problem to be overcome, and that the overcoming of it in human experience remains characteristically limited and precarious. From a different point of view, Hegel's discussion of the emergence of self-consciousness in conflict yields a general account of the conditions for its development as an ethical project. The most general condition is set by the nature of the project itself as arising out of the desire for recognition as a free and independent being. Its proper development therefore requires reciprocal acknowledgment on the part of others who are free and independent; its full realization presupposes the existence of a free society. In addition, Hegel proposes that work and discipline, education and art, and awareness of the finitude of life are the primary means by which the individual is raised to the universal level of spirit. At this point, it can be seen that the development of self-consciousness in an ethical order is precisely the task of education in family, civil society, and the State which Hegel sets out in the *The Philosophy of Right*. But this is historically possible only on the basis of the long process of education and cultural growth which followed on the collapse of the Greek ethical world.

FROM "MORALITY" TO "ETHICS"

Hegel's conception of ethics comes forward as the culmination of this historical process; it is presented as the dialectical synthesis of the divergent elements of individual and community which first emerged, separately and in opposition, in Socrates' confrontation with the common morality of Athens. Socrates, in Hegel's phrase, was the inventor of morality (as *Moralität*): he was the original voice of the individual subject, with immediate access, through reason, to universal value and obligation. But much had happened in European ethical experience since Socrates, and in the late eighteenth century, Kantian ethics provided the supreme expression of a morality of this sort. In coming to terms with the past, therefore, Hegel was especially concerned to show how Kantian morality was both superseded and completed in his own conception of ethics as *Sittlichkeit*. For reasons which have already emerged, the major question concerns the relationship of the individual to the community. Hegel welcomed especially the insistence on freedom, independence, and rational awareness which was associated with the Kantian moral agent (and the Rousseauian subject also). But he was critical of the idea that the

individual could construct a morality out of his own resources without
reference to the shared life of a community, a criticism which he applied
also to Utilitarianism and related theories of ethics. More generally, he saw
the isolation of the Kantian individual as symptomatic of the long historical
affliction which followed on the demise of the Greek *polis*. In the absence of
a community with a genuine common spirit, the individual is forced back
on himself:

> Isolated and on his own, it is he who is now the essence, no longer
> universal Spirit. . . . In thus establishing himself . . . the individual
> thereby placed himself in opposition to the laws and customs. These are
> regarded as mere ideas having no absolute essentiality, an abstract
> theory without any reality, while he as this particular "I" is his own
> living truth. (*PG* 355, 214)

The idea of the subject as free and independent moral agent eventually
arose out of this experience, especially in connection with the economic
achievements of modern civil society in satisfying human needs. But this
positive achievement was weighed down by negative factors. Hegel, who
was familiar with the writings of Adam Smith and other political econo-
mists, considered that the individualism of the modern market society also
posed a considerable threat to the well-being of the individuals who
composed it. In more general terms, he considered that the isolation of
individuals from an integrated community had long been manifested in
forms of alienation and fragmentation in cultural and personal experience.
What was needed was some way of harmonizing hard-won individual
independence and freedom of personality with a conscious attachment on
the part of individuals to the laws and customs of a community as the
substance of ethical life.

Hegel insisted that the great strength of Kant's philosophy in relation to
this goal was the significance it attached to the individual rational will as
the foundation of duty; its great weakness, he continued, was its empty
formalism and reduction of "the science of morals to the preaching of duty
for duty's sake" (*PR* 135, 90). It is not possible to examine Hegel's objec-
tions to Kantian formalism here in detail, but something of their character
was reflected in the critical discussion of Kant's ethics in chapter seven.[25]

Kant, as we saw, attempted to identify the moral law by the formal test
of universalizability, on the principle that what could not be universalized
without contradiction could be ruled out for consideration as a moral
maxim. Hegel objects, in brief, that contradiction arises in regard to a
universal maxim only if one assumes some content in the maxim in
question, that is, only if one treats it as realized concretely. There is
nothing contradictory as such, he observes, in the complete absence of
property or the non-existence of the human race. On the other hand, "if it
is already established on other grounds and presupposed that property

and human life are to exist and be respected, then indeed it is a contradiction to commit theft or murder" (PR 135, 90). In other words, the moral character and universal force of given maxims depend on natural and social considerations relating to human beings and presuppose the existence of social institutions. Again, the very possibility of recognizing that a universal maxim has *moral* relevance presupposes reference to its empirical content and hence its place within human relationships.

These considerations lead to the main burden of Hegel's criticism. This is the charge that Kantian formalism undermines the distinction between what is morally relevant and irrelevant and between good and evil, with the result that "any wrong or immoral line of conduct may be justified" (ibid.). In the end, the determination of morality is rendered arbitrary by being brought back to the decision of the individual will. The point of the charge, in spite of an appearance of unfairness, is that formal considerations alone cannot ground the desired distinctions. It might be said in Kant's defense that he recognizes that the moral law has content and that he invokes substantive moral considerations in the elaboration of his views. This is true (as we have already seen), but this acknowledgment concedes the substance of Hegel's objection.

The poverty of attempting to rely entirely on formal considerations becomes especially clear in relation to the problem of supplying a moral basis for social and political relations. At this point, Kant falls back on essentially Utilitarian and self-interested considerations. Society is portrayed as a collection of private wills, and morality is brought in at this level only as providing external restrictions on negative freedom to ensure some overall compatibility of wills. In the meantime, there is the fond hope on Kant's part that motivations of an unsociable sort (such as lust for power and avarice) will help to lead eventually to the establishment of a moral social order. What is missing from Kant's emphasis on the rational will and its radical freedom is any substantive moral conception of society, or recognition of the way in which social relationships provide the necessary ground of morality for the individual. It is this lacuna that Hegel seeks to overcome in his conception of ethical life.

THE STATE AS ETHICAL COMMUNITY

The insistence that morality needs to be grounded in social relationships is well taken; it is part of this idea that social milieus (family, school, and more generally, society) are themselves expressions of morality. We have seen how Hegel works out these ideas, to some extent at least, in relation to the family and the school in particular. The more problematic, and more controversial, question concerns his view of the role of the State in this domain. It is here above all that the laws and customs which constitute the character and content of ethics in the Hegelian view have their place. It is in relation to the State especially that the idea of virtue as simply carrying out the well-known and explicit rules of one's situation has its application.

In the view of many critics, Hegel completely repudiates the ideas of individual freedom and independence and critical awareness with the transition from morality to ethical life. In the words of Ernst Tugendhat, "Hegel does not allow for the possibility of a self-responsible, critical relationship to the community, to the state. Instead, we are told that the existing laws have an absolute authority, that a community determines what each individual must do, that each individual's conscience must cease to exist, and that trust must replace reflection."[26]

It is clear that there are some passages in Hegel, notably in *The Philosophy of Right*, to which these charges can be linked. It is equally clear that the task of assessing this interpretation adequately would be long and difficult, well beyond the scope of the present inquiry.[27] But I will try to say something about the topic by building on material already assembled. The focus of attention relates to aspects of Hegel's idea of the morally mature individual in the ethical community.

It is notable that Hegel supposes that, while the family has its own specific ethical character, the ethical principles which parents instill in their children are drawn from the wider community of which they are part. Children imbibe these "laws and customs" first in the form of immediate feeling and in a context of love and trust; later, and especially in the course of schooling, and then on through adult life, there is the task of appraising ethical principles rationally and acquiring ever deeper understanding of moral concepts. (For discussion of these themes see section 1 above.) In short, the whole character of Hegel's emphasis on education in the family and the school (and on self-education) is at odds with the idea that, for the adult, a critical relationship to the community is disallowed, or that individual conscience is ruled out, or that trust must take the place of reflection.

It would be completely false to Hegel's view, on the other hand, to think of the individual as standing over against the community and its ethical principles. What he stresses above all is that individuals are what they are essentially through involvement in the community, beginning with their primary relationships in the family. In the words of L. Siep, "for Hegel, the individual is never a *tabula rasa* who approaches a particular community with its customs and laws and then begins to analyse them. An individual is rather the particularization of a community being."[28] In this spirit, Hegel speaks of the relationship of the individual to the ethical order in the manner of an identity:

> [The ethical substance and its laws] are not something alien to the subject. On the contrary, his spirit bears witness to them as to its own essence, the essence in which he has a feeling of his selfhood, and in which he lives as in his own element which is not distinguished from himself. The subject is thus directly linked to the ethical order by a relation which is more like an identity than even the relation of faith or trust. (*PR* 147, 106)

There is no question, however, of the individual's being "swallowed up" or being merely passive in this relationship. Hegel goes on immediately to draw attention to the role of reflection, the acquisition of insight through reasoning and experience, and the achievement of adequate knowledge in its development.

The State as the ethical substance in which individuals inhere has to be interpreted, in important respects, as an ideal or standard. It is the State as idea, as the expression of what is universal, and especially the expression of an order of rational freedom. In this respect, the State is a community in which alienation and the fragmentation of cultural and personal life have been overcome; it is a community in which the constitution and institutions promote the self-realization of individuals and protect their rights. Actual states, it is clear, do not necessarily achieve this standard. It does not follow from this interpretation, however, that the State in the specified sense has *no* reality. Every state, understood basically as an autonomous and self-sufficient community, has a moral character which constitutes the general milieu within which its members are formed; some states may realize the ideal of the rational concept of freedom in a substantial way, even if others are highly unsatisfactory. There is obvious reason to think that the idea of the family as the basic institution in the ethical order has to be interpreted in the same manner. An approach of this sort makes sense of the many strong claims which Hegel makes on behalf of the family and the State in relation to ethical life. At the same time, it makes sense of his repudiation of an unreflective or blind trust in the ethical laws and spirit of one's State and his willingness to allow that an individual may be alienated by the laws and customs of his society. The spirit of Hegel's outlook, however, was to consider that cultured modern states realize the essential moments of the rational State.

It is true, in connection with the above interpretation of the rational State, that Hegel rejects the idea that he is concerned with teaching the State what it ought to be; similarly, he insists that the ethical order relates to what is, rather than to some unrealized standard. His concern, as he says in the preface of *The Philosophy of Right*, is with showing "how the state, the ethical universe, is to be understood," in keeping with the view that it is the task of philosophy to comprehend *what is* (PR Pref. 11). But in this same sense of "what is," he says of Plato's *Republic*, "which passes proverbially as an empty ideal," that it is "in essence nothing but an interpretation of the nature of Greek ethical life" (ibid., 10; cf. PR 185, 123). Hegel's account of the rational State, in this sense, relates to norms and practices realized (but not necessarily observed) in modern political communities. Thus the rational State, as noted above, is concerned to promote the self-realization of individuals and to uphold their rights. It is a State ruled by law, not caprice. It can have no place for slavery (PR 57, 48). So far as individuals are concerned, the State protects the right to property and, in association with this, the rights to life and liberty. In this connection,

Hegel speaks of the person as coming to "take possession of himself": "it is only through the development of his own body and mind, essentially through his self-consciousness's apprehension of itself as free, that he takes possession of himself and becomes his own property and no one else's" (PR 57, 47). This involves the constitution of one's own private personality, and related rights, as inalienable:

> Therefore those goods, or rather substantive characteristics, which constitute my own private personality and the universal essence of my self-consciousness are inalienable and my right to them is imprescriptible. Such characteristics are my personality as such, my universal freedom of will, my ethical life, my religion. (PR 66, 52).[29]

As part of "taking possession of oneself," the Hegelian conception of self-realization involves the central task of becoming a moral agent. In dealing with a range of relevant moral, legal, and psychological aspects, Hegel stresses the idea that action is central to the expression and fulfillment of the person: in addition to particular aims, activity is directed to self-realization and the expression of the person as a whole. This expression is nonetheless realized in particularity (a determinate action, a specific moment of the particularity of the agent), which constitutes subjective freedom in its more concrete sense, "the right of the subject to find his satisfaction in the action" (PR 123, 82). Hegel adds that, "it is on the strength of this particular aspect that the action has subjective worth or interest for me" (PR 122, 82). Translated into ends or goals, this interest relates to the expression of the subject in general as active being, and specifically to its status as a natural being with "needs, inclinations, passions, opinions, fancies, etc," the satisfaction of which constitutes welfare or happiness (PR 123, 83). Hegel thus supposes, contrary to Kant, that concern for one's own welfare is central to one's moral being. Reflection on welfare, so far as it concerns oneself, leads on logically to the concept of the welfare of others (and the welfare of all) and to the recognition that one's own welfare is tied in with the welfare of others (PR 125, 85). But Hegel does not allow that such reflection captures the nature of social unity or that it could provide an adequate ground of ethical relationships.

We are brought back to the idea that self-realization can be achieved only within an ethical community on the basis of its laws and customs. Hegel says in connection with the topic of good and conscience that "the right of giving recognition only to what my insight sees as rational is the highest right of the subject" (PR 132, 87). But he goes on to indicate that this right is subject to objective reason, in a system of principles and duties realized in the community. True conscience, which is "the disposition to will what is absolutely good" (PR 137, 90), is ultimately manifested in ethical life as political sentiment, patriotism properly understood in relation to the insti-

tutions existing in the state (*PR* 268, 163): in general, a trust or consciousness that "my interest, both particular or substantive" is contained and
preserved within the interests and ends of the community as a whole. The
proposal that individual insight should be referred to inter-subjective
standards is entirely reasonable. In any case, we need to remember that
Hegel is speaking of the rational State, that is, a State which is concerned
with protecting the rights of individuals and promoting the conditions in
which they are able to seek self-realization.

The ethical order is reflected in the individual character as virtue. With
regard to virtue and duty, Hegel says:

> In an *ethical* community, it is easy to say what man must do, what are the
> duties he has to fulfil in order to be virtuous: he has simply to follow the
> well-known and explicit rules of his own situation. (*PR* 150, 107)

In the major writings, however, he does not say a great deal about the
"well-known and explicit rules" of any given situation, or discuss in detail
the related laws and customs which give content to ethical life in one or
another ethical community. There is question, for example, of the extent to
which common elements might be expected across different communities.
Given that the State is the realization of the rational conception of freedom,
one would expect to find a broadly universal pattern in all such states at a
common point in history, consistent with considerable variation in history,
characteristic spirit in forms of cultural, artistic, and religious expression,
or in various modes of precedure and organization. The rational State, for
example, would everywhere uphold various individual rights and opportunities for self-development, and it would be characterized significantly
by the sorts of institutions and practices which are conditions for positive
social relationships, and by the development of a rich comprehension of
universal Spirit. In this light it is instructive to return finally to Hegel's
educational writings to consider briefly what he says about duties or
morals in "The Science of Laws, Morals and Religion" in *The Philosophical
Propaedeutic* (1–54).

What one finds in this source is the presentation of a range of familiar,
broadly universal duties (the performance of which is virtue) to oneself,
one's family, the State, and other people in general. With regard to oneself,
there is the duty to care for one's physical preservation and the development of one's universal nature as a spiritual and rational being through
theoretical and practical education. (In *The Philosophy of Right*, Hegel says
that the "growth of the universality of thought is the absolute value of
education" [*PR* 20, 29]). Practical education in particular involves the
acquisition of prudence and temperance; education more generally is the
preparation for one's choice of a calling or vocation, which "is something
universal and necessary, and constitutes a side of the social life of humanity" (*The Philosophical Propaedeutic*, 45). Duties to the family involve some

legal aspects, but they have their place in the moral feelings of love and confidence between husband and wife and parents and children, and consist fundamentally of care and obedience.

Legal relations are more significant in the State; even so, Hegel's emphasis falls on the State as a "moral commonwealth": "the union in customs, education and general form of thinking and acting, since one views and recognizes in the other his universality in a spiritual manner." The state as the embodiment of the "Spirit of a People" is the living whole which "*is* the universal spiritual nature or essence of each one as opposed to his individuality" (ibid. 47). On this basis, Hegel subscribes to the Greek view that the well-being of the community as a whole takes precedence over the well-being of the single individual. Along with the disposition to obey laws and established forms, one may be called on to sacrifice part of one's property for the preservation of others; patriotism may require the sacrifice of one's life. But these matters do not work well when they are imposed from above: the dispositions are the greater in a people, "the more the individuals can act for the whole from their *own will* and self-activity and the greater the confidence they have in the whole" (ibid. 48).

The outline of virtue and duty in *The Philosophical Propaedeutic* concludes with a section on "Duties towards Others." Hegel places the foundation of virtue in this context in *integrity*. This consists in a disposition to observe duties to others set by law, but it leads on to the "moral mode of thinking and acting" in which one regards others as possessing equal rights with oneself, and has concern for their well-being. Hegel makes particular mention of truthfulness in speech and action, the avoidance of harmful gossip and slander and hypocrisy, rendering help in appropriate circumstances, courtesy, and the universal love of humanity growing out of one's concrete relations with acquaintances and friends.

The list of duties to self, family, state, and other people, though it could hardly be taken as exhaustive, has interest in its own right. But it has significance also for the more general question of Hegel's understanding of *Sittlichkeit*. It is abundantly clear in this light that he considers that the laws and customs of the community, by which ethics is realized, need to manifest general moral principles.[30] The relevant principles, on the other hand, cannot be treated as purely formal deliverances of universal reason. Moral awareness grows out of communal experience, in family and society, and is realized in the same setting; ideally, one learns to be moral by growing up in a society which has good laws and customs (as the Pythagorean dictum supposed). This idea belongs to the substance of Hegel's particular emphasis on the State in relation to ethics. Its presentation is infused with his vision of the ethical world of the Greek *polis* and his conviction that the modern State could approach a similar (but now more fully self-conscious) ethical status. This latter conviction must appear naive and potentially dangerous in the light of twentieth-century experience, but the *idea* of family, community, society, state as the ground in which morality is realized is in no way impugned by that critical reflection.

On the evidence of *The Philosophical Propaedeutic*, Hegel's account of *Sittlichkeit* can be associated more closely with the teaching of Aristotle that there are two laws, particular and universal:

> Particular law is that which each community lays down and applies to its own members; this is partly written and partly unwritten. Universal law is the law of nature. For there really is, as everyone to some extent divines, a natural justice and injustice that is common to all, even to those who have no association or covenant with each other. (*Rhetoric*, I, 13)

In illustration of universal law, Aristotle cites Antigone's claim that the burial of Polynices was a just act in spite of Creon's prohibition; she means, he says, that it was just "by nature." He refers also to a remark of Empedocles which speaks of an eternal law of justice: "an all-embracing law, through the realms of the sky, unbroken it stretcheth, and over the earth's immensity."[31]

Hegel, as we have seen, did not advert to these considerations in his own interpretation of *Antigone*, in part because of the particular emphasis he placed on Socrates as the exemplar of the individual subject who gives expression to universal principles over against the family and the particular laws of the *polis*. An Aristotelian balance, however, pervades his conception of the possibility of *Sittlichkeit* in the modern world. The self-realization of the individual is achieved in and through the well-being of the community as a whole, and the laws and customs of the State need to reflect universal moral principles. The moral education of the individual in the family and the State opens up access to the universal sphere; the individual then acknowledges laws and customs in the light of this understanding. One could suppose that in unhappy times, in a corrupt State, particular individuals or groups become the primary bearers, in the manner of Sophocles' Antigone or Plato's Socrates, of universal values.

PART THREE
Concluding Thoughts

10. Moral and Developmental Themes in Review

The discussion of Carol Gilligan's "ethic of care" at the end of Part One led to the recovery of themes in Greek ethical thought and the idea of community. These same elements, as we have just seen, are given sustained expression in Hegel's writings. In each case, furthermore, the ideas can be linked most readily with themes in Greek tragedy and in the ethical and political thought of Aristotle.

This conjunction in the unfolding of the argument reflects the general character of my inquiry. That is, my treatment of questions regarding both morality and moral development has taken a broadly Aristotelian approach. There is much to criticize in regard to specific features of Aristotle's ethical and political thought and his general outlook, as I hope to have indicated in chapter four; furthermore, it would be necessary to re-think all of the issues in the light of the vastly changed conditions of our time. Nevertheless, I think that the Aristotelian understanding, with its emphasis on the place of the virtues and the realization of human powers and its accompanying account of moral development, offers the best approach and the most adequate sorts of answers to the two sets of questions from which we began.

I have not attempted to argue for this thesis exhaustively or even very directly; I do not propose to do so now. The historical and contextual study of a wide range of views about morality and moral development is worthwhile as a start, but such a study, as I have argued in relation to modern developmental accounts, cannot take place from a neutral standpoint or from one that is total or Olympian. My inquiry reflects an Aristotelian point of view, and in a rather indirect fashion, I have tried to indicate how this approach makes sense of the relevant issues regarding morality in human life, how it supplies grounds for criticism of some major accounts, how it has influenced or found an echo in later views, and how it is able to accommodate developments and ideas from other sources. The suggestion is that it provides substantially the right approach in regard both to morality and moral development. Its strength in both regards, furthermore, is not an accident precisely because it recognizes the necessity of approaching moral questions from within a developmental framework. My general argument for this account is very incomplete. But rather than attempting to set out the long argument which is still necessary, I will draw together some main threads of earlier discussion while taking note of some major open questions.

1. Community as the Condition of Moral Development

The idea of the Greek *polis*, as reflected in Aristotle's thought in particular, was a central influence in Hegel's conception of the rational State. The latter conception includes elements which are characteristically modern achievements, for example, the repudiation of slavery and the affirmation of the freedom of the individual, together with a range of features associated with the economic conditions of modern civil society. On the other hand, there is not the slightest advance in respect of the place of women; and Hegel came to hold that a direct democracy was unworkable because of the size and complexity of the modern State and the existence of domains of private and public life unknown in the Greek world. In its main terms, however, Hegel's rational State, and the ideal of self-realization which accompanies it, takes up the idea of its Greek counterpart and brings it into the modern world in the expression of the idea of community in the family and the State.

What Hegel shows is the need for community, and something of its significance in overcoming fragmentation and impoverishment in human life and providing the conditions for the realization of human powers. What especially strains credibility, however, is his conviction that modern states in some sense actually realize "the actuality of the ethical Idea." The difficulty is to see the modern State as an ethical community in any strong sense at all. On the contrary, there is widespread distrust of the State and an associated belief that it should not have any ethical role except in minimal and very general terms. Hegel's views about the State were very soon subjected to powerful criticism, not least by Marx; and a generation later, Nietzsche inveighed against the new German state as part of a radical critique of bourgeois-Christian society and the defense of established moral values undertaken in different ways by Kant and Hegel. Not so long after that, Freud's inquiries began to put in question the other basic ethical community, the family.

Marx's critique is not directed, however, against the idea of community. In fact, for all their considerable differences in regard to ethics and politics, Marx and Hegel shared common ground and a common Greek background in this matter. The other critics are themselves subject to criticism in this respect, as I sought to show in the discussion in chapters one and two. Nietzsche's conception of a moral ideal collapses because of his neglect of developmental and communal considerations. Freud, for all his insight into the problematic character of early development within the family, works with a questionable opposition between the individual and society which is characteristic of modern individualism. It is clear that one can recognize Hegel's claims in regard to the significance of ethical community without having to accept his general metaphysics or his particular political views. This is underlined by the prior expression of the idea in Greek life and understanding (and in numerous other societies, such as in Australian aboriginal tribal groups). Or again, one can look to its expression in the different context of John Dewey's ethical views. In words which bear comparison with F. H. Bradley's expression of Hegelian ethics (see discussion in chapter nine), Dewey observes in his own name:

> A child is born into an already existing family with habits and beliefs already formed, not indeed rigid beyond readaptation, but with their own order (arrangements). He goes to schools which have their established methods and aims; he gradually assumes membership in business, civic, and political organizations, with their own settled ways and purposes. Only in participating in already fashioned systems of conduct does he apprehend his own powers, appreciate their worth and realize their possibilities, and achieve for himself a controlled and orderly body of physical and mental habits.

More generally, Dewey shows how the inner quest suggested by the words of the Delphic oracle, "Know thyself," make sense only in a social context:

> Apart from the social medium, the individual would never "know himself"; he would never become acquainted with his own needs and capacities. He would live the life of a brute animal, satisfying as best he could his most urgent appetites of hunger, thirst, and sex, but being, as regards even that, handicapped in comparison with other animals.[1]

The mistake of modern individualism, as he suggests in a later source, is to think of the individual as something given, something already there, independent of social arrangements and relationships:

> Now it is true that social arrangements, laws, institutions are made for man, rather than that man is made for them; that they are means and agencies of human welfare and progress. But they are not means for obtaining something for individuals, not even happiness. They are the means of *creating* individuals.[2]

The distrust of government and the State, which is another side of modern individualism, is based in part on a well-founded concern about the abuse of power. But it also reflects the difficulties of achieving a reasonable form of democratic self-government and a corresponding sense of common good and common purpose and shared values across a society. There is a widespread sense that common purpose could be achieved only in response to an external threat, as can occur in time of war, or by an excessively powerful central authority abetted by a political or religious ideology. In this spirit, the Greek conception (in Plato's *Crito*, for example) that the State and its laws exercise a role of nurture and moral education can be seen only as a threat.

A characteristic response to these problems is to endorse a strong conception, in one form or another, of the detached, self-sufficient, autonomous individual. I have considered some historical versions of this ideal in connection with Rousseau, Kant, and Nietzsche, and also in the context of the development of Utilitarian theory from Hobbes to Mill. Rousseau also put particular emphasis on the general will as expressive of the community as a single unified whole, not a mere aggregate of individuals, but his conception of virtue (specifically male virtue) rests on a strong affirmation of detachment and self-sufficiency. Because social relations are seen as debilitating and corrupting (for men), he fails to consider the formative social conditions within which social passions and feelings could properly develop. An ethic of care is reserved for women, but only in conjunction with denying them full adult status and responsibility.

Each of the accounts noted above, Rousseau's included, goes wrong at an elementary level in failing to consider adequately the parent- or nurturer-child relationship. This is the basic human community in formation; furthermore its ethical status arises naturally and immediately in the conjunction of adult responsibility and the child's need in relation to their *common* good. In the accounts noted, though in different ways as we have seen, the child's original society is either ignored or misconstrued. The way is then open for the adoption of a framework in which the individual is set over against society and in which the whole basis of morality has to be conjured out of individual psychology (commonly in a conception of the passions in the Utilitarian tradition or in sovereign reason in Kantian ethics). This is accompanied by an idea of individual self-sufficiency and autonomy which, having set aside the original conditions of dependence, overlooks the continuing relations of dependence that are conditions of human existence, moral awareness, and well-being.

The setting aside of the role of nurturer involves the neglect of a task which has been exercised almost universally by women. The neglect is compounded by the view that women, who are accorded the primary responsibility for the care of children, are denied self-sufficiency. (This view does not depend on the assumption of the individualist standpoint, however, as we know from Aristotle and Hegel.) On the other hand, the idea of self-sufficiency, which is reserved for male individuals by Rousseau or Kant, for example, or for sovereign individuals and masters by Nietzsche, rests on a degree of illusion and moral distortion. What is needed is a balance in which self-sufficiency, in the sense of being responsible for one's behavior and being able to think for oneself and make decisions in the major spheres of one's life, goes along with the recognition of one's dependence on others and on the need to care about others if one is to live a human life. As with the Aristotelian virtue of practical wisdom, of which it is part, this balance cannot be set out in anything like exact rules, though laws relating to freedom and equality may be elements in its realization in a society.

The problem of morality in the individualist setting is characteristically conceived in terms of a dichotomy of egoism and altruism, or narrow self-interest and self-sacrifice. This dichotomy may well express attitudes which are widely manifested or expected, but it fails to capture the basic and normal forms of communal association which begin in the parent-child relationship, and which take on more developed character in friendships or among people who, on one basis or another, for longer or shorter periods of time, share common interests and engage in common undertakings. Communities may co-exist with considerable degrees of egoism, or may on occasions demand great sacrifice on the part of individuals; their basic character is expressed, however, by neither side of this dichotomy, but in the idea of something good or advantageous in which all concerned have a share. This goes with a conception of the individual as created, in Dewey's terms, through social practices, laws, and institutions; in other words, relationships with others and the sense of common or shared goods are properly an integral part of a person's identity. Again, community is the setting which is presupposed by the correlative legal and moral notions of rights and responsibilities.

Communities, beginning with the original society of nurturer and child, the family, may be good or bad, oppressive or liberating, more or less satisfactory, on a number of criteria which centrally include moral considerations. But the character of community, as Aristotle suggests, builds in the demand for some form of justice (as fair treatment of all) and appropriate types of friendship, and hence care and concern for others (see *NE* 8, 9). There is similarly the need for trust and truthfulness and courage, closely connected with concern for others, as basic qualities or virtues for involvement in common activities. One could suppose that just about everyone acquires a measure of these qualities in relation to their family, friends, and groups of one sort or another in which they find some fulfillment (engaged in work, cultural, or recreational activities, for example). In this light, the model of the purely self-interested individual appears to be quite rare. Thus Callicles, in Plato's *Gorgias*, who might be thought to speak for such an individual, admires the sort of "strong" person who can help himself and others about whom he cares (483C). This general consideration points to a more realistic moral problem than the one set by the dichotomy of egoism and altruism, viz., the problem of limited sympathies (exacerbated in some domains by competition for limited resources).[3]

2. The Problem of Limited Sympathies

This problem, in one of its main forms, is connected with the fact that communities frequently define themselves in opposition to outsiders. The development of the core qualities of justice and friendship, and so on, within a limited community may then go along with indifference or active hostility toward others beyond the group to which individuals maintain their primary loyalty. This consideration is linked with the difficulty of thinking of modern societies of any size as ethical communities. The problem of limited sympathy, however, is not peculiarly modern; opposition and occasional war was characteristic of the relations of the Greek city-states, for example, and there is a classical expression of the problem in relation to forming or maintaining a state at all in the views which Plato attributes to the Sophist Protagoras in his dialogue, *Protagoras*.[4]

In a discussion of this topic, J. L. Mackie assimilates Protagoras' account of the original human condition (prior to the development of social and moral virtues) to Hobbes's portrayal of the state of nature as "a war of every man, against every man." He links it also with Hume's contention that justice is an artificial virtue such that, "'tis only from the selfishness and confin'd generosity of men, along with the scanty provision nature has made for his wants, that justice derives its origin" (*Tr*. III, ii, [2], 495).[5] Perhaps all three accounts (and G. J. Warnock's treatment of the idea in *The Object of Morality*) can be treated as broadly the same for Mackie's purposes. But Hobbes's version is a radically individualist one in which the idea of limited sympathy is taken to an extreme to the exclusion of community. Sartre's account of concrete relations in Part III of *Being and Nothingness* — in which the possibility of genuine community is excluded and in which indifference, hatred, and sadism constitute a major cycle of relations — reflects a related view of human nature and a similarly extreme individualism. Again, human well-being and survival, in Hume's version, is treated as imaginable without reference to social and political virtue; justice, as an artificial virtue, is presented as merely instrumental to human ends otherwise specified.

With reference to Protagoras, however, I follow the view of those commentators who see his account as broadly Aristotelian, viz., as holding that human beings are social or political animals by nature, though moral education is necessary if their natural fitness for the requisite virtues is to be realized.[6] In referring to the idea of limited sympathy and the origin of justice, Protagoras was mainly concerned to defend his claim as a Sophist to teach political art and the qualities of good citizenship. He was also concerned to argue, as part of a defense of direct democracy, that ordinary people are able to engage intelligently in political life and government.

To this end, Protagoras presents a myth according to which human beings originally lacked political skill and wisdom. Indeed, the myth supposes that they would have lacked *all* abilities, even for basic survival, had Prometheus not stolen the capacity for crafts and the use of fire from the gods and given them to the human race. These original beings, equipped unequally with skills for survival and living in scattered groups, are imagined as developing religious practices, the use of language, and agriculture. Being unable to protect themselves against wild beasts, they were led to establish fortified cities, but then these first large communities began to tear themselves apart because their members, in their lack of political wisdom, injured one another. With the failure of the experiment and a return to scattered existence, Zeus, who feared that the race would be destroyed, then gave "conscience [*aidos*, respect for others] and justice [*dike*] to mankind, to be the principles of organization of cities and the bonds of friendship" (322C). Zeus insisted, furthermore, that these qualities, unlike practical skills, were to be distributed universally, for "cities could not come into being, if only a few shared in them as in the other crafts" (322D).

According to the myth, human beings need to live in large communities to survive and flourish, but the necessary qualities for this form of life are not natural to them in an original sense. This could be interpreted as meaning that human beings do not enter into the complex cooperative undertakings on which large communities depend in an automatic or instinctive way, in the manner of bees or ants, for example. It does not follow, however, that there is not a need set by the conditions of human existence for this sort of development (as Hobbes and Hume in different ways also allow); but nor does it exclude the further idea that human beings have the natural capacity to learn how to live in communities and that this is an essential element in *human* development, even if the learning process is slow and always a task to be achieved.

In this light, Zeus' decree, by which respect and justice are to be given to all, can be interpreted in W. K. C. Guthrie's words as standing "for what in the non-mythical anthropologies (and in Protagoras's mind) was the work of time, bitter experience, and necessity."[7] Thus the emphasis falls on moral education as the means by which human beings realize their full development. This is equally the basis of Protagoras' attempt to provide a solution to the problem of limited sympathies. His case is that human beings have a need for social and political virtues and a natural tendency toward them, but their realization depends on education. His related defense of democracy is linked especially with the idea that respect and justice are universal qualities; this is associated in turn with the view that nearly everyone acquires enough of these virtues in their moral formation from childhood to have a concern for common good and to be able to take a part in government.

Protagoras' expression of his views in the dialogue manifests a certain complacency and naive optimism. This is underlined by the Socratic challenge to his profession as a Sophist: How can he claim to be a teacher of political wisdom and good citizenship when democratic practices suppose that everyone — "be he carpenter, smith or cobbler, merchant or shipowner, rich or poor, noble or low-born" — is entitled to give advice on

these matters without benefit of instruction? (*Protagoras*, 319A–D). Socrates' challenge is given further edge by Plato's general conviction that a
democracy is a fragmented, factionalized society, without a strong common culture or a general sense of the common good.

Protagoras' reply does not need to be taken in a complacent, naive, or
particularly optimistic way. He goes on to claim that, beginning in early
childhood (and building on a natural basis), most people do get some
formation and instruction in the relevant matters through family and
public education; in this regard, he emphasizes moral formation, with
attention to music and poetry, along lines which Plato, elsewhere, and
Aristotle, in the *Politics*, developed in more detail, and with reference also
to the place of law and punishment. He holds furthermore that there are
certain values, summed up in the notions of respect and justice, which are
needed in every society. His defense of democracy in this regard could be
linked precisely with the importance he attaches to the social and political
dimension of human life and *his* conviction, as against Plato, that a
democracy develops this involvement best and allows for the emergence of
a collective wisdom.

This Protagorean-Aristotelian (and Deweyan) standpoint is compatible
with the idea that a society needs to find ways of sifting among a wide
variety of views in matters that bear on the common good. The role of the
teacher of political wisdom and moral virtue is relevant in this connection.
Protagoras compares his art to that of the teacher of the mother tongue in a
community: the suggestion is that one builds on ordinary beliefs and
practices, but seeks to provide a more reflective and more systematic grasp
of the issues and a deeper attachment to the primary values embodied in
the practices (*Protagoras*, 328A–B). This would include, one may assume, a
concern with trying to overcome harmful factionalism and the damaging
effects of fragmentation in a society. But concern with a basic sense of
common good across a society, in terms of respect and justice, does not
require anything like a totally unified community characterized by moral
unanimity. The problems of maintaining communities within the network
of associations which make up a society are considerable, and the lack of
rich community life impoverishes moral life. But the lack of a single,
centralized *moral* authority in a society as a whole is not a matter for regret.
For there are no genuine authorities of this sort, though governments,
parties, churches, particular interest groups, and sometimes an individual
may seek to occupy the role.

Protagoras, like Aristotle, does not see ethics and politics as constituting
an exact science, knowledge of which could guarantee a desired outcome.
This is connected, in Martha Nussbaum's summary of his speech, with the
attachment of value to vulnerable activities and objects such as friends,
families, and the city itself. It is connected also with the recognition of a
plurality of distinct values which are not commensurable, so that there is

the possibility of conflict and tragedy in the clash of values. It is connected finally with the recognition of the power of the passions as a source of conflict with common morality.[8] In these terms, Protagoras' views might be recommended for a modern society not with complacency, but in a spirit of sober realism in the recognition that the achievement of community, as the condition of moral life and development, is a difficult art which needs the involvement of every individual and which is subject to failure in many ways.

3. Stages of Moral Development

In a discussion of the growth of the moral sense, Richard Wollheim speaks of a fundamental intuition that he has about morality, viz., "that morality, if it is anything at all, is an achievement: it isn't something that can be learnt or inherited." Wollheim's account belongs to a mainly Freudian framework in which the evolution of morality consists in "the transition from the dominion of the superego to the cultivation of the ego ideal."[9] Whatever of that, the contrast between achievement and something learned or inherited seems forced. For the achievement is one which is possible only for beings with the capacities with which human beings are born, and in human beings, the achievement certainly involves a long and complex process of learning. What Wollheim's remark properly emphasizes is that in morality, as in many other domains, one learns by doing; furthermore, moral growth is not primarily a matter of learning a set of propositions or truths.

Is there a standard pattern of moral development? From many different accounts, a consensus emerges, with a certain air of inevitability, regarding three broad stages: a pre-moral (or perhaps proto-moral) stage; a middle stage in which one's moral beliefs and practices are based mainly on the authority of others and are not thought about in a very adequate way (heteronomous morality, to make use of Piaget's terminology); and a mature stage in which a person is able to assume responsibility for meeting certain common standards of behavior associated with virtues or rules (cooperative, autonomous morality in Piaget's terms). The Aristotelian account, to which I have given primary support, fits this pattern; so too do nearly all other accounts, allowing for rough boundaries and different emphases and sub-stages. In drawing threads together, I propose to conclude with some remarks about aspects of each of these stages, with brief reference to the main accounts of moral development, modern and ancient, discussed in Parts One and Two.

LOVE AND FEAR

Very young children are not moral agents. The first part of our life constitutes a pre-moral stage, but where this shades into a proto-moral stage is difficult to say, for community and the conditions of moral growth need to be established from the beginning. A primary focus of attention in the child's early years concerns the axis of pleasure and pain and the manifestation of passions. The appearance of the passions is distinctive at this stage, in part because of the lack of moral significance (and related features such as the absence of self-consciousness and the lack of relevant concepts, the concept of pleasure and of acting for pleasure, for example). At the same time, passions in the child are identified by reference to their later forms and cannot be properly considered in isolation from a social context; nor should they be accorded decisive significance, as if passions in the child, for example, determined what human beings are *really* like apart from a later surface phenomenon of consciousness and culture, as Nietzsche or Freud appear to suggest on occasions.

Another focus of study in this period would be those features of existence which, as Aristotle suggests, make us fit by nature to acquire the virtues. There would almost certainly be connections and overlap here with other factors such as the ability to learn to speak a language and the tendency to respond to other human beings in a distinctive way and to pick up expressions of feeling. A related major focus would concern the affective relationships in the early life of the child. There is a strong case for thinking that human learning presupposes relations with others in which feelings of affection, based on sharing a common form of life, play an essential part; that is, the emotions are closely related to cognitive development. In these terms, community is the basic condition of knowledge generally, in a conceptual as well as a causal sense. This is connected, in D. W. Hamlyn's account of early learning, with the idea that the possibility of knowledge depends on "the possibility of agreement over what is so and not so"; this "presupposes common reactions and attitudes to the world, something which . . . presupposes in turn common, though sometimes competing interests and wants." More generally, Hamlyn proposes:

> It would not be much of an exaggeration to say that one all-important factor in the development of children as persons is that they are treated as persons by persons.[10]

This approach can be found, as one would expect, in moral thinkers who emphasize the idea of community. Thus Aristotle speaks of mutual love and friendship between parents and children as the proper setting for moral formation. Hegel similarly stresses love and trust in the context of the family and the initial implanting of ethical ideas in the form of feeling. This positive emphasis relates to an ideal situation, no doubt, but one that is broadly achievable. It is in any case accompanied by a certain recognition of the presence of fear in the child's world, the fear of punishment and, perhaps most significantly, the fear of the loss of parental love.

This aspect becomes more dominant when one recognizes that an important part of the child's first grasp of morality is in the form of imperatives, especially prohibitions, which are communicated in a practical setting designed to elicit obedience. With a shift of emphasis, one may be drawn to conclude that morality, and proto-morality in particular, consists exhaustively of a set of rules which stand in opposition to the child's natural desires. Along with this, one may suppose that the dominant feeling which feeds the development of the moral sense is fear, with love occupying an essential but subordinate role. Piaget's account of heteronomous morality, with its strong emphasis on parental authority, exhibits both of these elements to an extent. But they are clearly more typical of versions of social learning theory, and are most characteristic perhaps of Freudian theory.

In Wollheim's account, for example, everything that relates to the growth of the moral sentiments, and the moral beliefs and habits of the individual, is made to turn on the establishment of the super-ego. This consists of the formation of an internal figure as an introjective response to a severe anxiety-situation posed by the menacing external figure of the parent:

> The external figure that is counterpart to the superego is a menacing rather than a menaced figure, it is a parent or someone upon whom the child feels utterly dependent, it is perceived as obstructing and threatening the child's sensual desire, in the most terrifying fashion. . . .

It is an important part of this picture that the dictates of the super-ego are originally utterly alien to the child, that the child's very desire characteristically provokes parental prohibition, and also that "the dominant response of the infant to the superego is terror: the superego controls the child by means of fear." Furthermore, the figure on whom the child projects its aggression and by whom it is terrorized is one whom it loves and on whom it depends; thus the child comes to be caught up in guilt feelings in respect of the parent, fear of the loss of love, and the urge to make reparation (emotions which are grounded in depressive anxiety).[11]

These ideas and claims are put forward in the Freudian manner in universal and necessary terms. But as we saw in chapter two, they reflect a narrow contextual picture in regard to the growth of a sense of morality in the child, together with a limited and unsatisfactory conception of morality itself, viz., as a set of rules laid down in opposition to the child's sensuous desires. It may well be that repressive elements are universal in the transmission of morality, sometimes in connection with preventing the child's harming itself or others, sometimes as the expression of a will to power or a sheer determination (in the name of "the need for discipline," for example) to oppose the child's desire. Inevitably too, the early stages of the process occur in a context of radical dependence by the child and of clouds of unknowing (on both sides) in which the child is bound to feel emotions of fear and awe. Manuals of child-rearing have not uncommonly encouraged this emphasis. Locke proposes that, "fear and Awe ought to give you the first Power over their Minds, and Love and Friendship in riper years to hold it" (*Concerning Education*, § 42).

More generally, the Western Christian tradition has been marked by a repressive regime in sexual morality, especially in the wake of Augustine's defeat of Pelagius in the fifth century.[12] It may be true then that morality is widely conceived or implemented in the way Wollheim depicts (Nietzsche, as we saw in chapter one, makes a similar claim). It is in any case almost incontestable that the growth of the moral sense is accompanied by major occasions of conflict and clash of will between parents (or whoever acts in their place) and child. (But is this true of all times and cultures?) For all that, the sort of developmental experience Wollheim portrays appears to be one in which children are likely to be emotionally disturbed or to be faced from the beginning with very severe difficulties in achieving ordinary maturity. The account is thus plausible for some cases, perhaps many, though explanation in terms other than the super-ego may be available. More generally, it is an account in which one dimension of the process is enlarged and projected on the basis of a limited and otherwise unsatisfactory conception of morality. Even if this does capture the form morality commonly takes, it is nonetheless relevant to say that moral growth does not *have* to proceed in this way and that morality so conceived or implemented is unsatisfactory. Attention to wider contexts and the nature of morality makes it at least feasible to take something like the Aristotelian conception of the early growth of morality as a realistic ideal.

To return to a matter of more universal agreement, morality in its first explicit stage is heteronomous: a morality not only derived from others, but based largely on their authority and sustained by their various educational procedures (rewards and punishments, habit formation, instruction, example). A morality of this form may remain influential or even dominant in a person's life, but it is necessarily a morality of an immature sort in cognitive and emotional and social terms. Among other things, a person at this stage lacks a well-established sense of the reasons on which moral beliefs and practices are based, if they are well-founded, and is unable to appreciate the point of morality in human life, engage in the practical reasoning which moral judgment requires, or assume adult responsibility for behavior, and is emotionally dependent on authority in a dominant pattern of conformity or rebellion.

SHAME

In the transition to a more mature morality, the acquisition of a sense of shame occupies a central place. There is witness to this in Aristotle's writings, as we saw in chapter four. Habit-formation, the major vehicle of change, could result in mere conformism in itself; hence the increasing importance of instruction and practical understanding. In this context, shame is associated with a way of thinking about one's behavior and assuming responsibility for it: it marks a primary contrast with commitment to shared values which is based primarily on the fear of punishment, and a further contrast with attitudes of indifference or contempt for shared values (shamelessness). On the other side, it points to a striving toward "fine things," the noble and the excellent in human life. Shame is similarly a basic element in what Plato says of Protagoras' idea of the bond of social and political life: *aidos*, respect for others, has connotations of self-respect, shame, modesty, and (social) conscience; it is a quality which everyone is thought to need. More generally, the notion of shame occupies a central place in Plato's ethical and political thought and in Greek culture.

There is a comparable emphasis on shame in the writings of some contemporary social learning theorists. Thus Aronfreed presents it as part of a motivational basis which is more developmentally advanced than the fear of punishment, but this recognition, as I argued in chapter two, is not integrated into a satisfactory account of moral agency. Shame also figures in Freudian accounts of moral development.

Maturity in the Freudian framework is linked importantly, as we saw, with the weakening of the power of the super-ego in relation to considerations of reason. Wollheim suggests that this growth could be interpreted as a transition in which the sentiment of shame modifies the feelings of guilt generated by the super-ego so as to give rise to the formation of the ego-ideal. (Freud tended to use the term "ego-ideal" as an alternative for the super-ego; Wollheim adapts it here to refer to its later, modified form.) The child who is under the primary influence of guilt, in the Freudian sense, is led to control its aggression by fear of retaliation. The development in which shame emerges as a distinctive motive rests on cognitive achievements (including the sense of the other and of oneself as complex wholes), increasing identification with external authority figures, and increasing familiarity and ease with the internal figure.

As with the other accounts we have considered, shame is reasonably treated here as an interiorized sentiment no less than guilt. It involves in particular the imagining of a figure with whom one identifies, together with the representation of oneself as falling under the gaze of the figure. The sentiment specifically relates, in Wollheim's words, "not to actions and how far they fall short of the person's internal prescriptions, but to the condition of the person himself and how far it meets or disappoints the ego-ideal." The general structure of this account of the place of shame reflects an interesting convergence with a range of different developmental views. But it suffers in general from the problems of narrow contextual focus in regard to moral experience which I considered in connection with Freudian theory in chapter two. In addition, the contrast which is built into the primary account of shame appears artificial. For the idea of the condition of the person as meeting or disappointing an ego-ideal can hardly be separated from the consideration of their actions in relation to standards. A further consideration is that the appropriateness of a person's satisfaction or disappointment is not a purely internal matter: the notion of shame needs to be referred to standards of behavior recognized and expected within a community.

While Wollheim treats shame fundamentally as an internal sentiment, his account draws attention to the public dimension of the notion in an indirect but interesting way. He suggests that the morality of the ego-ideal is permanently threatened by narcissism. This comes about in connection with envy as resentment of one's dependence on goodness in the world and the subsequent wish to destroy this goodness. "Envy," Wollheim says, "is largely prompted by the fear of loss, the fear of disappointment. But envy brings in train the fear of retaliation, and one reaction that a person may make to envy is to deny that there is anything good in the external world or to assert his own complete independence of anything outside himself." Narcissism in this case is manifested in the belief that one is completely independent of the external world, that one is the source of all the values one needs, that one is invulnerable.[13] One could say, however, that a conception of this sort, which, no doubt, admits of degrees, arises only when shame and morality are treated as psychological phenomena divorced from the social context in which they develop. But shame always has a social history in a culture; it is connected with the existence of communal standards according to which certain types of behavior are shameful and certain ways of acting exhibit shamelessness quite apart from how individuals might feel. In this way, the *sentiment* of shame needs to be referred to public criteria to provide the ground of its appropriateness.

Reference to communal standards is insufficient in itself, however, as I argued in connection with Aristotle's views in chapter four. The acquisition of a sense of shame is linked originally with the desire to win approval and avoid disgrace within a group. It may be related to a code of honor and practices which are far removed from virtue, as among a band of thieves. Aristotle's account thus presses on to the task of marking out a range of qualities which, while they can be realized only in community, have general validity in relation to human well-being (together with a notion of natural or universal justice across societies). This is connected with the idea that the individual needs to develop a love of these virtues, in part through the experience of shame and the realization, in association with others, that certain types of behavior are shameful and incompatible with the achievement of human good.

BETWEEN NARCISSISM AND SUBSERVIENCE

It is an important part of this conception of moral growth that individuals have to assume responsibility for their behavior within a communal setting; not to do so would itself be shameful. What is offered is perhaps a middle way between extremes: a narcissistic morality (as Wollheim describes it) which involves the illusion of complete individual self-sufficiency, on the one hand; and an unthinking or servile commitment to laws and moral practices of a community, with no place for critical appropriation, individual freedom, or autonomy, on the other. The Aristotelian conception of self-sufficiency is connected mainly with the idea of a life characterized by worthwhile activities. Such a life, it is clear, is fully compatible with the recognition of dependence on others, the need for friends, and so on. Its standpoint in regard to individual freedom and the community can be illustrated, as Martha Nussbaum suggests, by the contrast which Thucydides makes between Sparta and Athens. Nussbaum's summary of the contrast is as follows:

> Both cities [Sparta and Athens] agree that self-respect and the sense of shame are essential ingredients of human good living; but while one tries to secure it to citizens by teaching them to regard themselves as totally subservient to law, their minds as "not their own," the other insists on the importance of autonomous judgment, freedom from constraint.[14]

The contrast set out here is clear in itself, but if one allows that it captures the spirit of Sparta and Athens respectively, it would still be a mistake to interpret the Athenian point of view as the expression of an individualist conception of freedom.[15] In Aristotle's thought, for example, freedom is placed firmly within the context of the community and its laws. But, in taking a stand against too much unity and concentration of power in the State, he insisted that the *polis* consists of a plurality of communities, a network of kinship and local associations, religious, social, educational, recreational bodies, and so on, an arrangement which allows for a choice of different patterns of social existence. He also took the view that political association is properly an association of equals, a community of freemen, who take turns in ruling and being ruled. Finally, his conception of moral maturity holds that the choice of a good life needs to be made by the person concerned as part of assuming control of one's life.

These considerations are restricted for the most part in Aristotle's account to adult male citizens of the more leisured class; they alone are accorded "minds of their own" in the full sense, in keeping with "the natural order of things." His arguments in this connection in support of the institution of slavery are a threadbare piece of theory in the face of the evidence and the force of other elements in his moral theory. His arguments, and the arguments of the philosophers generally, for the subservient status of women are hardly less bereft of theoretical force. The task of turning around the beliefs and practices of ages in these concerns is not simply a matter of argument, of course, but so far as argument matters, there seems to be no reason why the middle path between narcissism and subservience should not be an entirely general possibility for adult morality. The conjunction of acknowledged dependence on others and the need to care about others, on the one hand, with freedom to engage in deliberative choice in regard to worthwhile activities, on the other, marks out a possible and desirable sense of individual self-sufficiency.

Where philosophical accounts of moral growth put the major emphasis on adult morality, the focus of attention in both social learning theory and psychoanalytic theory is fixed explicitly on the early stages of development. The study of the child is guided, nonetheless, by a conception of adult morality which is largely unstated. It consists, narrowly, of the acceptance of a truce, perhaps zealously pursued, perhaps unhappily borne, in which original desire is subordinated to the demands of the other by a set of restrictive rules. Early childhood in this setting constitutes the site of conflict until the child becomes a party to the truce. It is in fact possible to find in Freud's writings, and in the work of many social learning theorists, ideas toward a richer conception of moral agency and maturity. Freudian analysis points, in Nietzschean fashion, to the considerable scope for repression and other ill-effects, in traditional moral outlooks (an analysis which might lead to the search for a healthier moral basis). But these considerations are not brought into the formal accounts of development to any extent: the story is told within a narrow framework and a limited conception of morality in which large areas of moral experience and moral possibility are filtered out of consideration.

Piaget's study of moral judgment, which is also focused primarily on childhood, draws on a more explicit conception of morality in an ideal and desirable form. Morality, as Piaget presents it, consists of a system of rules; its character is then fixed by the way in which respect for these rules is established. The features which Piaget stresses as desirable in this context are democratic cooperativeness and individual autonomy. One could say that these are precisely the considerations which emerged in reflection on the Aristotelian conception of adult morality. In a broad sense this is true. In Piaget's case, however, morality is introduced as a set of rules without much attention to the demands set by association, and without consideration of the conditions of well-being for individual and community (which is the substance of the Aristotelian account of morality). In this sense, the vortex from which his account of the child's moral judgment hangs is almost empty. The account is then controlled by the need to respond to Durkheim's excessive emphasis on the centralized moral authority of society. In this context, Piaget turned to a conception of mature morality as the product of participatory democracy, in which set conditions and forms of authority are ignored or wished away.

Kohlberg's account of moral development is avowedly complete, as we have seen, from early childhood to maturity. Furthermore, the mature moral stages in the system are given full characterization as formal principles of justice and are accorded the determinative role as standards of moral progress. It is at this level, however, as I argued in chapter three, that the account collapses. The historical studies of Utilitarian theory and Kantian ethics in Part Two bring out the problems of Kohlberg's higher stages in further ways. One of the most pertinent and ironical considerations is that neither theory can allow for a satisfactory account of moral development in the first place.

Kohlberg turned to Stages 5 and 6 because of the inherent limitations, as he saw it, in thinking of morality within the context of a community. He thus sought a standpoint for the rational creation of moral laws *ex nihilo*.[16] This standpoint is illusory, and the mistake lies precisely in the attempt to escape from the conditions in which moral considerations make sense. Carol Gilligan brings out this criticism clearly in her focus on adult morality in the form of an ethic of care. But her views need to be modified and filled out, as I have argued, along lines drawn from an Aristotelian and Hegelian understanding of morality and its growth. In this way, there is the basis for a realistic ideal of adult morality as part of an equally illuminating treatment of moral development. But the achievement of the conditions of moral life and development is never complete and is always precarious and vulnerable, subject to failure in many ways.

Notes

Chapter 1. Morality in Question

1. There is a good philosophical discussion of the topic in D. W. Hamlyn, "The Concept of Development," *Proceedings of the Philosophy of Education Society of Great Britain*, IX (1975), 26–39; see also D. W. Hamlyn, *Experience and the Growth of Understanding* (London: Routledge & Kegan Paul, 1978), and I. Dilman, *Freud and Human Nature* (Oxford: Blackwell, 1983), Chaps. 7 and 8.
2. *The Dialogues of Plato*, trans. B. Jowett (London: Oxford University Press, 3rd. ed. 1892), 5 vols., vol. 2. The *Euthyphro* is available in numerous translations and editions.
3. See Anthony Skillen, *Ruling Illusions* (Hassocks, U.K.: Harvester Press, 1977), 129–30; also Richard Norman, *The Moral Philosophers* (Oxford: Clarendon Press, 1983), Chap. 9, 187ff. On Marx's account of ideology in general see J. Larrain, *The Concept of Ideology* (London: Hutchinson, 1979), Chap. 2; and W. A. Suchting, *Marx, An Introduction* (Brighton: Harvester Press, 1983), 136ff.
4. With reference to Marx's general moral orientation, see J. Elster, *Making Sense of Marx* (Cambridge: Cambridge University Press, 1985), 61ff and 82ff; S. Lukes, *Marxism and Morality* (Oxford: Oxford University Press, 1984); R. Norman, *The Moral Philosophers*.
5. Jean-Paul Sartre argued in the late 1950s that a neglect of this sort had become characteristic of Marxist thought in relation to the social sciences generally; see *Search for a Method*, trans. Hazel E. Barnes (New York: Vintage Books, 1968), Chap. 2.
6. Ronald de Sousa, "Norms and the Normal," in Richard Wollheim, ed., *Freud, A Collection of Critical Essays* (New York: Anchor Press, 1974), 196–221.
7. Sigmund Freud, *New Introductory Lectures in Psychoanalysis* (1933), Lecture 35, "The Question of a *Weltanschauung*," *The Standard Edition of the Complete Works of Sigmund Freud*, trans. and ed. James Strachey (London: Hogarth Press, 1964), vol. XXII, 158–82; 168, 164. All references to Freud are to this edition.
8. Sigmund Freud, *The Future of an Illusion* (1927), *Complete Works*, vol. XXI (1961), 34.
9. Freud, "The Question of a *Weltanschauung*," 160.
10. Freud, *The Future of an Illusion*, 41.
11. Sigmund Freud, "The Disillusionment of the War" (1915), *Thoughts for the Times on War and Death, Complete Works*, vol. XIV (1957), 281.
12. Sigmund Freud, *Civilization and Its Discontents, Complete Works*, vol. XXI (1930), 112.
13. Sigmund Freud, "Why War?", letter to Albert Einstein, *Complete Works*, vol. XXII, (1932), 205.
14. See *Civilization and Its Discontents*, 112ff. The topic has been discussed extensively in recent literature in anthropology, sociology, psychology, and philosophy, notably in connection with Karl Lorenz, *On Aggression*, trans. M. K. Wilson (London: Methuen, 1963); for a recent philosophical discussion, see Mary Midgley, *Beast and Man* (London: Methuen, 1979). The view that war and aggression are part of human nature is criticized in T. Trainer and H. Waite,

274

"Culture and the Production of Aggression," in Rachel Sharp (ed.), *Apocalypse No* (Sydney: Pluto Press, 1984), 205–26.

15. Friedrich Nietzsche, *Beyond Good and Evil* (1886), trans. R. J. Hollingdale (Harmondsworth: Penguin Press, 1973); cited here as *BGE* with section number.
16. On Nietzsche's use of the rhetorical trope of hyperbole, see Alexander Nehamas, *Nietzsche, Life as Literature*, (Cambridge, Mass.: Harvard University Press, 1985), Chap. 1.
17. Friedrich Nietzsche, *Thus Spoke Zarathustra* (1885), trans. R. J. Hollingdale (Harmondsworth: Penguin Books, 1961), 84–86.
18. Friedrich Nietzsche, *On the Genealogy of Morals* (1887) (with *Ecce Homo*), trans. W. Kaufmann and R. J. Hollingdale (New York: Random House, 1969); cited here as *GM* with essay and section number.
19. Ibid. I, 10ff. Nietzsche always used the French word *ressentiment* rather than a German equivalent; the Kaufmann-Hollingdale translation follows this practice. The significance of Nietzsche's treatment of the notion is discussed in Max Scheler, *Ressentiment*, trans. W. Holdheim and L. A. Coser (New York: Free Press, 1961).
20. Nietzsche marks the distinction by using different words: *Böse* (usually translated as "evil"), *Schlecht* ("bad").
21. Friedrich Nietzsche, *The Will to Power*, trans. W. Kaufmann and R. J. Hollingdale (New York: Vintage Books, 1968), § 765. This work, drawn from Nietzsche's notebooks, was published posthumously in 1901.
22. Seneca, the first century Roman Stoic, observes in this regard:

    At this point it is pertinent to ask what pity is. For many commend it as a virtue, and call a pitiful man good. But this too is a mental defect . . . Pity is the sorrow of the mind brought about by the sight of the distress or sadness caused by the ills of others which it believes come undeservedly. But no sorrow befalls the wise man.

    See J. L. Saunders (ed.), *Greek and Roman Philosophy after Aristotle* (New York: Free Press, 1966), 128.
23. Friedrich Nietzsche, *The Anti-Christ* (1889) (with *Twilight of the Idols*), trans. R. J. Hollingdale (Harmondsworth: Penguin Books, 1968), 118. Among other passages in which Nietzsche discusses pity, see *Daybreak*, section 134; *Thus Spoke Zarathustra*, 112ff; *BGE*, 222, 259, 260, 293; *GM*, Preface and III, 14 and 25; *The Will to Power*, 333.
24. Gilles Deleuze, *Nietzsche and Philosophy*, trans. H. Tomlinson (New York: Columbia University Press, 1983), 147ff.
25. Nietzsche's idea of the *Übermensch* — "superman," "overman," "beyond-man" — is a subject of considerable dispute. Alasdair MacIntyre says that it belongs "in the pages of a philosophical bestiary rather than in serious discussion" in *After Virtue* (Notre Dame: University of Notre Dame Press, 1981), 21; but MacIntyre does not appear to have given *Nietzsche's* use of the term the attention it deserves. I interpret it (but without argument here) as the embodiment of a human ideal, and hence as "beyond the human." The notion picks up some elements from Nietzsche's account of master morality, but it relates more strictly to the future as the idea of one who *goes beyond* nihilism and creates new meaning and values.
26. Alasdair MacIntyre, *After Virtue*, 107–08.
27. Ibid., 24–25; MacIntyre refers in this connection to Raymond Aron, *Main Currents in Sociological Thought: Durkheim, Pareto, Weber*, trans. R. Howard and H. Weaver (Harmondsworth: Penguin Books, 1967), 192, 206–10.

28. Friedrich Nietzsche, *Twilight of the Idols*, "Morality as Anti-Nature," 42, 45.
29. Ibid. 101.
30. Friedrich Nietzsche, *Ecce Homo* (with *On the Genealogy of Morals*), trans. W. Kaufmann (New York: Random House, 1969); see *The Gay Science*, sections 270, 335.
31. Alexander Nehamas, *Nietzsche*, 1.

Chapter 2. Moral Development: Social Learning and Psychoanalytic Theories

1. John Rawls, *A Theory of Justice* (London: Oxford University Press, 1972), 458–60.
2. For accounts of social learning theory in this context, see J. Aronfreed, *Conduct and Conscience* (New York and London: Academic Press, 1968); "Moral Development from the Standpoint of a General Psychological Theory," in Thomas Lickona (ed.), *Moral Development and Behavior* (New York: Holt, Rinehart and Winston, 1976), 54–69, and "Some Problems for a Theory of the Acquisition of Conscience," in C. M. Beck, B. Crittenden, E. V. Sullivan (eds.), *Moral Education: Interdisciplinary Approaches* (Toronto: University of Toronto Press, 1971), 183–99; R. Brown, *Social Psychology* (New York: Free Press, 1965); H. J. Eysenck, "The Biology of Morality," in Thomas Lickona, *Moral Development*, 108–23; and *Crime and Personality* (London: Routledge and Kegan Paul, 1964); D. Graham, *Moral Learning and Development* (Sydney: Angus and Robertson, 1972); M. L. Hoffman, "Moral Development," in P. H. Mussen (ed.) *Carmichael's Manual of Psychology*, 3rd. ed., vol. II (New York: Wiley, 1970), 261–359; Dennis Krebs, "Psychological Approaches to Altruism; An Evaluation," *Ethics* 92 (1982), 447–58; Walter Mischel and Harriet N. Mischel, "A Cognitive Social-Learning Approach to Morality and Self-Regulation," in Thomas Lickona, *Moral Development*, 84–107; J. Philippe Rushton, "Altruism and Society: A Social Learning Perspective," *Ethics*, 92 (1982), 425–46; Thomas E. Wren, "Social Learning Theory, Self-Regulation, and Morality," *Ethics*, 92, (1982), 409–24. From among many general sources, see Albert Bandura, *Social Learning Theory* (Englewood Cliffs: Prentice Hall, 1977).
3. See J. Aronfreed, "The Concept of Internalization," in D. Goslin (ed.), *Handbook of Socialization Theory and Research* (Chicago: Rand-McNally, 1969); J. Aronfreed, *Conduct and Conscience*. Two very different versions of the concept will be considered in this chapter.
4. H. J. Eysenck provides an example of this when he says: "It is pointless to ask why people behave in a selfish, aggressive, immoral manner; such behavior is clearly reinforcing in that it gives the person or organism acting in such a fashion immediate satisfaction. Furthermore such behavior is demonstrated by animals and young children without any need of teaching; it is 'natural' in a real and obvious sense" ("The Biology of Morality," 108).
5. Thomas E. Wren, "Social Learning Theory," 411.
6. H. J. Eysenck, *Fact and Fiction in Psychology* (Harmondsworth: Penguin Books, 1965), 260; see also "The Morality of Biology" and *Crime and Personality*.
7. H. J. Eysenck, "The Morality of Biology," 109, 127. Eysenck argues further that conditioning is dependent on cortical arousal: antisocial conduct results from a failure to form conditioned responses which is attributed in turn "to a genetically low level of cortical arousal" (117).
8. B. F. Skinner, *About Behaviorism* (New York: Knopf, 1974), 168.
9. B. F. Skinner, *Beyond Freedom and Dignity* (New York: Knopf, 1971), 188.
10. Walter Mischel and Harriet N. Mischel, "A Cognitive Social Learning Approach," in Thomas Lickona, *Moral Development*; also "Self-Control and the

Self," in T. Mischel (ed.), *The Self, Psychological and Philosophical Issues* (Oxford: Blackwell, 1977), 31–64.
11. J. Aronfreed, "Moral Development," in Thomas Lickona, *Moral Development*, 55.
12. The main references are cited in note 2 above; I will be particularly concerned with Aronfreed's book, *Conduct and Conscience*, cited here as *CC*.
13. Aronfreed remarks that, "in the classical Greek conceptions of morality (Plato, *The Republic*; Aristotle, *Nicomachean Ethics*), there was nothing that would really correspond to what we today might call conscience" (*CC* 2). This is arguably correct: the notion of conscience did not develop in a precise sense until the Stoics and the Christian era; but the absence is totally unrelated to any putative exclusion of affective elements from moral experience in Plato's and Aristotle's thought.
14. Thomas E. Wren, "Social Learning Theory," 411.
15. William P. Alston, "Self-Intervention and the Structure of Motivation," in T. Mischel, *The Self*, 65–102; 76, 96.
16. Thomas E. Wren, "Social Learning Theory," 422. Aronfreed discusses the criteria of moral cognition (and hence the scope and character of morality) only very briefly in *CC* 245–57; see also *CC* 25.
17. Thomas E. Wren, "Social Learning Theory," 422.
18. Thomas E. Wren says that the two action-guiding principles linked with Aronfreed's account of guilt and shame are "formal in that they are cherished by the agent prior to any specification of their contents" ("Social Learning Theory," 422); this claim reflects a Kantian orientation in ethics which will be discussed more fully in chapter seven. By way of an anticipatory criticism, it is difficult to see how the ideas could get established (or defended) except on the basis of experience (hence with reference to content and context).
19. Charles Taylor, "What Is Human Agency?," in T. Mischel *The Self*, 103–35, 104; see H. Frankfurt, "Freedom of the Will and the Concept of a Person," *Journal of Philosophy*, LXVII (1971), 5–20.
20. Augusto Blasi, "Bridging Moral Cognition and Moral Action: A Critical Review of the Literature," *Psychological Bulletin*, 88 (1980), 1–45, 37.
21. J. Aronfreed, "Moral Development," in Thomas Lickona, *Moral Development*, 64.
22. D. Graham, *Moral Learning and Development*, 158; see M. L. Hoffman, "Child-rearing Practices and Moral Development: Generalizations from Empirical Research," *Child Development*, 34 (1963), 295–318; and M. L. Hoffman and H. D. Salzstein, "Parent Discipline and the Child's Moral Development," *Journal of Personal and Social Psychology*, 5 (1967), 45–57.
23. No doubt everyone would agree with this very general claim; but it is forgotten in the many philosophical and psychological theories which treat the human individual in abstraction from social relationships.
24. Sigmund Freud, *Civilization and Its Discontents*, 124.
25. Sigmund Freud, *Three Essays on Sexuality* (1905/1920), *Complete Works* (1953), vol. VII, 226, note.
26. Sigmund Freud, *New Introductory Lectures on Psychoanalysis* (1933), *Complete Works*, vol. XXII, Lecture XXXI, "The Dissection of the Psychical Personality," 57–80; 64, 67. This lecture is particularly relevant to Freud's conception of the super-ego as heir to the Oedipus complex and to parental authority, on the one hand, and to his view of the preferred path of later development, on the other. One of Freud's general observations concerning education is that, "as a rule parents and authorities analogous to them follow the precepts of their own

super-egos in educating children. Whatever understanding their ego may have come to with their super-ego, they are severe and exacting in educating children"; in this way, "the past, the traditions of the race and of the people, lives on in the ideologies of the super-ego, and yields only slowly to the influences of the present and to new changes" (67). The preferred path of later development is for the ego to become more independent of the super-ego and "to appropriate fresh portions of the id. Where id was, there ego shall be. It is a work of culture — not unlike the draining of the Zuider Zee" (80).

27. The following essays in Freud's writings are particularly relevant: "The Dissolution of the Oedipus Complex" (1924), *Complete Works*, vol. XIX, 173–82; "Some Psychical Consequences of the Anatomical Distinction between the Sexes" (1925), ibid., vol. XIX, 241–60; "Female Sexuality" (1931), ibid., vol. XXI, 225–43; *New Introductory Lectures on Psychoanalysis*, Lecture XXXIII, "Femininity," 112–35.
28. "Femininity," 134.
29. "Some Psychical Consequences of the Anatomical Distinction between the Sexes," 257–58.
30. *Civilization and Its Discontents*, 125, 123.
31. Sigmund Freud, "The Disillusionment of the War," *Complete Works*, vol. XIV, 281.
32. J. R. Maze, *The Meaning of Behaviour* (London: Allen and Unwin), 1982.
33. I. Dilman, *Freud and Human Nature*, 187; also Chap. 8; Ronald de Sousa, "Norms and the Normal."
34. For Freud's treatment of character and its formation, see the following essays in *Complete Works*: vol. IX, 1959: "Character and Anal Erotism" (1908), 169–75; "On Transformations of Instinct as Exemplified in Anal Erotism" (1917), vol. XVII, 125–34; "Libidinal Types" (1931), vol. XXI, 217–20; "Anxiety and Instinctual Life" (1933), vol. XXII, 81–111.
35. "Libidinal Types," 219.
36. Sigmund Freud, "Analysis of a Phobia in a Five-Year-Old Boy ('Little Hans')" (1909), *Complete Works*, vol. X, 1955, *Two Case Histories I*, 5ff.
37. I. Dilman, *Freud and Human Nature*, 61; see B. Malinowski, *Sex and Repression in Savage Society* (New York: Meridian Books, 1955), Part Three.
38. I. Dilman, *Freud and Human Nature*, 63–64.
39. M. L. Hoffman, "Moral Development," in P. H. Mussen (ed.), *Carmichael's Manual of Psychology*, 317.

Chapter 3. Moral Development: Cognitive Developmental Theories

1. One well-known account is R. H. Peck and R. J. Havinghurst, *The Psychology of Character Development* (New York: Wiley, 1960). Peck and Havinghurst distinguish five ideal types: amoral; expedient (self-considering); irrational-conscientious (self-obeying); conforming (other-obeying); rational-altruistic (other-considering). These types are linked with developmental stages, in a broad sense, from infancy to maturity, but since the irrational-conscientious and conforming types are taken to be alternatives which are characteristic of middle and late adolescence, the developmental schema is non-linear. On the basis of research, Peck and Havinghurst added three mixed groups to yield an eight-point scale of maturity and character.
2. H. Hartshorne and M. A. May, *Studies in the Nature of Character* (New York: Macmillan, 1928–30).
3. Among relevant studies, see R. J. Havinghurst and H. Taba, *Adolescent Charac-*

ter and Personality (New York: Wiley, 1949); N. Emler, "Moral Character," in H. Weinreich-Haste and D. Locke (eds.), *Morality in the Making* (Chichester: John Wiley & Sons, 1983), 187–211.

4. L. Kohlberg, *Essays on Moral Development* (San Francisco: Harper and Row), vol. I, "Education for Justice: A Modern Statement of the Socratic View," 29–48; 39. Kohlberg portrays his account as Socratic, based on Plato's earlier dialogues; it is contrasted with what he calls Aristotle's "bag of virtues" account; see ibid. 9, 31, 184; I will discuss these ancestral claims later in the chapter.

5. C. Gilligan, *In a Different Voice* (Cambridge, Mass.: Harvard University Press, 1982).

6. See, for example, Jean Piaget, "The Mental Development of the Child," in *Six Psychological Studies* (Brighton: Harvester Press, 1968); "Piaget's Theory," in P. H. Mussen (ed.), *Carmichael's Manual of Child Psychology*, vol. I (New York: Wiley, 1970), 703–32; *Structuralism* (London: Routledge & Kegan Paul, 1971). Among secondary sources, see Margaret A. Boden, *Piaget* (Brighton, U.K.: Harvester Press, 1979); J. H. Flavell, *The Developmental Psychology of Jean Piaget* (Princeton, N.J.: Van Nostrand, 1963); L. S. Siegel and C. J. Brainerd, *Alternatives to Piaget: Critical Essays on the Theory* (New York: Academic Press, 1978); S. Modgil and C. Modgil (eds.), *Towards a Theory of Psychological Development* (Windsor: NFER, 1980); S. Modgil and C. Modgil (eds.), *Jean Piaget, Consensus and Controversy* (New York: Praeger, 1982).

7. Jean Piaget, *The Moral Judgment of the Child*, trans. M. Gabain (New York: Free Press, 1965), first published in 1932; to be cited as *MJC* with page number. Other writings of Piaget relevant to moral and social topics include *Etudes Sociologiques* (Geneva: Droz, 2nd. ed.), 1967.

8. See Jean Piaget, *Structuralism*, 34. For discussion of Piaget's views on morality, see Helen Weinreich-Haste, "Piaget on Morality: A Critical Perspective," in S. Modgil and C. Modgil, *Jean Piaget*, 1982, 181–206; Derek Wright, "Piaget's Theory of Moral Development," ibid. 207–17; and Wolfe Mays, "Piaget's Sociological Theory," ibid. 31–50.

9. *MJC* 13–76; for the report of the girl's game, see 76–84. Piaget's conclusion regarding substantial similarity between boys and girls in these matters is accompanied by the claim that, "the most superficial observation is sufficient to show that in the main the legal sense is far less developed in little girls than in boys" (*MJC* 77); he connects the loosely knit character of the girls' game with evidence that girls are more tolerant from an early age (*MJC* 80). Gilligan, *In a Different Voice* (10), interprets this as an element of male bias in Piaget's account of moral development since the development of a legal sense is treated as essential to the process; but this particular claim could be balanced by the fact that Piaget treats tolerance in regard to rules as an element of the more mature morality of cooperation.

10. Piaget puts particular stress on the idea of a time-lag between acting in keeping with rules and the conscious realization of them at each level, an idea which he explored in a number of writings both early and late.

11. For more detail regarding the respective features of moral realism and the morality of cooperation, see Thomas Lickona, "Research on Piaget's Theory of Moral Development," in Thomas Lickona, *Moral Development*, 219–40.

12. Surveys of research on Piaget's account of moral development include Thomas Lickona, "Research on Piaget's Theory"; M. L. Hoffman, "Moral Development"; S. Modgil and C. Modgil, *Piagetian Research*, vol. 6 (Windsor: NFER, 1976).

13. Margaret A. Boden, *Piaget*, 61; see Thomas Lickona, "Research on Piaget's Theory," 222–23.

14. Thomas Lickona notes that "a Piagetian dimension such as intentionality shows regular quantitative increases beginning at 5 to 6 years of age . . . and extending at least as late as 17 years" ("Research on Piaget's Theory", 229).
15. Ibid. 231–35.
16. *MJC* 396; Piaget's primary reference is to Léon Brunschvicg, *Le Progrès de la conscience dans la philosophie occidentale* (Paris: Presses Universitaires de France, 1927).
17. Piaget discusses Durkheim's views in *MJC* 327–71; his aim is to defend his stage-related account of morality through a critique of Durkheim's theory of responsibility and his views on moral authority and moral education. The primary reference is to Emile Durkheim, *Moral Education* (1925), trans. E. K. Wilson and H. Schnurer (Glencoe, Ill.: Free Press, 1961); and *Sociology and Philosophy* (1924), trans. D. F. Pocock (Glencoe, Ill.: Free Press, 1953). In discussing Durkheim's views, Piaget also refers extensively to P. Fauconnet, *La Responsabilité, étude de sociologie* (Paris: Alcan, 1920).
18. E. Durkheim, *Moral Education*, 96, 116; more generally, see Part I above, "The Elements of Morality," especially chaps. 7 and 8.
19. *MJC* 351. Piaget agrees with Durkheim to the effect that "the spirit of discipline . . . constitutes the starting-point of all moral life. There must be rules and rules clothed with sufficient authority. No one will seriously deny that this is the price to be paid for the development of the personality" (*MJC* 361). Durkheim, it could be said, does not advance beyond this starting point in his account of authority; Piaget, on the other hand, does not consider its relevance beyond the stage of heteronomous morality.
20. A table setting out relations between Piaget's cognitive-logical stages and Kohlberg's moral stages is given in L. Kohlberg and C. Gilligan, "The Adolescent as a Philosopher: The Discovery of the Self in a Postconventional World," in P. H. Mussen, J. J. Conger, and J. Kagan (eds.) *Basic and Contemporary Issues in Developmental Psychology* (New York: Harper and Row, 1974), 18–33; 28. The correlations allow for slippage: attainment of the logical stage is necessary but not sufficient for attainment of the related moral stage.
21. See C. Levine, L. Kohlberg, and A. Hewer, "The Current Formulation of Kohlberg's Theory and a Response to Critics," *Human Development*, 28 (1985), 94–100; 95; to be cited as *CFK*.
22. The specification of levels and stages here is taken from L. Kohlberg, "Moral Stages and Moralization," in Thomas Lickona, *Moral Development and Behavior*, 31–53, "The Six Moral Stages," Table 2.1, 34–35; also "The Six Moral Stages," Table 2 in L. Kohlberg, "A Current Statement on Some Theoretical Issues," in S. Modgil and C. Modgil (eds.), *Lawrence Kohlberg, Consensus and Controversy* (Lewes, U.K.: Falmer Press, 1985), 485–546; 488–9; with reference to L. Kohlberg, *Essays on Moral Development*, vol. I, *The Philosophy of Moral Development* (New York: Harper and Row, 1981), Appendix: "The Six Stages of Moral Judgment," 409–12. For major general accounts, see L. Kohlberg, "Stage and Sequence: The Cognitive-Developmental Approach to Socialization," in D. A. Goslin (ed.), *Handbook of Socialization Theory and Research* (Chicago: Rand McNally, 1969), 347–480; also "From Is to Ought: How to Commit the Naturalistic Fallacy and Get away with It," in T. Mischel (ed.), *Cognitive Development and Epistemology* (New York: Academic Press, 1971), 151–235.
23. These claims are made in many of Kohlberg's publications; immediate reference here is to "From Is to Ought," and "Development as the Aim of Education: The Dewey View," in *Essays in Moral Development*, vol. I, 49–96; 57ff; this text to be cited as *EMD*.

24. Scoring methods have been considerably revised over the years; for a complete recent treatment, see A. Colby and L. Kohlberg (eds.), *The Measurement of Moral Judgment*, vols. 1 and 2 (New York: Cambridge University Press, 1984). A good general account of the issues is given in J. Rest, "Moral Research Methodology," in S. Modgil and C. Modgil, *Lawrence Kohlberg*, 455–70. The dilemmas, which are drawn from a number of sources, are intended to cover questions relating to distributive, commutative, and corrective justice. The best known is the "Heinz dilemma": "In Europe, a woman was near death from a rare form of cancer. There was one drug that the doctors thought might save her, a form of radium that a druggist in the same town had recently discovered. The druggist was charging $2,000, ten times what the drug cost him to make. The sick woman's husband, Heinz, went to everyone he knew to borrow the money, but he could only get together about half of what [the drug] cost. He told the druggist that his wife was dying and asked him to sell it cheaper or let him pay later. But the druggist said "No." So Heinz got desperate and broke into the man's store to steal the drug for his wife." This version of the dilemma is quoted from L. Kohlberg, "Moral Stages and Moralization," 41–42. Kohlberg has a conception of morality as pertaining to situations of conflict, thought of typically as a clash of competing claims between individuals (in this case, a conflict of life and property); one of the most striking features of his presentation (and discussion) of the Heinz dilemma is the virtual absence of social context.

25. See L. Kohlberg, C. Levine, and A. Hewer, *Moral Stages: The Current Formulation of Kohlberg's Theory and a Response to Critics* (Basel: S. Karger, 1983), 64, 112–113; to be cited as *MSK*. Note: *CFK*, note 21 above, is a synopsis of this monograph. See also L. Kohlberg, "High School Democracy and Educating for a Just Society," in R. L. Mosher (ed.), *Moral Education* (New York: Praeger, 1980), 20–57; 21–25.

26. See L. Kohlberg, "Moral Stages and Moralization," 42–44; "Continuities in Childhood and Adult Moral Development Revisited," in P. B. Baltes and K. W. Schaie (eds.), *Life-Span Developmental Psychology: Personality and Socialization* (New York: Academic Press, 1973), 192; *EMD*, I, Appendix, 411. The (A) and (B) substages appear in *CFK* 96–97.

27. Kohlberg draws attention to the two main schools of ethical liberalism in "Development as the Aim of Education: The Dewey View," *EMD*, I, 73.

28. See L. Kohlberg, *EMD*, I, part 1, *Moral Stages and the Aims of Education*; "Stages of Moral Development as a Basis for Moral Education," in C. Beck, B. Crittenden, and E. Sullivan (eds.), *Moral Education: Interdisciplinary Approaches* (Toronto: University of Toronto Press, 1971), 29–72; "High School Democracy and Educating for a Just Society," in R. L. Mosher, *Moral Education*; and M. Blatt and L. Kohlberg, "The Effects of Classroom Moral Discussion upon Children's Level of Moral Judgment," *Journal of Moral Education*, 4 (1975), 129–61.

29. Bill Puka, "An Interdisciplinary Treatment of Kohlberg," *Ethics*, 92 (1982), 468–90; 474 and 481.

30. L. Kohlberg, "High School Democracy and Educating for a Just Society," in R. L. Mosher *Moral Education*, 21. Kohlberg supposes that Piaget's two moral stages correspond to Stages 1 and 2 on his scale; but this cannot be the case for Piaget's morality of cooperation incorporates elements relating to autonomy and justice which would link it more appropriately with a morality of principles.

31. William M. Sullivan, *Reconstructing Public Philosophy* (Berkeley and Los Angeles: University of California Press, 1982), 125, 122–23.

32. *MSK* 92.
33. See in particular L. Kohlberg, "Education for Justice: A Modern Statement of the Socratic View," in *EMD*, I, 29–48. In an earlier version of this paper (1970), Kohlberg had spoken of the *Platonic* view; he explains that the title was changed to indicate that the essay "draws on Socrates' views as portrayed in Plato's earlier *Dialogues*. These *Dialogues* present a view of moral education as democratic and based on dialogue" (in contrast with the more indoctrinative and hierarchical views of Plato's *Republic* and *Laws*). This claim is spoiled by the consideration that Socrates was anti-democratic in outlook and did not take a democratic view of education — as is clear, for example, in his criticism of Protagoras' defense of democracy in the *Protagoras*.

    For Kohlberg's account of Aristotle's "bag of virtues" approach (so-called), see *EMD*, I, 31.
34. L. Kohlberg, "From Is to Ought," 192.
35. See especially L. Kohlberg and D. Candee, "The Relation of Moral Judgment to Moral Action," in W. Kurtines and J. L. Gewirtz (eds.), *Morality, Moral Behavior and Moral Development: Basic Issues in Theory and Research* (New York: Wiley, 1984); and see P. Kutnick, "The Relationship of Moral Judgment and Moral Action: Kohlberg's Theory, Criticism and Revision," in S. Modgil and C. Modgil *Lawrence Kohlberg*, 125–48; A. Blasi, "Bridging Moral Cognition and Moral Action."
36. *CFK* 96. J. C. Gibbs, in a significant article, "Kohlberg's Moral Stage Theory, A Piagetian Revision," *Human Development*, 22 (1979), 89–112, argues that Kohlberg's Stages 5 and 6 belong to a level of "existential" understanding, in contrast to the natural (and Piagetian) character of Stages 1 to 4. Kohlberg rejected this classification of Stages 5 and 6, but he accepted the idea of "soft," "post-Piagetian" stages for a range of other developed moral outlooks. Gilligan's "ethic of care" is classified in this way as are forms of ethics discussed by W. F. Perry, *Forms of Intellectual and Ethical Development in the College Years* (New York: Holt, Rinehart and Winston, 1970), and J. W. Fowler, *Stages of Faith; the Psychology of Human Development and the Quest for Meaning* (San Francisco: Harper and Row, 1981). Kohlberg has postulated in particular a hypothetical "soft" Stage 7, described in *CFK* 96 as "an orientation based on ethical and religious thinking involving a cosmic or religious perspective on life"; see "Moral Development, Religious Thinking, and the Question of a Seventh Stage" (with Clark Power), in *EMD*, I, 311ff; and "The Aging Person as Philosopher" (with Richard Shulik), in *Essays on Moral Development*, vol. II (San Francisco: Harper and Row, 1984).
37. Among philosophical critiques, see Don Locke, "Cognitive Stages or Developmental Phases? A Critique of the Stage-Structural Theory of Moral Reasoning," *Journal of Moral Education*, 9 (1980), 103–09; "The Principle of Equal Interests," *Philosophical Review*, 90 (1981), 531–59; "A Psychologist among the Philosophers: Philosophical Aspects of Kohlberg's Theories," in S. Modgil and C. Modgil, *Lawrence Kohlberg*, 21–38; O. Flanagan, Jr., "Virtue, Sex, and Gender: Some Philosophical Reflections on the Moral Psychology Debate," *Ethics*, 92 (1982), 499–512; B. Crittenden, "The Limitations of Morality as Justice in Kohlberg's Theory," in D. B. Cochrane et al., *The Domain of Moral Education*, 251–66; R. S. Peters, "Moral Principles and Moral Education," ibid. 120–34; R. W. Miller, "Ways of Moral Learning," *Philosophical Review*, XCIV (1985), 507–56. The quotation is from *CFK* 97.
38. L. Kohlberg and D. Elfenbein, "Capital Punishment, Moral Development and the Constitution," in *EMD*, I, 243–93; 253. For a more complete account of Kohlberg's ideas in this matter, see "The Future of Liberalism as the Dominant

Ideology of the Western World," *EMD*, I, 231–42; for critiques of Kohlberg in this respect, see H. Weinreich-Haste, "Kohlberg's Contribution to Political Psychology," in S. Modgil and C. Modgil, *Lawrence Kohlberg*, 337–61; and N. Emler, "Morality and Politics: The Ideological Dimension in the Theory of Moral Development," in H. Weinreich-Haste and Don Locke, *Morality in the Making; Thought. Action and the Social Context*, 47–71.

39. L. Kohlberg, "From Is to Ought," 174, 177, 178, 173, 178.
40. *MSK* 113, 112–13. The main cross-cultural studies in question are: B. Parikh, "Development of Moral Judgment and its Relation to Family Environmental Factors in Indian and American families," *Child Development*, 51 (1980), 103–09; T. Leu and S. W. Cheng, "An Empirical Study of Kohlberg's Theory and Moral Judgment in Chinese Society" (Mimeo: Laboratory of Human Development, Harvard University, Cambridge Mass.); M. Nisan and L. Kohlberg, "Universality and Variation in Moral Judgment: A Longitudinal and Cross-Sectional Study in Turkey," *Child Development*, 53 (1982), 865–76; C. P. Edwards, "Social Experience and Moral Judgment in Kenyan Young Adults," *Journal of Genetic Psychology*, 133 (1978), 19–29; and "Moral Development in Comparative Cultural Perspective," in D. A. Wagner and H. Stevenson (eds.), *Cultural Perspectives on Child Development* (San Francisco: W. H. Freeman, 1982), 248–79; L. Kohlberg, J. Snarey, J. Reimer, "Cultural Universality of Moral Judgment Stages: A Longitudinal Study in Israel" (Mimeo: Laboratory of Human Development, Harvard University, Cambridge, Mass., 1983).
41. Ian Vine, "Moral Maturity in Socio-Cultural Perspective: Are Kohlberg's Stages Universal?", in S. Modgil and C. Modgil, *Lawrence Kohlberg*, 431–50. B. Parikh, "Development of Moral Judgment"; M. Nisan and L. Kohlberg, "Universality and Moral Judgment," 874, note 40.
42. L. Kohlberg, J. Snarey, J. Reimer, "Cultural Universality", C. P. Edwards, "Cross-Cultural Research on Kohlberg's Stages: The Basis for Consensus," in S. Modgil and C. Modgil, *Lawrence Kohlberg*, 419–30.
43. See L. Kohlberg, "From Is to Ought," 200.
44. See L. Kohlberg, *MSK, CFK,* and "A Current Statement on Some Theoretical Issues," in S. Modgil and C. Modgil, *Lawrence Kohlberg*, 517–21 and 527–42. For Habermas' use of Kohlberg's stages, see J. Habermas, *Communication and the Evolution of Society*, trans. T. McCarthy (Boston: Beacon, 1979); J. Habermas, "Interpretative Social Sciences vs Hermeneuticism," in N. Haan, R. W. Bellah, P. Rabinow, and W. M. Sullivan, (eds.), *Social Science as Moral Inquiry* (New York: Columbia, 1983), 251–69; and T. McCarthy, *The Critical Theory of Jürgen Habermas* (Cambridge: Polity Press, 1984).
45. *CFK* 95, 98. Kohlberg's meta-ethical assumptions (a set of nine) rest on the general assumption that, "the core of morality and moral development is deontological, that it is a matter of rights and duties as prescriptions. Furthermore, the core of mature deontological morality is justice or principles of justice" (*CFK* 95); the assumptions lead to a corollary assumption of the primacy of justice: "*Moral* judgments or principles have the central function of resolving interpersonal or social conflicts; that is, conflicts of claims or rights. Such judgments also define duties relative to these rights. Thus, moral judgments and principles imply a notion of equilibrium, balancing, or reversibility of claims" (*CFK* 98).
46. Among studies, see C. B. White, N. Bushell, and J. L. Regnemer, "Moral Development in Bahamian School Children: A Three-Year Examination of Kohlberg's Stages of Moral Development," *Developmental Psychology*, 14 (1978), 58–65; L. Kohlberg, "The Young Child as a Philosopher," *EMD*, II.
47. Martin Packer, Norma Haan, Paola Theodorou, and Gary Yabrove, "Moral

Action of Four-Year-Olds," in N. Haan, E. Aerts, and B. A. B. Cooper (eds.), *On Moral Grounds, The Search for Practical Morality* (New York and London: New York University Press, 1985), 276–305. Packer et al. refer to a number of studies which challenge the views of Piaget and Kohlberg, directly or indirectly, in regard to very young children.

48. Carol Gilligan, *In a Different Voice* (Cambridge, Mass., and London: Harvard University Press, 1982), 7; to be cited as *DV*. The reference is to Sigmund Freud, "Some Psychical Consequences of the Anatomical Distinction between the Sexes" (1925), *Complete Works* (1961), vol. XIX, 257–58.

49. Plato is the most notable exception among philosophers of the past. In the *Republic*, though not elsewhere, he works with the idea that men and women are equally endowed with intelligence and skills of government and moral virtue, and hence should share equally in the offices of the state; he proposes, as part of a general hypothesis in this connection, that the family be abolished. Ideas of this sort had had a limited currency in Athens, but, in addition, Plato was characteristically drawn to look for what is common or general beyond differences. In his thinking, then, moral virtue will be the same whether it is manifested in men or women: there is no proper place, or need, for a different voice. At the same time, the common standard which Plato had in mind in relation to virtue and the government of the state was set by the male world.

50. On the male character of the social contract theory, see Carole Pateman, "The Fraternal Social Contract," in J. Keane (ed.), *Civil Society and the State: New European Perspectives* (London and New York: Verso, 1988); and Carole Pateman, *The Sexual Contract* (Cambridge: Polity Press, 1988).

51. *DV* 18; reference is made there to views expressed in L. Kohlberg and R. Kramer, "Continuities and Discontinuities in Children and Adult Moral Development," *Human Development*, 12 (1969), 93–120.

52. For the earlier study, see J. M. Murphy and C. Gilligan, "Moral Development in Late Adolescence and Adulthood: A Critique and Reconstruction of Kohlberg's Theory," *Human Development*, 23 (1980), 77–104; 90–1. A similar conclusion is arrived at in a later report by Gilligan et al., "Contribution of Women's Thinking to Developmental Theory. The Elimination of Sex Bias in Moral Development Theory and Research" (Final Report to National Institute of Education, 1982). This study provided evidence that in relation to real-life dilemmas, women predominantly took an approach based on beneficence or care, while men responded predominantly in terms of rights or justice. Among other subsequent studies, see, N. Eisenberg and R. Lennon, "Sex Differences in Empathy and Related Capacities," *Psychological Bulletin*, 94 (1983), 100–31; L. Walker, "Sex Differences in the Development of Moral Reasoning: A Critical Review," *Child Development*, 55 (1984), 183–201; L. Walker, "Experiential and Cognitive Sources of Moral Development in Adulthood," *Human Development*, 29 (1986), 113–24. On the basis of such reports, Kohlberg strongly repudiated the charge of sexual bias; see *MSK* and *CFK*. Kohlberg's reflective view is nonetheless subject to some confusion in this area: in *MSK* 122, a denial that Kohlberg ever stated that males have a more developed sense of justice than females is followed by an explanation of why there is such a difference!

53. *DV* 18; Gilligan refers to J. Piaget, *Structuralism* (New York: Basic Books, 1970) in this connection and comments that Piaget, "challenging the common impression that a developmental theory is built like a pyramid from its base in infancy, points out that a conception of development instead hangs from its vortex of maturity, the point toward which progress is traced. Thus, a change in the definition of maturity does not simply alter the description of the highest stage but recasts the understanding of development, changing the entire account."

54. *DV* 7–8, Gilligan refers to Nancy Chodorow, *The Reproduction of Mothering: Psychoanalysis and the Sociology of Gender* (Berkeley: University of California Press, 1978), and also R. J. Stoller, "A Contribution to the Study of Gender Identity," *International Journal of Psychoanalysis*, 45 (1964), 220–26. While Gilligan cites these sources in support of her general thesis of the two paths of development, she does not discuss them in any detail; she does not consider, for example, how these views might affect her proposal for the eventual integration of an ethic of care with an ethic of justice.

55. In place of Kohlberg's stages, reference could be made rather to W. F. Perry's positional schema in W. F. Perry, *Forms of Intellectual and Ethical Development in the College Years: A Scheme* (New York: Holt, Rinehart, and Winston, 1968), or to Jane Loevinger's schema of stages of ego development, in Jane Loevinger and Ruth Wessler, *Measuring Ego Development* (San Francisco: Jossey-Bass, 1970).

56. *DV* 7–8; Gilligan cites Chodorow in this connection: "Girls emerge from this period with a basis for 'empathy' built into their primary definition of self in a way that boys do not. . . . Girls emerge with a stronger basis for experiencing another's needs or feelings as one's own. . . . Furthermore, girls do not define themselves in terms of the denial of preoedipal relational modes as do boys. Therefore, regression to these modes tends not to feel as much a basic threat to their ego. From very early on, then, because they are parented by a person of the same gender . . . girls come to experience themselves as less differentiated than boys, as more continuous with and related to the external object-world, and as differently oriented to their inner object-world as well" (167).

57. Gilligan refers to the complementarity thesis in various places, but the terms of the relationship are left unexplored. The origin of her version of the thesis lies in the questionable assumption that Kohlberg's account is applicable to male moral development. Once this assumption is withdrawn, the idea of the two distinct ethics and their supposed complementarity loses its rationale. There may be good independent grounds, however, for talking about characteristically different ways in which men and women think and act in the moral domain, connected, for example, with different conditions in identity-formation and roles; but that is another question.

58. Aristotle, *Nicomachean Ethics*, 8, 1 (1155a26–7); see 9, 1; to be cited as *NE*.

59. *NE* 9, 8, and 9, 4; Jean-Jacques Rousseau, *A Discourse on Inequality*, trans. M. Cranston (Harmondsworth: Penguin Books, 1984) 167.

60. Reference to this idea can be found in *DV* 101. The primary witness to situations of this sort is found in Greek tragedy. Philosophy, beginning with Plato, has usually rejected the tragic view in favor of looking for a science of ethics which will yield clear and definite conclusions in all situations. Kohlberg, drawing on philosophical sources, holds that tragedy represents an immature stage of moral development (see below).

61. *MSK* 92–93.

62. L. Kohlberg, "Moral Development and the Theory of Tragedy," in *EMD*, I, 373–99; 391, 386.

63. Aristotle, *Rhetoric*, I, 13, 1373b7–11; see Sophocles' *Antigone*, lines 450–70. Martha C. Nussbaum shows how criticism of aspects of Antigone's character is consistent with recognizing the moral depth of her position: "The belief that not all values are utility-relative, that there are certain claims whose neglect will prove deeply destructive of communal attachment and individual character, is a part of Antigone's position left untouched by the play's implicit criticism of her single-mindedness (Martha C. Nussbaum, *The Fragility of Goodness* [Cambridge University Press, 1986]). Insights of this sort are overlooked in the Kohlbergian assignment of ranks.

64. A recent argument in support of an Aristotelian approach can be found in Alasdair MacIntyre, *After Virtue*; in taking note of this book, Kohlberg et al. describe MacIntyre misleadingly as a "historically relativistic philosopher" (*MSK* 105); elsewhere in this source, the claim is made that Kohlberg's current position with reference to justice is "perhaps as close to that of Aristotle as it is to that of Plato" (*MSK* 118). Kohlberg's appropriation of Plato and Aristotle is made without attention to historical context.

65. Largely in response to Gilligan's critique, Kohlberg began to recognize a morality of care and response, as different from, but not opposed to, his morality of universal justice. In this approach, the morality of care is treated as supplementary to justice and as restricted properly to "the domain of personal care and response" (*MSK* and CFK 96). The implication is that the Kohlbergian account remains largely unaffected by Gilligan's critique; at one point, in fact, Kohlberg reverts to the view that justice is the only virtue! (*MSK* 18). This is replaced by the more defensible proposal that, "justice is the first virtue of a person or society." This idea echoes an Aristotelian remark, but the Aristotelian idea, that justice is primary in that it defines a community of people who agree in a common way of life and have a care for one another, is obscured: for the conception of justice which Kohlberg espouses is that of a universal principle defined from the point of view of the rational individual.

Chapter 4. Aristotle: Reason and the Passions

1. "Happiness" is the usual translation of the Greek *eudaimonia*, but it is somewhat misleading because of the connotation of happiness as a feeling. The Greek term conveys the broader and more active sense of an overall situation in which a person acts well and things go well in their regard in the major respects of human life. A number of excellent essays dealing with *eudaimonia* and other major themes in Aristotle's ethics can be found in A. O. Rorty (ed.), *Essays on Aristotle's Ethics* (Berkeley: University of California Press, 1980); among these essays, I am particularly indebted, in my account of developmental themes in Aristotle's ethics, to M. F. Burnyeat, "Aristotle on Learning to be Good," 69–92.

2. Aristotle's best known ethical work is the *Nicomachean Ethics*; the *Eudemian Ethics* is also important, and the *Politics* is especially relevant for developmental themes. The following abbreviations will be used in citations: NE (*Nicomachean Ethics*), EE (*Eudemian Ethics*), Pol. (*Politics*); references will ordinarily cite book and chapter, and the numerals from the Bekker edition of the Greek text (1831) which are given in most editions. Translations are from *The Complete Works of Aristotle*, Revised Oxford Translation, ed. Jonathan Barnes, 2 vols. (Princeton, N.J.: Princeton University Press, 1984).

3. Plato, *Meno*, 70A, in *The Dialogues of Plato*, trans. B. Jowett, 5 vols., 3rd. ed. (London: Oxford University Press, 1892), vol. II, 27.

4. Aristotle (from Stagira in Chalcide in the Macedonian region) was a resident foreigner, or metic, in Athens for much of his life, first as a student in Plato's Academy and later as head of his own school, the Lyceum. As a metic, he would have had full legal protection and most of the duties of a citizen other than the right to marry a citizen or own landed property. He was clearly a prominent identity in Athens, but in unstable conditions which involved periods of anti-Macedonian feeling he was forced to leave the City, notably a year or so before his death in 322.

5. Aristotle discusses the moral virtues and vices in Books 3-5 of *NE*, intellectual virtues in Book 6, and friendship in Books 8 and 9. The theme of the vulnerability of *eudaimonia* in Aristotelian thought is discussed in Martha C. Nussbaum, *The Fragility of Goodness*, Chaps. 11–12.

6. Aristotle's major study in psychology is *On the Soul* (*De Anima*); and with reference to the emotions, see also *Rhetoric* II. Some scholars hold that the account of the soul utilized in *NE* is quite different from the psychology in *On the Soul*; a version of the view can be found in W. W. Fortenbaugh, *Aristotle on Emotion* (London: Duckworth, 1975, 26ff); for argument against the view, see W. F. R. Hardie, *Aristotle's Ethical Theory*, 2nd. ed. (Oxford: Clarendon Press, 1981), Chap. 5. For a general discussion of Aristotle's psychology relevant to his ethics, see T. Engberg-Pedersen, *Aristotle's Theory of Moral Insight* (Oxford: Clarendon Press, 1983), Chap. 5.

7. For main passages in *NE*, see 2, 3–5; for discussion of this point, see D. Wiggins, "Deliberation and Practical Reason," in A. O. Rorty, *Essays*, 221–40; J. M. Cooper, *Reason and Human Good in Aristotle* (Cambridge, Mass.: Harvard University Press, 1975); and Martha C. Nussbaum, *Fragility of Goodness*, 297. The topic will be discussed in its modern setting in chapter eight.

8. In this connection, see *EE* 7, 15: 1248b26ff: "A good man, then, is one for whom natural goods are good. For the goods men fight for and think the greatest — honour, wealth, bodily excellences, good fortune and power — are naturally good, but may be to some hurtful because of their dispositions"; cf. *NE* 9, 8: 1168b15ff.

9. See the discussion of justice in *NE* 5 and of friendship in *NE* 8 and 9. In *NE* 10, 9 Aristotle stresses the importance of good laws in exercising a basic educative and deterrent role in regard to virtue; this connects with themes which he explores more fully in relation to family-household and the state in the *Politics*.

10. For critical discussion of Aristotle's views in this matter, see G. E. R. Lloyd, *Science, Folklore and Ideology: Studies in the Life-Sciences in Ancient Greece* (New York: Cambridge University Press, 1983), 128–64.

11. "For the sake of the noble": see *NE* 1115b12–13; 22–24; 116a11–12; 1116b2–3; 1117a16–17; 1119b16; 1120a22–24; 1122b6–7 (and elsewhere); "goodness of action itself": see 1139b3–4; 1140b7 (and elsewhere).

12. In *NE* 10, 6-8, Aristotle proposes that contemplation, specifically philosophical contemplation, is the highest form of human activity, the best, the most pleasant, the happiest. He had earlier proposed in Book 6 that theoretical wisdom is the highest kind of human excellence. The question of how this teaching is to be related to his account of the life of moral virtue and practical wisdom and the idea of a rich, multifaceted development of human powers has long been a subject of dispute. The juxtaposition of views may be witness to different tendencies and tensions in Aristotle's thought or to different layers of text in *NE* from different periods. But there seems to be no reason to think that the commendation of contemplative activity excludes or is at odds with the requirements of practical wisdom and the moral virtues. He could then be interpreted as saying (at least) that the life of practical wisdom, exercised in political life, needs to include a place for contemplative activity. Among many discussions of this topic, see J. M. Cooper, *Reason and Human Good in Aristotle*, and A. O. Rorty, "The Place of Contemplation in Aristotle's *Nicomachean Ethics*," in A. O. Rorty, *Essays*, 377–94.

13. For Aristotle's discussion of education, see *Politics*, 7, 17; and 8.

14. For discussion and criticism of this view, see R. Sorabji, "Aristotle on the Role

of Intellect in Virtue," in A. O. Rorty, *Essays*, 201–19; and T. Engberg-Pedersen, *Aristotle's Theory of Moral Insight*, Chaps. 6 and 7; I am indebted to both sources.

15. The topic of Aristotle on action, with particular reference to his notion of *orexis* (desire), is interestingly discussed by M. Nussbaum, *The Fragility of Goodness*, Chap. 9, "Rational Animals and the Explanation of Action," 264ff.

16. For discussion of this topic, see C. Lord, *Education and Culture in the Political Thought of Aristotle* (Ithaca, N.Y.: Cornell University Press, 1982), 85ff.

17. Aristotle arrives at this conclusion at *Pol.* 8, 5: 1340b11–12. The discussion of music is introduced in *Pol.* 8, 3, and taken up more fully in 5–7. The main passage relating to my summary of Aristotle's argument is *Pol.* 1340a14–25:

> Since then music is a pleasure, and excellence consists in rejoicing and loving and hating rightly, there is clearly nothing which we are so much concerned to acquire and cultivate as the power of forming right judgments, and of taking delight in good dispositions and noble actions. Rhythm and melody supply imitations of anger and gentleness, and also of courage and temperance, and of all the qualities contrary to these, and of the other qualities of character, which hardly fall short of the actual affections, as we know from our own experience, for in listening to such strains our souls undergo a change. The habit of feeling pleasure or pain at mere representations is not far removed from the same feelings about realities.

Aristotle's argument here reflects a passage in *Protagoras*, 326A-B, and ideas explored in the *Republic*; further discussion of the idea would need to take up themes discussed more fully in Aristotle's *Poetics*.

18. See T. Engberg-Pedersen, *Aristotle's Theory of Moral Insight*, 182–83.

19. Shame is a central concept in Greek ethical and political thought, and it remains a major topic in moral education (as we saw in relation to Aronfreed's account of conscience, *Conduct and Conscience*, Chap. 9, see chapter two above). Martha Nussbaum discusses aspects of shame in Platonist and Aristotelian thought, especially with reference to the notion of self-respect, in "Shame, Separateness, and Political Unity," in A. O. Rorty, *Essays*, 395–435; Nussbaum's discussion is also concerned with the examination of shame and self-respect in John Rawls, *A Theory of Justice*, §§ 29 and 67.

20. M. Nussbaum, *The Fragility of Goodness*, explores this theme in Chap. 13, "The Betrayal of Convention: A Reading of Euripides' *Hecuba*." The reading is avowedly Aristotelian, though it does not rely on Aristotle, and it is intended to "help us to assess Aristotle's attitude towards tragic events; and also to understand why he singles out Euripides as 'the most tragic of all', therefore the most suited for the educational function that he ascribes to tragedy" (399). There is a critical discussion of Nussbaum's reading in K. Lycos, "Hecuba's Newly-Learned Melody: Nussbaum on Philosophy Learning from Euripides," *Critical Philosophy*, 4 (1988), 161–80.

21. See Oswyn Murray, "Life and Society in Classical Greece," *The Oxford History of the Classical World*, ed. J. Boardman, J. Griffin, O. Murray (Oxford and New York: Oxford University Press, 1986), 204–33, 212–17.

22. A distinction of this sort is made by T. H. Irwin, "Reason and Responsibility in Aristotle," in A. O. Rorty, *Essays*, 117–55; Irwin argues that in espousing a broad concept of the voluntary which would include many actions of animals and children, Aristotle fails to provide an adequate account of ethical responsibility. Irwin's argument is criticized by Nussbaum, *The Fragility of Goodness*, 283–87, who argues (persuasively in my view) that, without attention to the broad or "common" notion, one cannot give a developmental account of full ethical responsibility.

23. M. F. Burnyeat, "Learning to Be Good," 82–88.
24. Ibid., 85.

Chapter 5. Locke: The Character of Modern Virtue

1. John Locke, *Some Thoughts Concerning Education*, § 1. Locke's treatise was first published in 1693; quotations and references here are taken from the text in J. L. Axtell (ed.), *The Educational Writings of John Locke* (Cambridge: Cambridge University Press, 1968). The text is that of the fifth edition, which was prepared for publication by Locke shortly before his death and appeared in 1705; it was included in the first edition of Locke's *Collected Works* in 1714. Locke divided the text into 216 sections; reference will be made to section number only in citations. This chapter draws on my paper, "Thoughts about Locke's Thought about Education," *Journal of Philosophy of Education*, 15 (1981), 149–60.
2. John Locke, *An Essay Concerning Human Understanding* (1690), critical edition by Peter H. Nidditch (Oxford: Clarendon Press, 1975), I, II, 1ff; cited either in full or as *Essay*.
3. Ibid. II, 1, 1; see I, II, 1ff.
4. John Passmore, "The Malleability of Man in Eighteenth-Century Thought," in E. R. Wasserman (ed.), *Aspects of the Eighteenth Century* (Baltimore: Johns Hopkins Press, 1965), 21–46; see also John Passmore, *The Perfectibility of Man* (London: Duckworth, 1970), Chap. 8.
5. John Locke, *The Reasonableness of Christianity, as Delivered in the Scriptures* (1695), §§ 1–9; ed. and abridged by I. T. Ramsey (London: A. and C. Black, 1958).
6. N. Chomsky, *Reflections on Language* (Glasgow: Fontana, 1976); H. Bracken, *Berkeley* (London: MacMillan, 1972), E. M. Wood, *Mind and Politics* (Berkeley: University of California Press, 1972).
7. John Passmore, "Malleability of Man," 23; John Locke, *Two Treatises of Government* (1690), critical edition by Peter Laslett (Cambridge: Cambridge University Press, 1963), § 61; see also § 63.
8. It would have to be assumed that Locke's strictures on the desire for property extend only to its unjustified or improper acquisition; it would otherwise be difficult to reconcile his remarks here with his defense of the universal right to property, based on the person and on labor, in the *Second Treatise of Government*, Chap. 5.
9. This passage is quoted from J. W. Yolton, *John Locke and the Way of Ideas* (London: Oxford University Press, 1956), 57, from Noah Porter, *Marginalia Lockeana*, in *New Englander and Yale Review*, July 1887.
10. John Passmore, *Perfectibility*, 161.
11. See J. W. Yolton, *John Locke and The Way of Ideas*, 55.
12. The more important of the letters can be found in J. L. Axtell, *Educational Writings*, Appendix 1, 341–91.
13. *Some Thoughts Concerning Education*, Dedicatory Letter to Edward Clarke, in J. L. Axtell, *Educational Writings*, 112–13.
14. J. L. Axtell (ed.), *Educational Writings*, Introduction, 51; cf. Peter Laslett, *The World We Have Lost — Further Explored*, 3rd. ed. (London: Methuen 1983), Chap. 2 (first published, 1965).
15. Public Records Office, Board of Trade Papers, London, 1697; see H. R. Fox-Bourne, *The Life of John Locke* (London, 1876), vol II, 337–91; there is an early draft in the Lovelace Collection, Bodleian Library, Oxford, c. 30, f. 94.
16. See J. L. Axtell, *Educational Writings*, 344ff.

17. See Philippe Ariès, *Centuries of Childhood: A Social History of Family Life*, trans. R. Baldick (New York: Vintage Books, 1962).

18. Locke put this idea forward in *An Essay Concerning Human Understanding*, IV, III, 18:

> The *Idea* of a supreme Being, infinite in Power, Goodness, and Wisdom, whose Workmanship we are, and on whom we depend; and the *Idea* of ourselves, as understanding, rational Beings, being such as are clear in us, would, I suppose, if duly considered, and pursued, afford such Foundations of our Duty and Rules of Action, as might place *Morality among the Sciences capable of Demonstration*: wherein I doubt not, but from self-evident Propositions, by necessary Consequences, as incontestable as those in Mathematicks, the measures of right and wrong might be made out, to anyone that will apply himself with the same Indifferency and Attention to the one, as he does to the Other of these Sciences.

Locke's friend, William Molyneux, was particularly taken with the idea and pressed him to produce a *Treatise of Morals* along the projected lines; but in correspondence with Molyneux, Locke kept deferring the project and became more reserved about its prospects, excusing himself on the grounds that, "the Gospel contains so perfect a body of Ethicks, that reason may be excused from that enquiry" (John Locke, *Correspondence*, 8 vols., ed. E. S. de Beer [Oxford, Clarendon Press, 1976 —], 5.595). For a recent study of Locke's moral theory, see John Colman, *John Locke's Moral Philosophy* (Edinburgh: Edinburgh University Press, 1983).

19. See § 185. John W. Yolton, *Locke, An Introduction* (Oxford: Basil Blackwell, 1985), 49, gives a list of rules which Locke presents in various places as derivable by reason from the law of nature, linked with the idea that the existence of God as supreme lawmaker can be known by reason: love and respect and worship God; obey your superiors; tell the truth and keep your promises; be mild and pure of character, and be friendly; do not offend or injure, without cause, any person's health, life, or possessions; be candid and friendly in talking about other people; do not kill or steal; love your neighbor and your parents; console a distressed neighbor; feed the hungry; that property is mine which I have acquired through my labor, so long as I can use it before it spoils; parents are to preserve, nourish, and educate their children (sources in Locke's early *Essays* and the *Second Treatise of Government*).

20. See especially *The Second Treatise of Government*, §§ 6 and 7.

21. In *An Essay Concerning Human Understanding*, II, XXVIII, 8, Locke speaks of the "*Divine* Law, whereby I mean, that Law which God has set to the actions of Men, whether promulgated to them by the light of Nature, or the voice of revelation. That God has given a Rule whereby Men should govern themselves, I think there is nobody so brutish as to deny. He has a Right to do it, we are his Creatures: He has Goodness and Wisdom to direct our Actions to that which is best; and he has Power to enforce it by Rewards and Punishments, of infinite weight and duration, in another Life . . . . This is the only true touchstone of *moral Rectitude*."

22. John Locke, *Essay Concerning Human Understanding*, II, 27, 11ff; see John Passmore, *Perfectibility*, 162.

23. John W. Yolton, *Locke: An Introduction*, 29.

24. On this topic, see Anthony Levi, *French Moralists* (Oxford: Oxford University Press, 1964), 225–33; Passmore discusses this connection in a brief but enlightening way in each of the sources cited.

25. Ibid. 229.

26. P. Nicole, *Essais de Morale* (1671–78) (Paris, 1755), vol. III, II Traite: "De la Charité et de l'amour-propre," Chap. XI, 181–82. The translation is quoted from John Passmore, "The Malleability of Man," 29, with the addition in brackets of the French phrase on the two occasions reference is made to *amour-propre*.
27. For argument about the way in which both of the treatises are directed against the views of Sir Robert Filmer (in his work *Patriarcha*, circulated in manuscript form in the 1640s and published in 1680) see Peter Laslett, introduction to the critical edition of *Two Treatises of Government*, 15ff.
28. Pierre Coste, Locke's French translator, wrote in the preface to the first French edition of 1695 (quoted from J. L. Axtell, *Educational Writings*, 52):

> It is certain that this Work was particularly designed for the education of Gentlemen, but this does not prevent its serving also for the education of all sorts of Children, of whatever class they are: for if you except that which the author says about Exercises that a young Gentleman ought to learn, nearly all the rules that he gives are universal.

Chapter 6. Rousseau: Natural Goodness and Virtue

1. Jean-Jacques Rousseau, *Discourse on the Origin and Foundations of Inequality* (*Second Discourse*), in *The First and Second Discourses*, ed. R. D. Masters, trans. R. D. and J. R. Masters (New York: St. Martin's Press, 1964), 180. The *Discourse on Inequality* was originally published in 1755.
2. Jean-Jacques Rousseau, *Discourse on the Sciences and Fine Arts* (*First Discourse*), 38; originally published in 1750.
3. Plato, *Protagoras*, 320Cff. For a survey of relevant ideas in the Greek world, see E. R. Dodds, *The Ancient Concept of Progress* (Oxford: Oxford University Press, 1973), Chap. 1.
4. The doctrine of original sin was of immense theological and *social* significance in the seventeenth and eighteenth centuries (as we have seen already in connection with Locke). Ernst Cassirer points out that the mandate in which the Archbishop of Paris condemned Rousseau's *Emile* soon after its publication in 1762 "laid the chief emphasis on Rousseau's denial of original sin"; see E. Cassirer, *The Question of Jean-Jacques Rousseau*, trans. and ed. by Peter Gay (New York: Columbia University Press, 1954), 74.
5. The remark occurs in a letter of 1764, quoted from P. D. Jimack's introduction to the Everyman edition of *Emile*, ix; for details of this edition, see note below.
6. *The Confessions of Jean-Jacques Rousseau*, trans. J. M. Cohen (Harmondsworth, U. K.: Penguin, 1975), Book IX, 377.
7. Jean-Jacques Rousseau, *The Social Contract*, trans. Maurice Cranston (Harmondsworth, U.K.: Penguin, 1980); originally published in 1762.
8. Jean-Jacques Rousseau, *Emile*, trans. Barbara Foxley (London: Dent, 1974); originally published in 1762. References to *Emile* will cite book and page number.
9. Most of the guiding ideas could also be located in the *Confessions*; on this, see Christopher Kelly, *Rousseau's Exemplary Life* (Ithaca and London: Cornell University Press, 1987).
10. Robert Derathé, *Le Rationalisme de J.-J. Rousseau* (Paris: Presses Universitaires de France, 1948), 106.
11. *The Creed of a Savoyard Priest*, in *Emile*, IV, 228–78. There is good reason to think that the *Creed* or *Profession of Faith* expresses Rousseau's own opinions for the most part, certainly in regard to what is said about the role of feeling in relation to conscience; on this, see R. D. Masters, *The Political Philosophy of Rousseau* (Princeton: Princeton University Press, 1968), 76ff.

12. E. Cassirer, *The Question of Jean-Jacques Rousseau*, 96.
13. There is an illuminating discussion of Rousseau's use of major theorists in the natural-law tradition in R. Derathé, *Le Rationalisme*, Chap. III, "La raison et la conscience"; Derathé concludes that Rousseau was a rationalist, but of a qualified sort, "a rationalist who is aware of the limits of reason" (176). See also R. Derathé, *Jean-Jacques Rousseau et la science politique de son temps* (Paris: Presses Universitaires de France, 1950).
14. I do not mean to suggest that Rousseau subscribed to a Thomistic account of natural law. He was critical of the traditional notion of natural law in the *Second Discourse*, in part because he held that human beings in the state of nature did not have moral knowledge and hence could not be said to act according to moral law. In *Emile*, by contrast, he makes use of natural-law terminology in his account of morality: the basis of morality in feeling remains, but reason, and hence moral knowledge, are brought into play and it becomes appropriate to speak of "precepts of the natural law," "duties of nature," and so on. In the *Profession of Faith* in *Emile*, this teaching is couched in the form of elements of a natural religion: Rousseau's ethical naturalism is thereby given the character of law. On this topic, see R. D. Masters, *Political Philosophy of Rousseau*, 74–89.
15. See *Discourse on Inequality*, note (i), 194.
16. Rousseau was not entirely consistent in maintaining his distinction between *amour de soi* and *amour-propre*; in *Emile*, IV, 197, he says: "The love of others, springing from self-love [*amour de soi*], is the source of human justice"; here at IV, 215 he says, "Extend self-love [*amour-propre*] to others and it is transformed into virtue." See Rousseau, *Oeuvres Completes* (Paris: Aux Editions du Seuil, 1971), vol. 3.
17. There is a good discussion of this topic in J. Charvet, *The Social Problem in the Philosophy of Rousseau* (Cambridge: Cambridge University Press, 1974); also in Elizabeth Rapaport, "On the Future of Love: Rousseau and the Radical Feminists," in C. C. Gould and M. W. Wartofsky (eds.), *Women and Philosophy* (New York: Perigree, 1980), 185–205; and in Anthony Skillen, "Rousseau and the Fall of Social Man," *Philosophy*, 60 (1985), 105–21.
18. In an unfinished sequel to *Emile*, entitled *Emile et Sophie ou les Solitaires*, Sophy is portrayed as unfaithful. Emile is at first heartbroken, but then regains in composure and happiness in a spirit of detached wisdom; see P. D. Jimack, introduction to *Emile*, xii.
19. For discussion of this topic, see Carole Pateman, *The Sexual Contract* (Cambridge: Polity Press, 1988); and "The Fraternal Social Contract," in J. Keane (ed.), *Civil Society and the State: New European Perspectives* (London and New York: Verso, 1988).
20. For discussion of these themes, see Genevieve Lloyd, "Rousseau on Reason, Nature and Women," *Metaphilosophy*, 14 (1983), 308–26, and *The Man of Reason* (London: Methuen, 1984), 58–64, 75–79; Joel Schwartz, *The Sexual Politics of Jean-Jacques Rousseau* (Chicago: University of Chicago Press, 1984).
21. This is precisely the issue which Carol Gilligan brings to light in *In a Different Voice* (Chapter 5 in particular) in connection with women's experience of an ethic of care; see chapter three above.

Chapter 7. Kant: the Sovereignty of Reason

1. Immanuel Kant, *Education*, trans. Annette Churton, (Michigan: University of Michigan Press, 1960), 8, 6. The University of Michigan Press edition, an Ann Arbor paperback, carries no information about the original text or the provenance of the translation. The original text is entitled *Immanuel Kant Über*

Pädagogik, edited by F. T. Rink (Königsberg, 1803), in vol. IX of the Academy edition of Kant's writings. Annette Churton's translation was originally published under the title *Kant on Education* (London, 1899); the translation was based on the text of Kant's *Pädagogik* in the Th. Vogt edition (Langensalza, 1883). I will refer to the text as *Kant on Education* and by the abbreviation *KE* in citations.

2. Immanuel Kant, *The Critique of Judgement,* trans. J. C. Meredith (Oxford: Oxford University Press, 1952), Part II, 97; the *Critique of Judgement,* Kant's third critique, was originally published in 1790; it will ordinarily be cited as *CJ.*

3. *KE* 7; Immanuel Kant, *Lectures on Ethics,* trans. Louis Infield (New York and London: The Century Co., 1930), 252; originally published in 1781; it will ordinarily be cited as *LE.*

4. Kant distinguishes *art* from *science* as *ability* from *knowledge,* "as a practical from a theoretical faculty"(*CJ* I, 63). Kant considered that most schools are bad because they work against nature and because they follow, in slavish fashion, stupid and ignorant traditions; this is brought out in a letter published in the Königsberg newspaper in 1777, in which he expressed support for an experimental school set up by the German educator, Basedow, at Dessau. See E. F. Buchner, *The Educational Theory of Immanuel Kant,* translation of *Immanuel Kant Über Pädagogik.* with introduction and notes (Philadelphia and London: J. B. Lippincott Co.), 1908, 242–45.

5. Immanuel Kant, *Foundations of the Metaphysics of Morals,* trans. L. W. Beck (Indianapolis: Bobbs-Merrill, 1959), 5; translation of *Grundlegung zur Metaphysik der Sitten,* originally published 1785; the text will ordinarily be cited as *FMM.*

6. Ralph C. S. Walker, *Kant* (London: Routledge and Kegan Paul, 1978), 155. This point tells most directly against R. M. Hare's attempt to formulate a more satisfactory account of universalizability than Kant supplied, viz., an account according to which the moral law applies to everyone with the additional requirement that no one is accorded special status in its regard — hence, the specification that moral principles not include singular terms in their expression; see R. M. Hare, *Freedom and Reason* (Oxford: Oxford University Press, 1963), Chap. 2. As a test for the universalizability of a principle relating to one's behavior, Hare proposes that one should look at the matter through the eyes of others who are affected by it and consider whether, in that case, one would be willing to be treated in the same way in the same circumstances. If not, one has evidence that a universal principle is involved. (Kohlberg highlights reasoning of this sort — playing musical chairs, putting oneself in the other person's shoes — in connection with Stage 6 of his schema.) It is clear, on the basis of Walker's example, that the test is inadequate even if there were no inherent difficulties in its execution.

7. Richard Norman, *The Moral Philosophers* (Oxford: Oxford University Press, 1983), Chap. 6, 119.

8. See Immanuel Kant, *The Doctrine of Virtue* (Pt. II of *The Metaphysic of Morals*), trans. Mary J. Gregor (New York: Harper & Row, 1964); originally published 1797; Introduction, IV, 44. Kant argues there that, "since every man (by virtue of his *natural* impulses) has *his own happiness* as his end, it would be contradictory to consider this an obligatory end." This would not show, however, that the pursuit of happiness could or should be excluded from the scope of morality. He argues equally that it would be contradictory for a person to consider himself obligated to promote the perfection of another on the grounds that this is something that the other alone can do. I will consider this claim in connection with Kant's treatment of moral education.

9. R. C. S. Walker, *Kant,* 158.

10. *Ibid.*
11. For a discussion of Kant's use of the concept of natural purposes, see R. Norman, *The Moral Philosophers*, 112–13.
12. See note 4. In his *Letter on the Philanthropinum at Dessau* (1777), Kant expressed the hope that this school might light the torch of revolution in education in Germany and beyond. By the time the school finally closed in 1794, its promise blighted, he had concluded that a complete scheme of education would require many generations. But he continued to insist on the need for experimentation: "The only experimental school which had in a measure made a beginning to clear the way [toward a complete scheme of education] was the Dessau Institute. This must be said in its praise, in spite of the many mistakes with which we might reproach it — mistakes which attend all conclusions from experiments—namely, that still more experiments are required" (*KE* 23). His enthusiasm for experimentation in education did not extend to the education of women, however; in their regard he wrote: "Until we shall have studied feminine nature better, it is best to leave the education of daughters to their mothers, and to let them off their books." See Kant, *Pedagogical Fragments*, quoted from E. Buchner, *Educational Theory of Immanuel Kant*, 226.
13. The headings in the text (as edited by Rink) are: "Introduction"; "Concerning Physical Education"; "Concerning Practical Education." English versions of the text follow the somewhat different chapter headings, together with the paragraph divisions, introduced by Th. Vogt in his German edition of the work.
14. Traugott Weisskopf, *Immanuel Kant und die Pädagogik* (Zurich: EZW Verlag, 1970), 349. Weisskopf's conclusions are summarized and discussed briefly by L. W. Beck in an illuminating essay, "Kant on Education," in *Essays on Kant and Hume* (New Haven: Yale University Press, 1978), 188–204.
15. Weisskopf's study, *Immanuel Kant*, makes this task relatively straightforward: it includes the text of the *Pädagogik* with relevant sources (where they have been traced).
16. *KE* 9; for a thorough discussion of the topic, see R. Vierhaus, *Bildung*, in O. Brunner, W. Conze, R. Koselleck (eds.), *Geschichtliche Grundbegriffe* (Stuttgart: Klett-Cotta, 1972), vol. 1, 508–51.
17. Immanuel Kant, *Conjectural Beginning of Human History*, in *Kant on History*, ed. L. W. Beck (Indianopolis: Bobbs-Merrill, 1977), 53ff.
18. Immanuel Kant, *Critique of Pure Reason*, trans. Norman Kemp Smith (London: MacMillan, 1953), 575, A709/B737; translation of *Kritik der reinen Vernunft*, first edition, 1781, second edition, 1787; the text will be cited as *CPR*, with page number and paragraph number of first and second editions, (A) and (B).
19. Immanuel Kant, *Idea for a Universal History from a Cosmopolitan Point of View*, in *Kant on History*, ed. L. W. Beck, 21; cf. *KE* 21: "We live in an age of discipline, culture, and refinement, but we are still a long way off from the age of moral training".
20. See *KE* 26; cf. *Conjectural Beginning of Human History*, ed. L. W. Beck, 61, note 2.
21. See Immanuel Kant, *Observations on the Feeling of the Beautiful and the Sublime* (1764), trans. J. T. Goldthwait (Berkeley: University of California Press, 1965).
22. On this matter, see E. F. Buchner, *Educational Theory of Immanuel Kant*, 90.
23. R. Wellek, "Aesthetics and Criticism," in C. W. Hendel (ed.), *The Philosophy of Kant in our Modern World* (New York: Liberal Arts Press, 1957), 75.
24. *Idea for a Universal History*, 17. See also Immanuel Kant, *Anthropology from a Pragmatic Point of View*, trans. V. L. Dowdell (Carbondale: Southern Illinois University Press, 1978), 242: "Man must, therefore, be educated to the good. But he who is to educate him is again a human who still finds himself in the crudity of nature. This human, now, is expected to bring about what he himself

is in need of. This accounts for man's continuous deviation from his destiny and his ever repeated return to it."

25. The same sort of harmony is postulated in Kant's treatment of *perfection* as an essential end of mankind in the *Metaphysics of Morals;* the term *perfection* in this text is close to what Kant means by *culture* in the *Critique of Judgement*.

26. W. Frankena, *Three Historical Philosophies of Education: Aristotle, Kant, Dewey* (Glenview, Ill.: Scott, Foresman, 1965), 91.

27. For Locke's view, see *Some Thoughts Concerning Education*, § 58; self-interest as a proper motivation of moral behavior is to be found, for example, in the writings of Fontenelle, Mandeville, Voltaire, d'Holbach, and Bayle, and it is strongly criticized, as we have seen, by Rousseau.

28. *Conjectural Beginning of Human History*, 57.

29. *Idea for a Universal History*, 16, 17.

30. Cf. N. Rotenstreich, *Practice and Realization: Studies in Kant's Moral Philosophy* (The Hague: Nijhoff, 1979). Rotenstreich comments (118), that in the Kantian world, "human beings are involved in a basic contradiction between the possibility of coming to a moral standstill and the need to ensure an ongoing historical process."

31. The existence of a duty to foster the moral development of the young is presented most explicitly in the *Lectures on Ethics*, in "Duties Arising from Differences of Age," 247–51.

32. F. E. and F. P. Manuel, *Utopian Thought in the Western World* (Oxford: Blackwell, 1979), 4, 519.

Chapter 8. From Hobbes to Mill: The General Happiness

1. John Stuart Mill, *Utilitarianism*, in *Collected Works of John Stuart Mill*, vol. X, *Essays on Ethics, Religion and Society*, ed. by J. M. Robson (Toronto: University of Toronto Press, 1969), 210; all quotations of Mill are from this edition.

2. Jeremy Bentham, *An Introduction to the Principles of Morals and Legislation*, in *The Works of Jeremy Bentham*, ed. by John Bowring (New York: Russell & Russell), vol. 1, Chap. 1, § 4, 2; all quotations of Bentham are from this edition.

3. One of the best known early critics of Hobbes's account of motivation was Bishop Joseph Butler, in the first of his *Fifteen Sermons Preached at the Rolls Chapel*, "Upon Human Nature," published in London in 1726; quotations here are from Joseph Butler, *Five Sermons Preached at the Rolls Chapel*, ed. by Stuart M. Brown (New York: Bobbs-Merrill, 1950), 21–23, note; the relevant passage is discussed briefly later in this section.

4. Thomas Hobbes, *Leviathan, or the Matter, Form and Power of a Commonwealth, Ecclesiastical and Civil*, ed. Michael Oakeshott (Oxford: Basil Blackwell, edition undated). Chap. VI, 39; *Leviathan* was originally published in 1651; reference will be by chapter and page number to this edition.

5. Thomas Hobbes, *The Elements of Law Natural and Politic*, ed. F. Tönnies (London: Simpkin & Marshall, 1899), I, ix, 21; written in 1640 and first published, without Hobbes's consent, in two parts in 1650.

6. Joseph Butler, *Sermons*, 21–23, note.

7. Butler refers to Hobbes, *Of Human Nature*, Chap. 9, section 17; this work is the first part of *The Elements of Law Natural and Politic*.

8. This is argued strongly by Bernard Gert in his introduction to Thomas Hobbes, *Man and Citizen* (Atlantic Highlands, N.J.: Humanities Press, 1978), 3ff; this work contains a recent translation of Thomas Hobbes, *De Homine*, Chaps. 10–15, and Hobbes's own translation of his work, *De Cive*. Tom Sorell, *Hobbes* (London: Routledge & Kegan Paul, 1986), also argues that Hobbes did not

espouse psychological egoism in his writings — see Chap. 8; others have argued that there is a thesis of egoism in some of Hobbes's writings, but not in *Leviathan*: see F. S. McNeilly, *The Anatomy of Leviathan* (London: Macmillan, 1968); also D. D. Raphael, *Hobbes: Morals and Politics* (London: Allen and Unwin, 1977).

9. See Hobbes, *On Man*, in Bernard Gert, *Man and Citizen*, XI, 6, 48 (translation of Hobbes, *De Homine*, Chaps. X–XV, by C. T. Wood, T. S. K. Scott-Craig, and B. Gert); *De Homine* was originally published in 1658; reference will be made to the Gert edition, with page number.

10. Hobbes, *De Cive*, in B. Gert, *Man and Citizen*, I, section 2 and note, 110ff. *De Cive* was originally published in 1642. In 1651, Hobbes published a translation under the title *Philosophical Rudiments Concerning Government and Society*; the translation is regularly referred to by the Latin title, *De Cive*. The work will be cited as *De Cive*, with page number in the Gert edition.

11. Hobbes is also critical in *De Cive*, and again in *Leviathan* XVII, of the Greek idea of human beings as *political animals*. The argument in *Leviathan* in particular assumes that human beings could be naturally sociable only if human societies developed naturally in the manner of colonies of bees or ants, in the absence of any features involving art or convention. In misinterpreting the Greek idea here (and Aristotle in particular), Hobbes sets an excessively limiting condition on the notion of natural sociability.

12. For accounts of the laws of nature in Hobbes, see *Leviathan*, XIV and XV; *De Cive*, Chaps. II, III, and IV; and *On Man*, Chap. XIII.

13. This passage shows that Hobbes distinguished clearly between behavior which is purely self-interested and behavior which arises from the love of virtue; the just person, for example, "scorns to be beholden for the contentment of his life, to fraud, or breach of promise" *Lev.* XV, 97. In a related consideration, Hobbes's view is that, while the civil law requires that a person do what the law requires, it is not its concern whether the person acts out of fear or from love of justice; the laws of nature, however, oblige *in foro interno*, that is, "they bind to a desire they should take place" (*Lev.* XV, 103).

14. See B. Gert (ed.), *Man and Citizen*, Introduction, 15f.

15. Alasdair MacIntyre, *After Virtue*, 160–61.

16. Alasdair MacIntyre, *A Short History of Ethics* (London: Routledge and Kegan Paul, 1967), 167.

17. Francis Hutcheson, *An Essay on the Nature and Conduct of the Passions and Affections* (New York: Garland Publishing, 1971), 208; first published, London, 1728. I will refer to the work in citations as *Essay*. Reference will also be made to Francis Hutcheson, *An Inquiry concerning the Original of our Ideas of Virtue or Moral Good*, 1725; quotations are taken from the selection of this work, reprinted from the second edition of 1726, in L. A. Selby-Bigge (ed.), *British Moralists*, 2 vols. (New York: Dover Publications, 1965), vol. 1; the work will be referred to in citations as *Inquiry*.

18. Bernard de Mandeville, *The Fable of the Bees*, abridged edition (Harmondsworth: Penguin Books, 1970). The text, originally published in 1714, included Mandeville's poem of 1705, *The Grumbling Hive*, with commentary and argument.

19. In his essay, *An Enquiry into the Origins of Moral Virtue*, first published in the second edition of *The Fable of the Bees* in 1723, de Mandeville tells a story according to which "the first rudiments of morality, broached by skilful politicians, to render men useful to each other as well as tractable, were chiefly contrived, that the ambitious might reap the more benefit from, and govern vast numbers with the greatest and security"; in L. A. Selby-Bigge, *British*

Moralists, vol. 2, 351. Variations on this theme were to become common in the eighteenth century.

20. Joseph Butler, *Sermons*, Sermon XI, 64 (and see Sermon XII, 77).
21. William Paley, *The Principles of Moral and Political Philosophy*, in L. A. Selby-Bigge, *British Moralists*, vol. 2, 357.
22. Hume's main ethical writings are *A Treatise of Human Nature*, Book II, "Of the Passions," and Book III, "Of Morals" (London, 1739), edited by L. A. Selby-Bigge (Oxford: Clarendon Press, 1967); and *An Enquiry Concerning the Principle of Morals* (London, 1751), edited by L. A. Selby-Bigge (Oxford: Clarendon Press, 1902), reprinted from the edition of 1777. For a useful collection of Hume's ethical writings, see Alasdair MacIntyre (ed.), *Hume's Ethical Writings* (New York: Collier Books, 1965). Quotations here are from the Selby-Bigge editions, with the abbreviations *Tr.* (with book, part, section, and page number) and *EPM* (with section, part, and page number). Among studies of Hume's ethical thought, note in particular J. L. Mackie, *Hume's Moral Theory* (London: Routledge & Kegan Paul, 1980).
23. Adam Smith, *The Theory of Moral Sentiments* (New Rochelle, N.Y.: Arlington House, 1969); originally published in 1759; reference will be made to the work in citations by the abbreviation *TMS* (with the part, section, chapter, and page number).
24. On this matter, see T. D. Campbell, *Adam Smith's Science of Morals* (London: Allen & Unwin, 1971). Campbell notes (153), that most critics consider that this claim destroys the whole basis of Smith's theory since it appears that he treats conscience as an ability to know what is right and wrong "independently of the empirically determinable judgments of the impartial spectator." Campbell argues, reasonably I think, that the desire to be worthy of love can be linked with the attitudes of actual spectators and does not have to be seen as "some rational, innate or non-sensory awareness of good and evil." But the sense in which the desire is "original" remains problematic.
25. May one assume that, in the case of women, Smith would say that reason, principle, conscience, the inhabitant of the breast is "the *woman* within"? The answer is not obvious.
26. Given that induction is an operation of reason, Smith holds that, "reason is undoubtedly the source of the general rules of morality" (*TMS*, VII, iii, 2, 470); what he insists on is that the first perceptions and subsequent experiences (to which reason is applied) are matters of immediate sense and feeling. At this point, Smith's account is unsatisfactorily confined to an (idealized) level of individual psychology; he would need to take up the place of communal relationships again, this time in the context of the development of general moral rules. On this, see J. L. Mackie, *Hume's Moral Theory*, 132.
27. On this topic, see Norbert Waszek, "Two Concepts of Morality: A Distinction of Adam Smith's Ethics and its Stoic Origin," *Journal of the History of Ideas*, XLV (1984) 591ff; see also T. D. Campbell, *Adam Smith's Science of Morals*, on the topic "Morality and Social Class," 174ff.
28. T. D. Campbell, *Adam Smith's Science of Morals*, 205, argues that while Smith rejected utility "as the explanation for the ordinary person's moral and political attitudes, his own normative moral and political philosophy turns out to be, in the end, a form of utilitarianism." In following their moral sentiments, human beings "play their part in a system which is conducive to the happiness of mankind"; hence the justification of the sentiments lies in their contribution to general happiness. If this interpretation is correct, Smith's account sets up a gap between theory and practice which is characteristic of Utilitarianism (see below).

29. Adam Smith, *An Inquiry into the Nature and Causes of the Wealth of Nations* (1776), 2 vols., ed. by E. Cannan (London: Methuen, 1961); V, i, art. 3, vol. I, 315.

30. Ibid., IV, ii, vol. I, 477f; on Smith's use of the metaphor of the "invisible hand" here and in *TMS*, see T. D. Campbell, *Adam Smith's Science of Morals*, 60ff.

31. For a comparison with Kant's views on this topic, see the discussion of "pragmatic education" in chapter seven above.

32. Jeremy Bentham, *A Fragment on Government* (1776), Chap. 1, § 36, in *The Works of Jeremy Bentham*, vol. I, 268, note. For a discussion of Hume's (limited) Utilitarianism, see J. L. Mackie, *Hume's Moral Theory*, 151ff.

33. In *The Works of Jeremy Bentham*, vol. 10, 142; Francis Hutcheson, as we have seen, used a similar phrase in his *Inquiry concerning the Original of our Ideas of Virtue or Moral Good*, as early as 1725. In his memoirs, in fact, Bentham traces the great turning point in his life back to the reading of Fenelon's *Telemachus*: "That romance may be regarded as the foundation-stone of my whole character; the starting-point from whence my career of life commenced. The first dawning of the principle of utility may, I think, be traced to it" (*Works*, vol. 10, 10).

34. *An Introduction to the Principles of Morals and Legislation* (1789), Chap. 1, § 4, in *The Works of Jeremy Bentham*, vol. 1, 2; this text will be referred to as *Princ.* (with chapter, section and page reference).

35. *Panopticon; or The Inspection House*, in *The Works of Jeremy Bentham*, vol. 4, 66; for Bentham's summary of the idea, see Letter V, "Essential Points of the Plan," 45f.; and for a critical discussion, see Michel Foucault, *Discipline and Punish, The Birth of the Prison*, trans. Alan Sheridan (New York: Pantheon Books, 1977), Chap. 3, "Panopticism," 195ff.

36. Joseph Butler, *Sermons*, Sermon XII, 79, note.

37. Stuart Hampshire, in his essay, "Morality and Pessimism," in S. Hampshire, *Public and Private Morality* (Cambridge: Cambridge University Press, 1982), presses a version of Butler's argument — that there are types of actions which are base and detestable in themselves — against contemporary Utilitarianism; he refers to the following sorts of cases: "In addition to certain fairly specific types of killing, certain fairly specific types of sexual promiscuity, certain takings of property, there are also types of disloyalty and of cowardice, particularly disloyalty to friends, which are very generally, almost universally, forbidden and forbidden absolutely: they are forbidden as being intrinsically disgraceful and unworthy, and as being, just for these reasons, ruled out: ruled out because they would be disgusting, or disgraceful, or shameful, or brutal, or inhuman, or base, or an outrage"(9).

38. *Plan of Parliamentary Reform*, in *Works*, vol. 3, 459.

39. John Stuart Mill, *Collected Works*, vol. X (Toronto: University of Toronto Press, 1969), Chap. V, 257; all quotations are from this edition.

40. Henry Sidgwick, *The Methods of Ethics* (1874), 7th. edition, 1907 (London: Macmillan, 1967), 382.

41. Bernard Williams, *Ethics and the Limits of Philosophy* (Glasgow: Collins, 1985), 105.

42. For a recent discussion, see Benjamin Gibbs, "Higher and Lower Pleasures," *Philosophy*, 61 (1986), 31ff.

43. *Rationale of Reward*, in *Works*, vol. 2, 253; Bentham added: "If the game of push-pin furnish more pleasure, it is more valuable than either. Everybody can play at push-pin: poetry and music are relished only by a few." Apart from the character of Bentham's argument, one might be inclined to question the factual claim inasmuch as poetry and music are of immense significance for almost all peoples and play a basic part in the lives of children. Mill makes a point of this

sort (while remarking that Bentham himself loved music); he cites this passage somewhat freely in his essay on Bentham as, "quantity of pleasure being equal, pushpin is as good as poetry"; *Collected Works*, vol. X, 113.

44. See B. Gibbs, "Higher and Lower Pleasures."

45. Mary Warnock, "On Moore's Criticism of Mill's Proof," in J. B. Schneewind (ed.), *Mill, A Collection of Critical Essays* (New York: Doubleday, 1968), 199–203, 200.

46. *Collected Works*, vol. XVI, Letter to Henry Jones, 1868, 1414.

47. Mill's most critical remarks concerning the idea of an innate moral sense are in his essay on some views of Adam Sedgwick, *Sedgwick's Discourse* (1835), *Collected Works*, vol. X, 33ff. In response to Sedgwick's claim that "moral feelings are often strongest in very early life," Mill comments that if he means "that they are strongest in children, he only proves his ignorance of children. Young children have affections but not moral feelings; and children whose will is never resisted, never acquire them. There is no selfishness equal to that of children, as every one who is acquainted with children well knows. . . . If a child restrains the indulgence of any wish, it is either from affection or sympathy, which are quite other feelings than those of morality; or else (whatever Mr Sedgwick may think) because he has been taught to do so. And he only learns the habit gradually, and in proportion to the assiduity and skill of the teaching" (60f).

48. Bernard Williams, *Ethics and the Limits of Philosophy*, 106; the main relevant discussion in Sidgwick is in *The Methods of Ethics*, Bk. IV, Chaps. 3 and 5. My discussion here draws heavily on Williams's argument; my contribution is to apply it more specifically to the developmental context.

49. Bernard Williams, *Ethics*, 215, note 12; with reference to these forms of Utilitarianism, Williams asks: "Is there anywhere in the mind or in society that a theory of this kind can be coherently or acceptably located?" (107–08). The topic is also discussed in Bernard Williams, "Utilitarianism and Moral Self-Indulgence," in H. D. Lewis (ed.), *Contemporary British Philosophy* (London: Allen & Unwin, 1976), 306ff; see 318f.

50. Bernard Williams, *Ethics*, 108; Henry Sidgwick, *Methods of Ethics*, 589, 490.

51. This problem remains pertinent to contemporary Utilitarianism. Many Utilitarians allow that those who would administer a society in terms of utility would need to be secretive about their practices. Others, especially indirect Utilitarians such as R. M. Hare, resist the idea of distinguishing between different groups within a society along such lines. Hare's proposal is for a distinction between two levels of moral thinking: practical moral thinking which draws on simple general principles for immediate use and which is inculcated in moral education and is ordinarily treated as binding; and a more leisurely, more critical, more theoretical moral thinking which is Utilitarian (up to an ideal degree) but is sensitive, on Utilitarian grounds, to the need for maintaining the ordinary level of moral thinking. The moral formation of children would proceed at the first level under the guidance of educators who are capable of second-level thinking to some degree; and the prospect is that each individual, and the society at large, will manifest both levels of thinking while approximating more and more to Utilitarian awareness. (Hare's distinction is set out in "Principles," *Proceedings of the Aristotelian Society*, 72 (1972–73) 1–18; also "Ethical Theory and Utilitarianism," in H. D. Lewis, *Contemporary British Philosophy*, 122ff.) This proposal, so far as children are concerned, does not escape the pedagogical problem. The problem for enlightened individuals would also appear to be acute, for the individual is required to have dispositional commitments to certain values in ordinary behavior ("principles which they will not be

able to break without the greatest repugnance, and whose breach by others will arouse in them the highest indignation"; see R. M. Hare, "Ethical Theory and Utilitarianism," 122). Yet the individual, in the cool hour of critical reflection, is to appraise these commitments in the very different instrumental framework of Utilitarian thought. For more general discussion of modern Utilitarianism, see J. J. C. Smart and Bernard Williams, *Utilitarianism: For and Against* (New York: Cambridge University Press, 1973); and A. Sen and B. Williams (eds.), *Utilitarianism and Beyond* (New York: Cambridge University Press, 1982).

Chapter 9. Hegel: The Ethical Community

1. The addresses were first published in the first edition of Hegel's *Samtliche Werke* (*Complete Works*), (1832–45), in volumes XVI and XVII; in the jubilee publication of this edition, they were relocated, with some related writings, in vol. 3: G. W. F. Hegel, *Samtliche Werke*, ed. H. Glockner (Stuttgart: Fromanns, 1927–30). For an English translation, see M. Mackenzie, *Hegel's Educational Theory and Practice* (London: Swan Sonneschein, 1909). References will be made to the addresses under the title *School Addresses*; translations are my own, made from the Glockner edition, with reference to a recent French translation, G. W. F. Hegel, *Textes Pédagogiques*, trans. Bernard Bourgeois (Paris: J. Vrin, 1977); page references in citation are to the Glockner edition.

2. G. W. F. Hegel, *The Philosophical Propaedeutic*, trans. by A. V. Miller, ed. M. George and A. Vincent (Oxford: Blackwell, 1986); originally published in vol. XVIII of the *Samtliche Werke* (1840) and relocated in vol. 3 of the Glockner edition.

3. Bernard Bourgeois, *La Pédagogie de Hegel*, in G. W. F. Hegel, *Textes Pédagogiques*, trans. B. Bourgeois (Paris: J. Vrin, 1978); 7–74; 8. This work contains a French translation from the Glockner edition of Hegel's Nuremburg addresses and some of his other writings on the teaching of philosophy in schools and universities.

4. Karl Löwith, *From Hegel to Nietzsche*, trans. D. E. Green (London: Constable, 1965), 290.

5. G. W. F. Hegel, *Phenomenology of Spirit*, trans. A. V. Miller (New York: Oxford University Press, 1977); first published in 1807. The abbreviation PG (*Phänomenologie des Geistes*) will be used in citations, with section and page numbers.

6. For discussion of this concept (in connection with Kant), see chap. seven, 2 above.

7. Jean Hyppolite, *Genèse et Structure de la Phénomenologie de l'esprit de Hegel* (Paris: Aubier, 1942), 16. Hyppolite draws attention to Hegel's remark in the introduction to PG, where he says of his work: "This exposition can be regarded as the path of the natural consciousness which presses forward to true knowledge; or as the way of the Soul which journeys through the series of its own configurations as though they were the stations appointed for it by its own nature, so that it may purify itself for the life of the Spirit, and achieve finally, through a completed experience of itself, the awareness of what it really is in itself" (PG 77, 49).

8. See *Hegel's Philosophy of Right*, trans. T. M. Knox (New York: Oxford University Press, 1967), Additions, para. 151, 260, and paras. 173ff., 117ff. The work was originally published in 1821; the translation, based on that edition, has an appendix which includes additional paragraphs (Additions) from notes taken at Hegel's lectures and published by Gans in Hegel's *Collected Works*, vol. viii

(Berlin, 1833). All quotations are from this translation; and the work is cited as *PR*, with paragraph and page numbers.

9. Hegel discusses these topics in the third address (1811), 264ff; the theme of the address is announced as *"the relation of the school and of school instruction to the ethical formation [Bildung] of human beings in general"* (265; emphasis in original).

10. J. G. Fichte, *Reden an die deutsche Nation* (*Addresses to the German Nation*), in Fichte's *Sammtliche Werke* (Berlin: Weit, 1845), vol. 3, 422.

11. For discussion of this theme, see B. Bourgeois, *La Pédagogie de Hegel*, 24ff.

12. Hans-Georg Gadamer, *Philosophical Hermeneutics*, trans. D. E. Linge (Berkeley: University of California Press, 1977), 113. The origin of Hegel's idea of objective spirit, as Gadamer suggests, is the concept of *pneuma* in the New Testament, the idea of the Holy Spirit as the spirit and source of unity in the community.

13. G. W. F. Hegel, *The Philosophy of Fine Art*, trans. F. P. B. Osmaston (London: G. Bell & Sons, 1920), 4 vols; references here are taken from *Hegel on Tragedy*, ed. by Anne and Henry Paolucci (Westport, Conn.: Greenwood Press, 1978), 68, 178, 133.

14. Ibid., 73, 71.

15. Martha C. Nussbaum, *The Fragility of Goodness*, 63ff, 67.

16. For background information and references, see Nussbaum, ibid., 55 and 437–38.

17. A. C. Bradley, "Hegel's Theory of Tragedy," Appendix in A. and H. Paolucci, *Hegel on Tragedy*, 381; originally published in A. C. Bradley, *Oxford Lectures on Poetry* (London: Macmillan, 1950), 69–95.

18. G. W. F. Hegel, *The Philosophy of History*, trans. J. Sibree (New York: Dover, 1956), 269–70.

19. *Hegel's Lectures on the History of Philosophy*, ed. and trans. E. S. Haldane (London: Routledge & Kegan Paul, 1955, reprinted), vol. I; references here are taken from A. and H. Paolucci, *Hegel on Tragedy*, 347ff, 354.

20. Ibid., 356, 357, 358.

21. Ibid., 364.

22. Hegel's major discussion of this much discussed theme is in *The Phenomenology of Spirit*, "Independence and Dependence of Self-Consciousness: Lordship and Bondage," sections 178ff. The topic of master and slave is an important theme in Aristotle, *Politics*, I, 4–7; and the moral ideal of self-sufficiency (of masters) in the *Nicomachean Ethics* is defined in relation to the status of the slave, *NE*, X, 6–7; on this, see Judith N. Shklar, *Freedom and Independence* (Cambridge: Cambridge University Press, 1976), 60f, 93–95. Hegel largely ignored the question of slavery in the ancient world, turning a blind eye in effect to the way in which the Greek *polis* and its ideal of civic freedom rested on this extreme form of exploitation.

23. *Hegel's Philosophy of Mind*, from *The Encyclopaedia of the Philosophical Sciences* (1830), trans. by William Wallace, with the *Zusätze* in Boumann's text (1845), trans. by A. V. Miller (Oxford: Clarendon Press, 1971), § 433, 173.

24. Ibid. §§ 436–37, 176–77.

25. For discussion of Hegel's critique of Kant's ethics, see W. H. Walsh, *Hegelian Ethics* (London: St. Martin's Press, 1969), 21–34; M. J. Petry, "Hegel's Criticism of the Ethics of Kant and Fichte," in L. S. Stepelevich and D. Lamb (eds.), *Hegel's Philosophy of Action* (Atlantic Highlands, N.J.: Humanities Press, 1983), 125–36.

26. Ernst Tugendhat, *Selbstbewusstsein und Selbstbestimmung* (Frankfurt: Suhrkampf, 1979), 349; translation quoted from L. Siep, "The 'Aufhebung' of Morality in Ethical Life," in L. S. Stepelevich and D. Lamb, *Hegel's Philosophy of Action*, 137.

27. For discussion, see Ludwig Siep, "The 'Aufhebung' of Morality in Ethical Life,"

137–56; and Charles Taylor, *Hegel* (Cambridge: Cambridge University Press, 1975), Chap. XIV, 365ff.
28. L. Siep, "The 'Aufhebung' of Morality in Ethical Life," 150. Siep's words carry an echo of F. H. Bradley's Hegelian account of the individual as "the specification or particularization of that which is common," in *Ethical Studies* (1876) (Oxford: Oxford University Press, 2nd. ed., 1962), 171. Richard Norman has suggested that "the best defence of a specifically Hegelian ethical theory remains one which is provided not by Hegel but by Bradley, in the early part of 'My Station and Its Duties'" (*Hegel's Phenomenology* [London: Sussex University Press, 1976], 84). The passage in Bradley to which Norman draws attention is as follows:

> The child . . . is born not into a desert but a living world, a whole which has a true individuality of its own. . . . He does not even think of his separate self; he grows with his world, his mind fills and orders itself; and when he can separate himself from that world, and knows himself apart from it, then by that time his self, the object of his self-consciousness, is penetrated, infected, characterized by the existence of others. Its content implies in every fibre relations of community. He learns, or already has learnt, to speak, and here he appropriates the common heritage of his race, the tongue that he makes his own is his country's language, . . . and it carries into his mind the ideas and sentiments of the race . . . and stamps them in indelibly. He grows up in in an atmosphere of example and general custom. . . . The soul within him is saturated, is filled, is qualified by, it has assimilated, has got its substance, has built itself up from, it *is* one and the same life with the universal life, and if he turns against this he turns against himself. (F. H. Bradley, *Ethical Studies*, 171–72)

Norman also discusses the Hegelian character of Bradley's ethics in "Hegelian Ethics: Self-Realization," in Richard Norman, *The Moral Philosophers*, 145–170.
29. On this topic, see Peter G. Stillman, "Person, Property, and Civil Society in the *Philosophy of Right*," in D. P. Verene (ed.), *Hegel's Social and Political Thought* (Atlantic Highlands, N.J.: Humanities Press, 1980), 103ff.
30. At the beginning of the section on religion in *The Philosophical Propaedeutic*, Hegel says that "the *Moral Law* within us is *The Eternal Law of Reason*" (52).
31. See G. S. Kirk, J. E. Raven, M. Schofield, *The Presocratic Philosophers* (Cambridge: Cambridge University Press, 1984), section 413, 319 (fragment 135 in H. Diels and W. Kranz, *Die Fragmente der Vorsokratiker* [Berlin: Weidmann, 1952]); the passage, in Aristotle's explanation, relates to a prohibition on the killing of living things.

Chapter 10. Moral and Developmental Themes in Review

1. John Dewey, *Ethics* (1908), in *The Middle Works, 1899–1924*, vol. 5: 1908, ed. Jo Ann Boydston (Carbondale and Edwardsville: Southern Illinois University Press, 1978), Part III, Chap. 20, 386, 388.
2. John Dewey, *Reconstruction in Philosophy* (1920) (Boston: Beacon Press, 1957), 194.
3. This topic is discussed in an illuminating way by G. J. Warnock, *The Object of Morality* (London: Methuen, 1971), 21ff. Versions of the problem, as I will note shortly, have had a long history in ethics.
4. Plato, *Protagoras*, trans. with notes by C. C. W. Taylor (Oxford: Clarendon Press, 1976), 319Aff. Among discussions of the topic (in addition to the notes in this edition), see W. K. C. Guthrie, *A History of Greek Philosophy*, III, 1969, 63ff; G. B. Kerferd, *The Sophistic Movement* (Cambridge: Cambridge University Press,

1981), Chaps. 11 and 12; Martha C. Nussbaum, *The Fragility of Goodness*, Chap. 4. I follow Guthrie (and many others) in assuming that the views put forward by Protagoras in the dialogue are substantially the views of the historical Protagoras; but nothing turns on this identification here.

5. J. L. Mackie, *Ethics, Inventing Right and Wrong* (Harmondsworth: Penguin Books, 1977), 108ff.

6. For argument on this matter see Martha C. Nussbaum, *The Fragility of Goodness*, 102ff; and W. K. C. Guthrie, *A History of Greek Philosophy*, III, 68.

7. W. K. C. Guthrie, *A History of Greek Philosophy*, III, 66.

8. Martha C. Nussbaum, *The Fragility of Goodness*, 104f.

9. Richard Wollheim, *The Thread of Life* (Cambridge, Mass.: Harvard University Press, 1984), 224.

10. D. W. Hamlyn, *Experience and the Growth of Understanding*, 86–87, 84.

11. Richard Wollhéim, *The Thread of Life*, 201, 211.

12. For discussion of this topic, see Peter Brown, *The Body and Society: Men, Women and Sexual Renunciation in Early Christianity* (New York: Columbia University Press, 1988).

13. Richard Wollheim, *The Thread of Life*, 218ff, 221.

14. Martha C. Nussbaum, "Shame, Separateness, and Political Unity: Aristotle's Criticism of Plato," in A. O. Rorty, *Essays on Aristotle's Ethics*, 395–435; 396. Nussbaum refers to Thucydides, *History of the Peloponnesian War*, 1.84.3 and 2.43.4; also 1.70.6–7, 2.37.2–3, 2.41.1 and 5.

15. In the Funeral Oration, Pericles speaks of freedom and tolerance in private life and deep respect for the law in public affairs as characteristic of Athens (Thucydides, *Peloponnesian War*, 2.37); and again, there is the claim that, "each single one of our citizens, in all the manifold aspects of life, is able to show himself the rightful Lord and owner of his own person" (ibid. 2.41).

16. L. Kohlberg, "From Is to Ought," 200.

Bibliography

Aeschylus. *The Oresteia*. Trans. by R. Fagles. Harmondsworth, U.K.: Penguin Books, 1987.

Alston, William P. "Self-Intervention and the Structure of Motivation." In *The Self, Psychological and Philosophical Issues*, edited by T. Mischel, 65–102. Oxford: Blackwell, 1977.

Aristotle. *The Complete Works of Aristotle, The Revised Oxford Translation*. Edited by Jonathan Barnes. 2 vols. Princeton: Princeton University Press, 1984.

Ariès, Philippe. *Centuries of Childhood: A Social History of Family Life*. Trans. R. Baldick. New York: Vintage Books, 1962.

Aron, Raymond. *Main Currents in Sociological Thought: Durkheim, Pareto, Weber*. Trans. R. Howard and H. Weaver. Harmondsworth, U.K.: Penguin Books, 1967.

Aronfreed, Justin. *Conduct and Conscience*. New York and London: Academic Press, 1968.

———. "The Concept of Internalization." In *Handbook of Socialization Theory and Research*, edited by D. Goslin, 263–323. Chicago: Rand-McNally, 1969.

———. "Some Problems for a Theory of the Acquisition of Conscience." In *Moral Education: Interdisciplinary Approaches*, edited by C. Beck et al., 183–99. Toronto: University of Toronto Press, 1971.

———. "Moral Development from the Standpoint of a General Psychological Theory." In *Moral Development and Behavior*, edited by Thomas Lickona, 54–69. New York: Holt, Rinehart and Winston, 1976.

Axtell, J. L., ed. *The Educational Writings of John Locke*. Cambridge: Cambridge University Press, 1968.

Baltes, P. B. and Schaie, K. W., eds. *Life-Span Developmental Psychology: Personality and Socialization*. New York: Academic Press, 1973.

Bandura, Albert. *Social Learning Theory*. Englewood Cliffs: Prentice-Hall, 1977.

Beck, C. M., Crittenden, B., Sullivan, E. V., eds. *Moral Education: Interdisciplinary Approaches*. Toronto: University of Toronto Press, 1971.

Beck, L. W. *Essays on Kant and Hume*. New Haven: Yale University Press, 1978.

Bentham, Jeremy. *The Works of Jeremy Bentham*, edited by John Bowring, 11 vols. New York: Russell and Russell, 1962:
A Fragment on Government (1776). Vol. 1.
An Introduction to the Principles of Morals and Legislation (1789). Vol. 1.
Panopticon; or the Inspection House. Vol. 4.

Blasi, Augusto. "Bridging Moral Cognition and Moral Action: A Critical Review of the Literature." *Psychological Bulletin* 88 (1980): 1–45.

Blatt, M. and Kohlberg, L. "The Effects of Classroom Moral Discussion upon Children's Level of Moral Judgment." *Journal of Moral Education* 4 (1975), 129–61.

Boardman, J., Griffin, J., Murray, O., eds. *The Oxford History of the Classical World*. Oxford: Oxford University Press, 1986.

Boden, M. *Piaget*. Brighton: Harvester Press, 1979.

Bourgeois, B. *La Pédagogie de Hegel*. In G. W. F. Hegel, *Textes Pédagogiques*, 7–74. Trans. by B. Bourgeois. Paris: J. Vrin, 1978.

Bracken, H. *Berkeley*. London: Macmillan, 1972.

Bradley, A. C. "Hegel's Theory of Tragedy." In *Oxford Lectures on Poetry*, 69–95. London: Macmillan, 1950.

Bradley, F. H. *Ethical Studies* (1876). 2nd. edition. Oxford: Oxford University Press, 1962.

Brown, Peter. *The Body and Society: Men, Women and Sexual Renunciation in Early Christianity*. New York: Columbia University Press, 1988.

Brown, R. *Social Psychology*. New York: Free Press, 1965.

Brown, S. M., ed. *Joseph Butler, Five Sermons Preached at the Rolls Chapel* (1726). New York: Bobbs-Merrill, 1950.

Brunner, O., Conze, W., Koselleck, R., eds. *Geschichtliche Grundbegriffe*. Stuttgart: Klett-Cotta, 1972.

Brunschvicg, L. *Le Progrès de la conscience dans la philosophie occidentale*. Paris: Presses Universitaires de France, 1927.

Buchner, E. *The Educational Theory of Immanuel Kant*. Philadelphia and London: J. B. Lippincott Co., 1908.

Burnet, J., ed. *Aristotle on Education*. Cambridge: Cambridge University Press, 1967.

Burnyeat, M. F. "Aristotle on Learning to be Good." In *Essays on Aristotle's Ethics*, edited by A. O. Rorty. Berkeley: University of California Press, 1980.

Butler, Joseph. *Fifteen Sermons Preached at the Rolls Chapel* (1726). In *The Works of Joseph Butler*, edited by W. E. Gladstone, 2 vols. Oxford, 1897.

Campbell, T. D. *Adam Smith's Science of Morals*. London: Allen & Unwin, 1971.

Cassirer, E. *The Question of Jean-Jacques Rousseau*. Trans. and edited by Peter Gay. New York: Columbia University Press, 1954.

Charvet, J. *The Social Problem in the Philosophy of Rousseau*. Cambridge: Cambridge University Press, 1974.

Chodorow, Nancy. *The Reproduction of Mothering: Psychoanalysis and the Sociology of Gender*. Berkeley: University of California Press, 1978.

Chomsky, Noam. *Reflections on Language*. Glasgow: Fontana, 1976.

Cochrane, D. B. et al., eds. *The Domain of Moral Education*. New York: Paulist Press, 1979.

Colby, A. and Kohlberg, L., eds. *The Measurement of Moral Judgment*. 2 vols. New York: Cambridge University Press, 1984.

Colman, John. *John Locke's Moral Philosophy*. Edinburgh: Edinburgh University Press, 1983.

Cooper, J. M. *Reason and Human Good in Aristotle*. Cambridge, Mass.: Harvard University Press, 1975.

Crittenden, Brian. *Parents, the State and the Right to Educate*. Melbourne: Melbourne University Press, 1988.

———. "Lawrence Kohlberg: Developmental Psychology and Moral Education." In *Perceptions of Excellence*, edited by J. V. D'Cruz and Wilma Hannah, 255–80. Melbourne: Polding Press, 1979.

———. "The Limitations of Morality as Justice in Kohlberg's Theory." In *The Domain of Moral Education*, edited by D. B. Cochrane et al., 251–66. New York: Paulist Press, 1979.

Crittenden, P. J. "Morality and the Moral Development of the Child." In *The Developing Child*, edited by G. Taylor, 109–52. Canberra: Australian Government Publishing Service, 1981.

———. "Thoughts about Locke's Thoughts about Education." *Journal of Philosophy of Education* 15 (1981): 149–60.

Deleuze, Gilles. *Nietzsche and Philosophy*. Trans. by H. Tomlinson. New York: Columbia University Press, 1983.

Derathé, R. *Le Rationalisme de J.-J. Rousseau*. Paris: Presses Universitaires de France, 1948.

Dewey, John. *Ethics* (1908). In *The Middle Works, 1899–1924*, vol. 5: 1908. Edited by Jo Ann Boydston. Carbondale and Edwardsville: Southern Illinois University Press, 1978.

———. *Democracy and Education*. New York: Macmillan, 1916.

———. *Reconstruction in Philosophy* (1920). Boston: Beacon Press, 1957.

Diels, H. and Kranz, W. *Die Fragmente der Vorsokratiker*. Berlin: Weidmann, 1952.

Dilman, I. *Freud and Human Nature*. Oxford: Blackwell, 1983.

Dodds, E. R. *The Concept of Progress*. Oxford: Oxford University Press, 1973.

Durkheim, E. *Moral Education* (1925). Trans. by E. K. Wilson and H. Schnurer. Glencoe, Ill.: Free Press, 1961.

———. *Sociology and Philosophy* (1924). Trans. by D. F. Pocock. Glencoe, Ill.: Free Press, 1953.

Edwards, C. P. "Social Experience and Moral Judgment in Kenyan Young Adults." *Journal of Genetic Psychology* 133 (1978): 19–29.

———. "Moral Development in Comparative Cultural Perspective." In *Cultural Perspectives on Child Development*, edited by D. A. Wagner and H. Stevenson, 248–79. San Francisco: W. H. Freeman, 1982.

———. "Cross-Cultural Research on Kohlberg's Stages: The Basis for Consensus." In *Lawrence Kohlberg, Consensus and Controversy*, edited by S. Modgil and C. Modgil, 431–50. Lewes, U.K.: Falmer Press, 1985.

Eisenberg, N. and Lennon, R. "Sex Differences in Empathy and Related Capacities." *Psychological Bulletin* 94 (1983): 100–31.

Elster, J. *Making Sense of Marx*. Cambridge: Cambridge University Press, 1985.

Emler, N. "Moral Character." In *Morality in the Making*, edited by H. Weinreich-Haste and D. Locke, 187–211. Chichester: John Wiley & Sons, 1983.

———. "Morality and Politics: The Ideological Dimension in the Theory of Moral Development." In *Morality in the Making*, edited by H. Weinreich-Haste and D. Locke, 47–71. Chichester: John Wiley & Sons, 1983.

Engberg-Pedersen, T. *Aristotle's Theory of Moral Insight*. Oxford: Clarendon Press, 1983.

Eysenck, H. J. *Crime and Personality*. London: Routledge and Kegan Paul, 1964.

———. *Fact and Fiction in Psychology*. Harmondsworth: Penguin Books, 1965.

———. "The Biology of Morality." In *Moral Development and Behavior*, edited by Thomas Lickona, 108–23. New York: Holt, Rinehart and Winston, 1976.

Fauconnet, P. *La Responsabilité, étude de sociologie*. Paris: Alcan, 1920.

Flanagan, O., Jr. "Virtue, Sex and, Gender: Some Philosophical Reflections on the Moral Psychology Debate." *Ethics* 92 (1982): 499–512.

Flavell, J. H. *The Developmental Psychology of Jean Piaget*. Princeton: Van Nostrand, 1963.

Fichte, J. G. *Reden an die deutsche Nation*. In J. G. Fichte, *Sammtliche Werke*, vol. 3. Berlin, 1845.

Fortenbaugh, W. W. *Aristotle on Emotion*. London: Duckworth, 1975.

Foucault, Michel. *Discipline and Punish, The Birth of the Prison*. Trans. by Alan Sheridan. New York: Pantheon Books, 1977.

Fox-Bourne, H. R. *The Life of John Locke*. London, 1876.

Fowler, J. W. *Stages of Faith: The Psychology of Human Development and the Quest for Meaning*. San Francisco: Harper and Row, 1981.

Frankena, W. *Three Historical Philosophies of Education: Aristotle, Kant, Dewey*. Glenview, Ill.: Scott, Foresman, 1965.

Frankfurt, H. "Freedom of the Will and the Concept of the Person." *Journal of Philosophy* LXVII (1971): 5–20.

Freud, Sigmund. *The Standard Edition of the Complete Works of Sigmund Freud.* 24 vols. Trans. and edited by James Strachey. London, Hogarth Press, 1948–74:
Three Essays on the Theory of Sexuality (1905). Vol. VII.
"Character and Anal Erotism" (1908). Vol. IX.
Analysis of a Phobia in a Five-year-Old Boy (1909). Vol. X.
Thoughts for the Times on War and Death (1915). Vol. XIV.
"On Transformations of Instinct as Exemplified in Anal Erotism" (1917). Vol. XVII.
"The Dissolution of the Oedipus Complex" (1924). Vol. XIX.
"Some Psychical Consequences of the Anatomical Distinction between the Sexes" (1925). Vol. XIX.
The Future of an Illusion (1927). Vol. XXI.
Civilization and Its Discontents (1930). Vol. XXI.
"Female Sexuality" (1931). Vol. XXI.
"Libidinal Types" (1931). Vol. XXI.
"The Dissection of the Psychical Personality" (1933), Vol. XXII.
"Anxiety and Instinctual Life" (1933). Vol. XXII.
"Femininity" (1933). Vol. XXII.
"The Question of a *Weltanschauung*" (1933). Vol. XXII.
Gadamer, H.-G. *Philosophical Hermeneutics.* Trans. by D. E. Linge. Berkeley: University of California Press, 1977.
Gibbs, Benjamin. "Higher and Lower Pleasures." *Philosophy* 61 (1986): 31–59.
Gibbs, J. C. "Kohlberg's Moral Stage Theory, A Piagetian Revision." *Human Development* 22 (1979): 89–112.
Gilligan, Carol. *In a Different Voice.* Cambridge, Mass.: Harvard University Press, 1982.
Goslin, D. A., ed. *Handbook of Socialization Theory and Research.* Chicago: Rand McNally, 1969.
Graham, D. *Moral Learning and Development.* Sydney: Angus & Robertson, 1972.
Guthrie, W. K. C. *A History of Greek Philosophy.* Cambridge: Cambridge University Press, 1969 (Vol. III), 1975 (Vol. IV).
Haan, N., Aerts, E., Cooper, B. A. B., eds. *On Moral Grounds, The Search for Practical Morality.* New York and London: New York University Press, 1985.
Haan, N., Bellah, R. W., Rabinow, P., Sullivan, W. M., eds. *Social Science as Moral Inquiry.* New York: Columbia University Press, 1983.
Habermas, J. *Communication and the Evolution of Society.* Trans. by T. McCarthy. Boston: Beacon Press, 1979.
———. "Interpretative Social Sciences vs. Hermeneuticism." In *Social Science as Moral Inquiry,* edited by N. Haan et al., 251–69. New York: Columbia University Press, 1983.
Hamlyn, D. W. *Experience and the Growth of Understanding.* London: Routledge and Kegan Paul, 1978.
———. "The Concept of Development." *Proceedings of the Philosophy of Education Society of Great Britain* IX (1975): 26–39.
Hampshire, S. *Public and Private Morality.* Cambridge: Cambridge University Press, 1982.
Hardie, W. F. R. *Aristotle's Ethical Theory.* 2nd. ed. Oxford: Oxford University Press, 1981.
Hare, R. M. *Freedom and Reason.* Oxford: Oxford University Press, 1962.
———. "Principles." *Proceedings of the Aristotelian Society* 72 (1972–73): 1–18.
———. "Ethical Theory and Utilitarianism." In *Contemporary British Philosophy,* edited by H. D. Lewis, 113–31. London: Allen & Unwin, 1976.
Hartshorne, H. and May, M. A. *Studies in the Nature of Character.* New York: Macmillan, 1928–30.

Havinghurst, R. J. and Taba, H. *Adolescent Character and Personality*. New York: Wiley, 1949.

Hegel, G. W. F. *Samtliche Werke*. Edited by H. Glockner. Stuttgart: Fromanns, 1927–30.

————. *Phenomenology of Spirit* (1807). Trans. by A. V. Miller. New York: Oxford University Press, 1977.

————. *Textes Pédagogiques*. Trans. by B. Bourgeois. Paris: J. Vrin, 1978.

————. *Hegel's Educational Theory and Practice*. Trans. by M. Mackenzie. London: Swan Sonneschein, 1909.

————. *The Philosophical Propaedeutic*. Trans. by A. V. Miller, edited by M. George and A. Vincent. Oxford: Blackwell, 1986.

————. *Philosophy of Right* (1821). Trans. by T. M. Knox. New York: Oxford University Press, 1967.

————. *Philosophy of Mind*, from *The Encyclopaedia of the Philosophical Sciences* (1830). Trans. by W. Wallace. With the *Zusätze* in Bouman's text (1845) trans. by A. V. Miller. Oxford: Clarendon Press, 1971.

————. *The Philosophy of History*. Trans. by J. Sibree. New York: Dover, 1956.

————. *Lectures on the History of Philosophy*. Trans. and edited by E. S. Haldane. London: Routledge and Kegan Paul, 1955.

————. *The Philosophy of Fine Art*. Trans. by F. P. B. Osmaston. London: G. Bell & Sons, 1920.

————. *Hegel on Tragedy*. Edited by Anne and Henry Paolucci. Westport, Conn.: Greenwood Press, 1978.

Hendel, C. W., ed. *The Philosophy of Kant in our Modern World*. New York: Liberal Arts Press, 1975.

Hobbes, Thomas. *Leviathan, or the Matter, Form and Power of a Commonwealth, Ecclesiastical and Civil* (1651). Edited by Michael Oakeshott. Oxford: Blackwell, undated.

————. *Man and Citizen*: Thomas Hobbes's *De Homine*, trans. by C. T. Woods, T. S. K. Scott-Craig, and B. Gert; and *De Cive*, trans. by Thomas Hobbes. Edited by Bernard Gert. Atlantic Highlands, N.J.: Humanities Press, 1978.

————. *The Elements of Law Natural and Politic*. Edited by F. Tönnies. London: Simpkin & Marshall, 1899.

Hoffman, M. L. "Childrearing Practices and Moral Development: Generalizations from Empirical Research." *Child Development* 34 (1963): 295–318.

————. "Moral Development." In *Carmichael's Manual of Psychology*, 3rd. ed., edited by P. H. Mussen, Vol. II, 261–359. New York: Wiley, 1970.

Hoffman, M. L. and Salzstein, H. D. "Parent Discipline and the Child's Moral Development." *Journal of Personal and Social Psychology* 5 (1967): 45–57.

Hume, David. *A Treatise of Human Nature* (1739). Edited by L. A. Selby-Bigge. Oxford: Clarendon Press, 1967.

————. *An Enquiry concerning the Principles of Morals* (1751). Edited by L. A. Selby-Bigge. Oxford: Clarendon Press, 1902.

Hutcheson, Francis. *An Essay on the Nature and Conduct of the Passions and Affections* (1725). New York: Garland Publishing, 1971.

————. *An Inquiry concerning the Original of our Ideas of Virtue or Moral Good* (1725). Included in part in *British Moralists*, vol. I, edited by L. A. Selby-Bigge. New York: Dover Publications, 1965.

Hyppolite, Jean. *Genèse et Structure de la Phénomenologie de l'Esprit de Hegel*. Paris: Aubier, 1942.

Kant, Immanuel. *Immanuel Kant über Pädagogik*. Edited by F. T. Rink. Königsberg, 1803. In *Kant's gesammelte Schriften*. Edited by the *Königlich Preussiche Akademie der Wissenschaften*, vol. IX. Berlin: Georg Reimer and W. de Gruyter, 1902—.

———. *Kant on Education*. Trans. by Annette Churton. London: 1899.

———. *Education*. Trans. by Annette Churton. Michigan: University of Michigan Press, 1960.

———. *Observations on the Feeling of the Beautiful and the Sublime* (1764). Trans. by J. T. Goldthwait. Berkeley: University of California Press, 1965.

———. *Lectures on Ethics*. Trans. by Louis Infield. New York and London: The Century Company, 1930.

———. *Critique of Pure Reason* (1781/1787). Trans. by Norman Kemp Smith. London: Macmillan, 1953.

———. *Foundations of the Metaphysics of Morals* (1785). Trans. by L. W. Beck. Indianapolis: Bobbs-Merrill, 1959.

———. *The Critique of Judgement* (1790). Trans. by J. C. Meredith. Oxford: Oxford University Press, 1952.

———. *The Doctrine of Virtue* (1797). Trans. by Mary J. Gregor. New York: Harper and Row, 1964.

———. *Anthropology from a Pragmatic Point of View*. trans. V. L. Dowdell. Carbondale; Southern Illinois Press, 1978.

———. *Conjectural Beginning of Human History*. In *Kant on History*. Trans. and edited by L. W. Beck. Indianapolis: Bobbs-Merrill, 1977.

———. *Idea for a Universal History from a Cosmopolitan Point of View*. In *Kant on History*. Trans. and edited by L. W. Beck. Indianapolis: Bobbs-Merrill, 1977.

Keane, J., ed. *Civil Society and the State: New European Perspectives*. London and New York: Verso, 1988.

Kelly, C. *Rousseau's Exemplary Life*. Ithaca and London: Cornell University Press, 1987.

Kerferd, G. B. *The Sophistic Movement*. Cambridge: Cambridge University Press, 1981.

Kirk, G. S., Raven, J. E., Schofield, M., *The Presocratic Philosophers*. Cambridge: Cambridge University Press, 1984.

Kohlberg, Lawrence. *Essays on Moral Development*. Vol. I: *The Philosophy of Moral Development*. San Francisco: Harper & Row, 1981.

———. *Essays on Moral Development*. Vol. II. San Francisco: Harper and Row, 1984.

———. "Stage and Sequence: The Cognitive-Developmental Approach to Socialization." In *Handbook of Socialization Theory and Research*, edited by D. A. Goslin, 347–480. Chicago: Rand McNally, 1969.

———. "From Is to Ought: How to Commit the Naturalistic Fallacy and Get Away with It." In *Cognitive Development and Epistemology*, edited by T. Mischel, 151–235. New York: Academic Press, 1971.

———. "Stages of Moral Development as a Basis for Moral Education." In *Moral Education: Interdisciplinary Approaches*, edited by C. Beck et al., 29–92. Toronto: University of Toronto Press, 1971.

———. "Continuities in Childhood and Adult Moral Development Revisited." In *Life-Span Developmental Psychology: Personality and Socialization*, edited by P. B. Baltes and K. W. Schaie. New York: Academic Press, 1973.

———. "Moral Stages and Moralization." In *Moral Development and Behavior*, edited by Thomas Lickona, 31–53. New York: Holt, Rinehart, and Winston, 1976.

———. "High School Democracy and Educating for a Just Society." In *Moral Education*, edited by R. L. Mosher, 20–57. New York: Praeger, 1980.

———. "Indoctrination Versus Relativity in Value Education." In *Essays on Moral Development*, I, 6–28.

———. "Education for Justice: A Modern Statement of the Socratic View." In *Essays on Moral Development*, I, 29–48.

———. "Justice as Reversibility: The Claim to Moral Adequacy of a Highest Stage of Moral Judgment." In *Essays on Moral Development*, I, 190–226.

———. "The Future of Liberalism as the Dominant Ideology of the Western World." In *Essays on Moral Development*, I, 231–42.

———. "Moral Development and the Theory of Tragedy." In *Essays on Moral Development*, I, 373–99.

———. "The Young Child as a Philosopher." In *Essays on Moral Development*, II, Chap. 13.

———. "A Current Statement on Some Theoretical Issues." In *Lawrence Kohlberg, Consensus and Controversy*, edited by S. Modgil and C. Modgil, 485–546. Lewes, U.K.: Falmer Press, 1985.

Kohlberg, L., Levine, C., Hewer, A. *Moral Stages: The Current Formulation of Kohlberg's Theory and a Response to Critics*. Basel: S. Karger, 1983.

Kohlberg, L. and Kramer, R. "Continuities and Discontinuities in Children and Adult Moral Development. *Human Development* 12 (1969): 93–120.

Kohlberg, L. and Gilligan, C. "The Adolescent as Philosopher: The Discovery of the Self in a Postconventional World." In *Basic and Contemporary Issues in Developmental Psychology*, edited by P. H. Mussen, J. J. Conger, and J. Kagan, 18–33. New York: Harper & Row, 1974.

Kohlberg, L. and Candee, D. "The Relation of Moral Judgment to Moral Action." In *Morality, Moral Behavior and Moral Development: Basic Issues in Theory and Research*, edited by W. Kurtines and J. L. Gewirtz. New York: Wiley, 1984.

Kohlberg, L. with Mayer, R. "Development as the Aim of Education: The Dewey View." In *Essays on Moral Development*, I, 49–96. San Francisco: Harper & Row, 1981.

Kohlberg, L., with Elfenbein, D. "Capital Punishment, Moral Development, and the Constitution." In *Essays on Moral Development*, I, 243–93.

Kohlberg, L. with Power, C. " Moral Development, Religious Thinking, and the Question of a Seventh Stage." In *Essays on Moral Development*, I, 311–72.

Kohlberg, L. with Shulik, R. "The Aging Person as Philosopher." In *Essays on Moral Development*, II, Chap. 15.

Krebs, D. "Psychological Approaches to Altruism; An Evaluation." *Ethics* 92 (1982): 447–58.

Kurtines, W. and Gewirtz, J. L., eds. *Morality, Moral Behavior and Moral Development: Basic Issues in Theory and Research*. New York: Wiley, 1984.

Kutnick, P. "The Relationship of Moral Judgment and Moral Action: Kohlberg's Theory, Criticism and Revision." In *Lawrence Kohlberg, Consensus and Controversy*, edited by S. Modgil and C. Modgil, 125–48. Lewes, U.K.: Falmer Press, 1985.

Laslett, P. *The World We Have Lost — Further Explored*. 3rd. ed. London: Methuen, 1983.

Levine, C., Kohlberg, L., Hewer, A. "The Current Formulation of Kohlberg's Theory and a Response to Critics." *Human Development* 28 (1985): 94–100.

Levi, Anthony. *French Moralists*. Oxford: Oxford University Press, 1964.

Lewis, H. D., ed. *Contemporary British Philosophy*. London: Allen & Unwin, 1976.

Lickona, Thomas, ed. *Moral Development and Behavior*. New York: Holt, Rinehart, and Winston, 1976.

———. "Research on Piaget's Theory of Moral Development." In *Moral Development and Behavior*, edited by Thomas Lickona, 219–40. New York: Holt, Rinehart, and Winston, 1976.

Lloyd, Genevieve. *The Man of Reason*. London: Methuen, 1984.

———. "Rousseau on Reason, Nature and Women." *Meta-Philosophy* 14 (1983): 308–26.

Lloyd, G. E. R. *Science, Folklore and Ideology: Studies in the Life-Sciences in Ancient Greece*. New York: Cambridge University Press, 1983.

Locke, Don. "Cognitive Stages or Developmental Phases? A Critique of the Stage-Structural Theory of Moral Reasoning." *Journal of Moral Education* 9 (1980): 103–09.

——. "The Principle of Equal Interests." *Philosophical Review* 90 (1981): 531–59.

——. "A Psychologist among the Philosophers: Philosophical Aspects of Kohlberg's Theories." In *Lawrence Kohlberg, Consensus and Controversy*, edited by S. Modgil and C. Modgil, 21–38. Lewes, U.K.; Falmer Press, 1985.

Locke, John. *An Essay Concerning Human Understanding* (1690). Critical edition by P. H. Nidditch. Oxford: Clarendon Press, 1975.

——. *Two Treatises of Government* (1690). Critical edition by Peter Laslett. Cambridge: Cambridge University Press, 1963.

——. *Some Thoughts Concerning Education* (1693). In *The Educational Writings of John Locke*, edited by J. L. Axtell. Cambridge: Cambridge University Press, 1968.

——. *The Reasonableness of Christianity as Delivered in the Scriptures* (1695). Edited and abridged by I. T. Ramsey. London: A. and C. Black, 1958.

Loevinger, Jane, and Wessler, Ruth. *Measuring Ego Development*. San Francisco: Jossey-Bass, 1970.

Lord, C. *Education and Culture in the Political Thought of Aristotle*. Ithaca: Cornell University Press, 1982.

Lorenz, Karl. *On Aggression*. Trans. by M. K. Wilson. London: Methuen, 1963.

Löwith, Karl. *From Hegel to Nietzsche*. Trans. by D. E. Green. London: Constable, 1965.

Lukes, S. *Marxism and Morality*. Oxford: Oxford University Press, 1984.

Lycos, K. "Hecuba's Newly-Learned Melody: Nussbaum on Philosophy Learning from Euripides." *Critical Philosophy* 4 (1988): 161–80.

MacIntyre, Alasdair. *After Virtue, A Study in Moral Theory*. Notre Dame: University of Notre Dame Press, 1981.

McCarthy, Thomas. *The Critical Theory of Jürgen Habermas*. Cambridge: Polity Press, 1984.

McNeilly, F. S. *The Anatomy of Leviathan*. London: Macmillan, 1968.

Mackie, J. L. *Ethics, Inventing Right and Wrong*. Harmondsworth, U.K.: Penguin Books, 1977.

——. *Hume's Moral Theory*. London: Routledge and Kegan Paul, 1980.

Malinowski, B. *Sex and Repression in Savage Society*. New York: Meridian Books, 1955.

Mandeville, B. de. *The Fable of the Bees* (1714). Abridged edition. Harmondsworth, U.K.: Penguin Books, 1970.

——. *An Enquiry into the Origins of Moral Virtue*. In *British Moralists*, edited by L. A. Selby-Bigge, vol. 2. New York: Dover Publications, 1965.

Manuel, Frank E. and Manuel, Fritzie P. *Utopian Thought in the Western World*. Oxford: Blackwell, 1979.

Marx, Karl. *Collected Works*. Moscow: Progress Publishers, 1975—.

Masters, R. D. *The Political Philosophy of Rousseau*. Princeton: Princeton University Press, 1968.

Mays, Wolfe. "Piaget's Sociological Theory." In *Jean Piaget, Consensus and Controversy*, edited by S. Modgil and C. Modgil, 31–50. New York: Praeger, 1982.

Maze, J. R. *The Meaning of Behavior*. London: Allen & Unwin, 1982.

Midgley, Mary. *Beast and Man*. London: Methuen, 1979.

Mill, John Stuart. *Utilitarianism*. In *Collected Works of John Stuart Mill*, vol. X. Edited by J. M. Robson, Toronto: University of Toronto Press, 1969.

Miller, R. W. "Ways of Moral Learning." *Philosophical Review* XCIV (1985): 507–56.

Mischel, T., ed. *Cognitive Development and Epistemology.* New York: Academic Press, 1971.

———, ed. *The Self, Psychological and Philosophical Issues.* Oxford: Blackwell, 1977.

Mischel, W. and Mischel, H. N. "A Cognitive Social Learning Approach to Morality and Self-Regulation." In *Moral Development and Behavior,* edited by Thomas Lickona, 84–107. New York: Holt, Rinehart, and Winston, 1976.

Mischel, W. and Mischel, H. N. "Self-Control and the Self." In *The Self, Psychological and Philosophical Issues,* edited by T. Mischel, 31–64. Oxford: Blackwell, 1977.

Modgil, S. and Modgil, C. *Cognitive-Developmental Approach to Morality. Piagetian Research,* vol. 6. Windsor: NFER, 1976.

Modgil, S. and Modgil, C., eds. *Towards a Theory of Psychological Development.* Windsor: NFER, 1980.

Modgil, S. and Modgil, C., eds. *Jean Piaget, Consensus and Controversy.* New York: Praeger, 1982.

Modgil, S. and Modgil, C., eds. *Lawrence Kohlberg, Consensus and Controversy.* Lewes, U.K.: Falmer Press, 1985.

Mosher, R. L., ed. *Moral Education.* New York: Praeger, 1980.

Murphy, J. M., and Gilligan, C. "Moral Development in Late Adolescence and Adulthood: A Critique and Reconstruction of Kohlberg's Theory." *Human Development* 23 (1980): 77–104.

Murray, O. "Life and Society in Classical Greece." In *The Oxford History of the Classical World,* edited by J. Boardman et al., 204–33. Oxford and New York: Oxford University Press, 1986.

Mussen, P. H., ed. *Carmichael's Manual of Psychology.* 3rd. edition. New York: Wiley, 1970.

Mussen, P. H., Conger, J. J., Kagan, J., eds. *Basic and Contemporary Issues in Developmental Psychology.* New York: Harper & Row, 1974.

Nehamas, Alexander. *Nietzsche, Life as Literature.* Cambridge, Mass.: Harvard University Press, 1985.

Nietzsche, Friedrich. *Daybreak* (1882). Trans. by R. J. Hollingdale. Cambridge: Cambridge University Press, 1982.

———. *Thus Spoke Zarathustra* (1885). Trans. by R. J. Hollingdale. Harmondsworth, U.K.: Penguin Books, 1961.

———. *Beyond Good and Evil* (1886). Trans. by R. J. Hollingdale. Harmondsworth, U.K.: Penguin Books, 1973.

———. *On the Genealogy of Morals* (1887) (with *Ecce Homo*). Trans. by W. Kaufmann and R. J. Hollingdale. New York: Vintage Books, 1969.

———. *The Gay Science* (2nd. edition, 1887). Trans. by W. Kaufmann. New York: Vintage Books, 1974.

———. *The Anti-Christ* (1889). Trans. by R. J. Hollingdale. Harmondsworth, U.K.: Penguin Books, 1968.

———. *The Will to Power* (1901). Trans. by W. Kaufmann and R. J. Hollingdale. New York: Vintage Books, 1968.

Nisan, M., and Kohlberg, L. "Universality and Variation in Moral Judgment: A Longitudinal and Cross-Sectional Study in Turkey." *Child Development* 53 (1982): 865–76.

Norman, Richard. *Hegel's Phenomenology, A Philosophical Introduction.* London: Sussex University Press, 1976.

———. *The Moral Philosophers.* Oxford: Oxford University Press, 1983.

Nussbaum, Martha C. *The Fragility of Goodness, Luck and Ethics in Greek Tragedy and Philosophy.* Cambridge: Cambridge University Press, 1986.

————. "Shame, Separateness, and Political Unity: Aristotle's Criticism of Plato." In *Essays on Aristotle's Ethics*, edited by A. O. Rorty, 395–435. Berkeley: University of California Press, 1980.

Packer, M., et al. "Moral Action of Four-Year-Olds." In *On Moral Grounds, The Search for Practical Morality*, edited by N. Haan et al., 276–305. New York and London: New York University Press, 1985.

Paley, William. *The Principles of Moral and Political Philosophy*. In *British Moralists*, edited by L. A. Selby-Bigge, vol. 2. New York: Dover Publications, 1965.

Paolucci, A. and H., eds. *Hegel on Tragedy*. Westport, Conn.: Greenwood Press, 1978.

Parikh, B. "Development of Moral Judgment and Its Relation to Family Environmental Factors in Indian and American Families." *Child Development* 51 (1980): 103–09.

Passmore, John. *The Perfectibility of Man*. London: Duckworth, 1970.

————. "The Malleability of Man in Eighteenth-Century Thought." in *Aspects of the Eighteenth Century*, edited by E. R. Wasserman, 21–46. Baltimore: Johns Hopkins Press, 1965.

Pateman, Carole. *The Sexual Contract*. Cambridge: Polity Press, 1988.

————. "The Fraternal Social Contract." In *Civil Society and the State: New European Perspectives*, edited by J. Keane. London and New York: Verso, 1988.

Peck, R. H. and Havinghurst, R. J. *The Psychology of Character Development*. New York: Wiley, 1960.

Perry, W. F. *Forms of Intellectual and Ethical Development in the College Years*. New York: Holt, Rinehart, and Winston, 1968.

Peters, R. S. *Psychology and Ethical Development*. London: Allen & Unwin, 1974.

————. "Moral Principles and Moral Education." In *The Domain of Moral Education*, edited by D. B. Cochrane, 120–34. New York: Paulist Press, 1979.

Petry, M. J. "Hegel's Criticism of the Ethics of Kant and Fichte." In *Hegel's Philosophy of Action*, edited by L. S. Stepelevich and D. Lamb, 125–36. Atlantic Highlands, N. J.: Humanities Press, 1983.

Piaget, Jean. *The Moral Judgment of the Child* (1932). Trans. by Marjorie Gabain. New York: The Free Press, 1965.

————. *Études Sociologiques*. 2nd. edition. Geneva: Droz, 1967.

————. *Structuralism* (1968). Trans. by C. Maschler. London: Routledge and Kegan Paul, 1971.

————. *Six Psychological Studies*. Trans. by Anita Tenzer. Brighton: Harvester Press, 1968.

————. "The General Problem of the Psychological Development of the Child." In *Discussions on Child Development*, vol. IV, edited by J. M. Tanner and B. Inhelder, 3–27. New York: International Universities Press, 1960.

————. "Piaget's Theory." In *Carmichael's Manual of Child Psychology*, edited by P. H. Mussen, vol. I, 703–32. New York: Wiley, 1970.

Plato. *The Dialogues of Plato*. 5 vols. Trans. by B. Jowett. 3rd. edition. Oxford: Clarendon Press, 1892.

————. *Protagoras*. Trans. by C. C. W. Taylor. Oxford: Clarendon Press, 1976.

Poole, R. "Reason, Self-interest and 'Commercial Society': The Social Content of Kantian Morality." *Critical Philosophy* I (1984): 24–46.

Puka, Bill. "An Interdisciplinary Treatment of Kohlberg." *Ethics* 92 (1982): 468–90.

Rapaport, Elizabeth. "On the Future of Love: Rousseau and the Radical Feminists." In *Women and Philosophy*, edited by C. C. Gould and M. W. Wartofsky, 185–205. New York: Perigree, 1980.

Raphael, D. D. *Hobbes: Morals and Politics*. London: Allen & Unwin, 1977.

Rawls, John. *A Theory of Justice*. London: Oxford University Press, 1972.

Rest, J. "Moral Research Methodology." In *Lawrence Kohlberg, Consensus and Controversy*, edited by S. Modgil and C. Modgil, 455–70. Lewes, U.K.: Falmer Press, 1985.

Rorty, A. O., ed. *Essays on Aristotle's Ethics*. Berkeley: University of California Press, 1980.

———. "The Place of Contemplation in Aristotle's *Nicomachean Ethics*." In *Essays on Aristotle's Ethics*, edited by A. O. Rorty, 377–94.

Rotenstreich, N. *Practice and Realization: Studies in Kant's Moral Philosophy*. The Hague: Nijhoff, 1979.

Rousseau, J.-J. *Oeuvres Completes*. Paris: Aux Editions du Seuil, 1971.

———. *The First and Second Discourses: Discourse on the Sciences and Fine Arts* (1750) and *Discourse on the Origin and Foundation of Inequality* (1755). Edited by R. D. Masters. Trans. by R. D. and J. R. Masters. New York: St. Martin's Press, 1964.

———. *The Social Contract* (1762). Trans. by Maurice Cranston. Harmondsworth, U.K.: Penguin Books, 1980.

———. *Emile*. Trans. by Barbara Foxley, with introduction by P. D. Jimack. London: Dent, 1974.

———. *The Confessions of Jean-Jacques Rousseau*. Trans. by J. M. Cohen. Harmondsworth, U.K.: Penguin Books, 1975.

Sartre, J.-P. *Being and Nothingness* (1943). Trans. by Hazel E. Barnes. London: Methuen, 1958.

———. *Search for a Method* (1958). Trans. by Hazel E. Barnes. New York: Vintage Books, 1968.

Saunders, J. L., ed. *Greek and Roman Philosophy after Aristotle*. New York: Free Press, 1966.

Scheler, Max. *Ressentiment*. Trans. by W. Holdheim and L. A. Coser. New York: Free Press, 1961.

Schneewind, J. B., ed. *Mill, A Collection of Critical Essays*. New York: Doubleday, 1968.

Schwartz, J. *The Sexual Politics of Jean-Jacques Rousseau*. Chicago: University of Chicago Press, 1984.

Selby-Bigge, L. A., ed. *British Moralists*. 2 vols. New York: Dover Publications, 1965.

Sen, A. and Williams, B., eds. *Utilitarianism and Beyond*. New York: Cambridge University Press, 1982.

Sharp, R., ed. *Apocalypse No*. Sydney: Pluto Press, 1984.

Shklar, Judith N. *Freedom and Independence*. Cambridge: Cambridge University Press, 1976.

Sidgwick, Henry. *The Methods of Ethics* (1874). 7th. edition, 1907. London: Macmillan, 1967.

Siegel, L. S. and Brainerd, C. J. *Alternatives to Piaget: Critical Essays on the Theory*. New York: Academic Press, 1978.

Siep, Ludwig. "The 'Aufhebung' of Morality in Ethical Life." In *Hegel's Philosophy of Action*, edited by L. S. Stepelevich and D. Lamb, 137–56. Atlantic Highlands, N.J.: Humanities Press, 1983.

Skillen, Anthony. *Ruling Illusions*. Hassocks, U.K.: Harvester Press, 1977.

———. "Rousseau and the Fall of Social Man." *Philosophy* 60 (1985): 105–21.

Skinner, B. F. *Science and Human Behavior*. New York: Macmillan, 1953.

———. *Beyond Freedom and Dignity*. New York: Knopf, 1971.

———. *About Behaviorism*. New York: Knopf, 1974.

Smart, J. J. C. and Williams, B., eds. *Utilitarianism: For and Against*. New York: Cambridge University Press, 1973.

Smith, Adam. *The Theory of Moral Sentiments* (1759). New Rochelle, N.Y.: Arlington House, 1969.

————. *An Inquiry into the Nature and Causes of the Wealth of Nations* (1776). Edited by E. Cannan. London: Methuen, 1961.

Sophocles. *Antigone*. In *The Three Theban Plays*. Trans. by R. Fagles. Harmondsworth, U.K.: Penguin Books, 1984.

Sorabji, R. "Aristotle on the Role of Intellect in Virtue." In *Essays on Aristotle's Ethics*, edited by A. O. Rorty, 201–19. Berkeley: University of California Press, 1980.

Sousa, Ronald de. "Norms and the Normal." In *Freud, A Collection of Critical Essays*, edited by R. Wollheim, 196–221. New York: Doubleday, 1974.

Stepelevich, L. S. and Lamb, D., eds. *Hegel's Philosophy of Action*. Atlantic Highlands, N.J.: Humanities Press, 1983.

Stillman, P. G. "Person, Property, and Civil Society in the *Philosophy of Right*." In *Hegel's Social and Political Thought*, edited by D. P. Verene, 103–18. Atlantic Highlands, N.J.: Humanities Press, 1980.

Stoller, R. J. "A Contribution to the Study of Gender Identity." *International Journal of Psychoanalysis* 45 (1964): 220–26.

Suchting, W. A. *Marx, an Introduction*. Brighton: Harvester Press, 1983.

Sullivan, W. M. *Reconstructing Public Philosophy*. Berkeley: University of California Press, 1982.

Tanner, J. M. and Inhelder, B., eds. *Discussions on Child Development*, vol. IV. New York: International Universities Press, 1960.

Taylor, Charles. *Hegel*. Cambridge: Cambridge University Press, 1975.

————. "What Is Human Agency?" In *The Self, Psychological and Philosophical Issues*, edited by T. Mischel, 103–35. Oxford: Blackwell, 1977.

Thucydides. *History of the Peloponnesian War*. Trans. by Rex Warner. Harmondsworth, U.K.: Penguin Books, 1982.

Tugendhat, E. *Selbstbewusstsein und Selbstbestimmung*. Frankfurt: Suhrkampf, 1979.

Verene, D. P., ed. *Hegel's Social and Political Thought*. Atlantic Highlands, N.J.: Humanities Press, 1980.

Vierhaus, R. "Bildung." In *Geschichtliche Grundbegriffe*, edited by O. Brunner, W. Conze, R. Koselleck, 508–51. Stuttgart: Klett-Cotta, 1972.

Vine, Ian. "Moral Maturity in Socio-Cultural Perspective: Are Kohlberg's Stages Universal?" In *Lawrence Kohlberg, Consensus and Controversy*, edited by S. Modgil and C. Modgil, 431–50. Lewes, U.K.: Falmer Press, 1985.

Wagner, D. A. and Stevenson, H., eds. *Cultural Perspectives on Child Development*. San Francisco: W. H. Freeman, 1982.

Walker, L. "Sex Differences in the Development of Moral Differences." *Child Development* 55 (1984): 183–201.

————. "Experiential and Cognitive Sources of Moral Development in Adulthood." *Human Development* 29 (1986): 113–24.

Walker, R. C. S. *Kant*. London: Routledge and Kegan Paul, 1978.

Walsh, W. H. *Hegelian Ethics*. London: St. Martin's Press, 1969.

Warnock, G. J. *The Object of Morality*. London: Methuen, 1971.

Warnock, Mary. "On Moore's Criticisms of Mill's 'Proof'." In *Mill, A Collection of Critical Essays*, edited by J. B. Schneewind, 199–203. New York: Doubleday, 1968.

Wasserman, E. R., ed. *Aspects of the Eighteenth Century*. Baltimore: Johns Hopkins Press, 1965.

Waszek, N. "Two Concepts of Morality: A Distinction of Adam Smith's Ethics and its Stoic Origin." *Journal of the History of Ideas* XLV (1984): 591–606.

Weinreich-Haste, H. "Piaget on Morality: A Critical Perspective." In *Jean Piaget, Consensus and Controversy*, edited by S. Modgil and C. Modgil, 181–206. New York: Praeger, 1982.

————. "Kohlberg's Contribution to Political Psychology." In *Lawrence Kohlberg, Consensus and Controversy*, edited by S. Modgil and C. Modgil, 337–61. Lewes, U.K.: Falmer Press, 1985.

Weinreich-Haste, H. and Locke, Don., eds. *Morality in the Making; Thought, Action, and the Social Context*. Chichester: Wiley and Sons, 1983.

Weisskopf, T. *Immanuel Kant und die Pädagogik*. Zurich: EZW Verlag, 1970.

Wellek, R. "Aesthetics and Criticism." In *The Philosophy of Kant in our Modern World*, edited by C. W. Hendel. New York: Liberal Arts Press, 1957.

White, C. B., Bushell, N., Regnemer, J. L. "Moral Development in Bahamian School Children: A Three-Year Examination of Kohlberg's Stages of Moral Development." In *Developmental Psychology* 14 (1978): 58–65.

Wiggins, D. "Deliberation and Practical Reason." In *Essays on Aristotle's Ethics*, edited by A. O. Rorty, 221–40. Berkeley: University of California Press, 1980.

Williams, Bernard. *Ethics and the Limits of Philosophy*. Glasgow: Collins, 1985.

————. "Utilitarianism and Moral Self-Indulgence." In *Contemporary British Philosophy*, edited by H. D. Lewis, 306–21. London: Allen & Unwin, 1976.

Wollheim, Richard. *The Thread of Life*. Cambridge, Mass.: Harvard University Press, 1984.

————, ed. *Freud, A Collection of Critical Essays*. New York: Doubleday, 1974.

Wollheim, Richard and Hopkins, J., eds. *Philosophical Essays on Freud*. Cambridge: Cambridge University Press, 1982.

Wood, E. M. *Mind and Politics*. Berkeley: University of California Press, 1972.

Wren, Thomas E. "Social Learning Theory, Self-Regulation, and Morality." *Ethics* 92 (1982): 409–24.

Wright, D. "Piaget's Theory of Moral Development." In *Jean Piaget, Consensus and Controversy*, edited by S. Modgil and C. Modgil, 207–17.

Yolton, John. *John Locke and the Way of Ideas*. London: Oxford University Press, 1956.

————. *Locke, An Introduction*. Oxford: Blackwell, 1985.

Index

adult morality, 73, 270–73; and *see* moral maturity
Aerts, E., 284
Aeschylus, 95
affections, 40, 48, 59, 123, 163, 203, 208, 229, 266, 299 n. 47; *see also* emotions, feelings, passions
affectivity, idea of in J. Aronfreed, 39–43
agency, moral, 1, 15, 31, 37, 43, 59, 88, 211, 272; conception of, in Aristotle, 108, 112, 115, 120, 124–27, 288 n. 15; in Hegel, 252; and in Kant, 181–2, 184, 186, 190–92, 194, 248; disappearance of, in Eysenck and Skinner, 36–7, and Hobbes, 202; and notion of person, in Locke, 140; and self-intervention and control, 43, 45–7, 121, 218, 277 n. 19; *see also* moral maturity, responsibility, self, self-intervention.
aggressiveness, 17, 51, 58, 267, 269, 274 n. 17
alienation, 13, 246, 248, 251
Alston, William, 43, 277
altruism, 33, 38, 52, 176, 261, 276 n. 2
amour de soi, as natural self-love in Rousseau's thought, 155, 159, 164, 172, 292. *See also amour-propre*, self-love
amour-propre, as artificial, selfish self-love in Rousseau's thought, 155–56, 164, 170–71, 292; in French moral thought, 143–45; in context of Locke's moral thought, 143–44. *See also amour de soi*, self-love, vanity
animality, animal nature in Kant's thought, 174, 181–3
Antigone, in Sophocles' *Antigone*, 94–5, 240–41
appetite, 107, 112, 115, 120, 133–34, 141, 197; *see also* desire, pleasure
Aquinas, Thomas, 101, 138, 139, 161, 204, 292 n. 14
Aries, P., 290
Aristotle, x, 8, 13, 14, 27–8, 39, 41, 44, 58, 97, 100–01; 103–27, 286–89, *passim*; on agency and moral responsibility, 115, 120–21, 124–6, 288 n. 22; on character, 115–18, 121, 123–25; on community, 108–09, 258, 261; on contemplation, 287 n. 12; on education, stages of, 115; on education of emotions through music, 115–17, 288 n. 17; on education and status of women, 87, 105, 111, 123–24, 287 n. 10; on emotions, 106–08, and *see* passions; ethical writings and life, 286–87 n. 26; on family, 244; on friendship, 108, 261, 287 n. 9; on habit-formation (habituation), 112–15, 118, 120–21, 122; on happiness (*eudaimonia*), 103, 112, 226, 286 n. 1; on justice, 108, 186, 255, 261, 287 n. 9; on morality, nature of, 103ff.; on moral development, stages of, 111, 120–23, 126–27; on moral excellence, 105–07, 113, 117–18, 120, 123; on moral failure, 111–12, 118–19, 121, 124–27, on moral goodness, 92, 103–04, and virtue, 105–06, 110, 118, 145, 204–05, and measure of, 108–09, and practical wisdom, 109, and as life "according to reason" 106, 109; on moral maturity, 105–12, 123; on moral responsibility, 124–26, and *see* agency; on motivation, 109–11; on human nature, 103, 105ff; on the noble and the good, 110; on passions 106–08, education of the passions, 115–17, living "by the passions", 106, 118–19, 120–21; on pleasure 106, 109–12, 118–19, 126–27; on practical wisdom, 106–07, 109, 114; on public education, 113–14; on reason, 106, as practical, 39, 107, 109, 123, 126, life "according to reason", 106; on two forms of self-love, 108; on shame, 44, 121–22, 288 n. 19; on slavery, 109, 111, 271, 301 n. 22; on the soul, 107; on

317

326 INDEX

Hampshire, 298 n. 37; Aristotle on absolute prohibitions, obligations, 108–09

moral development, 2–4, 5–7, 100–02; accounts of, in Aristotle 104–05, 112–27; in Cognitive Developmental Theory, 63–73, 73–9, 81–6, 89–91; in Freudian theory, 48–56, 58–60; in Hegel, 232–38, 243, 244–47, 250, 252; in Hobbes, 199–202; in Hume, 213–14; in Kant, 180–83, 184–86; 187–94; in Mill, 227–30; in Rousseau, 153, 154–58, 159–60, 163–65, 168–69, 173; in Smith, 215–17; in Social Learning Theory, 33–46; classification of theories of, 31–3, 78; community as condition of, 258–65; stages of, 2, 265–73, as presented by Aristotle, 117–27, by Aronfreed, 41, by Kohlberg, 74–6, 78, 82–6, by Piaget, 64–8, 69, 71–2

moral education, Aristotle on, 103–05, 112–17, 118–19; Hegel, on, 231–38, 253–54; Kant on, 174–75, 191–94; Kohlberg on, 77–9, 85–6, 281 n. 28; Locke on, 128–30, 135–39, 142; Rousseau on, 163–69; 201–02, 213–14; 263

moral failure, 111–12, 118, 119, 121, 124–27, 273

moral goodness, 92, 104–05, 110, 118, 145, 204–05; see virtue, happiness

moral knowledge, 104, 117, 134, 202

moral law: see law

moral maturity, 2, 3, 5, 6, 12, 48; idea of, in Aristotle, 105–09; Freud, 49, 54–6, 269; Gilligan, 89–93, 96–7, 273; Hegel, 232–33, 238, 251–52, 254, 258; Kant, 193–94; Kohlberg, 77, 81–4, 272; Locke, 140; Piaget, 66, 68–70, 71–3, 272; Rousseau, 32, 154–55, 167–68; 269, 270–73

moral psychology, x–xii, 2–4, 100, 265–66, 267–70; in Aristotelian context, 106–08, 109–11, 126–27; Bentham, 220; Dewey, 259; Freudian theory, 17–18, 48–54, 55–60; Gilligan, 87, 90–1; Hegel, 232–33, 248, 302 n. 28; Hobbes, 197–200; Hume, 210–12; Hutcheson, 207–08; Kant, 174, 181–82, 187–88; Kohlberg, 78–9; Locke, 130–35, 138, 141–42; de Mandeville, 206; Mill, 224, 225, 228, 299 n. 47; Piaget,

32, 62–3, 67; Rousseau, 155, 163–64, 169; Smith, 214–16

moral realism, Piaget's notion of, 65, 67

moral relativism, 77, 93–4, 97

moral rules, 5, 7, 10–11, 17, 33–5, 65–68, 71–3, 74, 217, 267; list of rules, in Locke, 290 n. 19

moral sense (sentiment), account of, in ethics of Hume, 211–12; of Hutcheson, 207–08; of Smith, 214; criticized by Mill, 228, 299 n. 47

moral understanding, according to Aristotle, 119, 122

Moralität, Hegel's notion of, 238, 241–3, 247, 248–49

morality, character and scope of, 2–4, 103, 257; controversy about, 4–5, 9–10; as concerned with well-being of individual and community, 103; as essentially other-directed, 38–9, 207, 261 (*see also* altruism); as a set of rules: see moral rules

Mosher, R. L., 281 n. 25, n. 30

motivation, 43, 45, 206; in Aristotelian ethics, 109–11, 126–27; in Bentham, 220–21; in Cognitive Developmental Theory, 62; in Freud, 49, 51–2, 58, 62–3; in Hobbes, 196–99, 201–03; in Kant, 176, 187–90; in Locke, 140–45

Murphy, J. M., 284 n. 52

Murray, O., 288 n. 21

music, role in education of the passions according to Aristotle, 115–17

Mussen, P. H., 276 n. 2, 279 n. 6, 280 n. 20

narcissism, 270–73

natural law: see law

naturalism, ethical, 8, 78; in Aristotle's ethics, 27, 103–04, 257; Hobbes, 195–96, 201, 203–04; Kant on, 175; in Nietzsche, 26–8; Rousseau, 160–62, 172–73, 292 n. 13–14

nature, human, 5, 6, 8, 147–50; Aristotle on, 103, 105–08; Bentham on, 220; Butler on, 209; in Cognitive Developmental Theory, 62; Freud on, 15, 17–18, 48, 52, 54–5, 57–8; Hobbes on, 146, 195–99, 200–01; individualist conception of, 203–06;

Sharp, R., 275 n. 14
Shklar, J., 301 n. 22
Shulik, R., 282 n. 36
Sidgwick, H., on impartial
  benevolence, 223–24, 227, 229; on
  teaching Utilitarianism, 229–30, 299
  n. 48–51
Siegel, L. S., 279 n. 6
Siep, L., 250, 301 n. 26, 302 n. 28
sin, 11, *see also* original sin
Sittlichkeit, 238, 241–42, 244, 247, 255,
  301 n. 27, 28
skepticism, 246
Skillen, A., 274 n. 3, 292 n. 17
Skinner, B. F., 32, 35, 37, 139, 276
  n. 8–9
slave morality, Nietzsche's idea of,
  19–24
slavery, 11, 271, 301 n. 22
Smart, J. J. C., 300 n. 51
Smith, Adam, on conscience, 215–16,
  217; impartiality, 216; impartial
  spectator, 214–16; invisible hand
  metaphor, 219, 298 n. 30; moral
  agency and the self, 215, 218; moral
  development, 215–18; moral
  sentiment, 214; origin of moral
  rules, 217; on twofold system of
  morality, 218; propriety, 215, 217,
  219; self-command, 215, 218;
  self-deceit, 216; self-interest, 217–19;
  self-love, 216; sympathy, 214; as
  theological Utilitarian, 217, 297
  n. 28; on virtues, 213–14, 218
Snarey, J., 283 n. 40
sociability, as natural, 6, 18; Aristotle
  on, 103, 296 n. 11; Hobbes on,
  199–201, 296 n. 11; Locke on, 203;
  Rousseau on, 159, 161, 165; 204,
  262–63; Kant on unsociability, 190, 249
Social Contract, idea of, 75, 81, 87–8;
  as male in character, 284 n. 50, 292
  n. 19
Social Learning Theory, x, 31–48
  passim; summary of, 335; a
  cognitivist version of, 37–46; a
  noncognitivist version of, 35–7; 48,
  57, 272
Socialism, 13
socialization, 33, 41–2, 48, 52
Socrates, 10; Hegel on, 241–44, 247;
  255, 263–64; as invoked by

Kohlberg, 79–80, 282 n. 33; 104, 126,
  143
Sophists, 103–4, 242, 262–63
Sophocles, *Antigone*, 94–5; Hegel on,
  239–41; 285 n. 63
Sorabji, R., 287 n. 14
Sorell, T., 290 n. 8
soul, as form of body, 107
Sousa, Ronald de, on Freud, 15, 274 n. 6
Spinoza, B., 101
spirit, universal, Hegel's notion of,
  232, 238, 248, 254, 301 n. 12
State, in Hegelian context, as ethical
  community, 236–38, 249–53, 258–59;
  as rational, 251, 253–54, 258
Stepelevich, L. S., 301 n. 26
Stillman, P. G., 302 n. 29
Stoic morality, 8, 23, 27, 29, 101, 163,
  169, 231, 246, 248, 277 n. 13
Stoller, R. J., 285 n. 54
subservience, 270–71
Suchting, W. A., 274 n. 3
Sullivan E. V., 276 n. 2, 281 n. 28
Sullivan, W. M., 281 n. 31, 283 n. 44
super-ego, 48–54, 277 n. 24–26; in
  Wollheim's account, 267–69
sympathy, 32, 115; Hume on, 212–14;
  Smith on, 214–15; problem of limited
  sympathy, 261–65

Taba, H., 278 n. 3
taste, Kant on, 183–85
Taylor, C. C. W., 302 n. 4
Taylor, Charles, 277 n. 19, 301 n. 25
teaching, in moral developmental
  context, 2; in Aristotle, 116, 118,
  119, 120; Hegel, 234, 253–54;
  Hobbes, 202; Hume, 214; Kant, 184,
  185, 189, 192–93; Locke, 134; Mill,
  299 n. 47; Plato's *Meno*, 104;
  Protagoras, 262–64; Utilitarian ethics,
  228, 229–30, 299 n. 48–51
technico-practical rationality, 190
Teiresias, in Sophocles' *Antigone*, 241
Theodorou, P., 283 n. 47
Thucydides, 303 n. 15
Trainer, H., 274 n. 14
tragedy, themes in, 94–5, 97–8, 231,
  239–41, 243–44, 257, 285 n. 63, 301
  n. 13–17
truth, moral, 9–10
Turgot, 396